Please Put Them On, Takamine-San

1

Yuichi Hiiragi

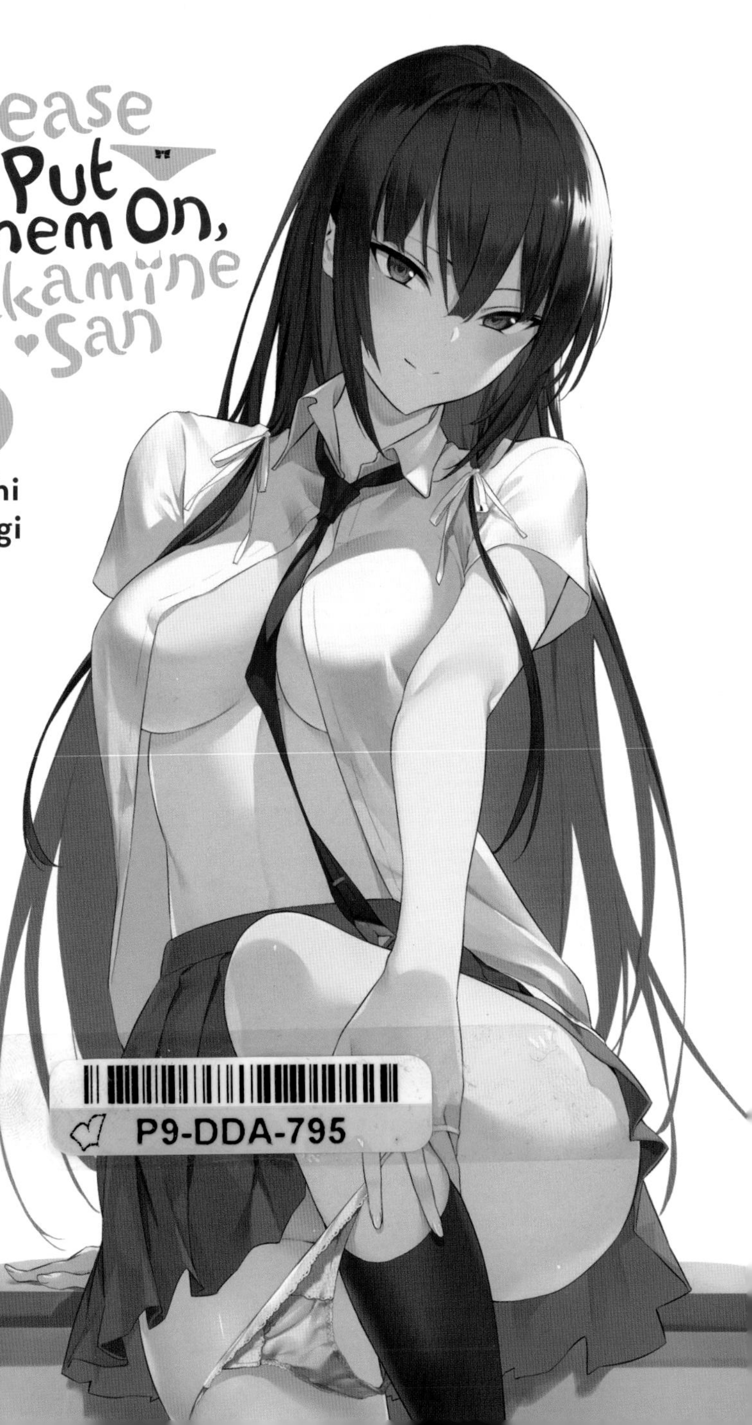

please
put them on,
takamine-
san

Contents

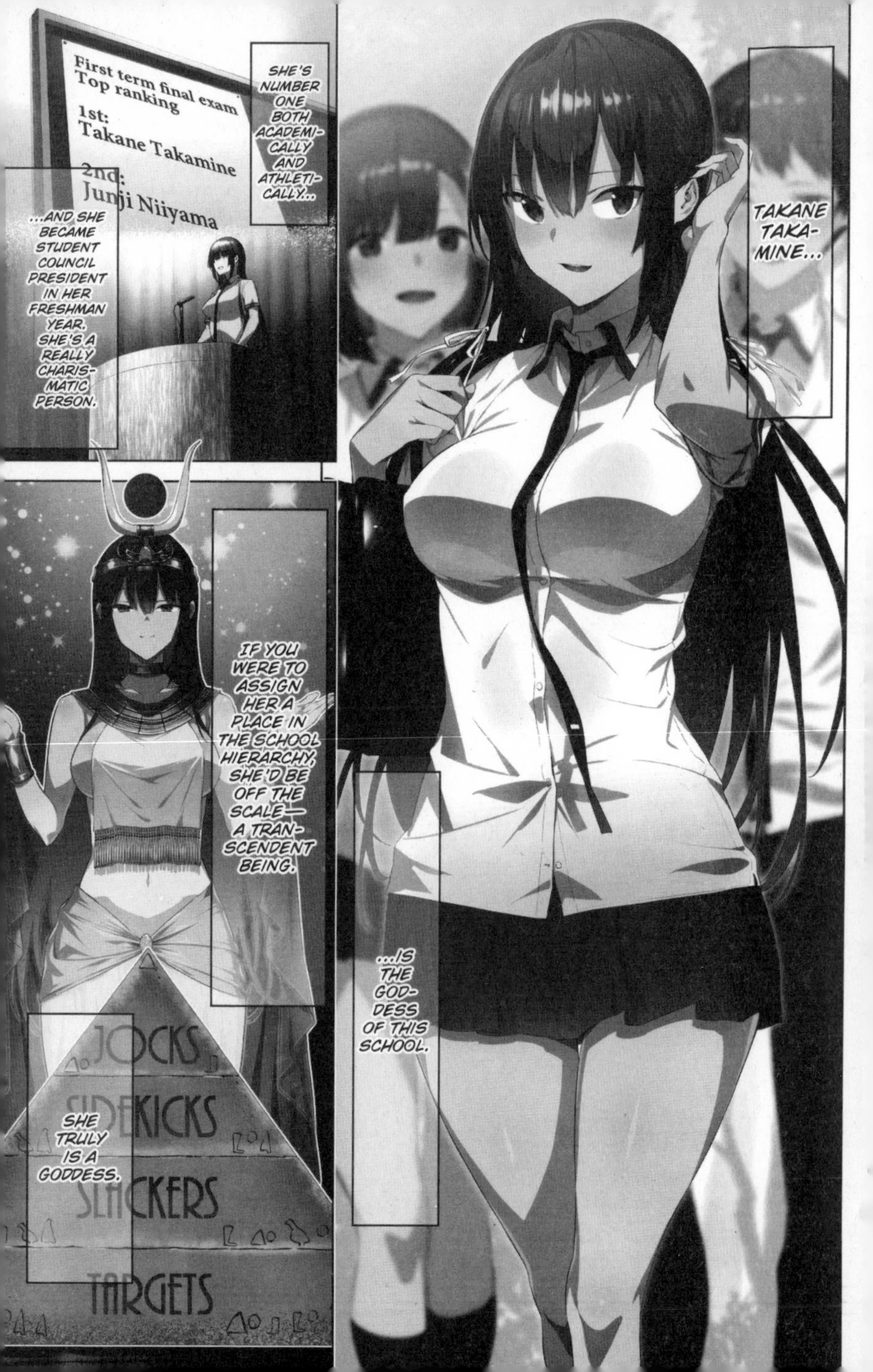
TAKANE TAKAMINE...
...IS THE GODDESS OF THIS SCHOOL.
First term final exam Top ranking
1st: Takane Takamine
2nd: Junji Niiyama
SHE'S NUMBER ONE BOTH ACADEMICALLY AND ATHLETICALLY...
...AND SHE BECAME STUDENT COUNCIL PRESIDENT IN HER FRESHMAN YEAR. SHE'S A REALLY CHARISMATIC PERSON.
IF YOU WERE TO ASSIGN HER A PLACE IN THE SCHOOL HIERARCHY, SHE'D BE OFF THE SCALE— A TRANSCENDENT BEING.
SHE TRULY IS A GODDESS.
JOCKS
SIDEKICKS
SLACKERS
TARGETS

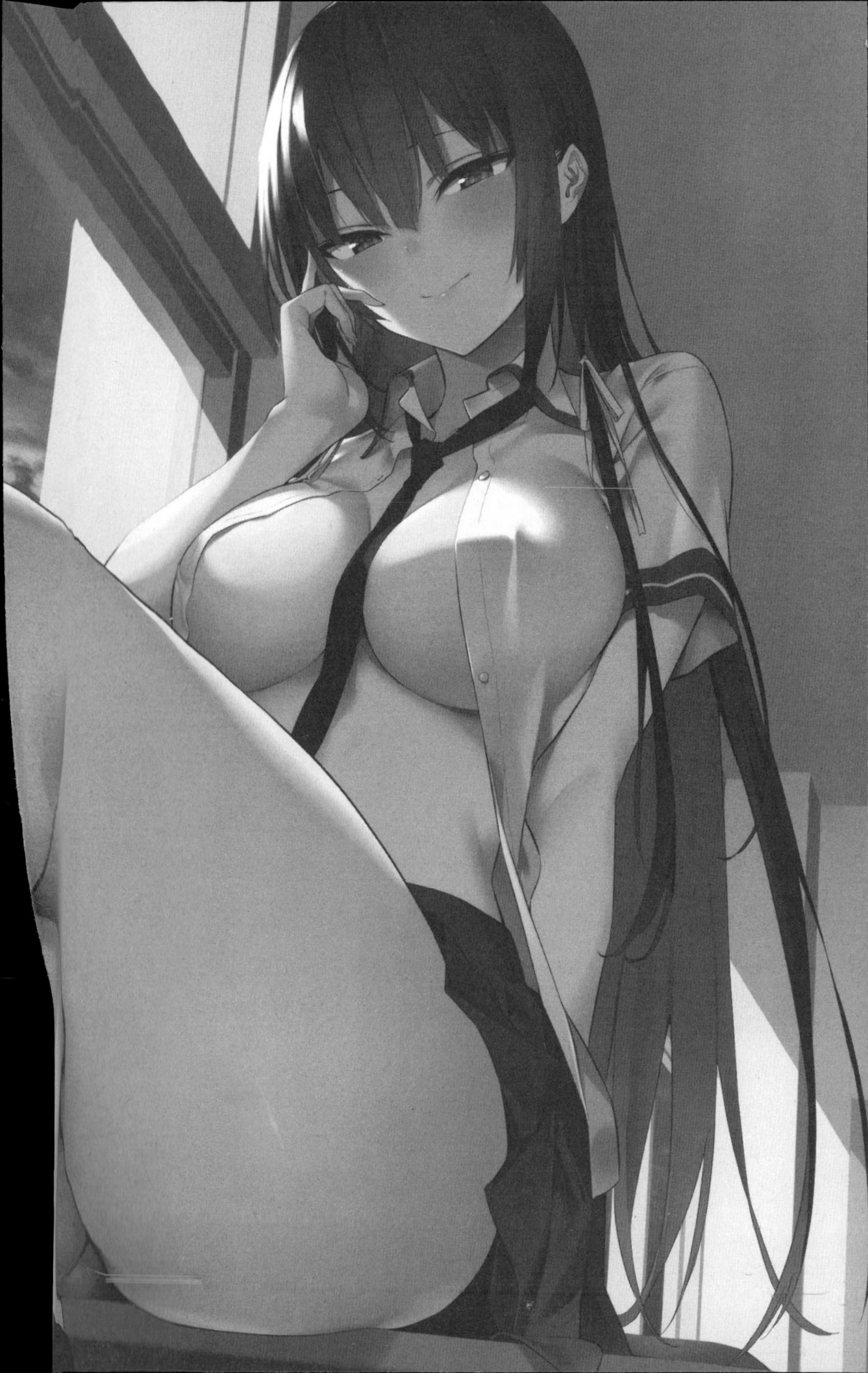

Chapter 1 Be my closet.

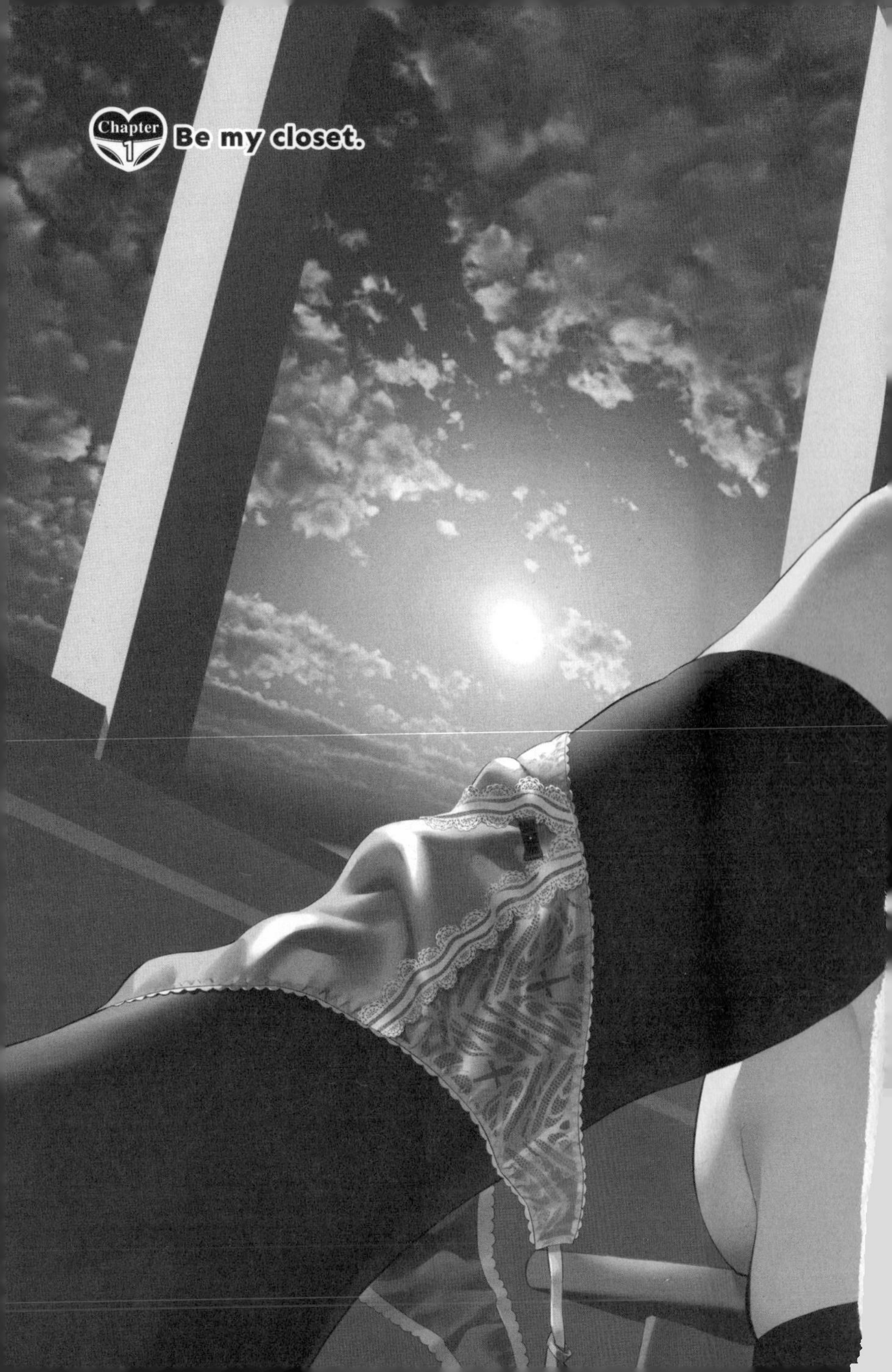

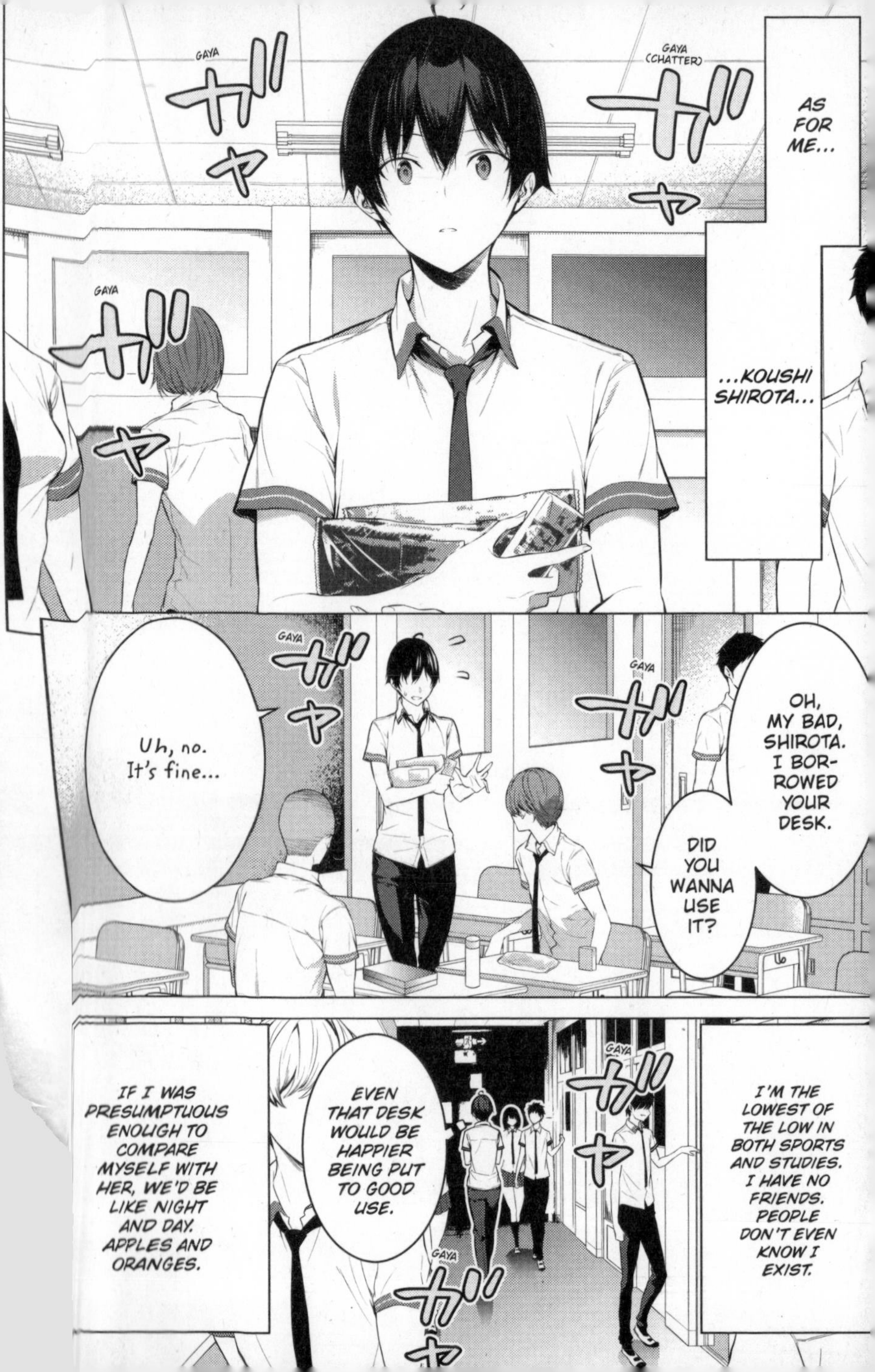
GAYA (CHATTER)
AS FOR ME...
...KOUSHI SHIROTA...
GAYA
GAYA
GAYA
OH, MY BAD, SHIROTA. I BOR-ROWED YOUR DESK.
DID YOU WANNA USE IT?
GAYA
Uh, no. It's fine...
I'M THE LOWEST OF THE LOW IN BOTH SPORTS AND STUDIES. I HAVE NO FRIENDS. PEOPLE DON'T EVEN KNOW I EXIST.
GAYA
EVEN THAT DESK WOULD BE HAPPIER BEING PUT TO GOOD USE.
IF I WAS PRESUMPTUOUS ENOUGH TO COMPARE MYSELF WITH HER, WE'D BE LIKE NIGHT AND DAY. APPLES AND ORANGES.
GAYA

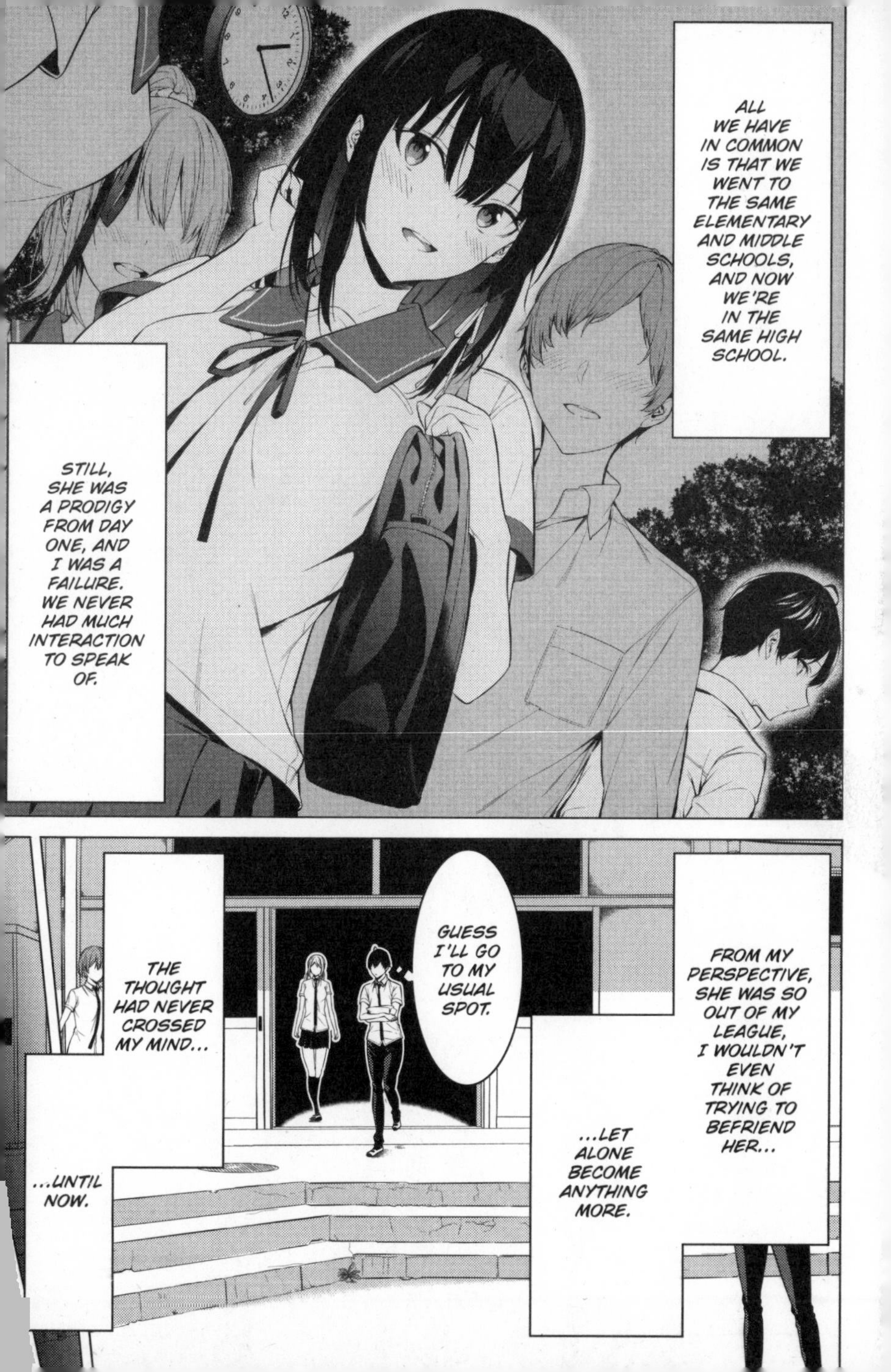
ALL WE HAVE IN COMMON IS THAT WE WENT TO THE SAME ELEMENTARY AND MIDDLE SCHOOLS, AND NOW WE'RE IN THE SAME HIGH SCHOOL.
STILL, SHE WAS A PRODIGY FROM DAY ONE, AND I WAS A FAILURE. WE NEVER HAD MUCH INTERACTION TO SPEAK OF.
FROM MY PERSPECTIVE, SHE WAS SO OUT OF MY LEAGUE, I WOULDN'T EVEN THINK OF TRYING TO BEFRIEND HER...
GUESS I'LL GO TO MY USUAL SPOT.
...LET ALONE BECOME ANYTHING MORE.
THE THOUGHT HAD NEVER CROSSED MY MIND...
...UNTIL NOW.

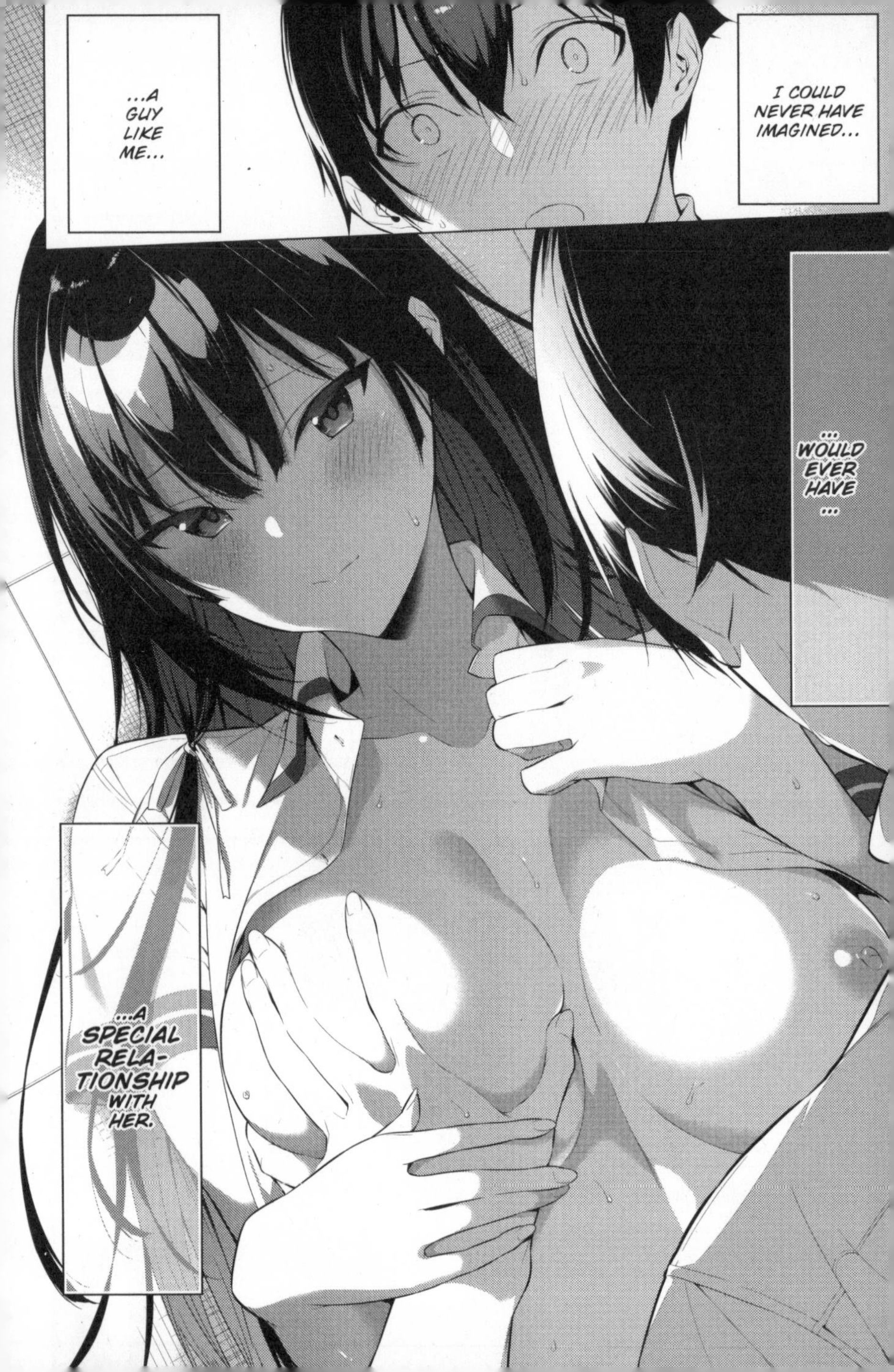
I COULD NEVER HAVE IMAGINED...
...A GUY LIKE ME...
...WOULD EVER HAVE ...
...A SPECIAL RELA-TIONSHIP WITH HER.

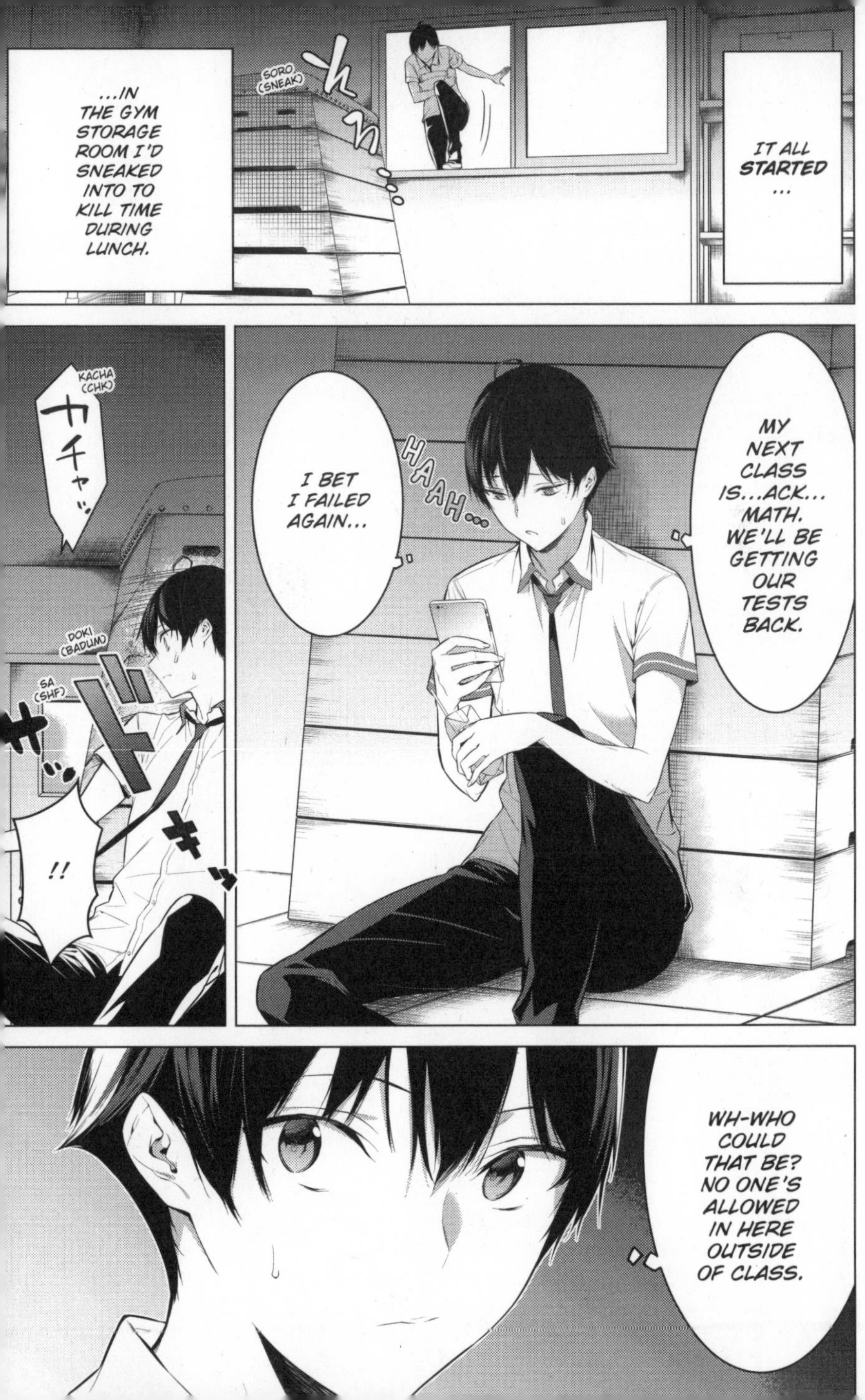
IT ALL STARTED...
SORO (SNEAK)
...IN THE GYM STORAGE ROOM I'D SNEAKED INTO TO KILL TIME DURING LUNCH.
MY NEXT CLASS IS...ACK... MATH. WE'LL BE GETTING OUR TESTS BACK.
HAAAH...
I BET I FAILED AGAIN...
KACHA (CHK)
カチャッ
DOKI (BADUM)
SA (SHF)
!!
WH-WHO COULD THAT BE? NO ONE'S ALLOWED IN HERE OUTSIDE OF CLASS.

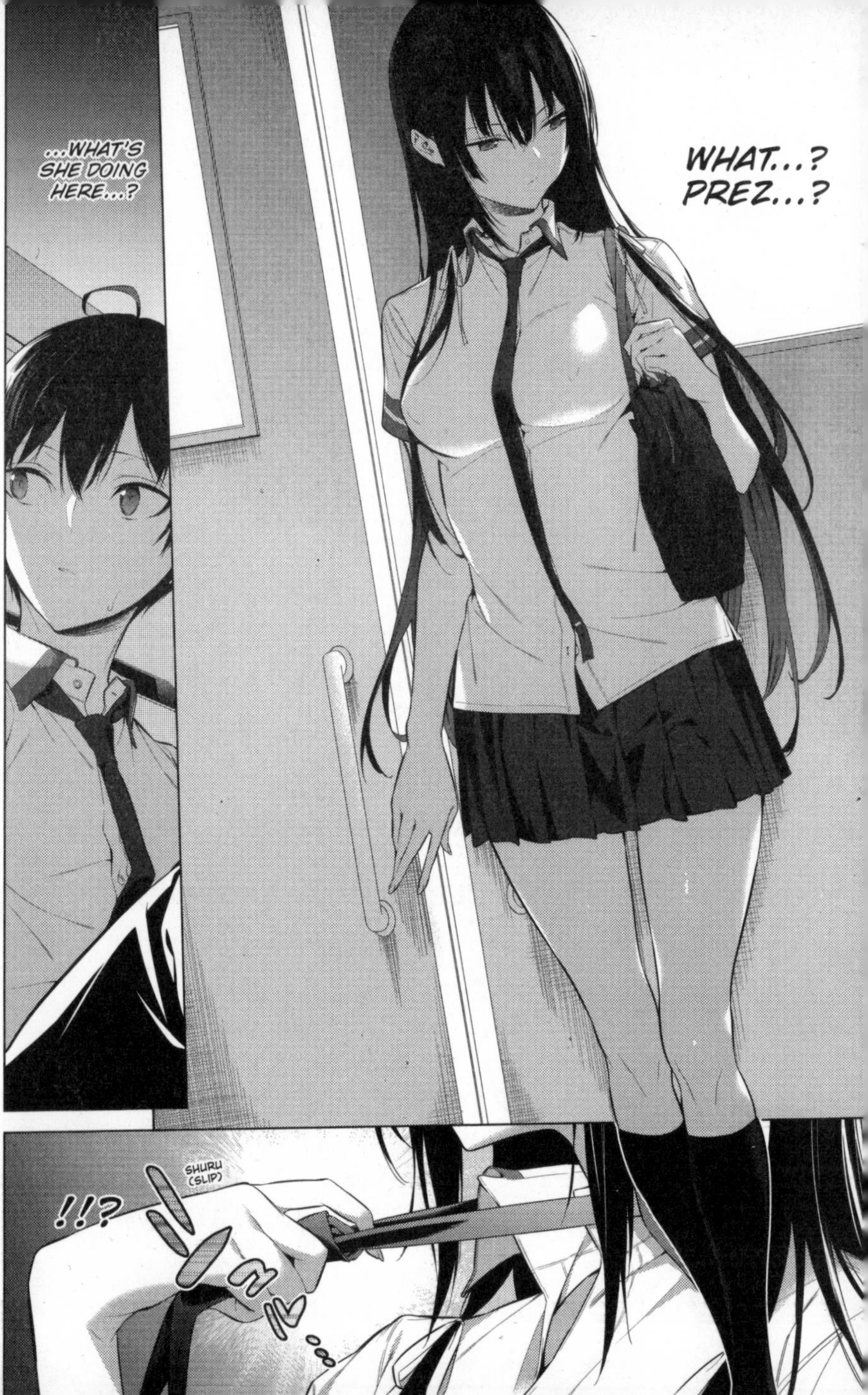
WHAT...?
PREZ...?
...WHAT'S SHE DOING HERE...?
SHURU (SLIP)
!!?

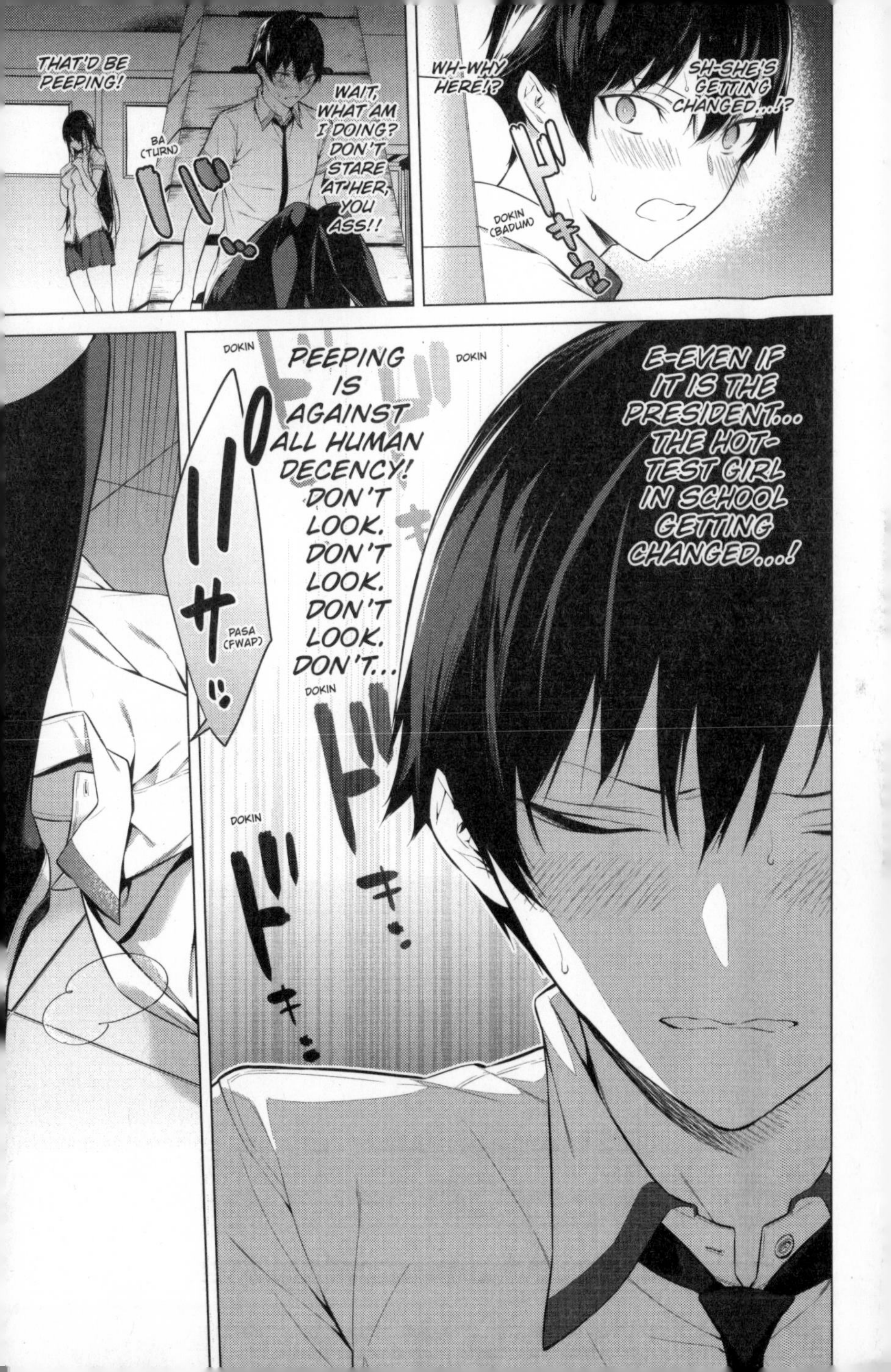
SH-SHE'S GETTING CHANGED...!?
WH-WHY HERE!?
DOKIN (BADUM)
WAIT, WHAT AM I DOING? DON'T STARE AT HER, YOU ASS!!
THAT'D BE PEEPING!
BA (TURN)
E-EVEN IF IT IS THE PRESIDENT... THE HOT-TEST GIRL IN SCHOOL GETTING CHANGED...!
DOKIN
PEEPING IS AGAINST ALL HUMAN DECENCY! DON'T LOOK. DON'T LOOK. DON'T LOOK. DON'T...
DOKIN
PASA (FWAP)
DOKIN
DOKIN

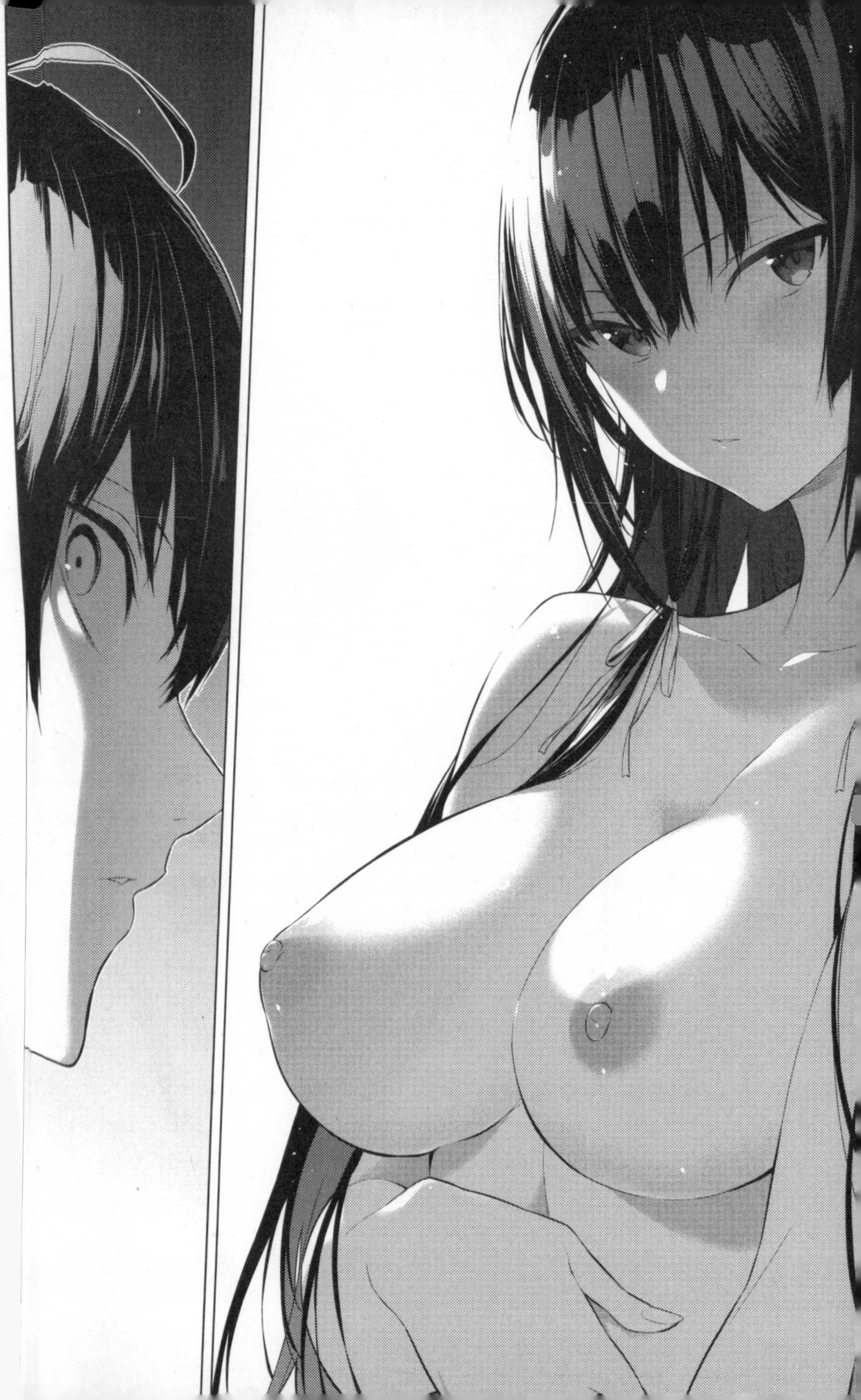

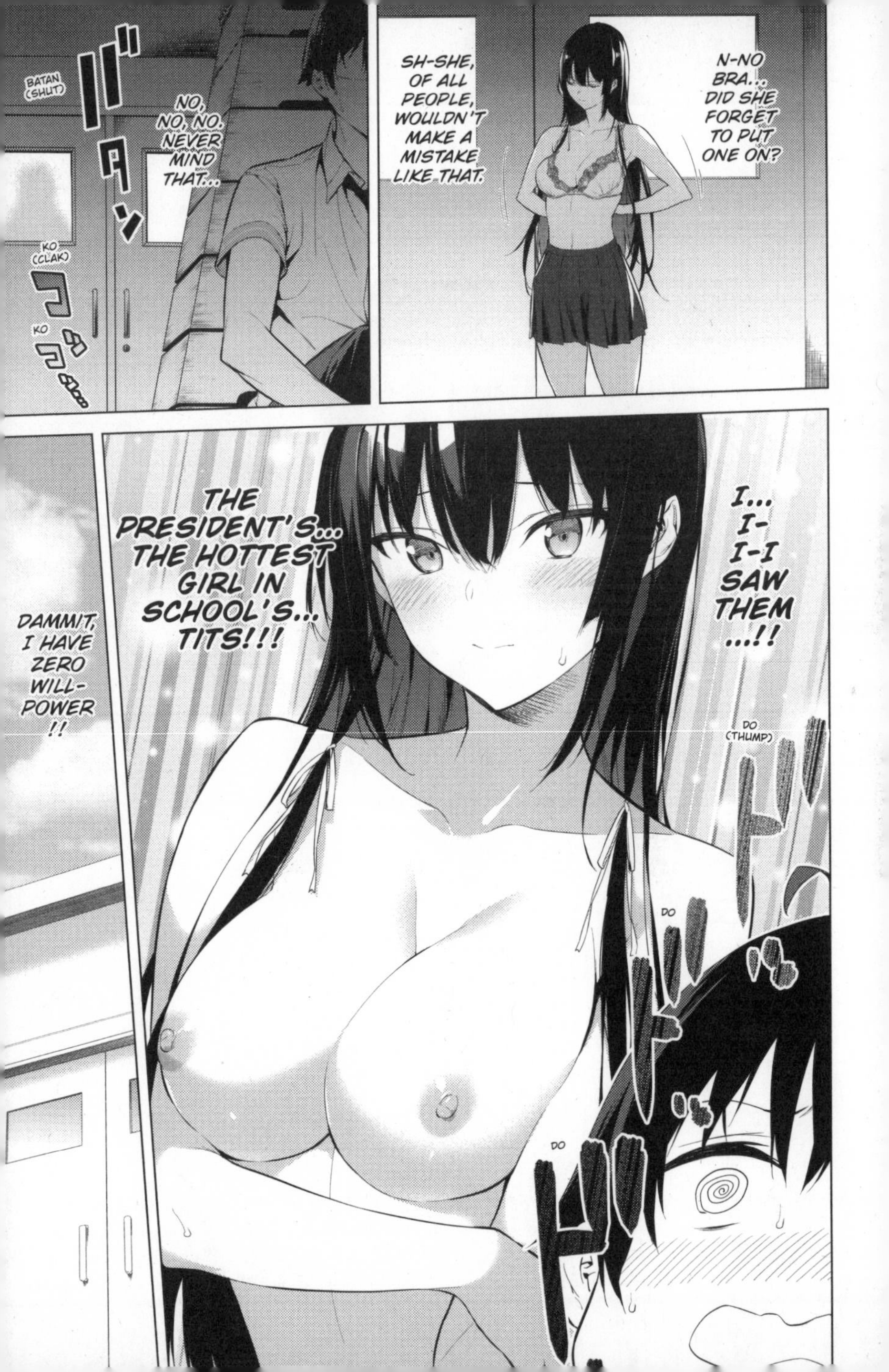
N-NO BRA... DID SHE FORGET TO PUT ONE ON?
SH-SHE, OF ALL PEOPLE, WOULDN'T MAKE A MISTAKE LIKE THAT.
BATAN (SHUT)
NO, NO, NO. NEVER MIND THAT...
KO (CLAK)
KO
I... I-I-I SAW THEM...!!
THE PRESIDENT'S... THE HOTTEST GIRL IN SCHOOL'S... TITS!!!
DAMMIT, I HAVE ZERO WILL-POWER!!
DO (THUMP)
DO
DO

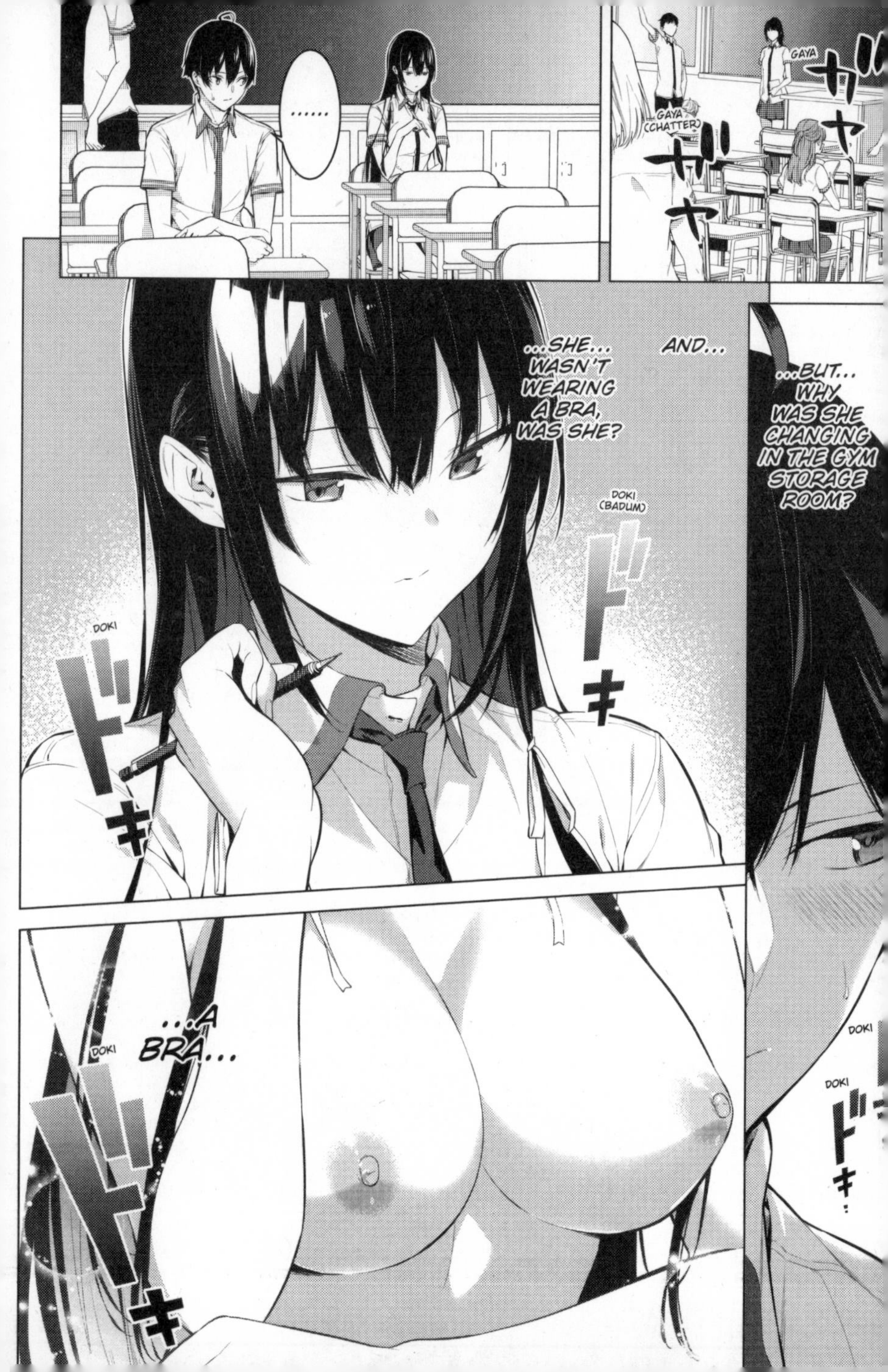
GAYA
GAYA (CHATTER)
......
...BUT... WHY WAS SHE CHANGING IN THE GYM STORAGE ROOM?
DOKI
DOKI
...SHE... WASN'T WEARING A BRA, WAS SHE?
AND...
DOKI (BADUM)
DOKI
...A BRA...
DOKI

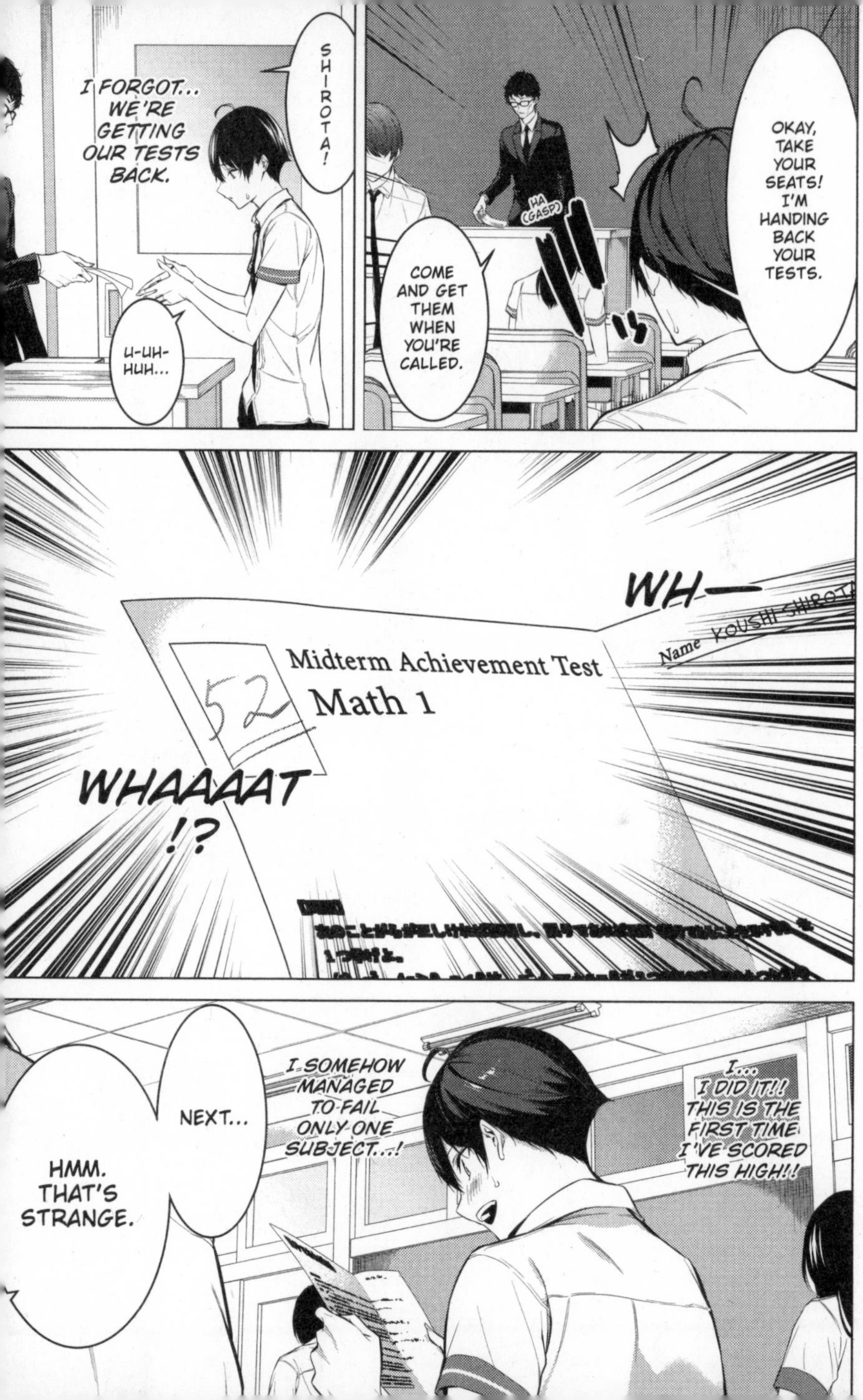
OKAY, TAKE YOUR SEATS! I'M HANDING BACK YOUR TESTS.
HA (GASP)
COME AND GET THEM WHEN YOU'RE CALLED.
SHIROTA!
I FORGOT... WE'RE GETTING OUR TESTS BACK.
U-UH-HUH...
WH—
Name KOUSHI SHIROTA
Midterm Achievement Test
Math 1
52
WHAAAAT!?
I... I DID IT!! THIS IS THE FIRST TIME I'VE SCORED THIS HIGH!!
I SOMEHOW MANAGED TO FAIL ONLY ONE SUBJECT...!
NEXT...
HMM. THAT'S STRANGE.

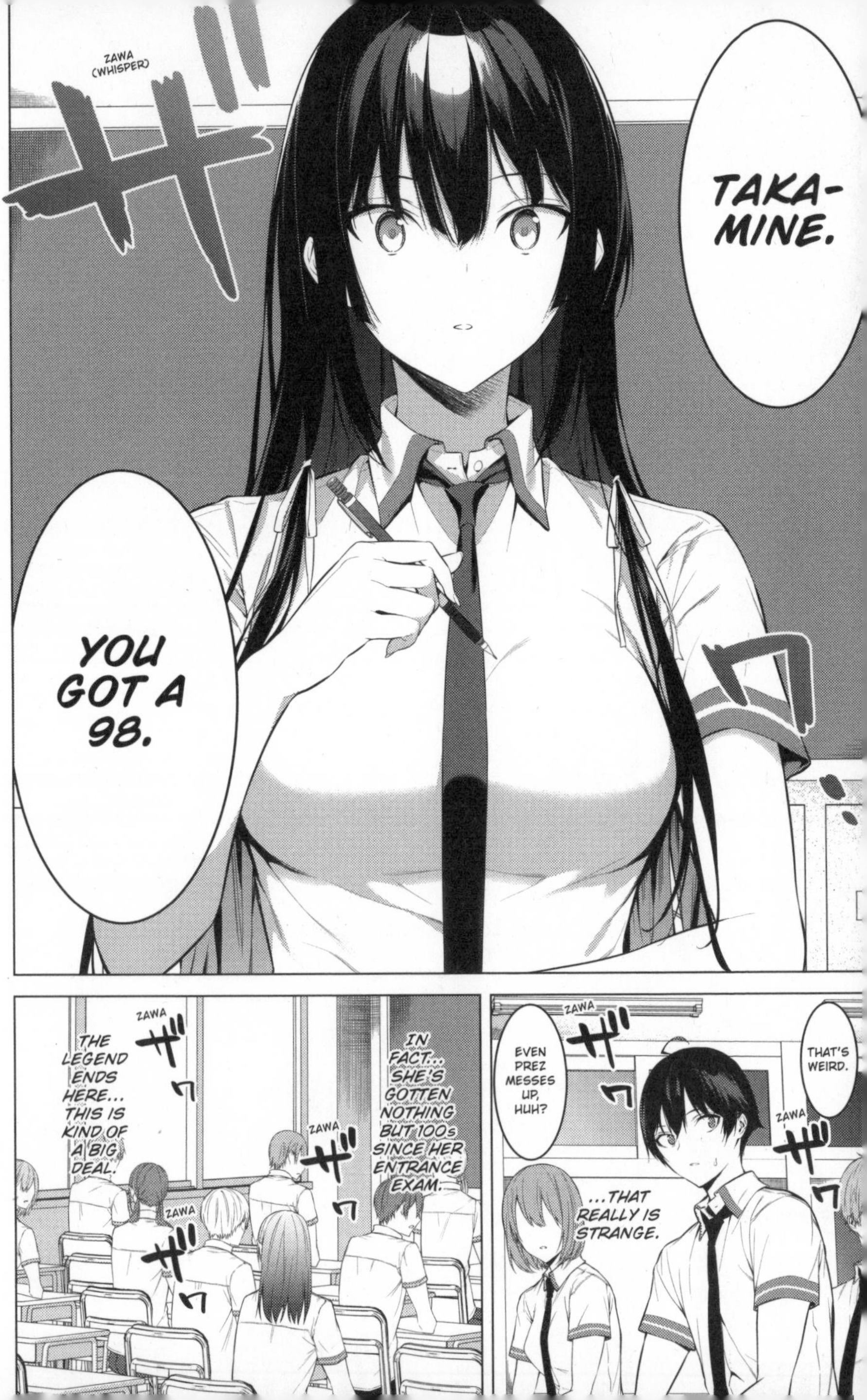
TAKA-MINE.
ZAWA (WHISPER)
YOU GOT A 98.
THAT'S WEIRD.
ZAWA
ZAWA
EVEN PREZ MESSES UP, HUH?
...THAT REALLY IS STRANGE.
IN FACT... SHE'S GOTTEN NOTHING BUT 100s SINCE HER ENTRANCE EXAM.
ZAWA
ZAWA
THE LEGEND ENDS HERE... THIS IS KIND OF A BIG DEAL.
ZAWA

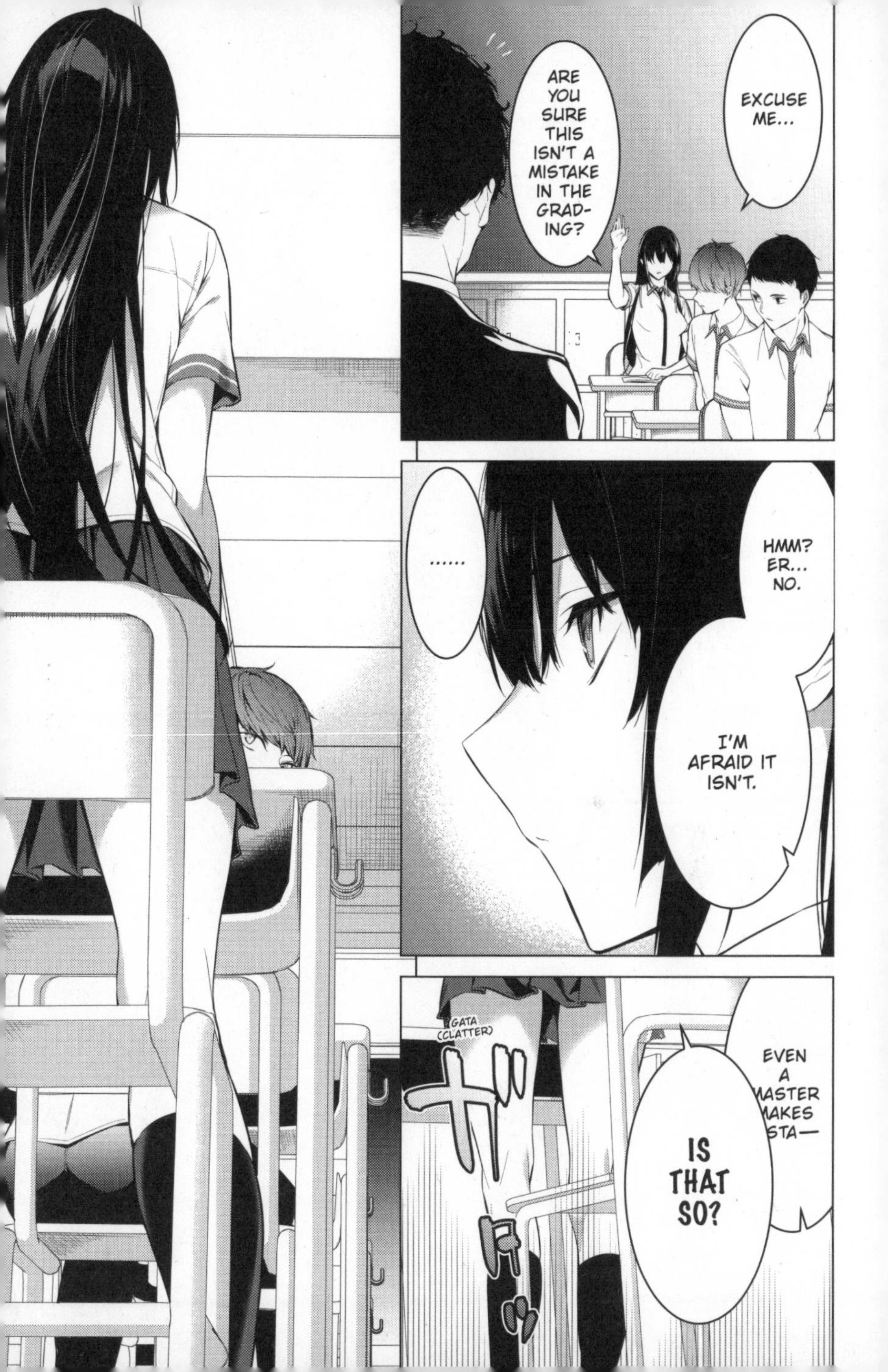
EXCUSE ME...
ARE YOU SURE THIS ISN'T A MISTAKE IN THE GRAD-ING?
HMM? ER... NO.
I'M AFRAID IT ISN'T.
......
EVEN A MASTER MAKES STA—
GATA (CLATTER)
IS THAT SO?

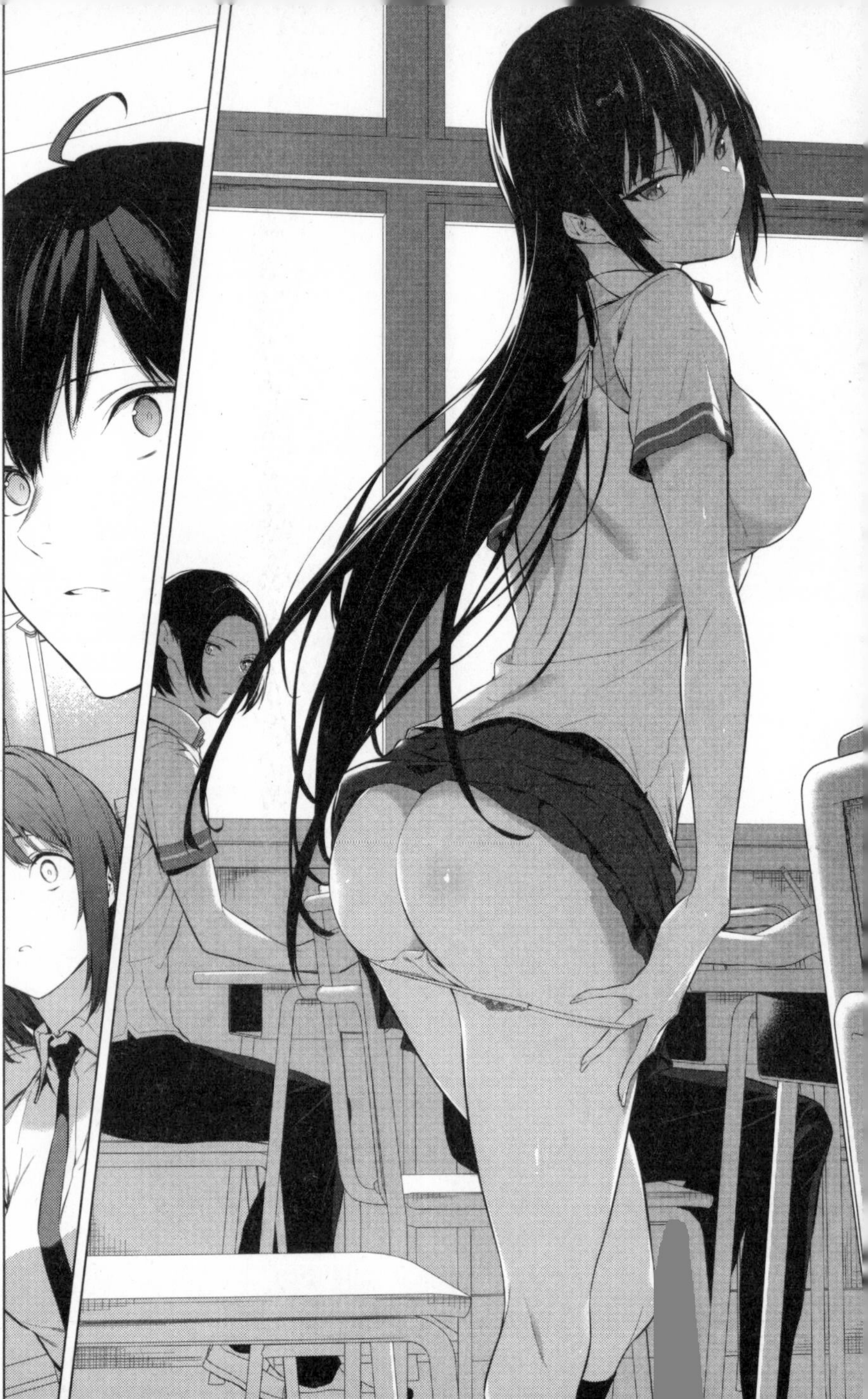

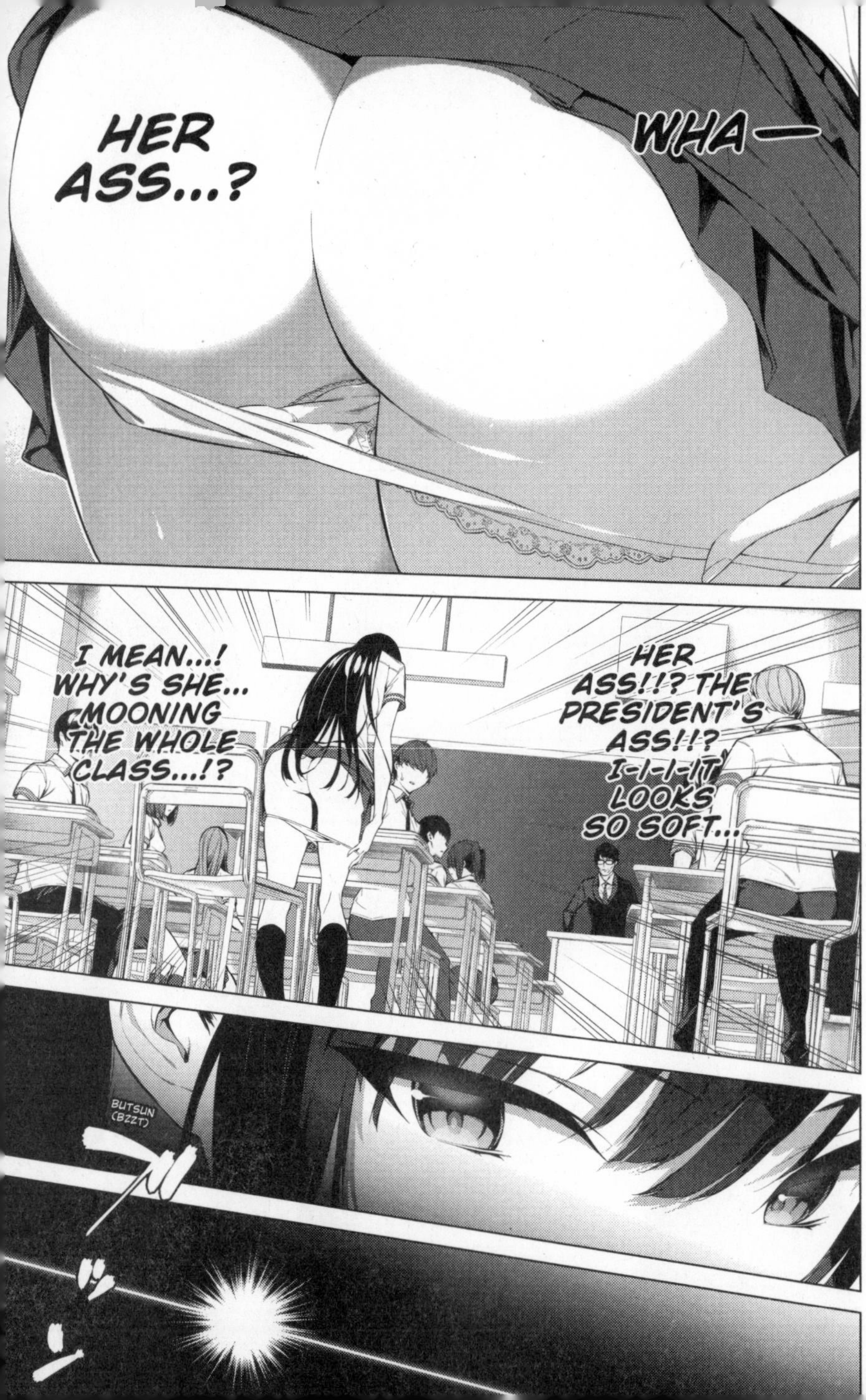
WHA—
HER ASS...?
HER ASS!!? THE PRESIDENT'S ASS!!? I-I-I-IT LOOKS SO SOFT...
I MEAN...! WHY'S SHE... MOONING THE WHOLE CLASS...!?
BUTSUN (BZZT)

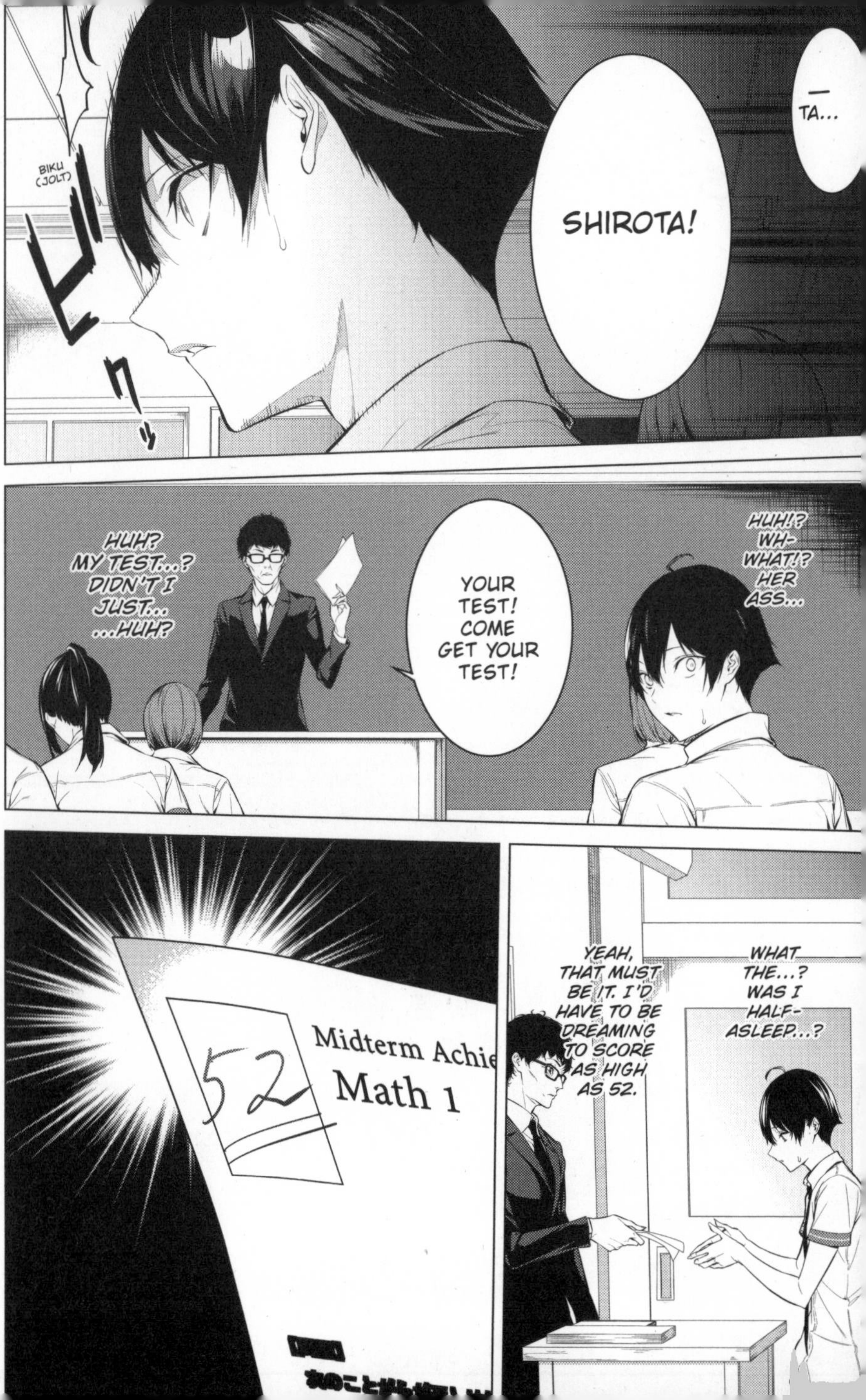
—TA...
SHIROTA!
BIKU (JOLT)
HUH!? WH-WHAT!? HER ASS...
YOUR TEST! COME GET YOUR TEST!
HUH? MY TEST...? DIDN'T I JUST... ...HUH?
WHAT THE...? WAS I HALF-ASLEEP...?
YEAH, THAT MUST BE IT. I'D HAVE TO BE DREAMING TO SCORE AS HIGH AS 52.
52
Midterm Achie
Math 1

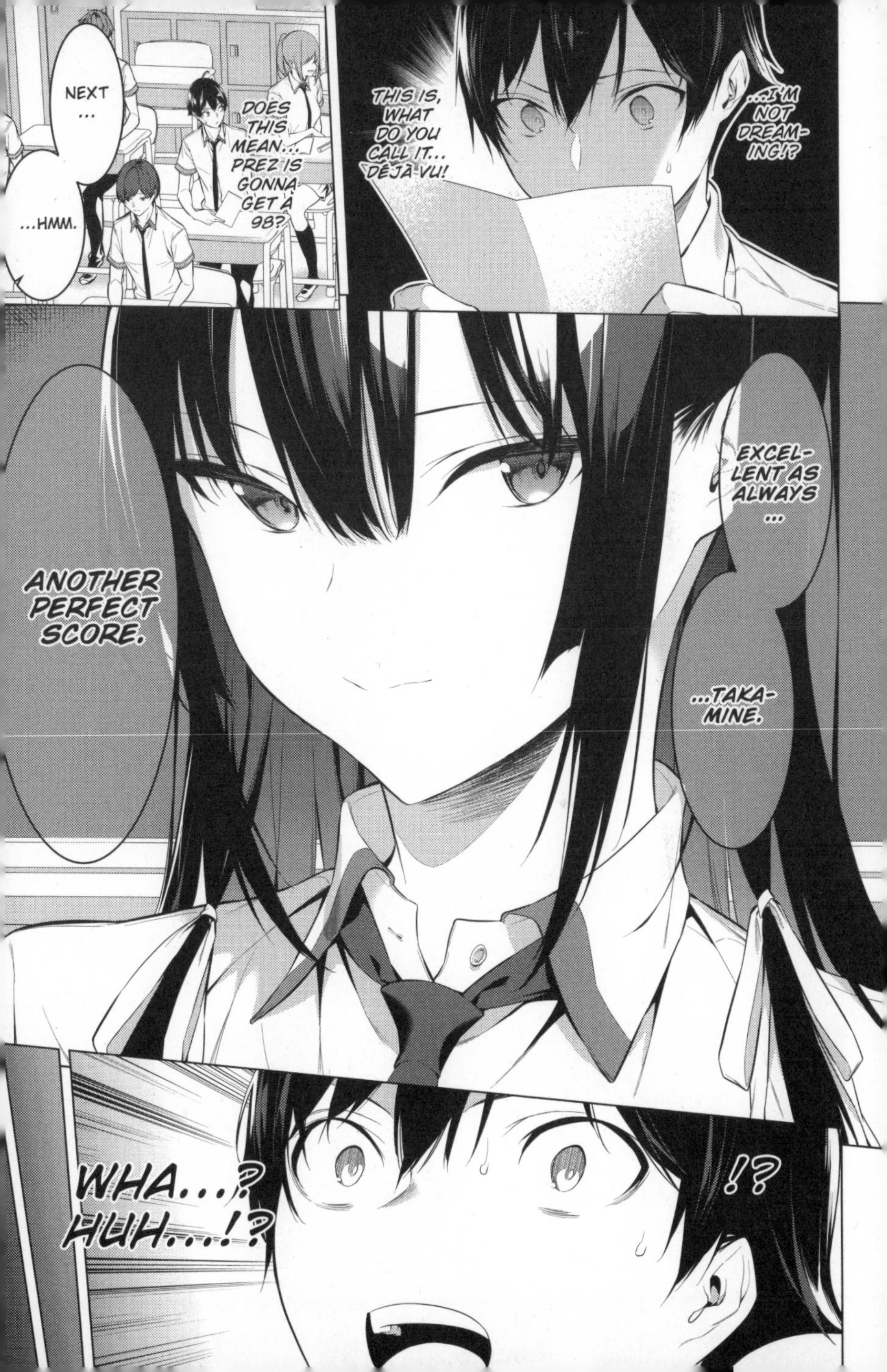
...I'M NOT DREAMING!?
THIS IS, WHAT DO YOU CALL IT... DÉJÀ VU!
DOES THIS MEAN... PREZ IS GONNA GET A 98?
NEXT...
...HMM.
EXCELLENT AS ALWAYS...
...TAKAMINE.
ANOTHER PERFECT SCORE.
!?
WHA...? HUH...!?

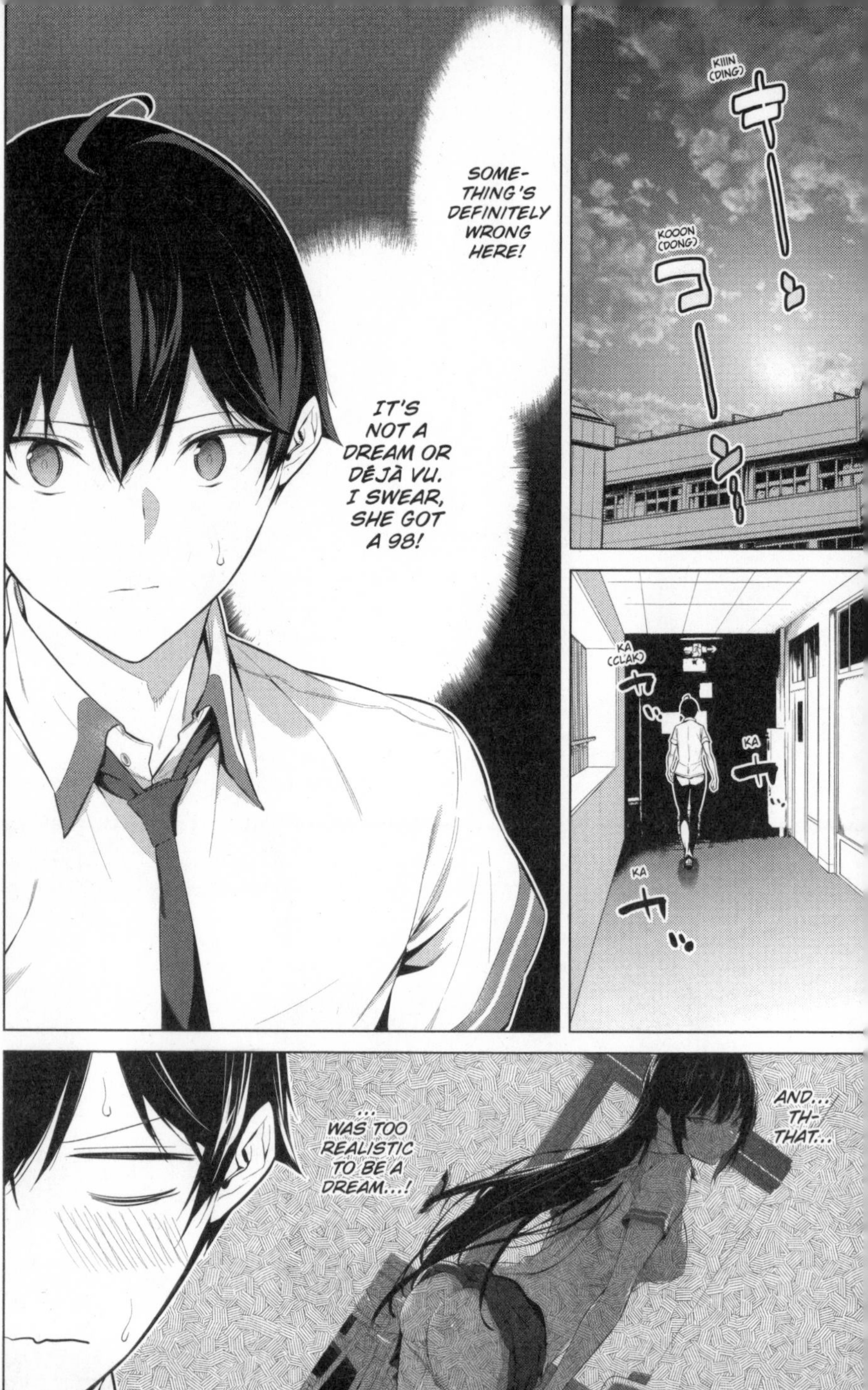
KIIN (DING)
KOOON (DONG)
KA (CLAK)
KA
KA
SOME-THING'S DEFINITELY WRONG HERE!
IT'S NOT A DREAM OR DÉJÀ VU. I SWEAR, SHE GOT A 98!
AND... TH-THAT...
...WAS TOO REALISTIC TO BE A DREAM...!

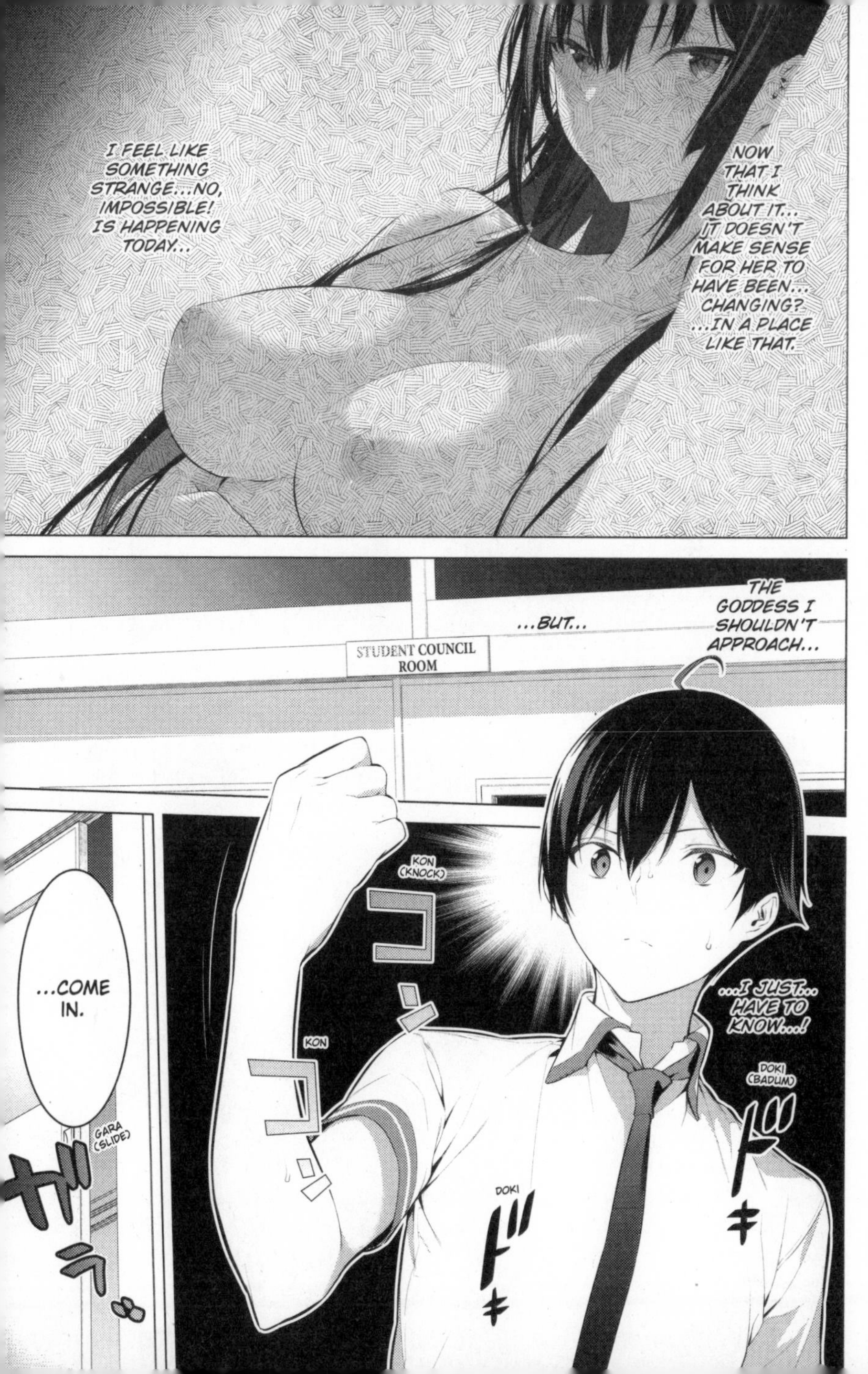
NOW THAT I THINK ABOUT IT... IT DOESN'T MAKE SENSE FOR HER TO HAVE BEEN... CHANGING? ...IN A PLACE LIKE THAT.
I FEEL LIKE SOMETHING STRANGE...NO, IMPOSSIBLE! IS HAPPENING TODAY...
THE GODDESS I SHOULDN'T APPROACH...
...BUT...
STUDENT COUNCIL ROOM
...I JUST... HAVE TO KNOW...!
DOKI (BADUM)
DOKI
KON (KNOCK)
KON
...COME IN.
GARA (SLIDE)

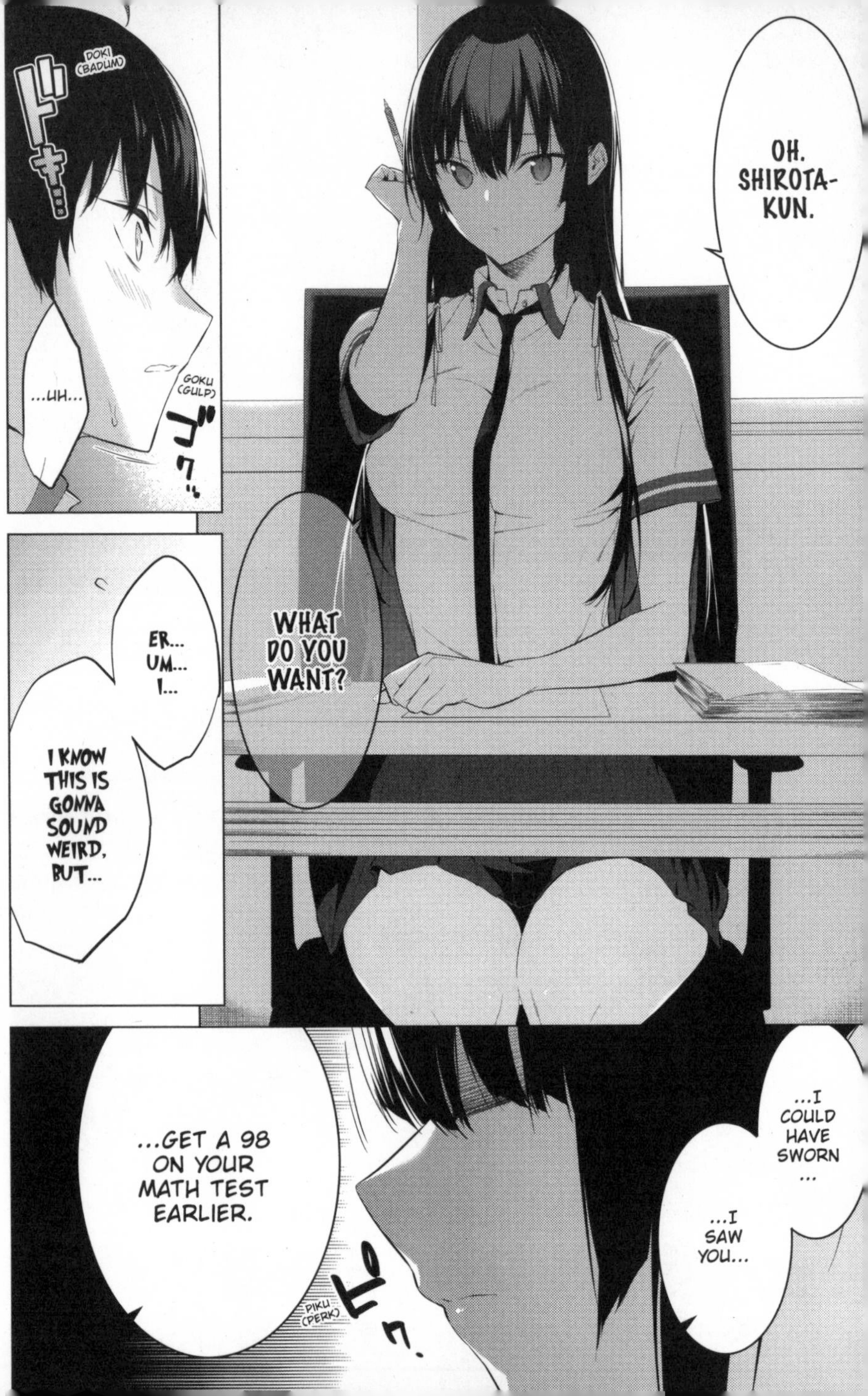
OH. SHIROTA-KUN.
WHAT DO YOU WANT?
DOKI (BADUM)
...UH...
GOKU (GULP)
ER... UM... I...
I KNOW THIS IS GONNA SOUND WEIRD, BUT...
...I COULD HAVE SWORN...
...I SAW YOU...
PIKU (PERK)
...GET A 98 ON YOUR MATH TEST EARLIER.

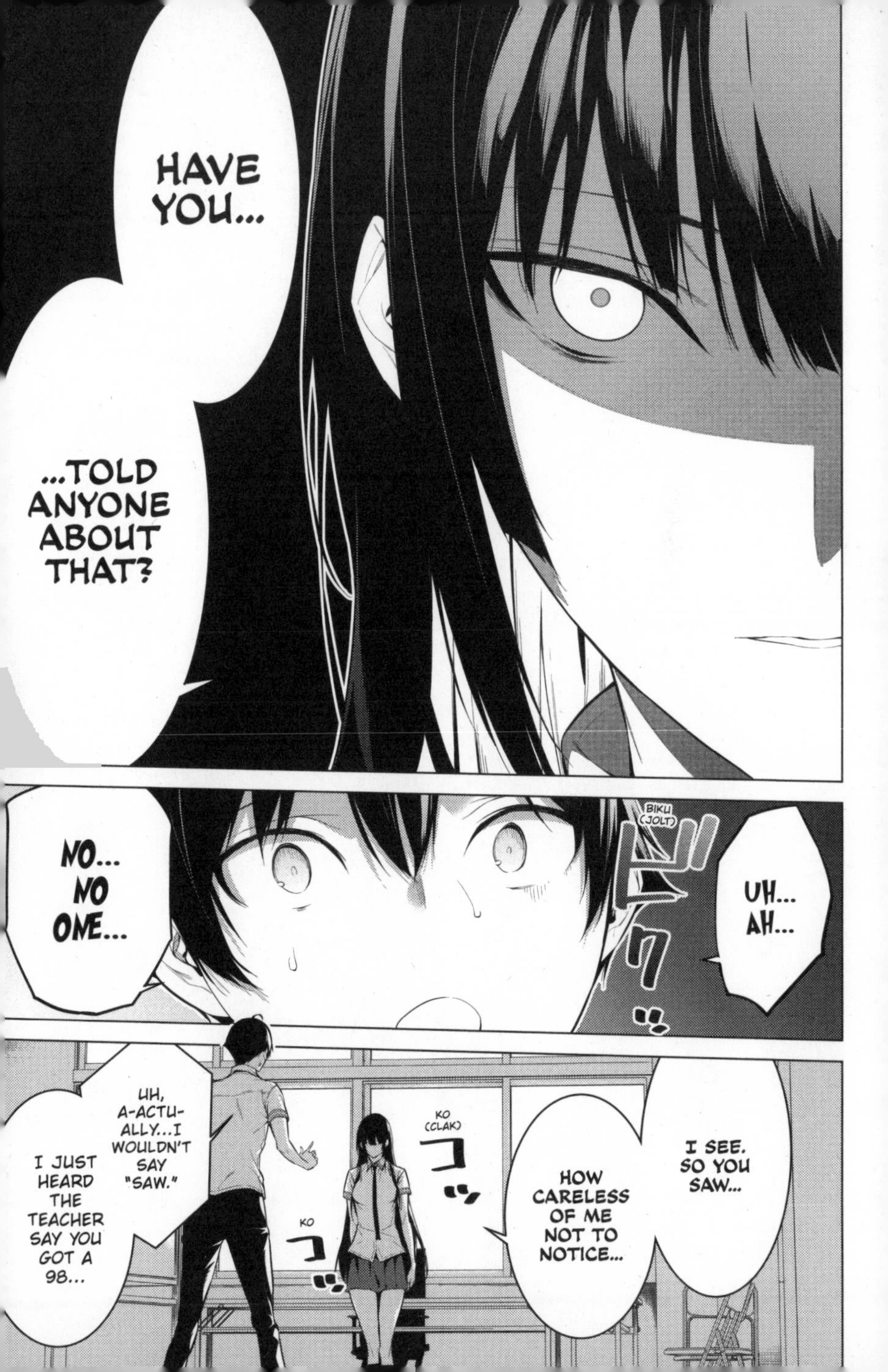
HAVE YOU...
...TOLD ANYONE ABOUT THAT?
BIKU (JOLT)
UH... AH...
NO... NO ONE...
I SEE. SO YOU SAW...
HOW CARELESS OF ME NOT TO NOTICE...
KO (CLAK)
KO
UH, A-ACTU-ALLY...I WOULDN'T SAY "SAW."
I JUST HEARD THE TEACHER SAY YOU GOT A 98...

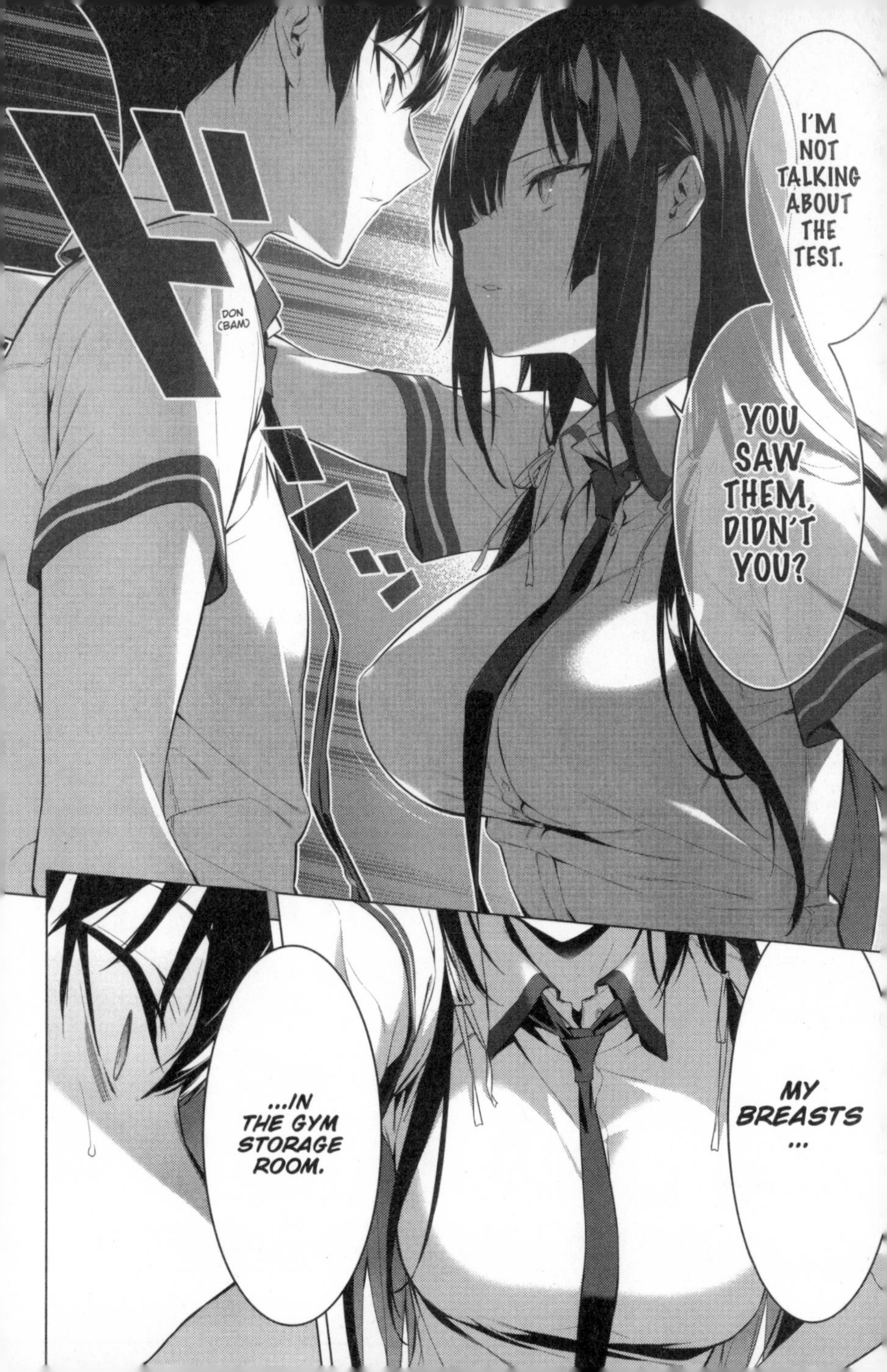
I'M NOT TALKING ABOUT THE TEST.
YOU SAW THEM, DIDN'T YOU?
DON (BAM)
MY BREASTS ...
...IN THE GYM STORAGE ROOM.

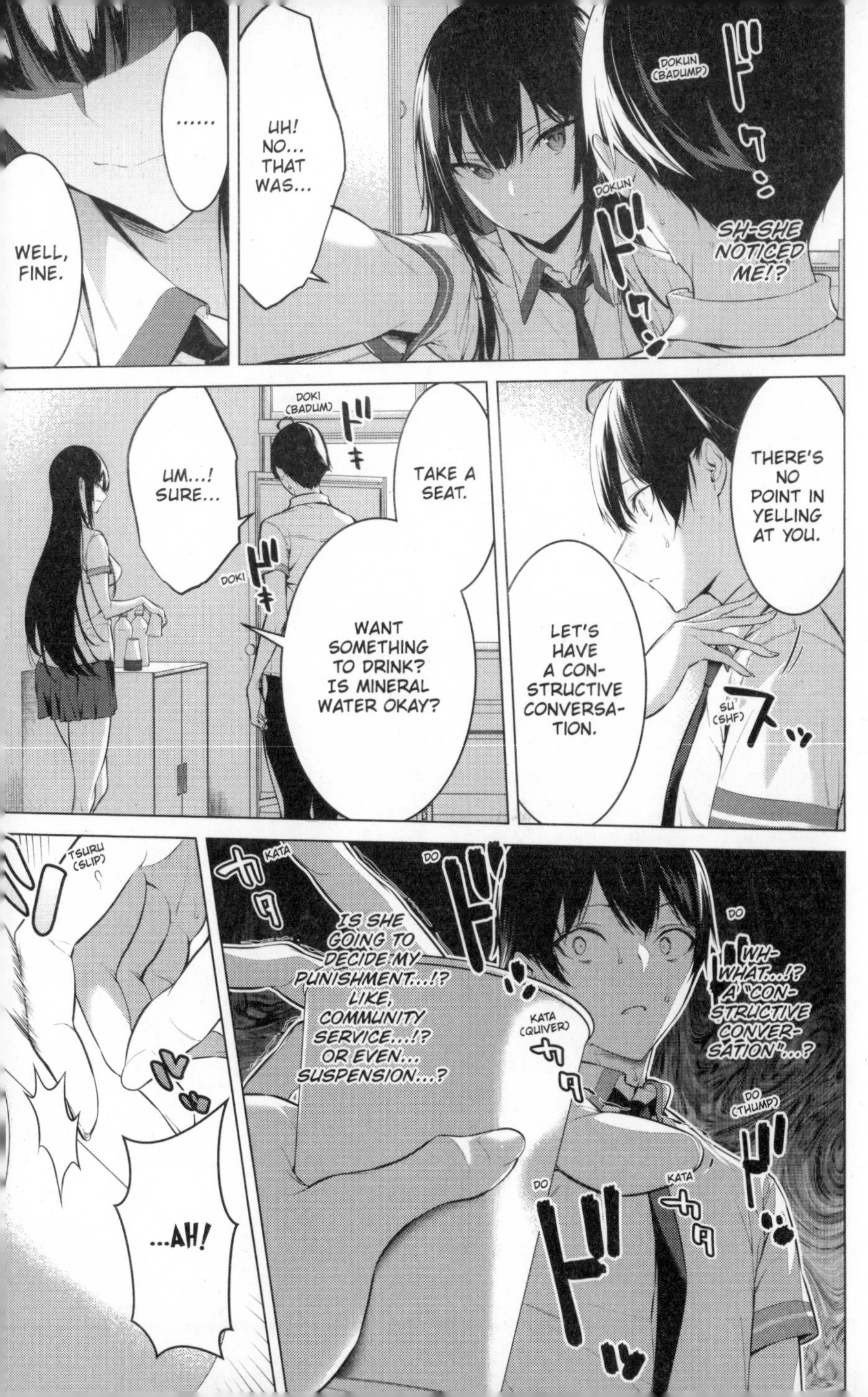
DOKUN (BADUMP)
DOKUN
SH-SHE NOTICED ME!?
UH! NO... THAT WAS...
......
WELL, FINE.
THERE'S NO POINT IN YELLING AT YOU.
LET'S HAVE A CON-STRUCTIVE CONVERSA-TION.
SU (SHF)
DOKI (BADUM)
TAKE A SEAT.
UM...! SURE...
DOKI
WANT SOMETHING TO DRINK? IS MINERAL WATER OKAY?
DO
DO
WH-WHAT...!? A "CON-STRUCTIVE CONVER-SATION"...?
KATA
IS SHE GOING TO DECIDE MY PUNISHMENT...!? LIKE, COMMUNITY SERVICE...!? OR EVEN... SUSPENSION...?
KATA (QUIVER)
DO (THUMP)
KATA
DO
TSURU (SLIP)
...AH!

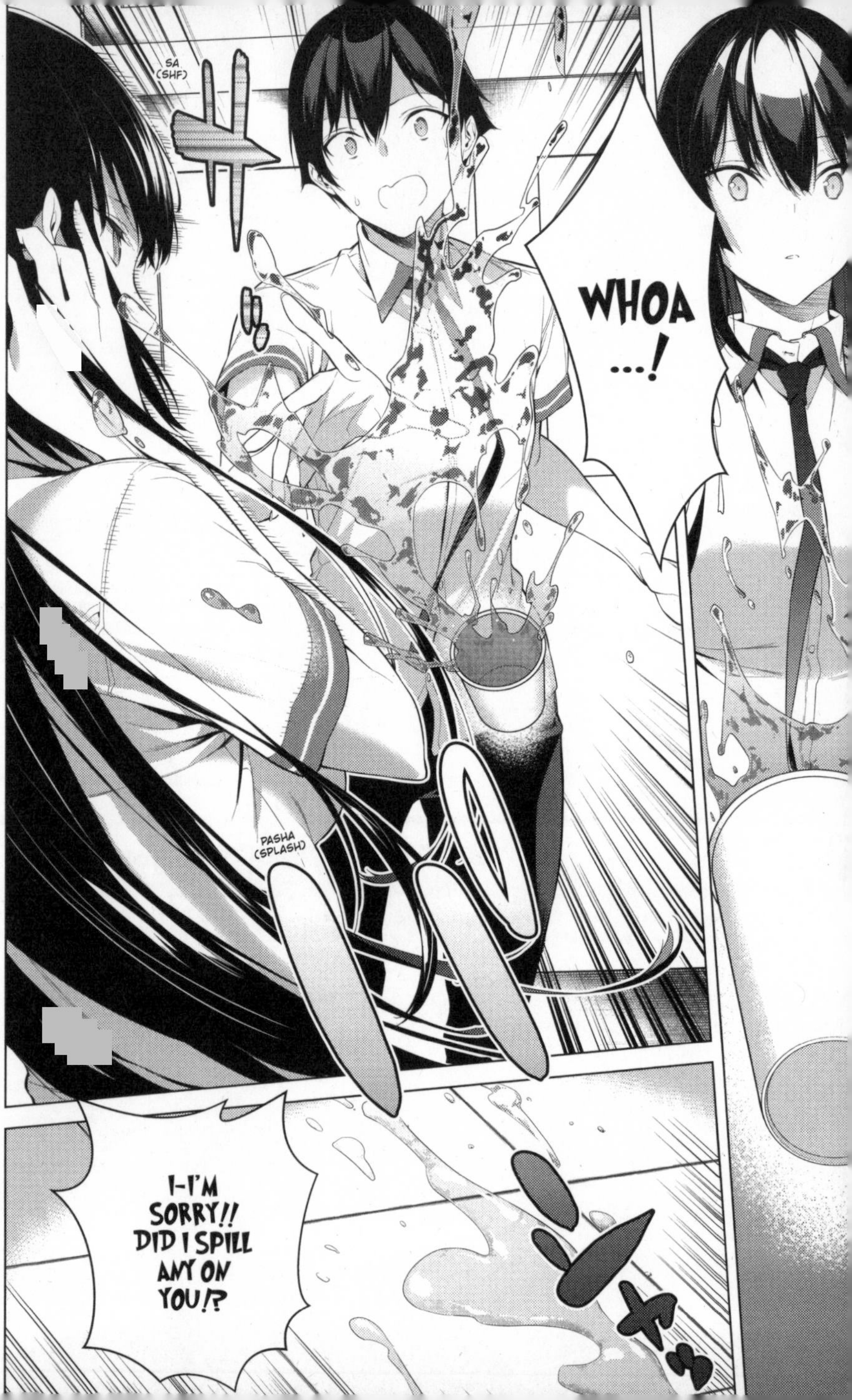
WHOA ...!
SA (SHF)
PASHA (SPLASH)
I-I'M SORRY!! DID I SPILL ANY ON YOU!?

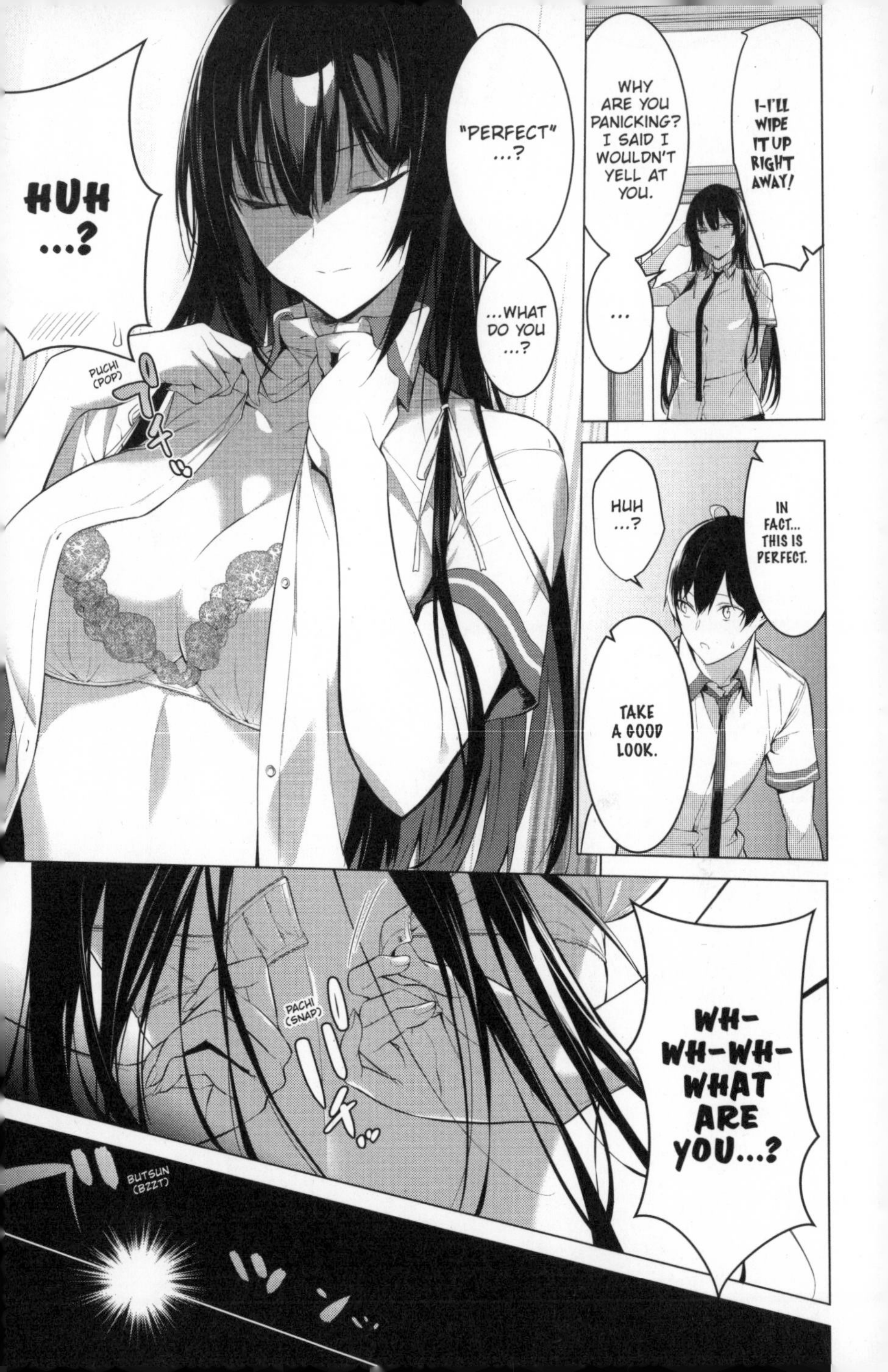
I-I'LL WIPE IT UP RIGHT AWAY!
WHY ARE YOU PANICKING? I SAID I WOULDN'T YELL AT YOU.
...
IN FACT... THIS IS PERFECT.
HUH ...?
TAKE A GOOD LOOK.
"PERFECT" ...?
...WHAT DO YOU ...?
HUH ...?
PUCHI (POP)
WH-WH-WH-WHAT ARE YOU...?
PACHI (SNAP)
BUTSUN (BZZT)

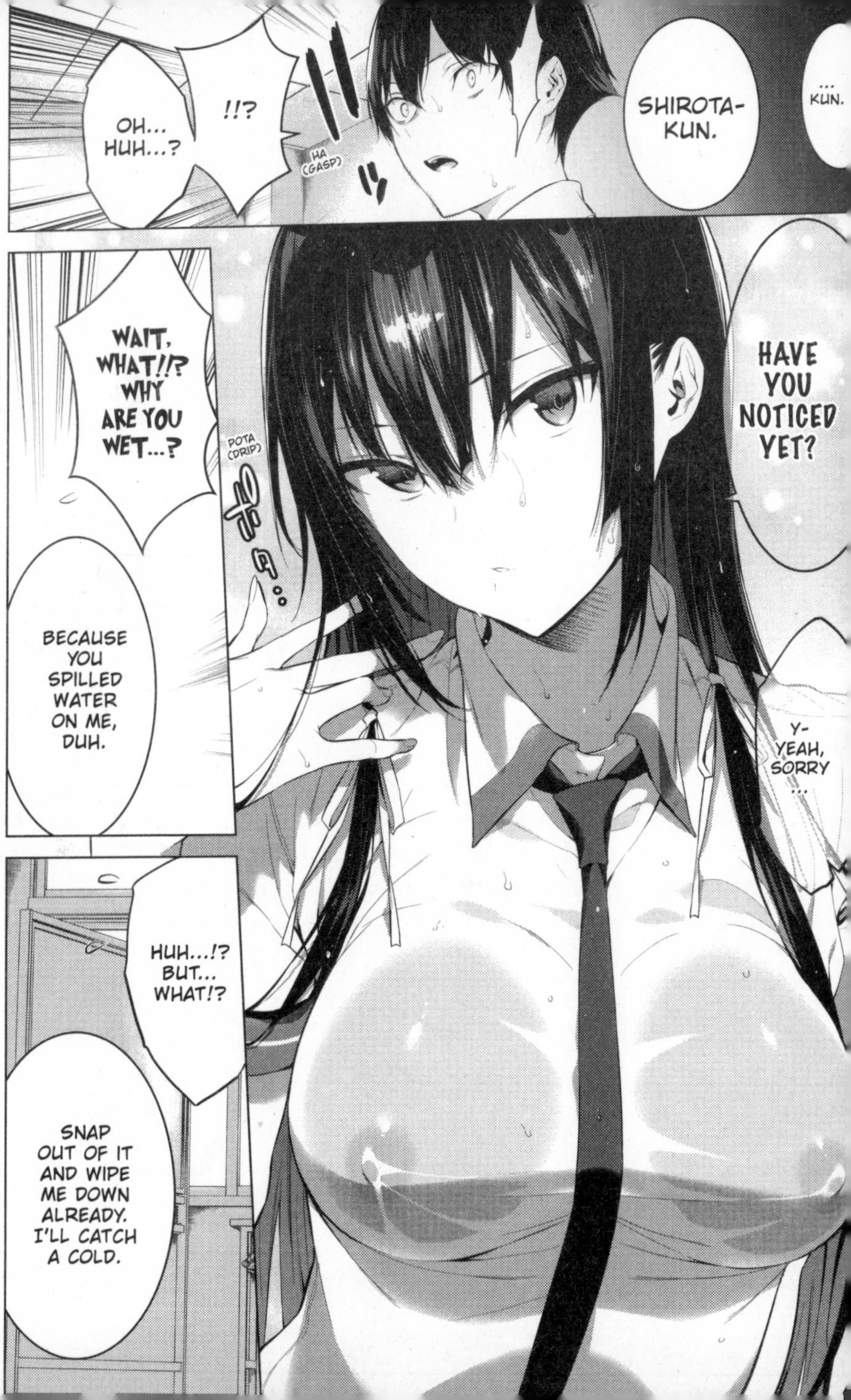
...KUN.
SHIROTA-KUN.
HA (GASP)
!!?
OH... HUH...?
HAVE YOU NOTICED YET?
POTA (DRIP)
Y-YEAH, SORRY...
WAIT, WHAT!!? WHY ARE YOU WET...?
BECAUSE YOU SPILLED WATER ON ME, DUH.
HUH...!? BUT... WHAT!?
SNAP OUT OF IT AND WIPE ME DOWN ALREADY. I'LL CATCH A COLD.

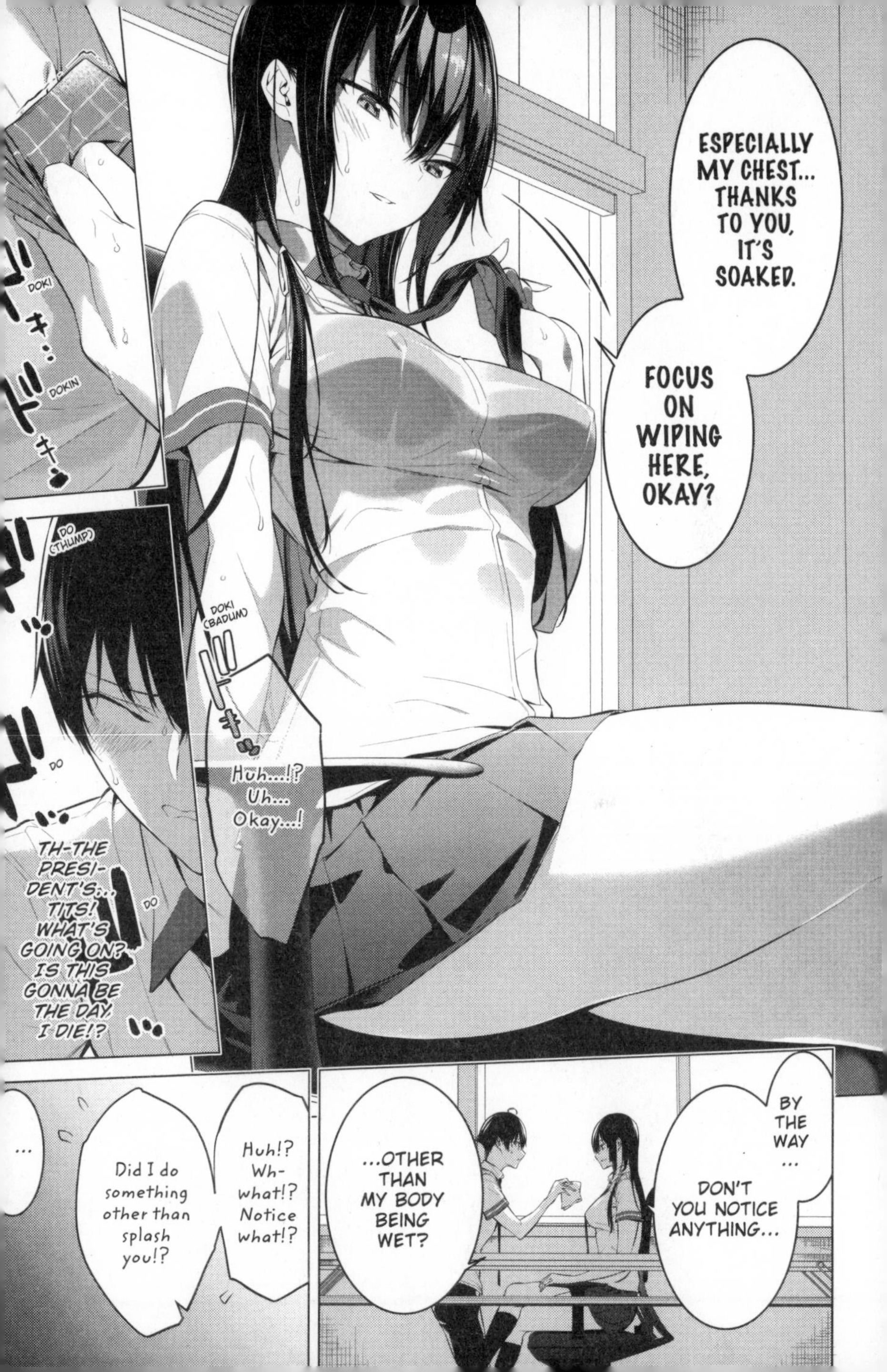
ESPECIALLY MY CHEST... THANKS TO YOU, IT'S SOAKED.
FOCUS ON WIPING HERE, OKAY?
DOKI
DOKIN
DO (THUMP)
DOKI (BADUM)
Huh...!? Uh... Okay...!
DO
DO
TH-THE PRESIDENT'S... TITS! WHAT'S GOING ON? IS THIS GONNA BE THE DAY I DIE!?
BY THE WAY...
DON'T YOU NOTICE ANYTHING...
...OTHER THAN MY BODY BEING WET?
Huh!? Wh-what!? Notice what!?
Did I do something other than splash you!?
...

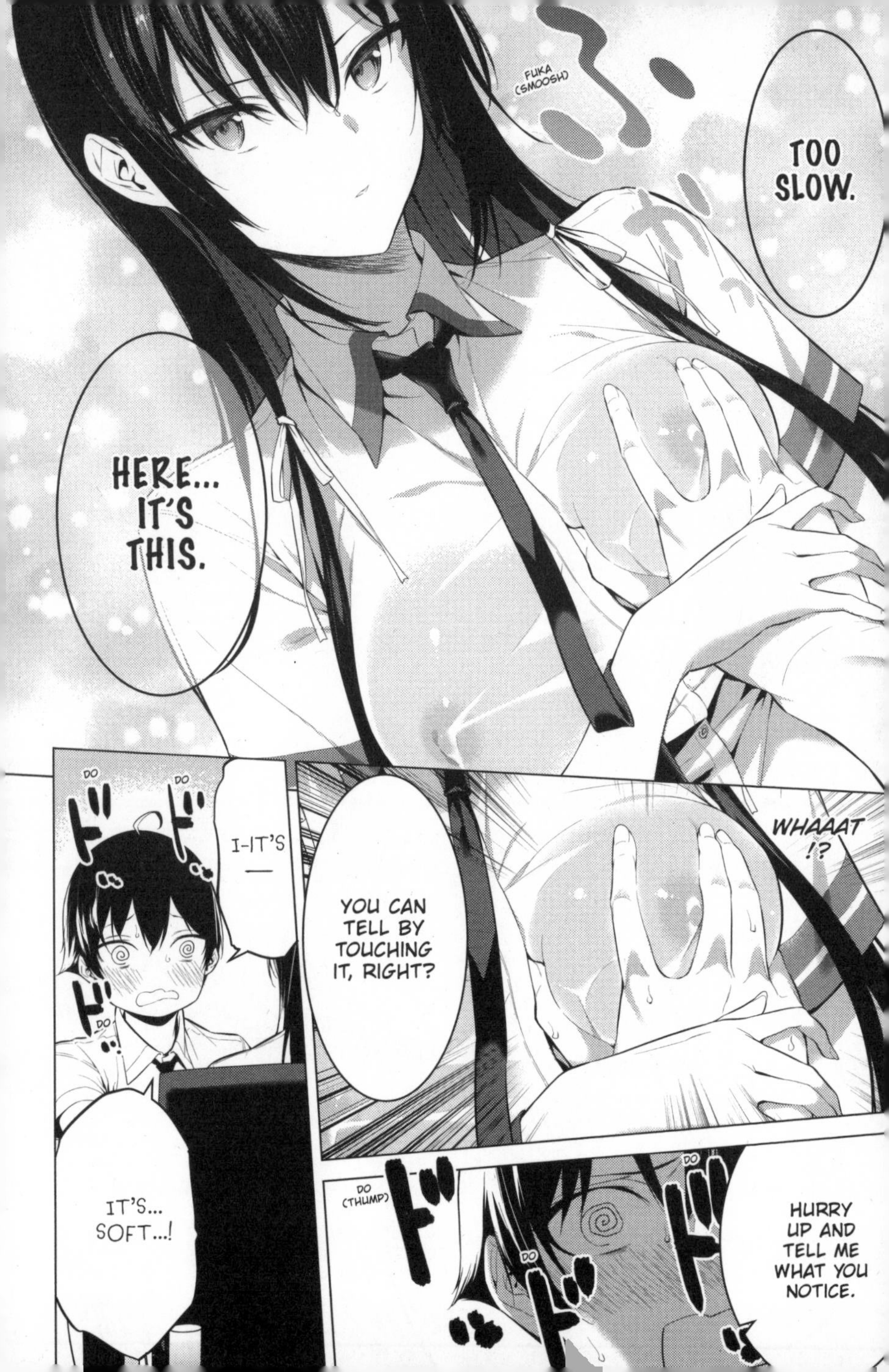
TOO SLOW.
FUKA (SMOOSH)
HERE... IT'S THIS.
WHAAAT!?
YOU CAN TELL BY TOUCHING IT, RIGHT?
HURRY UP AND TELL ME WHAT YOU NOTICE.
DO (THUMP)
DO
DO
DO
DO
I-IT'S —
DO
IT'S... SOFT...!

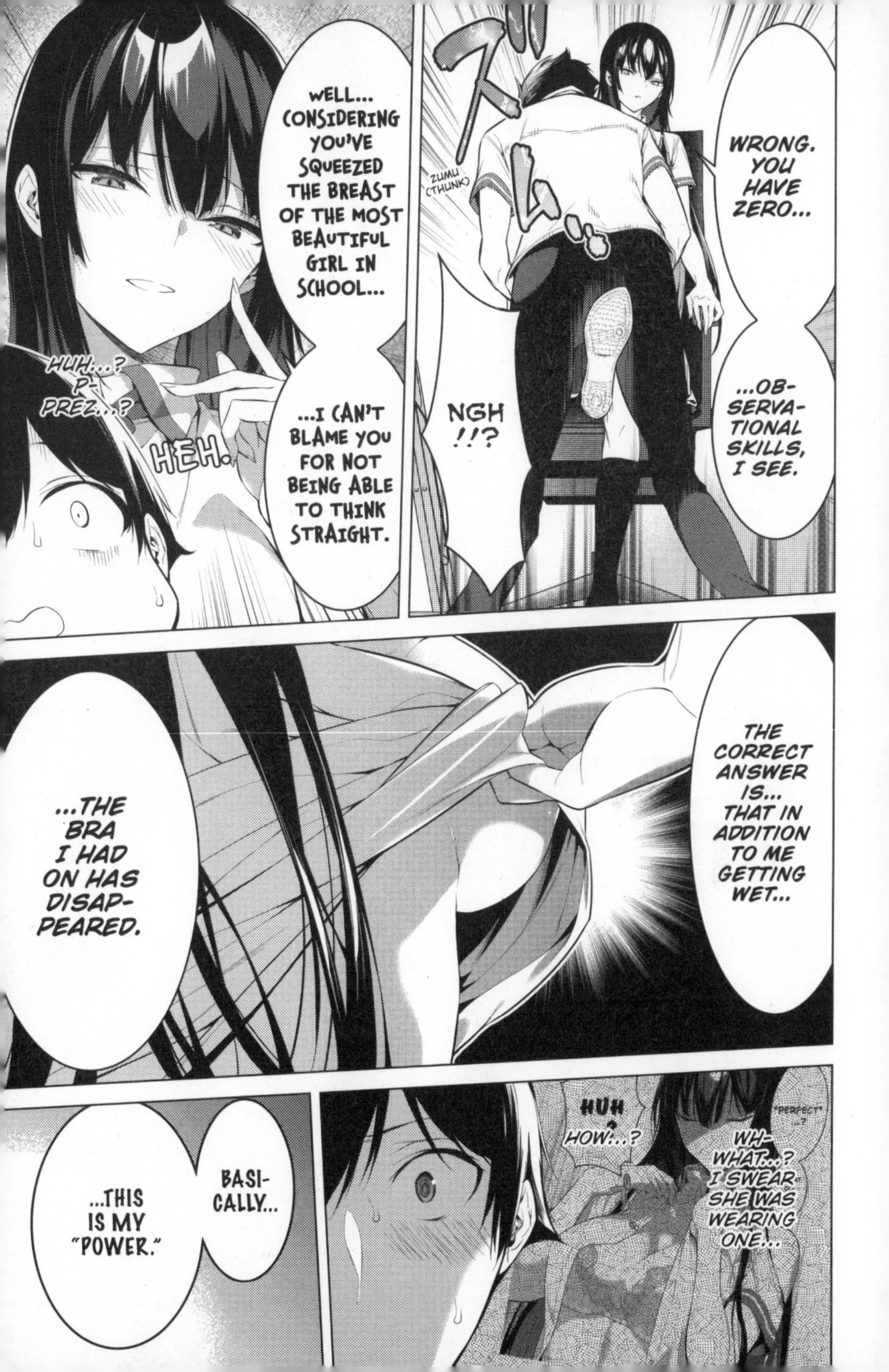

WRONG. YOU HAVE ZERO...
ZUMU (THUNK)
NGH!!?
...OBSERVATIONAL SKILLS, I SEE.
WELL... CONSIDERING YOU'VE SQUEEZED THE BREAST OF THE MOST BEAUTIFUL GIRL IN SCHOOL...
...I CAN'T BLAME YOU FOR NOT BEING ABLE TO THINK STRAIGHT.
HEH.
HUH...? P-PREZ...?
THE CORRECT ANSWER IS... THAT IN ADDITION TO ME GETTING WET...
...THE BRA I HAD ON HAS DISAPPEARED.
"PERFECT"...?
WH-WHAT...? I SWEAR SHE WAS WEARING ONE...
HUH HOW...?
BASICALLY...
...THIS IS MY "POWER."

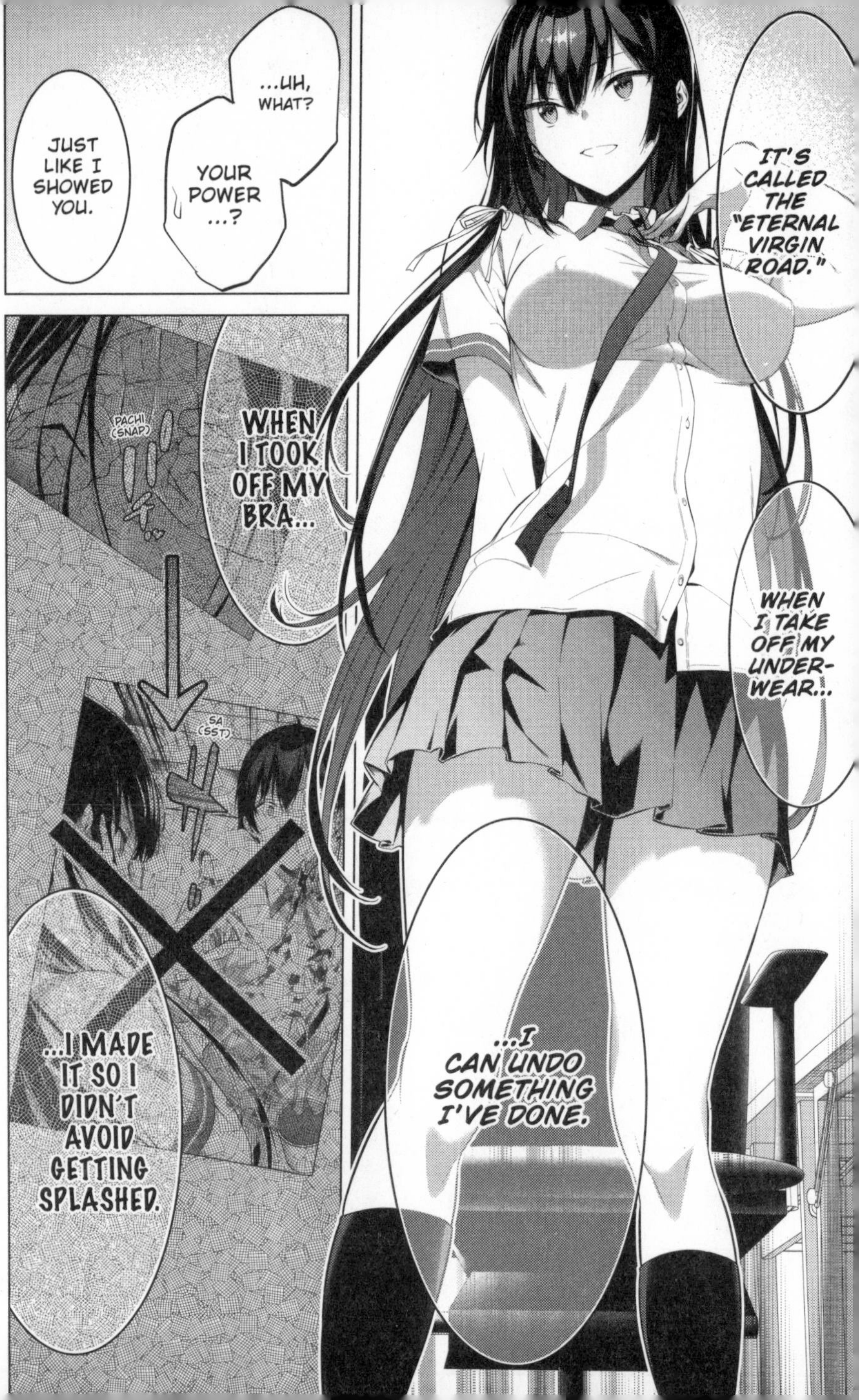

IT'S CALLED THE "ETERNAL VIRGIN ROAD."
WHEN I TAKE OFF MY UNDER-WEAR...
...I CAN UNDO SOMETHING I'VE DONE.
...UH, WHAT?
YOUR POWER ...?
JUST LIKE I SHOWED YOU.
WHEN I TOOK OFF MY BRA...
PACHI (SNAP)
SA (SST)
...I MADE IT SO I DIDN'T AVOID GETTING SPLASHED.

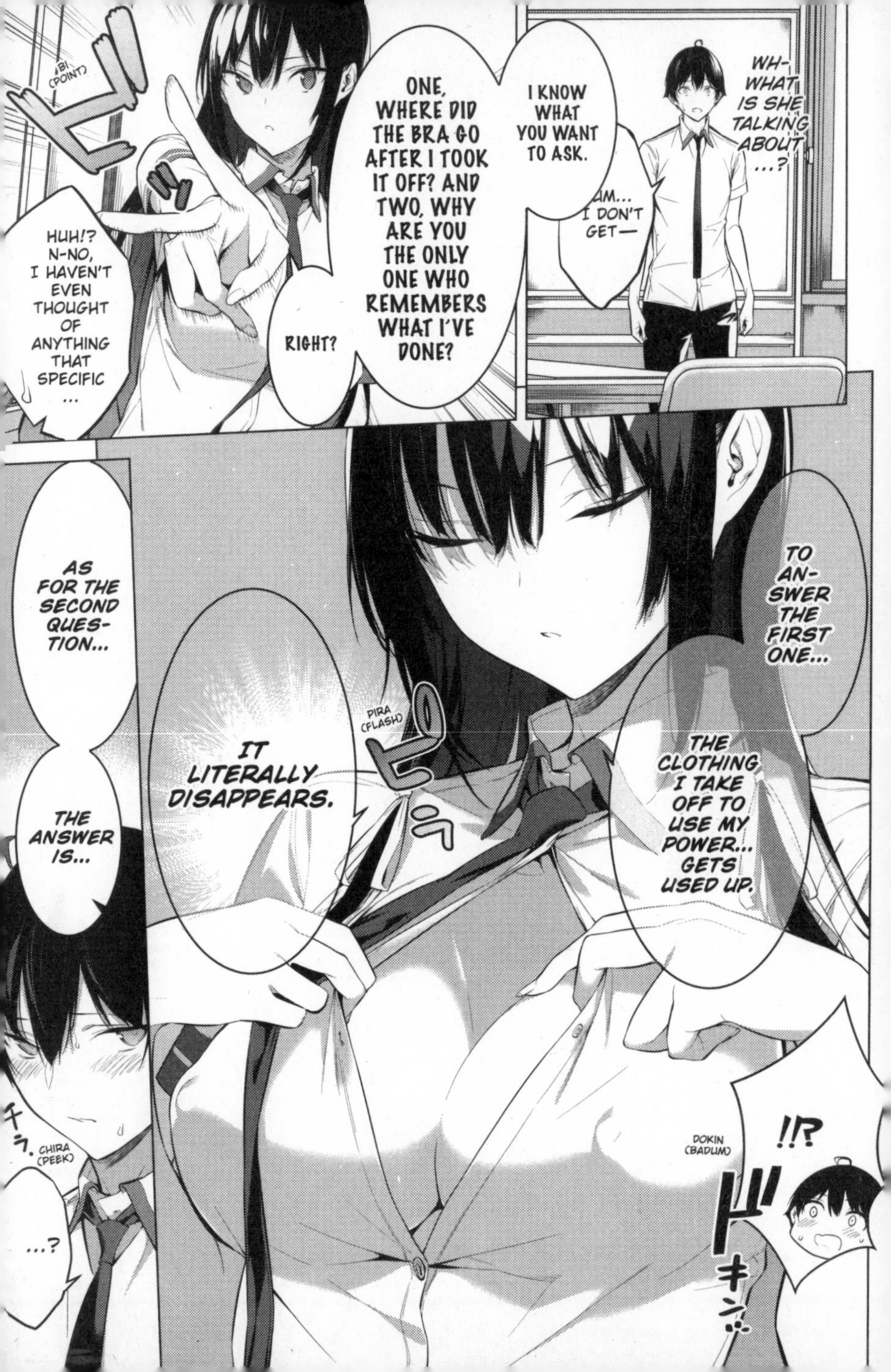
WH-WHAT IS SHE TALKING ABOUT …?
I KNOW WHAT YOU WANT TO ASK.
UM… I DON'T GET—
ONE, WHERE DID THE BRA GO AFTER I TOOK IT OFF? AND TWO, WHY ARE YOU THE ONLY ONE WHO REMEMBERS WHAT I'VE DONE?
RIGHT?
BI (POINT)
HUH!? N-NO, I HAVEN'T EVEN THOUGHT OF ANYTHING THAT SPECIFIC …
TO AN-SWER THE FIRST ONE…
THE CLOTHING I TAKE OFF TO USE MY POWER… GETS USED UP.
PIRA (FLASH)
IT LITERALLY DISAPPEARS.
AS FOR THE SECOND QUES-TION…
THE ANSWER IS…
!!?
DOKIN (BADUM)
CHIRA (PEEK)
…?

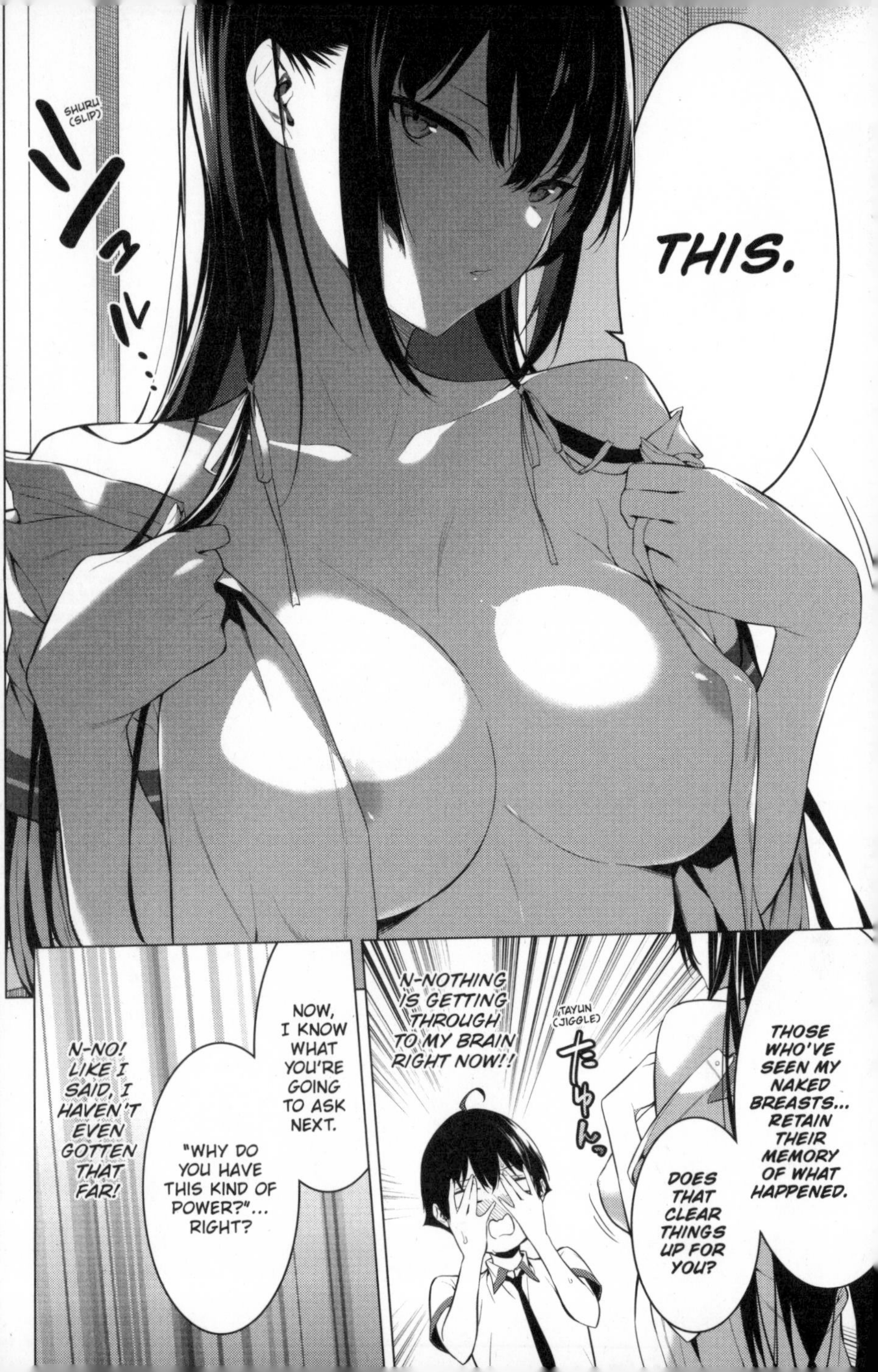
THIS.
SHURU (SLIP)
THOSE WHO'VE SEEN MY NAKED BREASTS... RETAIN THEIR MEMORY OF WHAT HAPPENED.
DOES THAT CLEAR THINGS UP FOR YOU?
TAYUN (JIGGLE)
N-NOTHING IS GETTING THROUGH TO MY BRAIN RIGHT NOW!!
NOW, I KNOW WHAT YOU'RE GOING TO ASK NEXT.
"WHY DO YOU HAVE THIS KIND OF POWER?"... RIGHT?
N-NO! LIKE I SAID, I HAVEN'T EVEN GOTTEN THAT FAR!

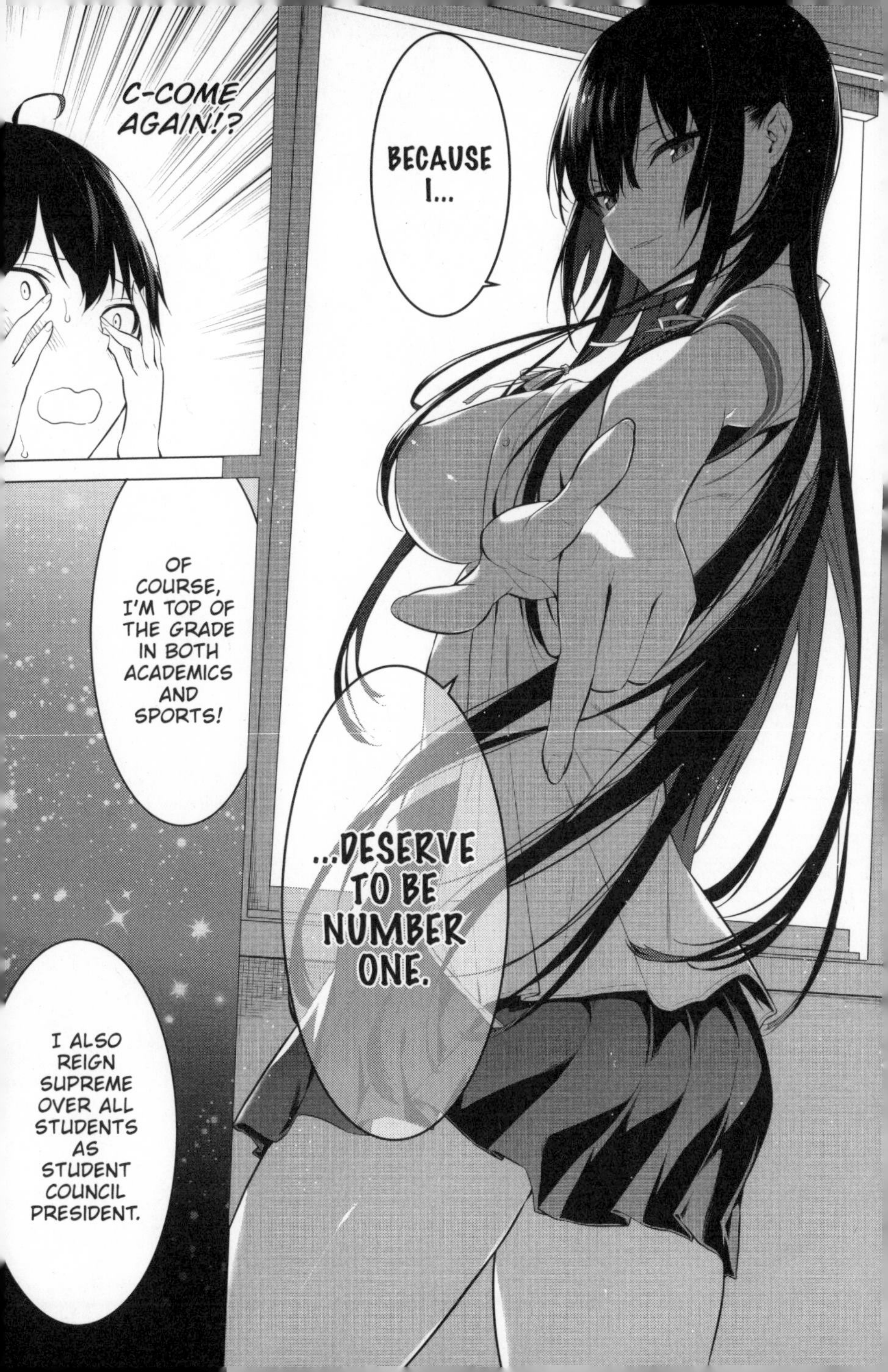
BECAUSE I...
...DESERVE TO BE NUMBER ONE.
C-COME AGAIN!?
OF COURSE, I'M TOP OF THE GRADE IN BOTH ACADEMICS AND SPORTS!
I ALSO REIGN SUPREME OVER ALL STUDENTS AS STUDENT COUNCIL PRESIDENT.

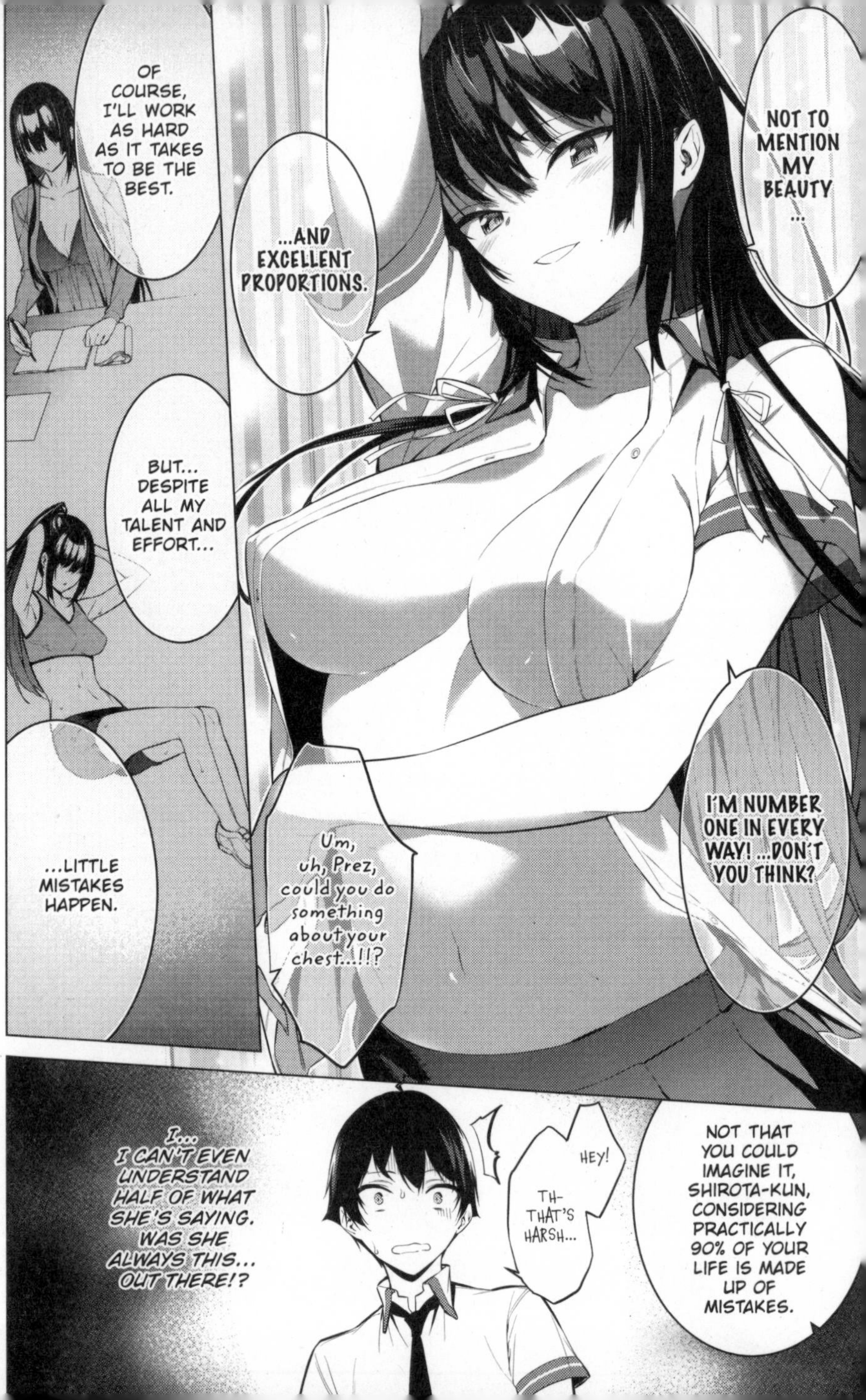
NOT TO MENTION MY BEAUTY ...
...AND EXCELLENT PROPORTIONS.
I'M NUMBER ONE IN EVERY WAY! ...DON'T YOU THINK?
Um, uh, Prez, could you do something about your chest...!!?
OF COURSE, I'LL WORK AS HARD AS IT TAKES TO BE THE BEST.
BUT... DESPITE ALL MY TALENT AND EFFORT...
...LITTLE MISTAKES HAPPEN.
NOT THAT YOU COULD IMAGINE IT, SHIROTA-KUN, CONSIDERING PRACTICALLY 90% OF YOUR LIFE IS MADE UP OF MISTAKES.
HEY!
TH-THAT'S HARSH...
I... I CAN'T EVEN UNDERSTAND HALF OF WHAT SHE'S SAYING. WAS SHE ALWAYS THIS... OUT THERE!?

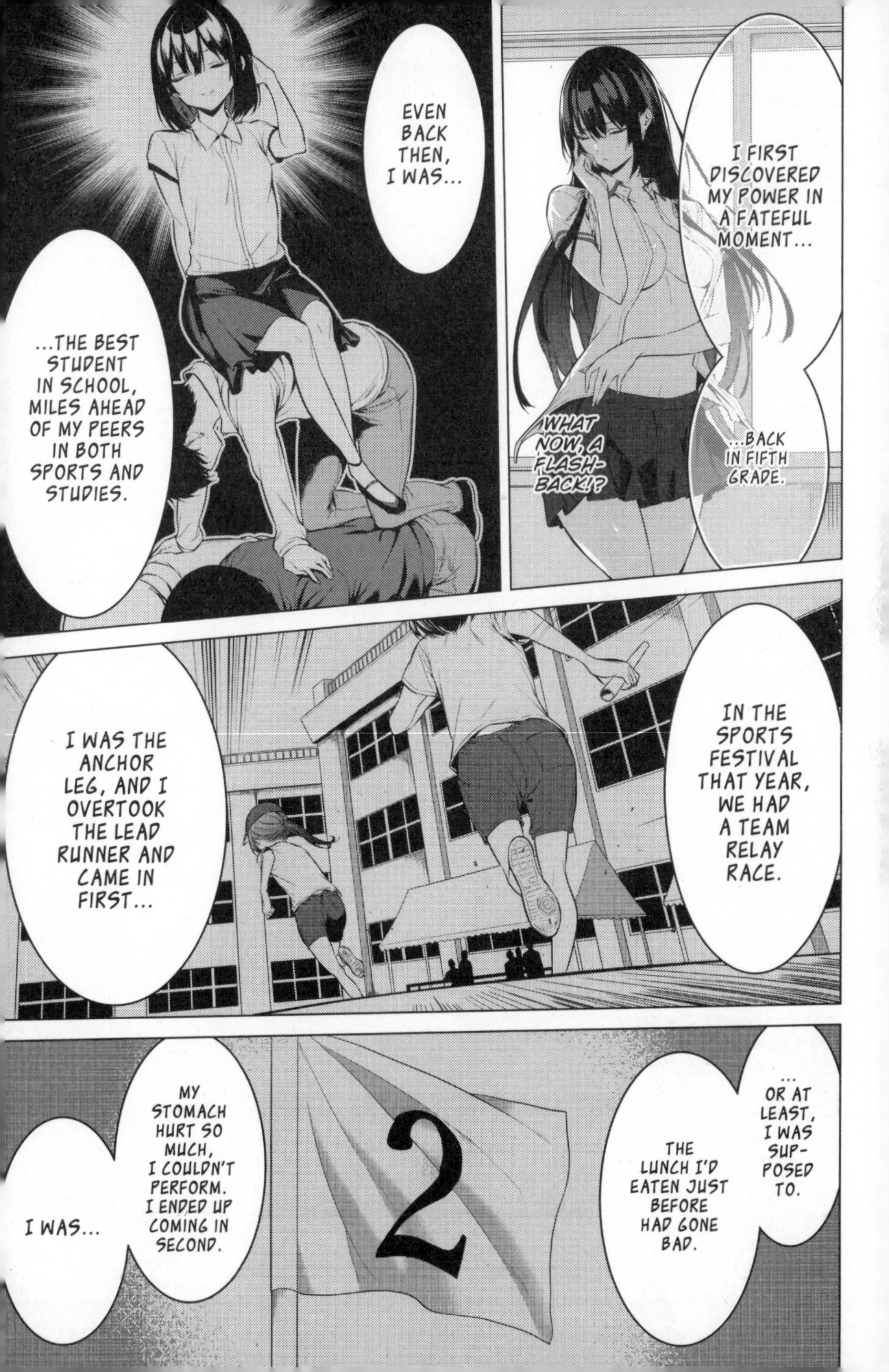
I FIRST DISCOVERED MY POWER IN A FATEFUL MOMENT...
...BACK IN FIFTH GRADE.
WHAT NOW, A FLASH-BACK!?
EVEN BACK THEN, I WAS...
...THE BEST STUDENT IN SCHOOL, MILES AHEAD OF MY PEERS IN BOTH SPORTS AND STUDIES.
IN THE SPORTS FESTIVAL THAT YEAR, WE HAD A TEAM RELAY RACE.
I WAS THE ANCHOR LEG, AND I OVERTOOK THE LEAD RUNNER AND CAME IN FIRST...
...OR AT LEAST, I WAS SUP-POSED TO.
THE LUNCH I'D EATEN JUST BEFORE HAD GONE BAD.
MY STOMACH HURT SO MUCH, I COULDN'T PERFORM. I ENDED UP COMING IN SECOND.
2
I WAS...

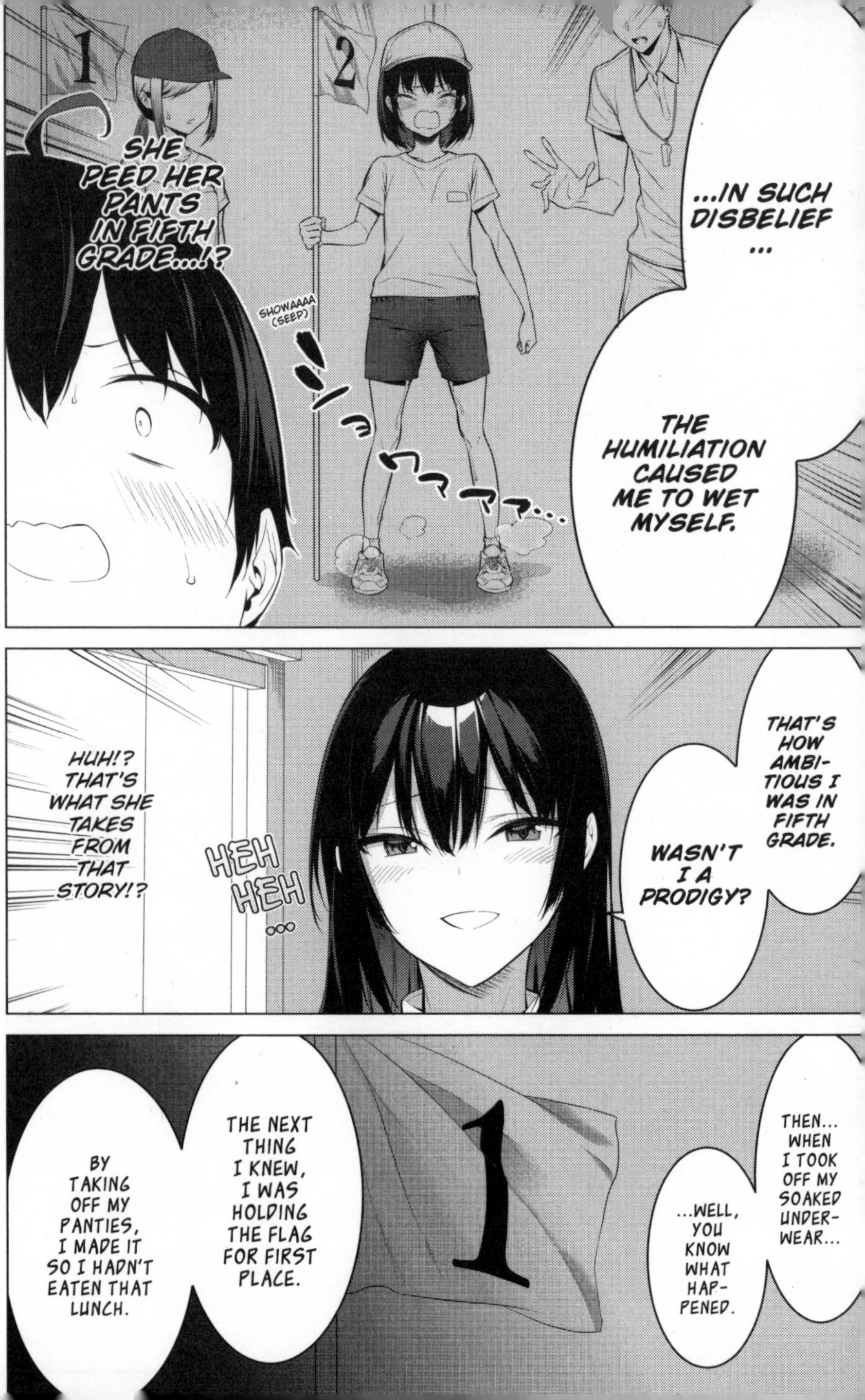
...IN SUCH DISBELIEF ...
THE HUMILIATION CAUSED ME TO WET MYSELF.
SHOWAAAA (SEEP)
SHE PEED HER PANTS IN FIFTH GRADE...!?
THAT'S HOW AMBI-TIOUS I WAS IN FIFTH GRADE.
WASN'T I A PRODIGY?
HEH HEH...
HUH!? THAT'S WHAT SHE TAKES FROM THAT STORY!?
THEN... WHEN I TOOK OFF MY SOAKED UNDER-WEAR...
...WELL, YOU KNOW WHAT HAP-PENED.
THE NEXT THING I KNEW, I WAS HOLDING THE FLAG FOR FIRST PLACE.
BY TAKING OFF MY PANTIES, I MADE IT SO I HADN'T EATEN THAT LUNCH.

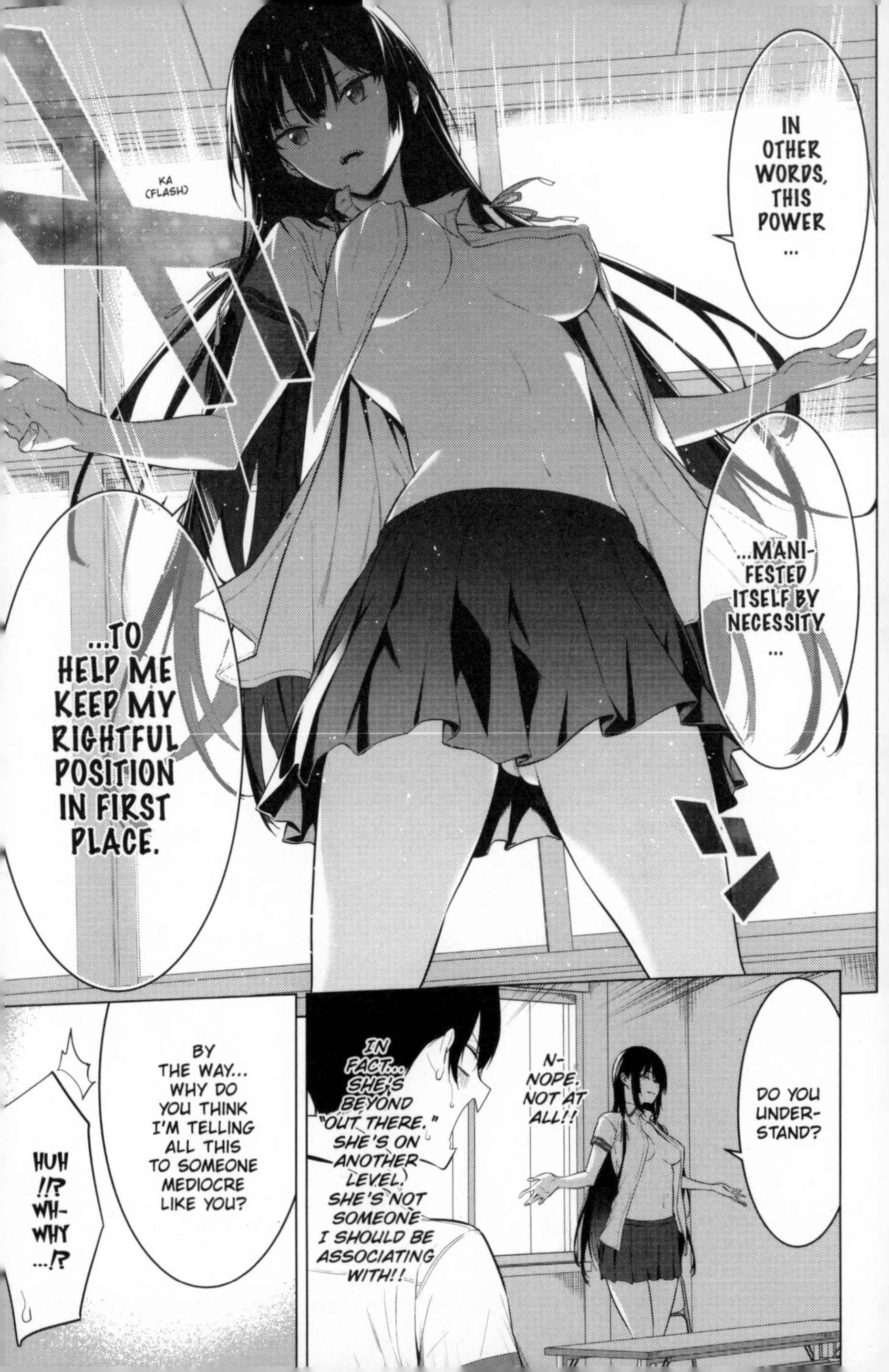
IN OTHER WORDS, THIS POWER ...
KA (FLASH)
...MANIFESTED ITSELF BY NECESSITY ...
...TO HELP ME KEEP MY RIGHTFUL POSITION IN FIRST PLACE.
DO YOU UNDERSTAND?
N-NOPE. NOT AT ALL!!
IN FACT... SHE'S BEYOND "OUT THERE." SHE'S ON ANOTHER LEVEL. SHE'S NOT SOMEONE I SHOULD BE ASSOCIATING WITH!!
BY THE WAY... WHY DO YOU THINK I'M TELLING ALL THIS TO SOMEONE MEDIOCRE LIKE YOU?
HUH!!? WH-WHY ...!?

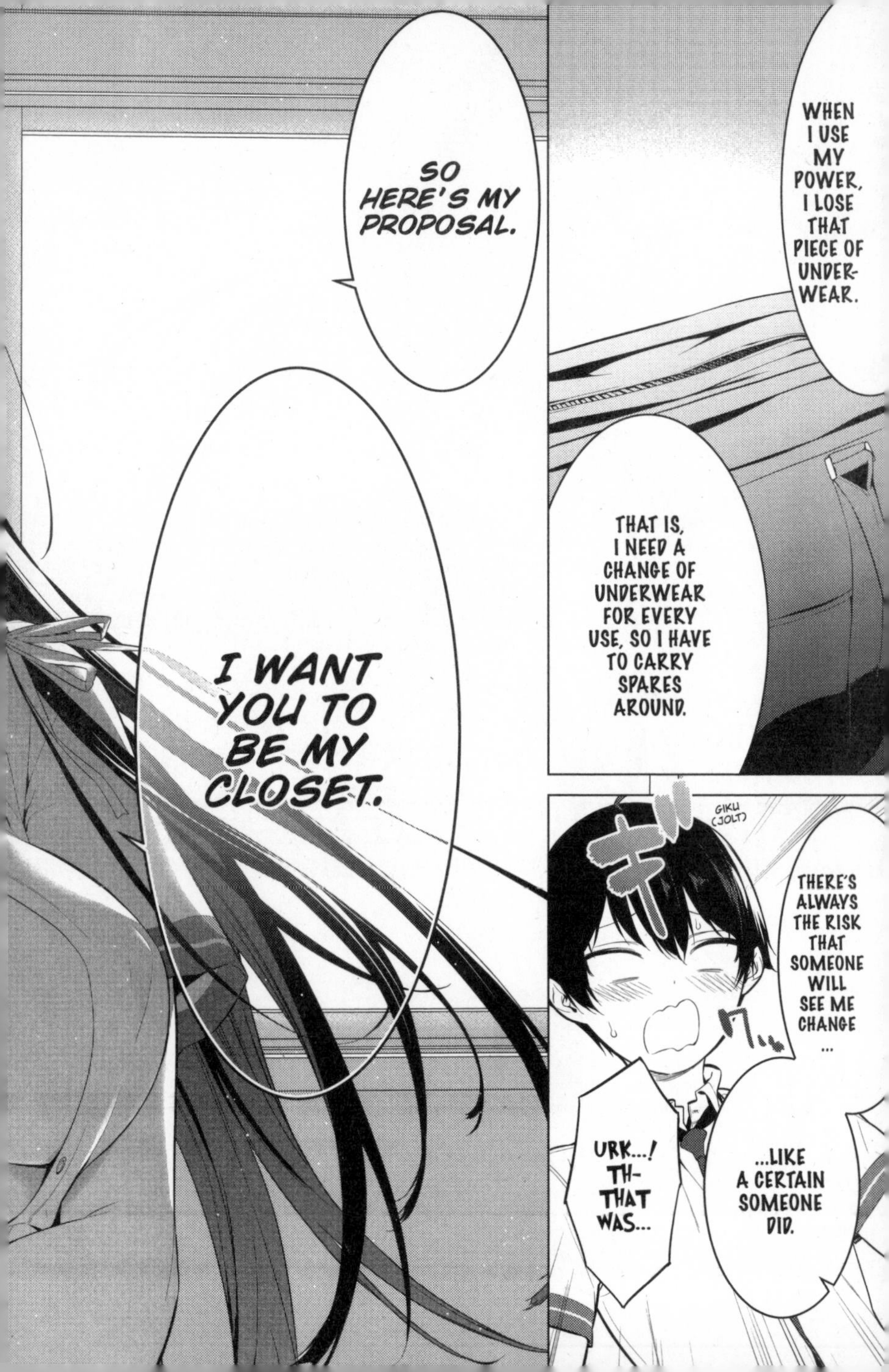
WHEN I USE MY POWER, I LOSE THAT PIECE OF UNDER-WEAR.
THAT IS, I NEED A CHANGE OF UNDERWEAR FOR EVERY USE, SO I HAVE TO CARRY SPARES AROUND.
GIKU (JOLT)
THERE'S ALWAYS THE RISK THAT SOMEONE WILL SEE ME CHANGE...
...LIKE A CERTAIN SOMEONE DID.
URK...! TH-THAT WAS...
SO HERE'S MY PROPOSAL.
I WANT YOU TO BE MY CLOSET.

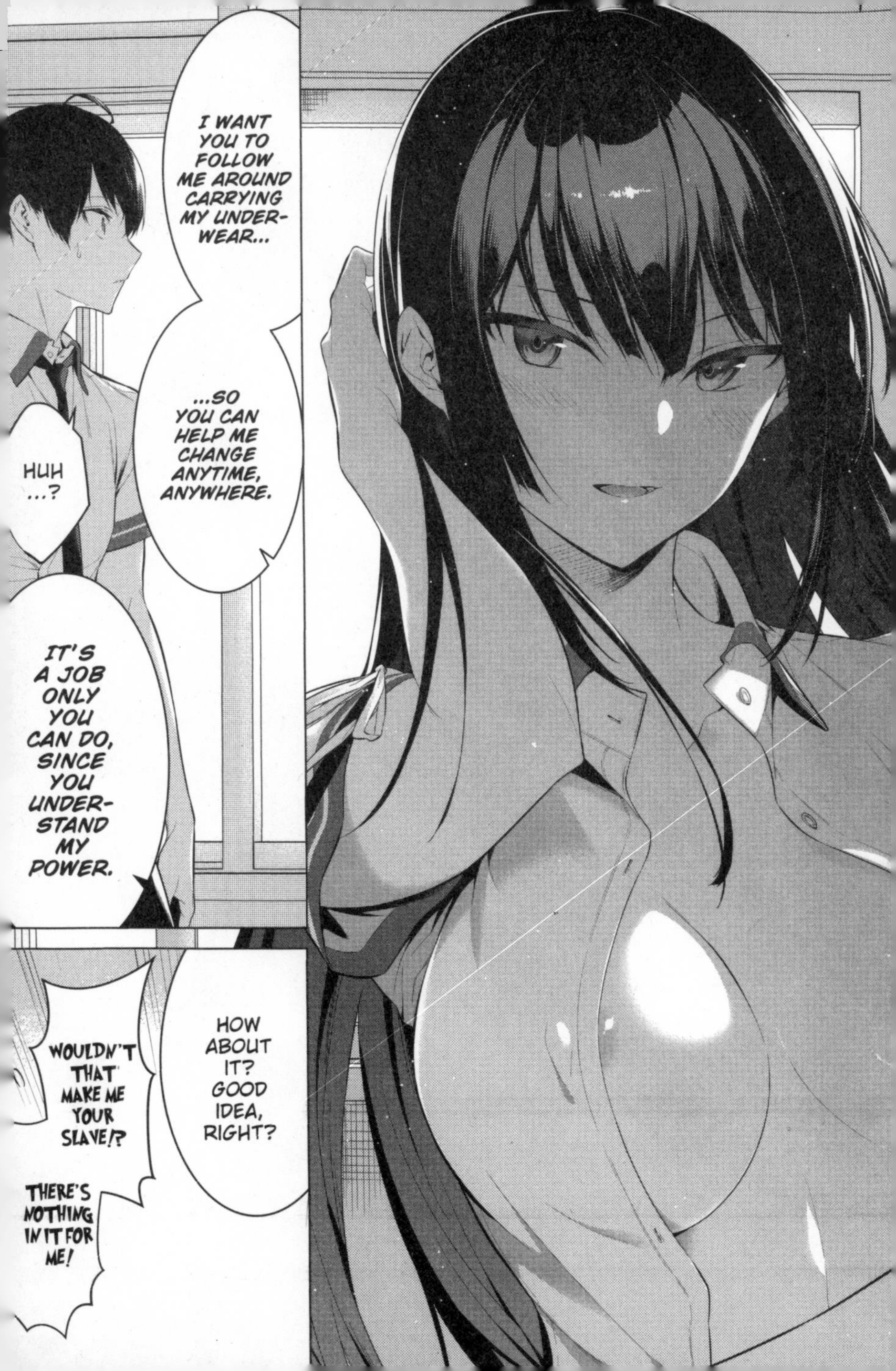
I WANT YOU TO FOLLOW ME AROUND CARRYING MY UNDER-WEAR...
...SO YOU CAN HELP ME CHANGE ANYTIME, ANYWHERE.
HUH ...?
IT'S A JOB ONLY YOU CAN DO, SINCE YOU UNDER-STAND MY POWER.
HOW ABOUT IT? GOOD IDEA, RIGHT?
WOULDN'T THAT MAKE ME YOUR SLAVE!?
THERE'S NOTHING IN IT FOR ME!

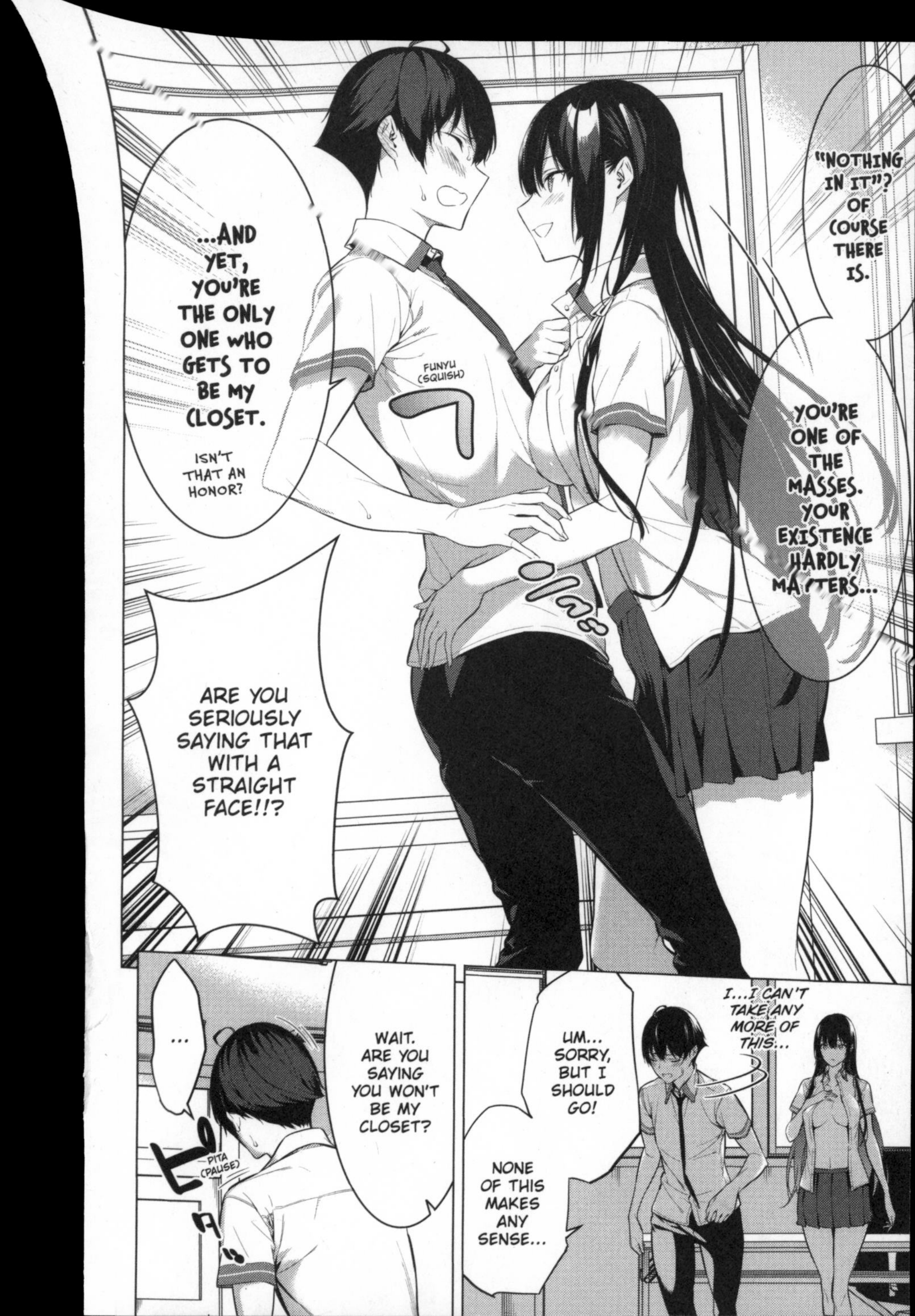
"NOTHING IN IT"? OF COURSE THERE IS.
YOU'RE ONE OF THE MASSES. YOUR EXISTENCE HARDLY MA TERS...
...AND YET, YOU'RE THE ONLY ONE WHO GETS TO BE MY CLOSET.
ISN'T THAT AN HONOR?
FUNYU (SQUISH)
ARE YOU SERIOUSLY SAYING THAT WITH A STRAIGHT FACE!!?
I...I CAN'T TAKE ANY MORE OF THIS...
UM... SORRY, BUT I SHOULD GO!
NONE OF THIS MAKES ANY SENSE...
WAIT. ARE YOU SAYING YOU WON'T BE MY CLOSET?
...
PITA (PAUSE)

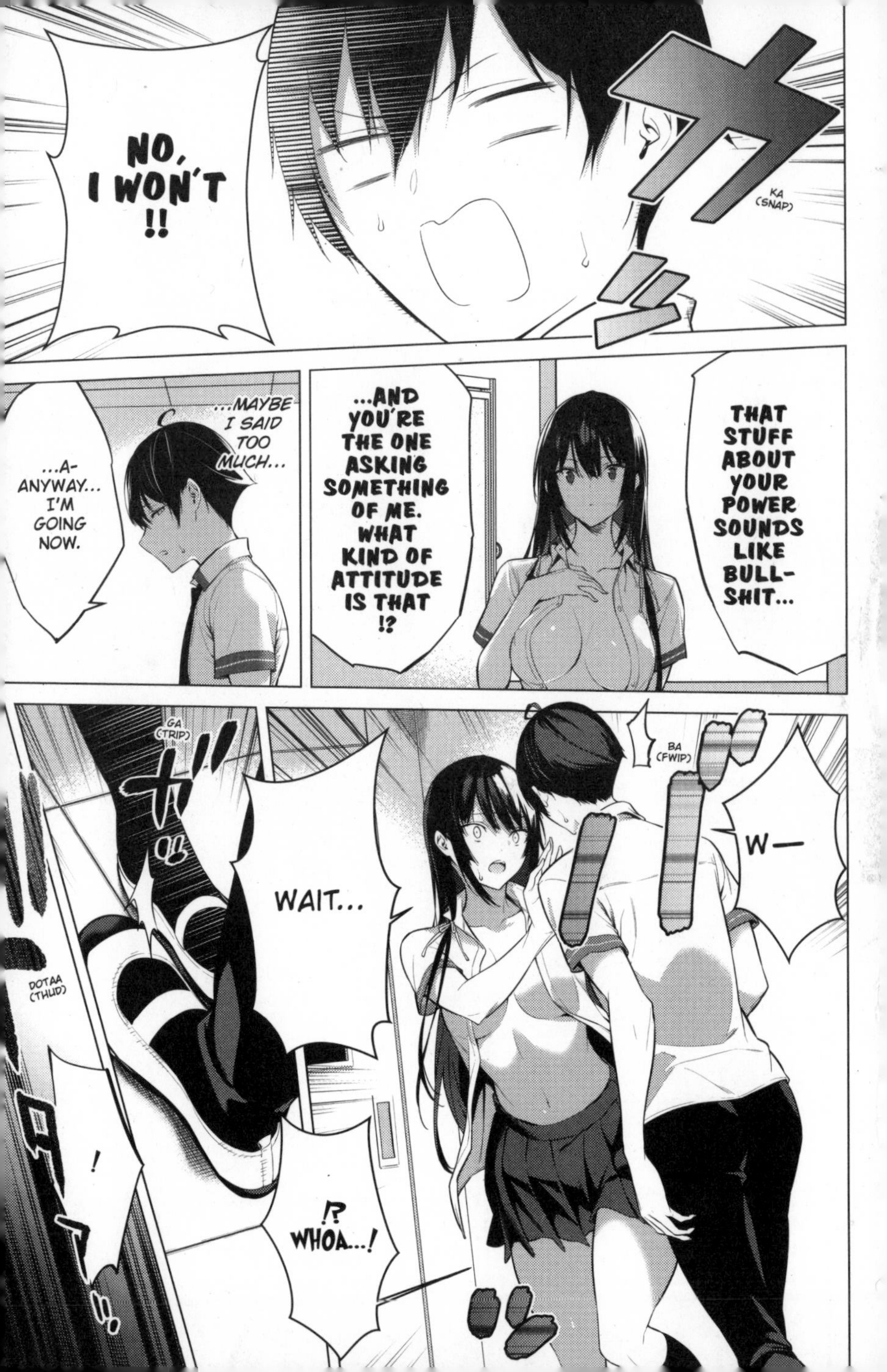
NO, I WON'T !!
KA (SNAP)
THAT STUFF ABOUT YOUR POWER SOUNDS LIKE BULL-SHIT...
...AND YOU'RE THE ONE ASKING SOMETHING OF ME. WHAT KIND OF ATTITUDE IS THAT !?
...MAYBE I SAID TOO MUCH...
...A- ANYWAY... I'M GOING NOW.
W—
BA (FWIP)
WAIT...
!? WHOA...!
GA (TRIP)
DOTAA (THUD)
!

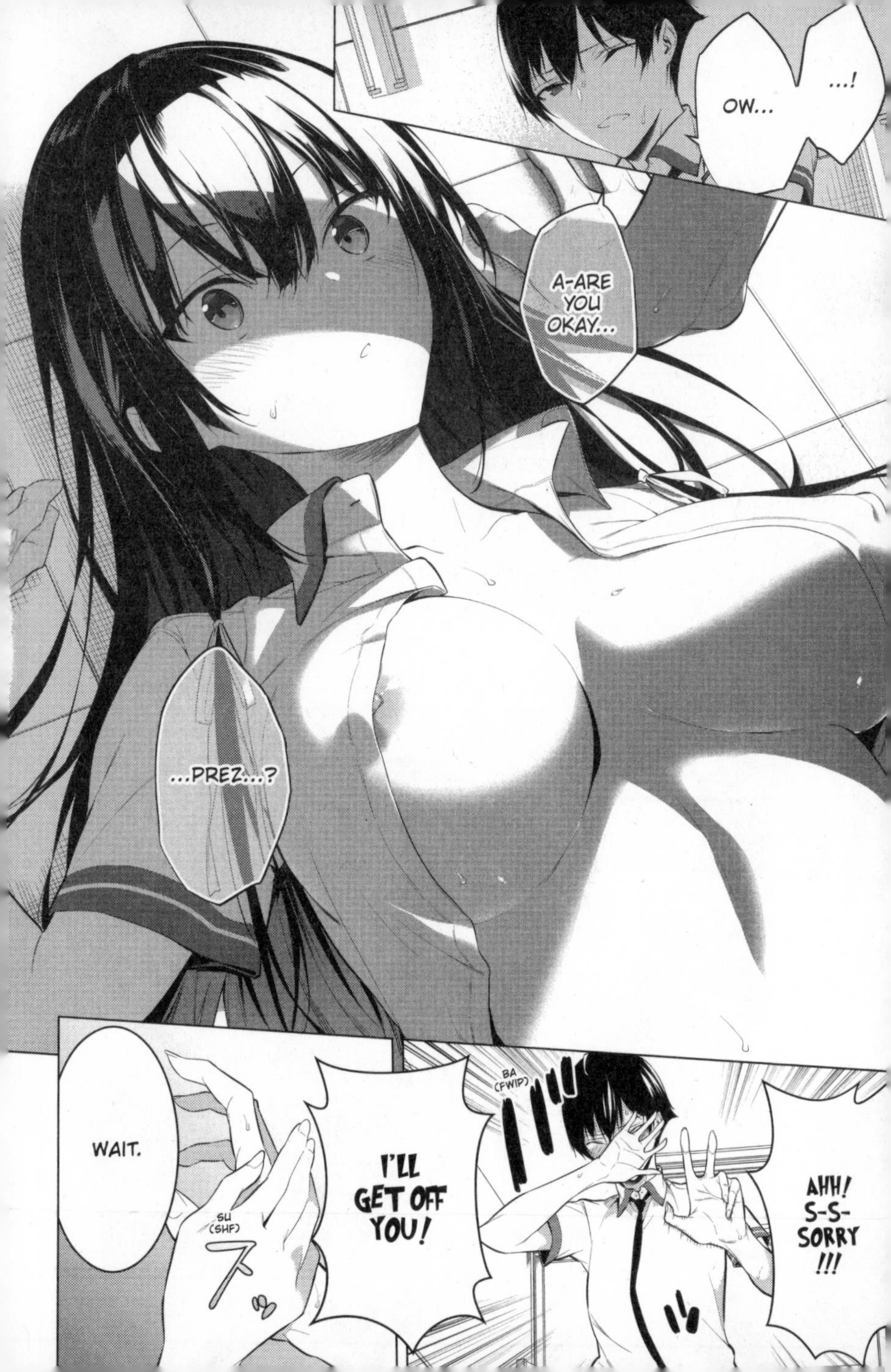
...!
OW...
A-ARE YOU OKAY...
...PREZ...?
AHH! S-S-SORRY!!!
BA (FWIP)
I'LL GET OFF YOU!
WAIT.
SU (SHF)

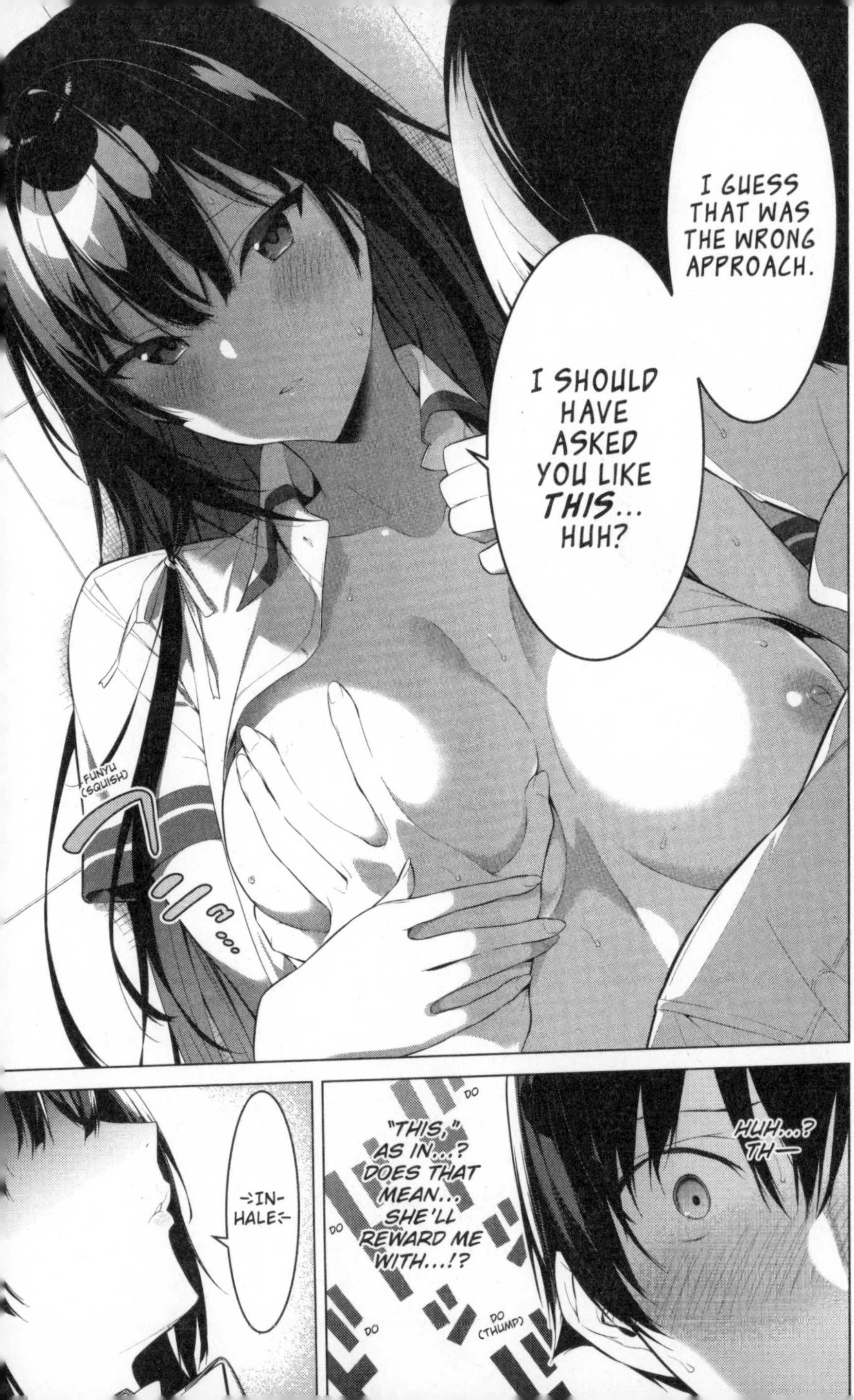
I GUESS THAT WAS THE WRONG APPROACH.
I SHOULD HAVE ASKED YOU LIKE THIS... HUH?
FUNYU (SQUISH)
HUH...? TH—
DO
"THIS," AS IN...? DOES THAT MEAN... SHE'LL REWARD ME WITH...!?
DO
DO
DO (THUMP)
-IN-HALE-

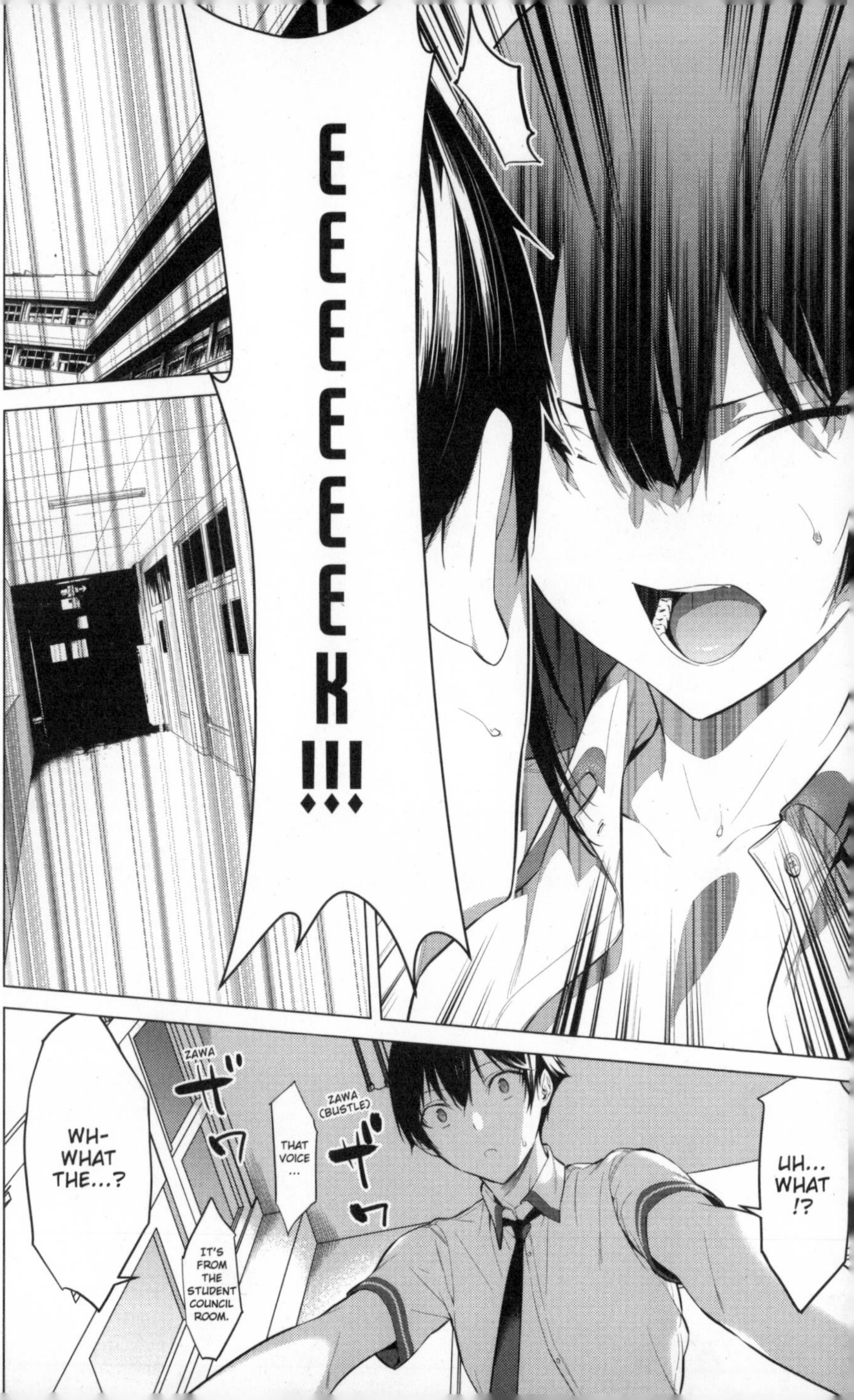
EEEEEEK!!!
UH... WHAT!?
ZAWA (BUSTLE)
THAT VOICE...
ZAWA
WH- WHAT THE...?
IT'S FROM THE STUDENT COUNCIL ROOM.

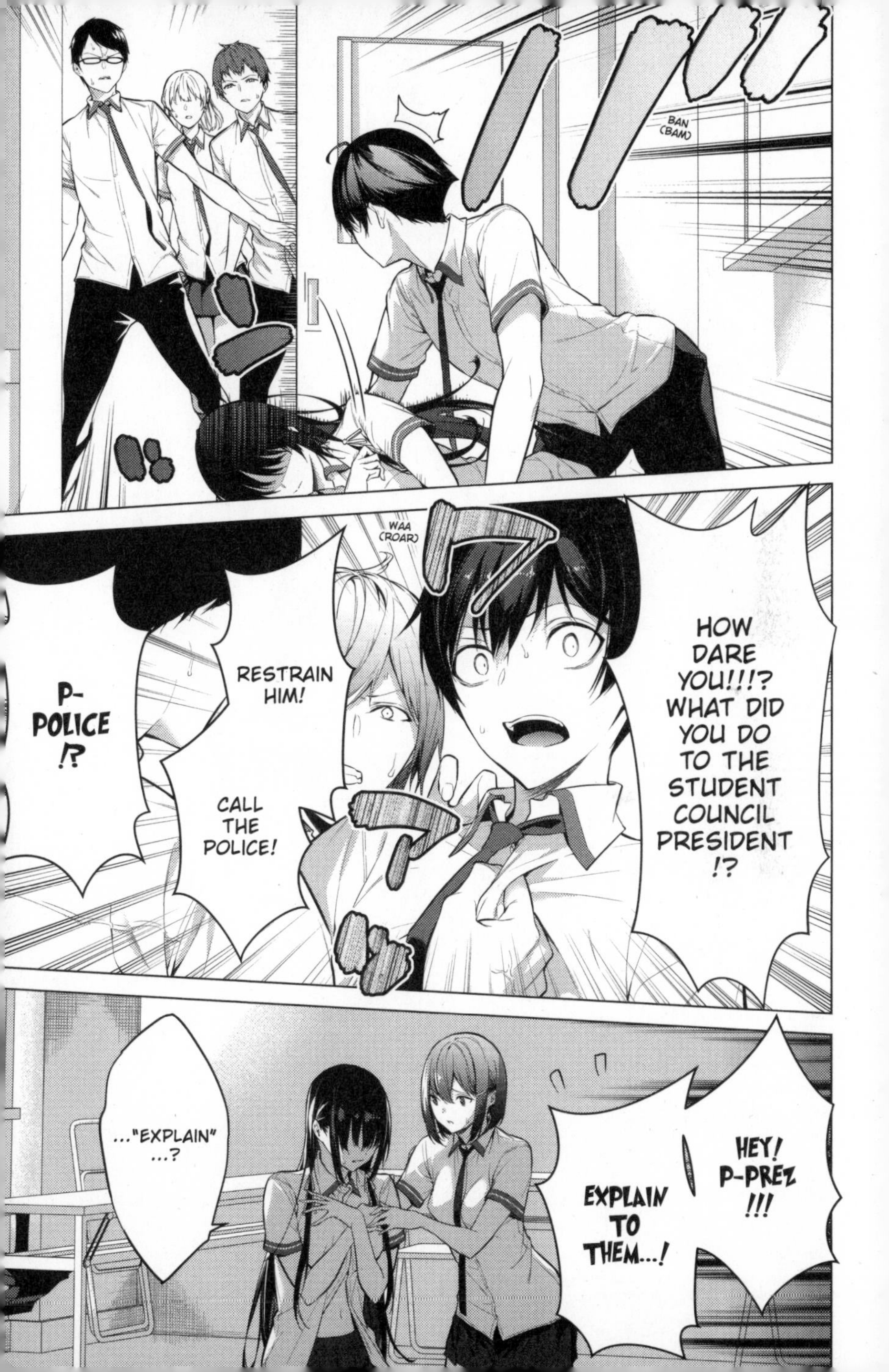
BAN (BAM)
HOW DARE YOU!!!? WHAT DID YOU DO TO THE STUDENT COUNCIL PRESIDENT!?
WAA (ROAR)
RESTRAIN HIM!
CALL THE POLICE!
P-POLICE!?
HEY! P-PREZ!!!
EXPLAIN TO THEM...!
..."EXPLAIN"...?

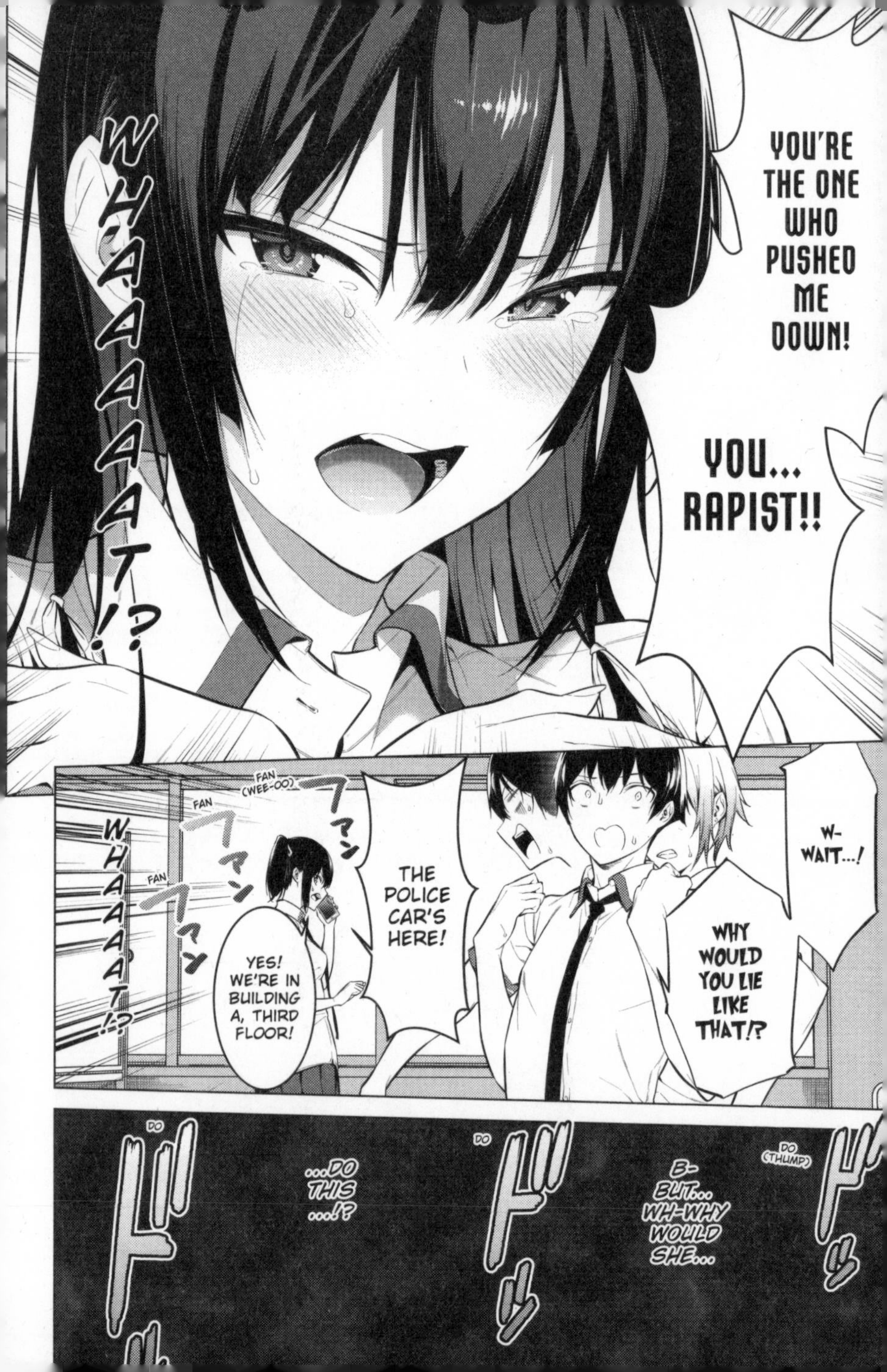
YOU'RE THE ONE WHO PUSHED ME DOWN!
YOU... RAPIST!!
WHAAAAAAAT!?
W-WAIT...!
WHY WOULD YOU LIE LIKE THAT!?
THE POLICE CAR'S HERE!
FAN (WEE-OO)
ファン
FAN
ファン
FAN
ファン
YES! WE'RE IN BUILDING A, THIRD FLOOR!
WHAAAAAT!?
DO (THUMP)
B-BUT... WH-WHY WOULD SHE...
DO
...DO THIS ...!?
DO

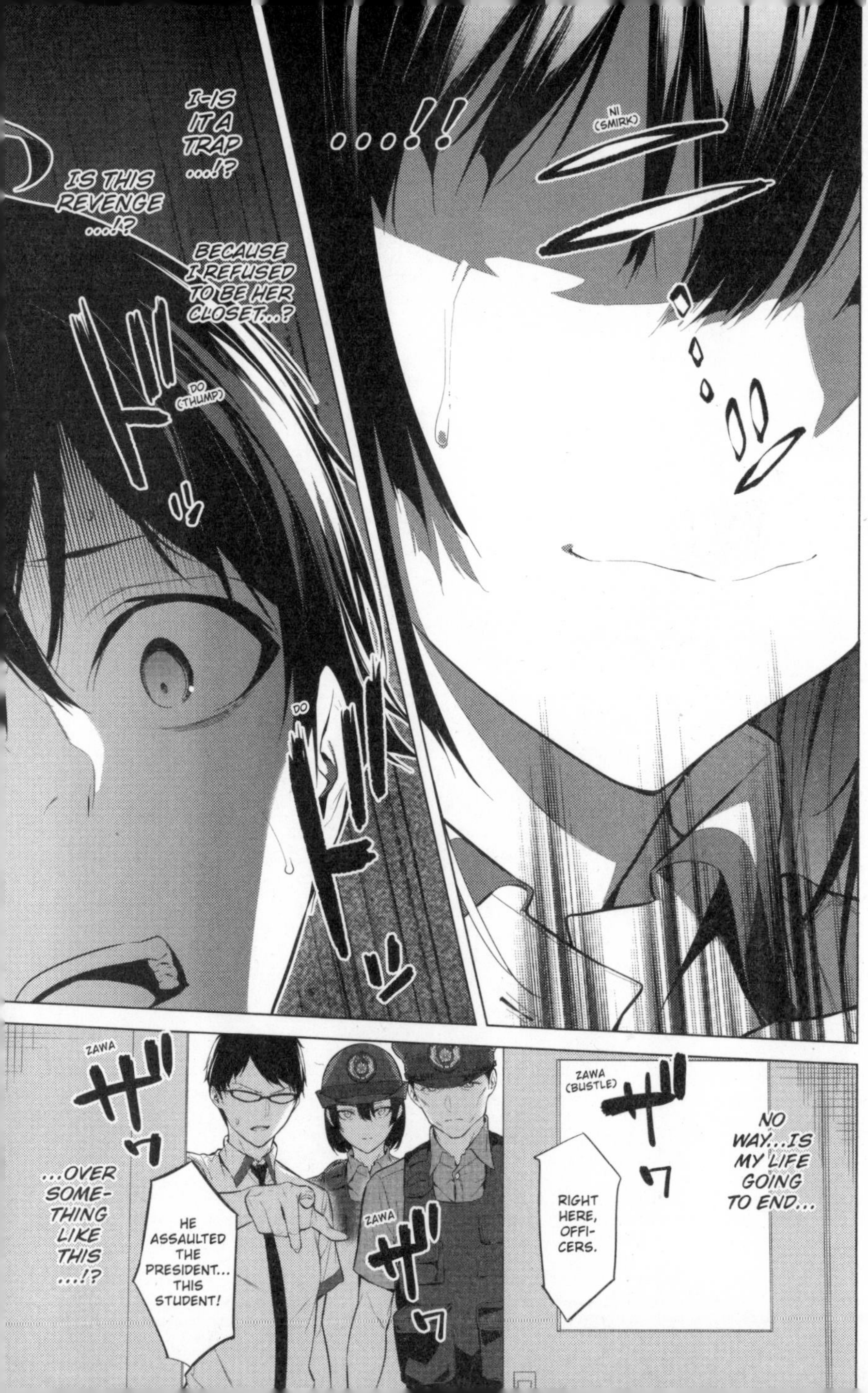
...!!
NI (SMIRK)
I-IS IT A TRAP ...!?
IS THIS REVENGE ...!?
BECAUSE I REFUSED TO BE HER CLOSET...?
DO (THUMP)
DO
NO WAY...IS MY LIFE GOING TO END...
ZAWA (BUSTLE)
RIGHT HERE, OFFICERS.
ZAWA
HE ASSAULTED THE PRESIDENT... THIS STUDENT!
ZAWA
...OVER SOMETHING LIKE THIS ...!?

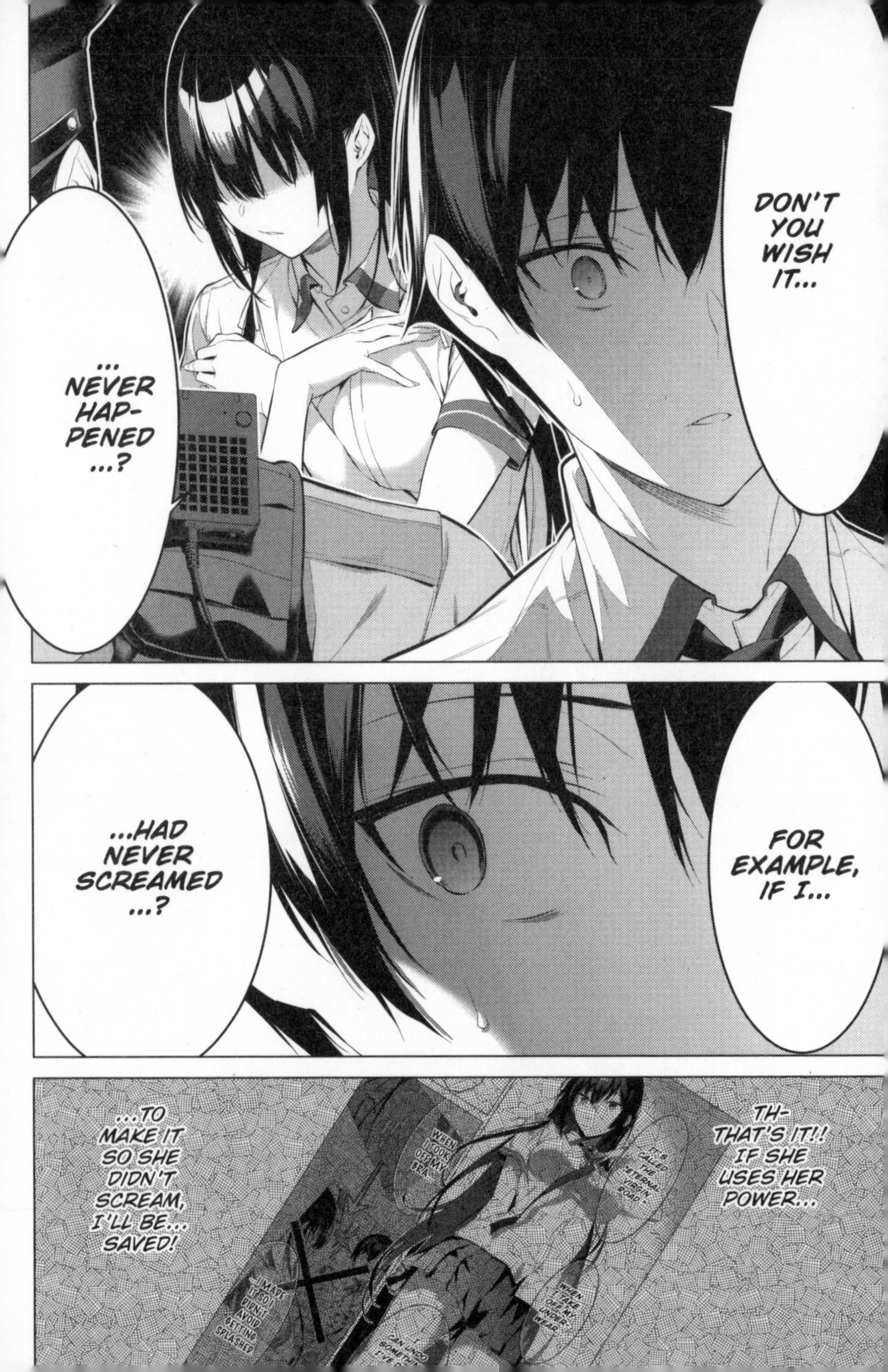
DON'T YOU WISH IT...
...NEVER HAPPENED...?
FOR EXAMPLE, IF I...
...HAD NEVER SCREAMED...?
TH-THAT'S IT!! IF SHE USES HER POWER...
IT'S CALLED THE "ETERNAL VIRGIN ROAD."
WHEN I TOOK OFF MY BRA...
WHEN I TAKE OFF MY UNDERWEAR...
...I MADE IT SO I DIDN'T AVOID GETTING SPLASHED
...TO MAKE IT SO SHE DIDN'T SCREAM, I'LL BE... SAVED!

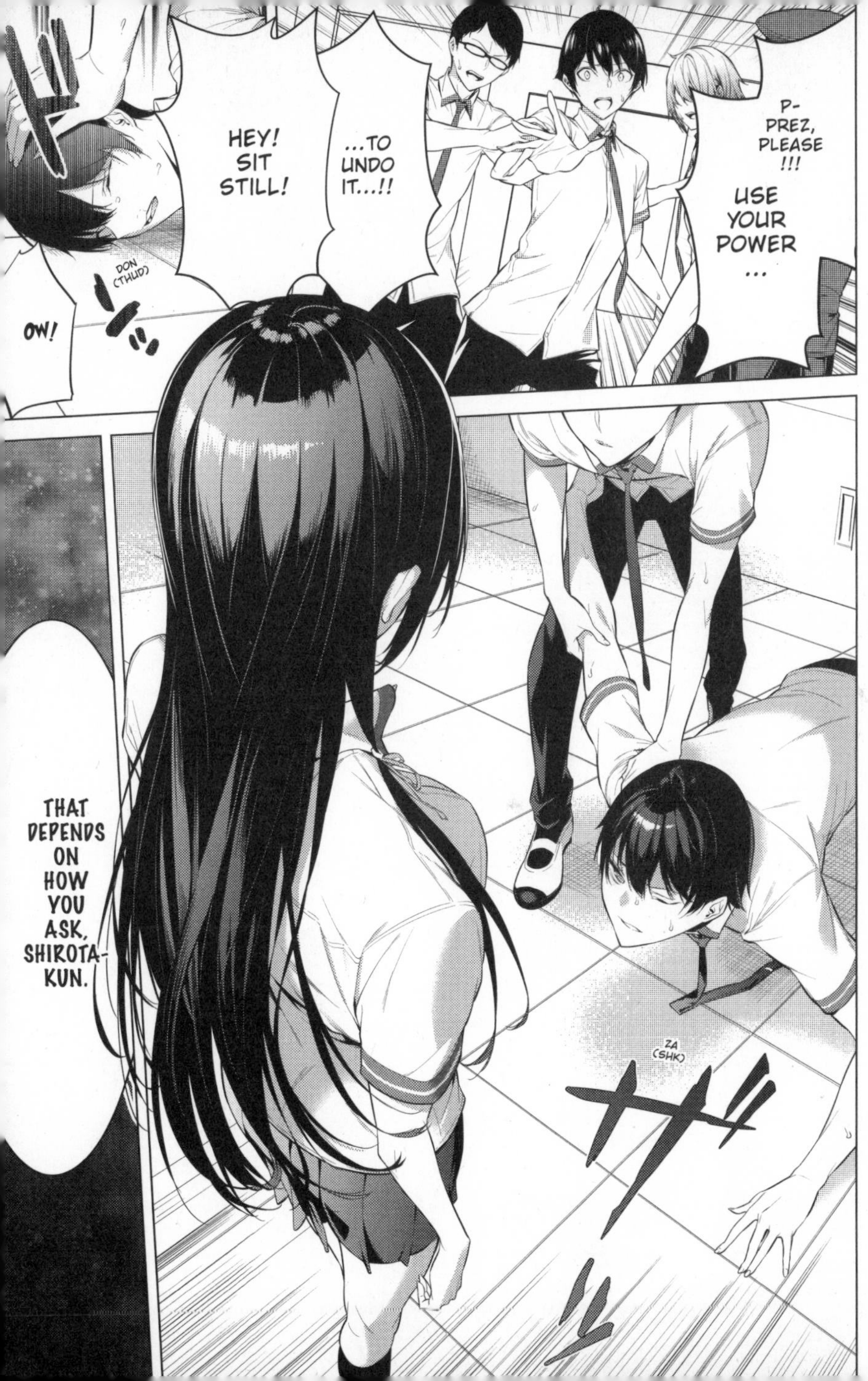
P-PREZ, PLEASE!!!
USE YOUR POWER...
...TO UNDO IT...!!
HEY! SIT STILL!
DON (THUD)
OW!
ZA (SHK)
THAT DEPENDS ON HOW YOU ASK, SHIROTA-KUN.

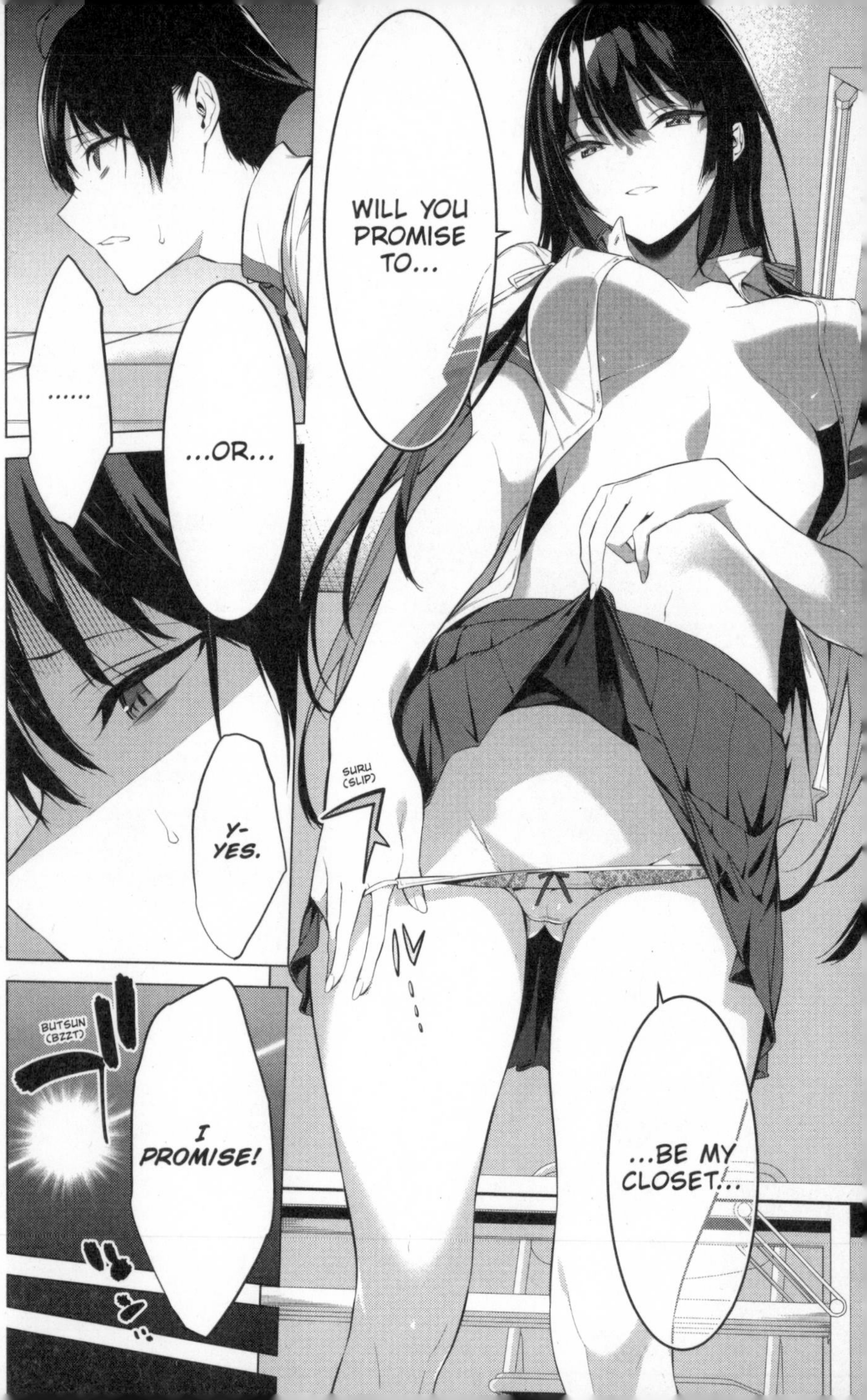
WILL YOU PROMISE TO...
SURU (SLIP)
...BE MY CLOSET...
......
...OR...
Y-YES.
BUTSUN (BZZT)
I PROMISE!

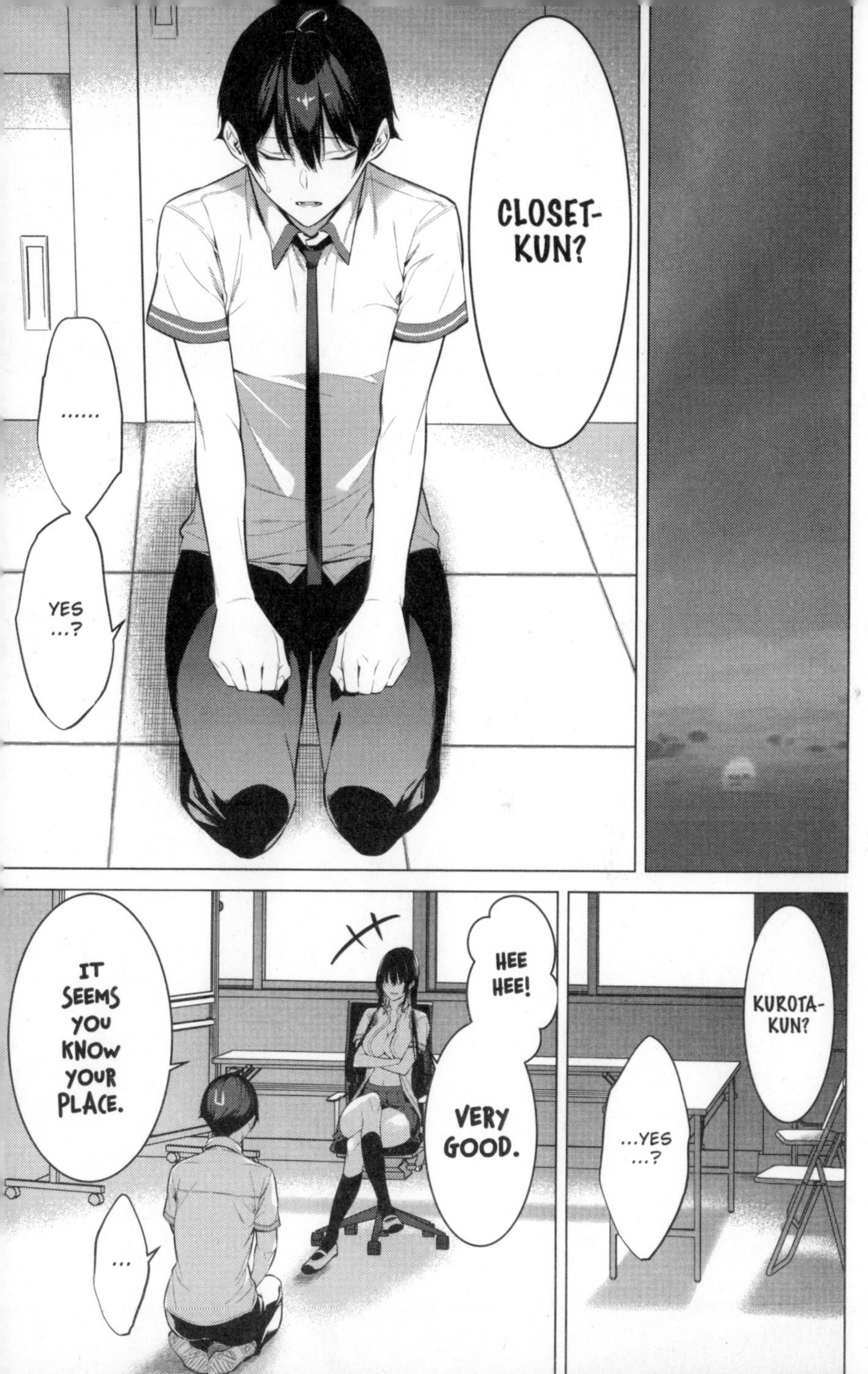
CLOSET-KUN?
......
YES ...?
KUROTA-KUN?
...YES ...?
HEE HEE!
VERY GOOD.
IT SEEMS YOU KNOW YOUR PLACE.
...

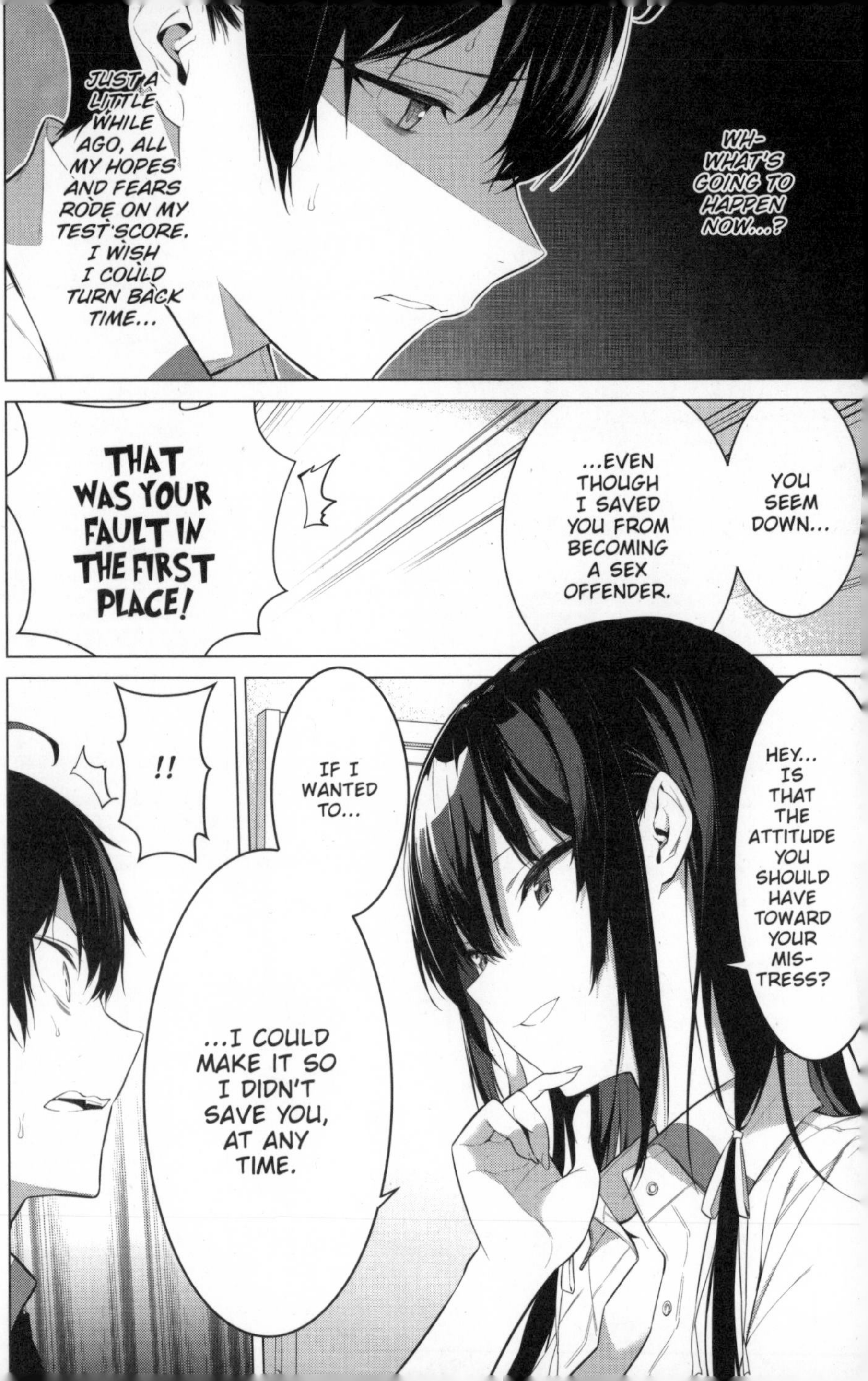
WH-WHAT'S GOING TO HAPPEN NOW...?
JUST A LITTLE WHILE AGO, ALL MY HOPES AND FEARS RODE ON MY TEST SCORE. I WISH I COULD TURN BACK TIME...
YOU SEEM DOWN...
...EVEN THOUGH I SAVED YOU FROM BECOMING A SEX OFFENDER.
THAT WAS YOUR FAULT IN THE FIRST PLACE!
HEY... IS THAT THE ATTITUDE YOU SHOULD HAVE TOWARD YOUR MISTRESS?
IF I WANTED TO...
...I COULD MAKE IT SO I DIDN'T SAVE YOU, AT ANY TIME.
!!

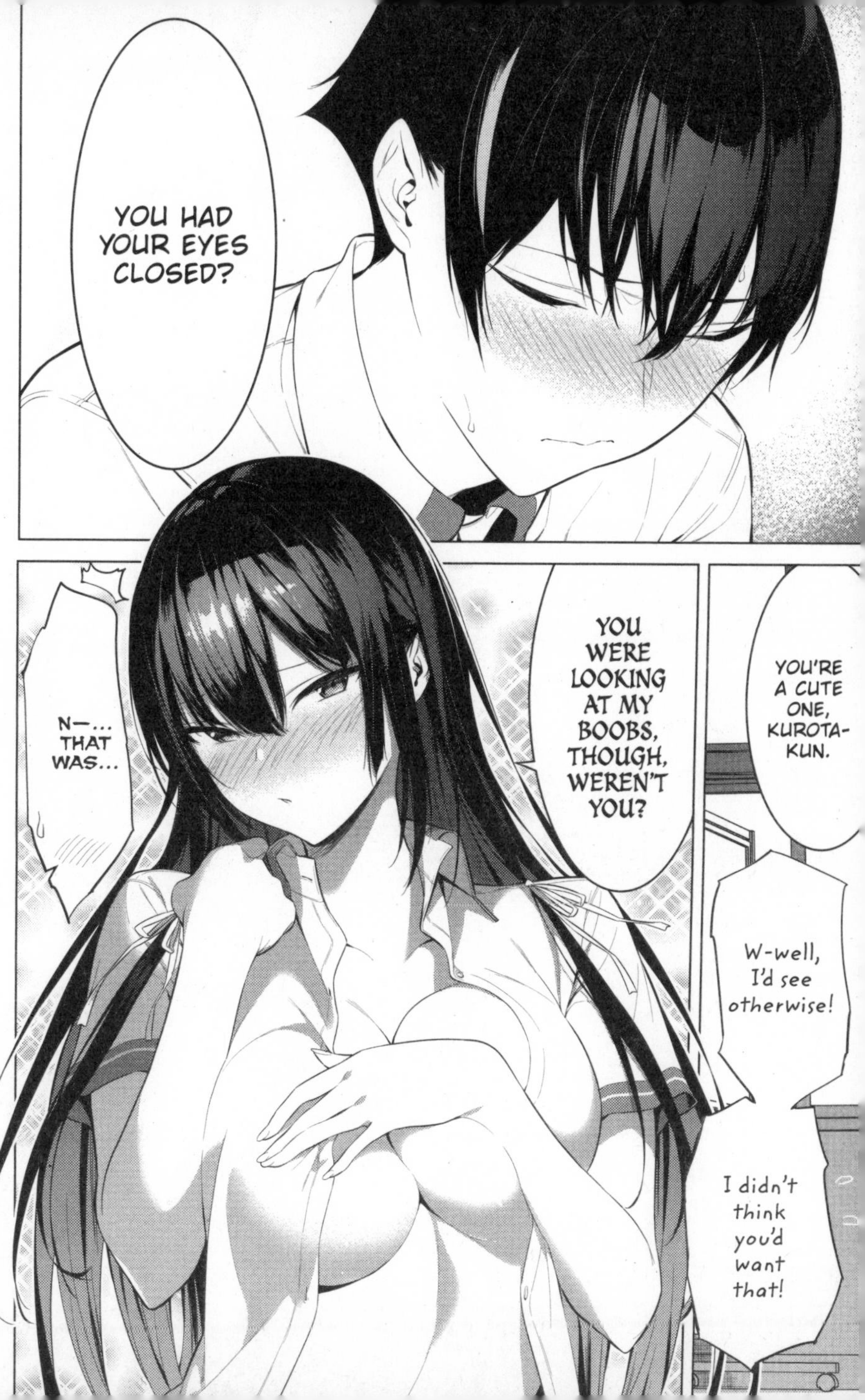
YOU HAD YOUR EYES CLOSED?
YOU'RE A CUTE ONE, KUROTA-KUN.
W-well, I'd see otherwise!
I didn't think you'd want that!
YOU WERE LOOKING AT MY BOOBS, THOUGH, WEREN'T YOU?
N—... THAT WAS...

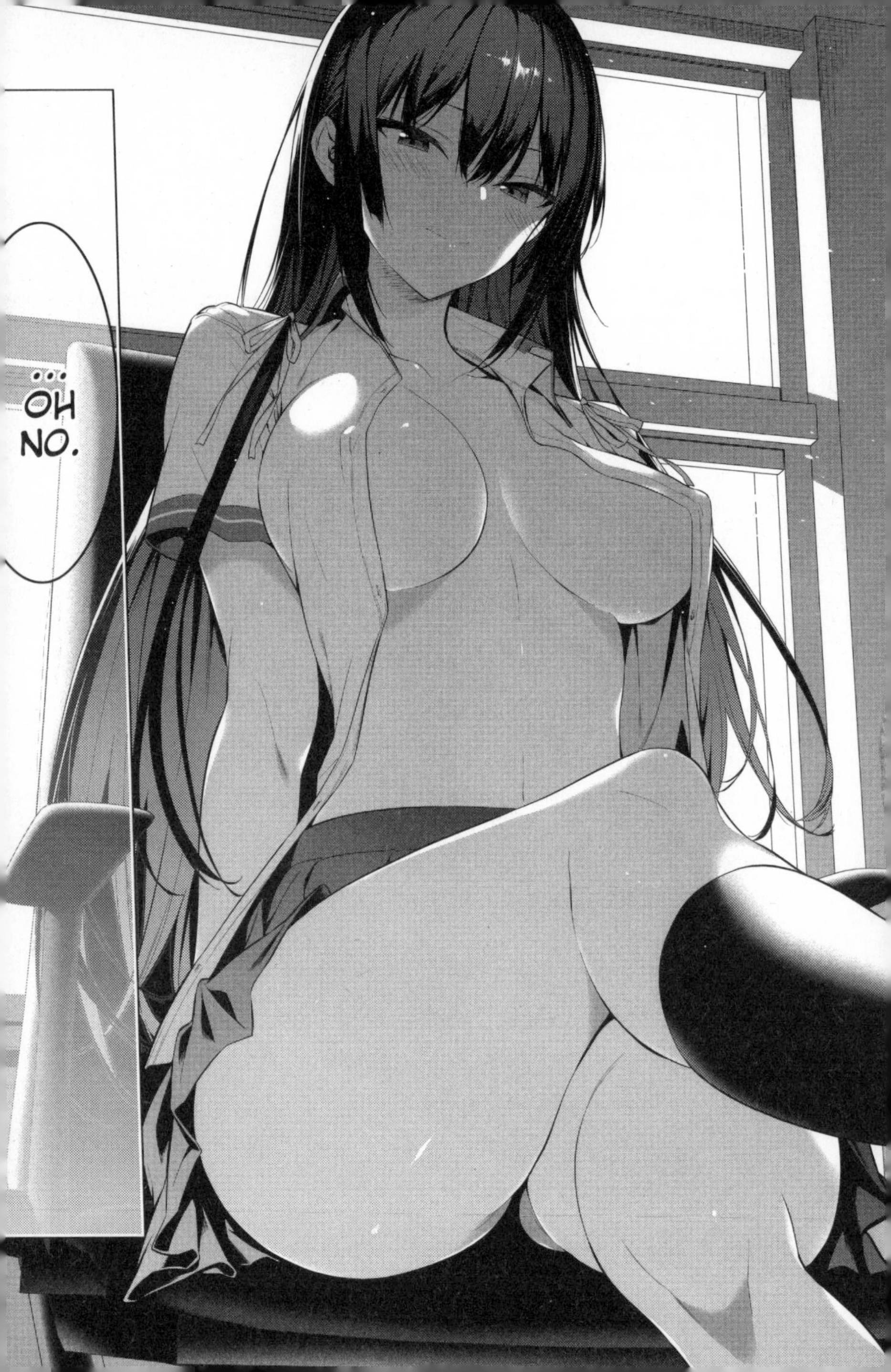
...OH NO.

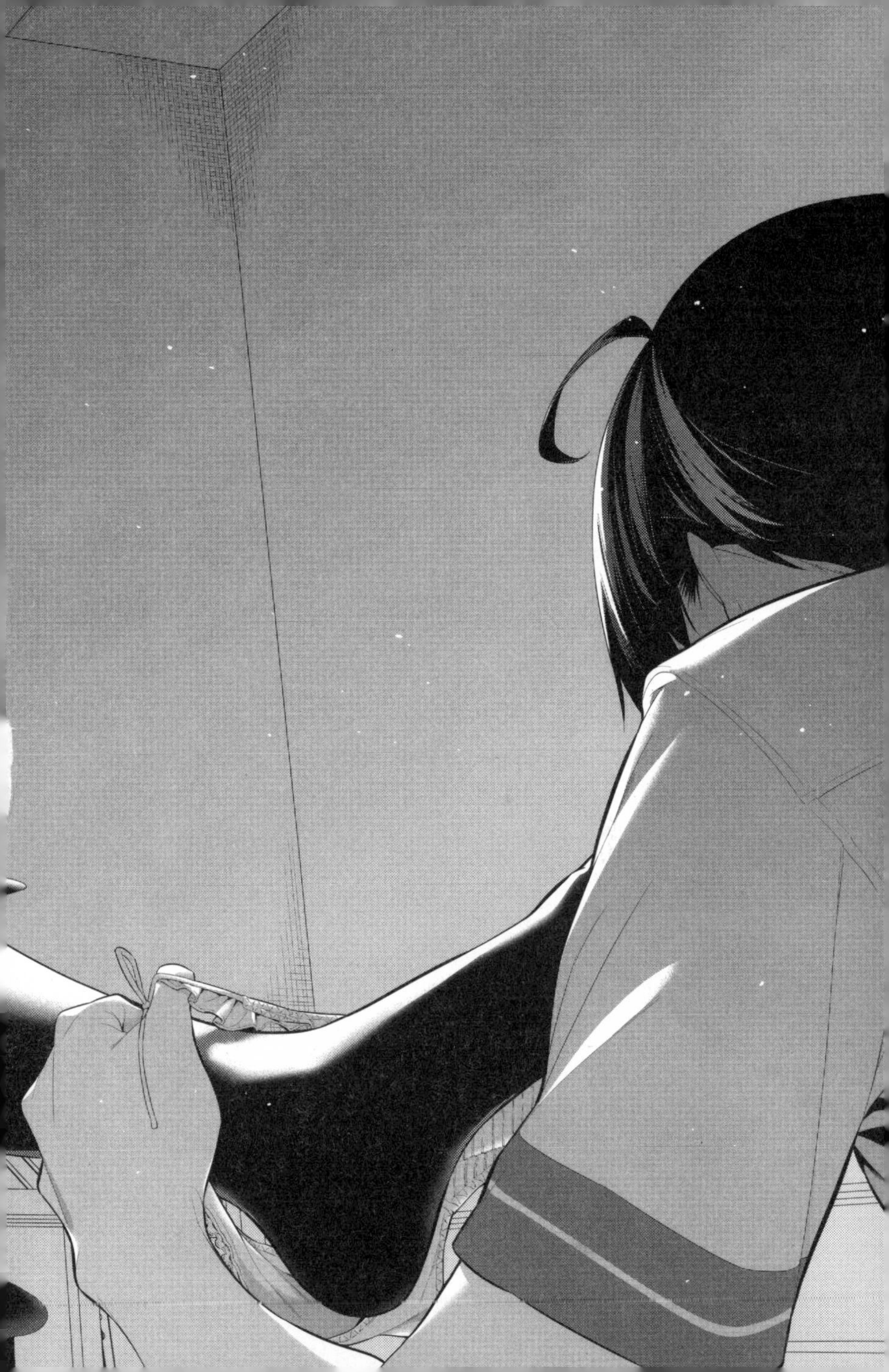

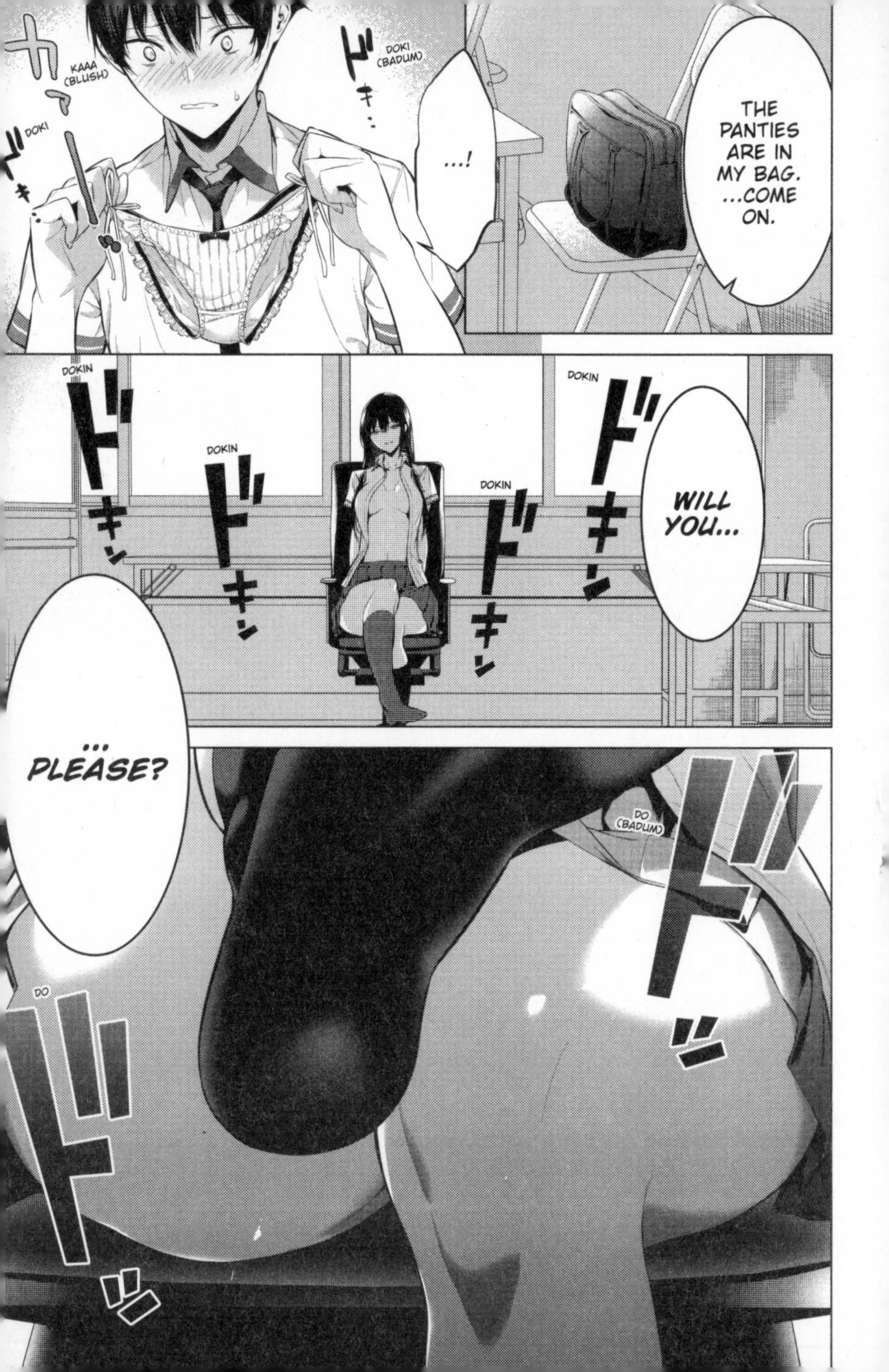
THE PANTIES ARE IN MY BAG. ...COME ON.
...!
DOKI (BADUM)
KAAA (BLUSH)
DOKI
DOKIN
WILL YOU...
DOKIN
DOKIN
DOKIN
...PLEASE?
DO (BADUM)
DO

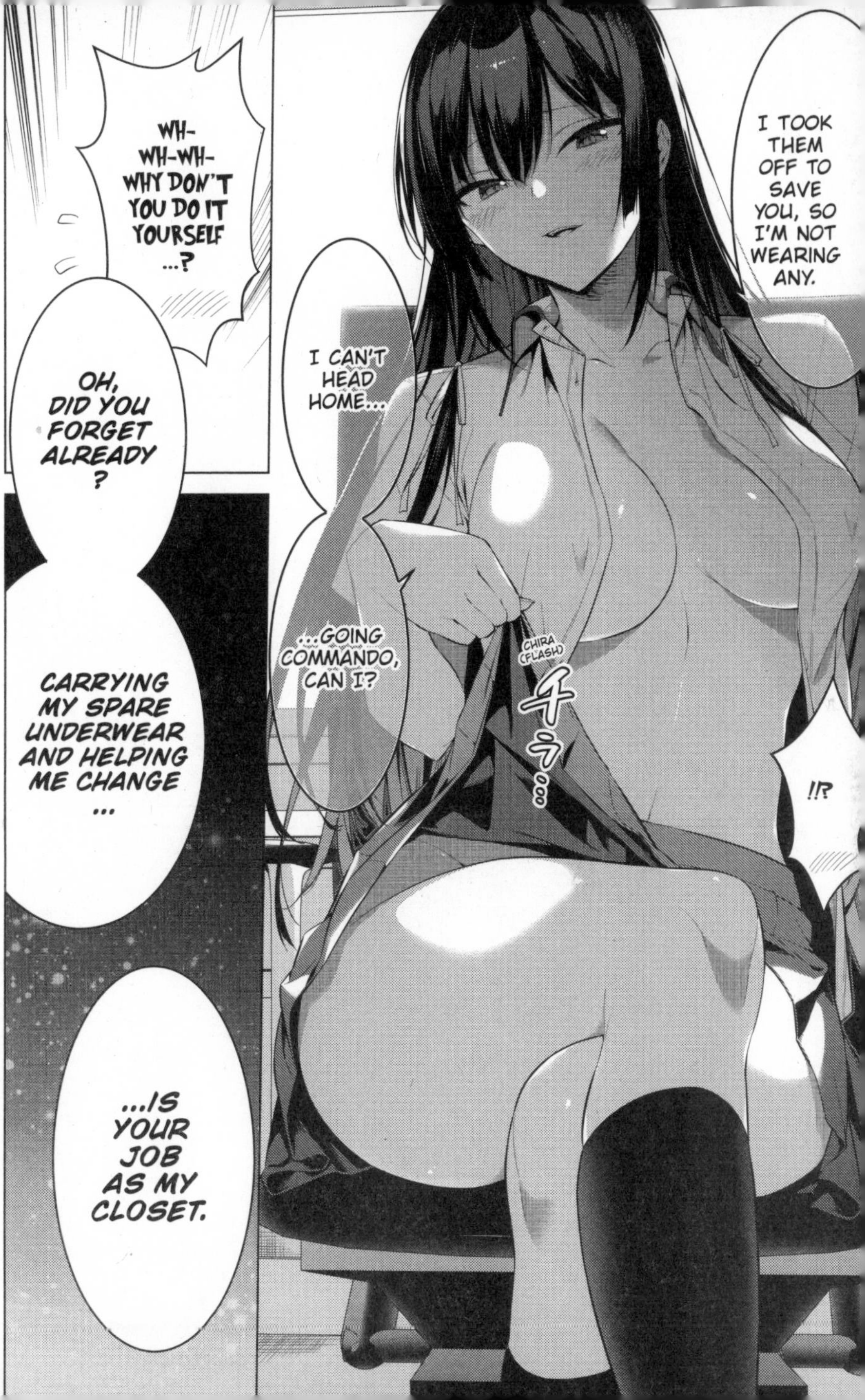
I TOOK THEM OFF TO SAVE YOU, SO I'M NOT WEARING ANY.
I CAN'T HEAD HOME...
...GOING COMMANDO, CAN I?
CHIRA (FLASH)
チラ...
!!?
WH-WH-WH-WHY DON'T YOU DO IT YOURSELF...?
OH, DID YOU FORGET ALREADY?
CARRYING MY SPARE UNDERWEAR AND HELPING ME CHANGE...
...IS YOUR JOB AS MY CLOSET.

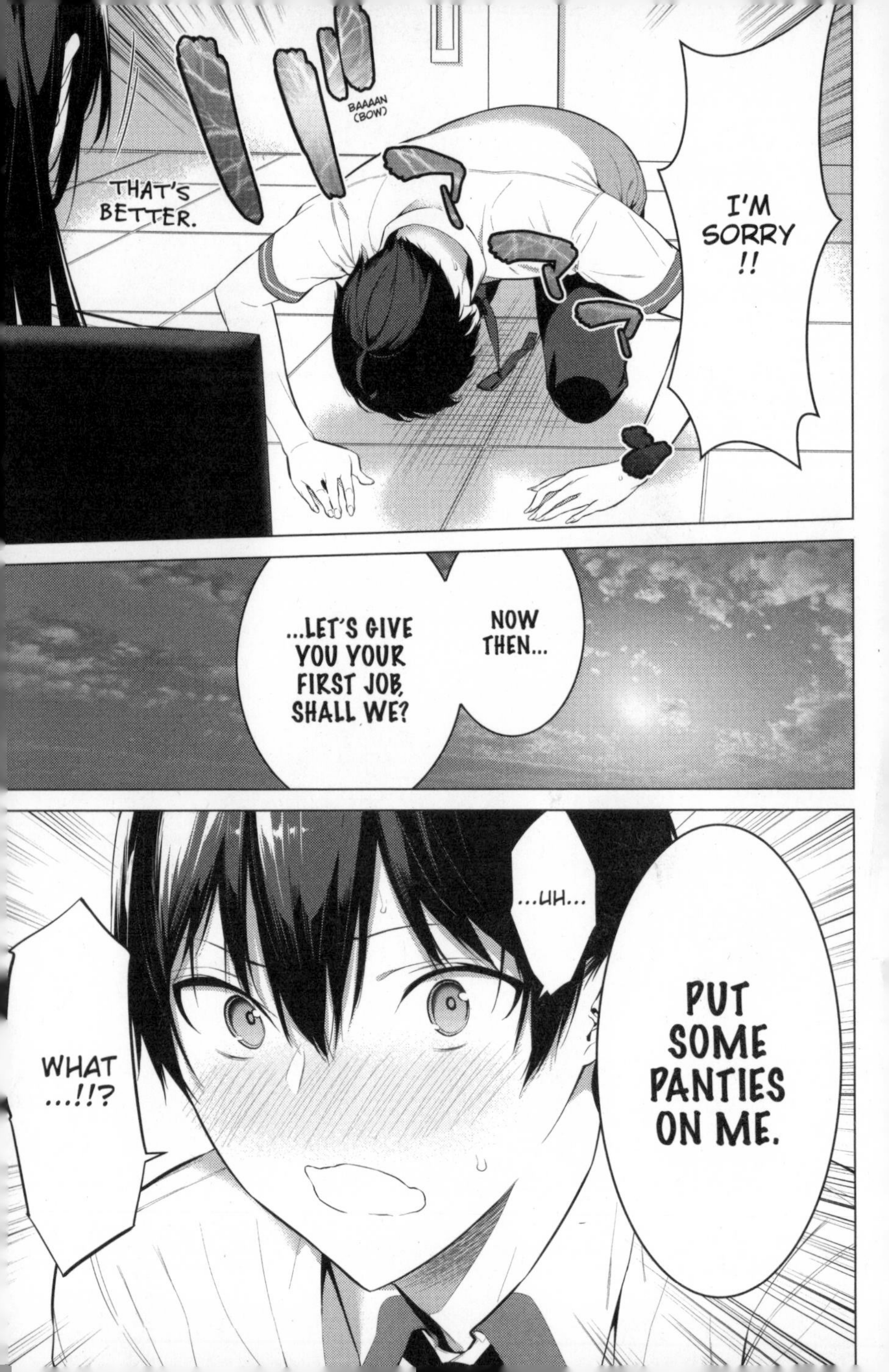
I'M SORRY!!
BAAAAN (BOW)
THAT'S BETTER.
NOW THEN...
...LET'S GIVE YOU YOUR FIRST JOB, SHALL WE?
PUT SOME PANTIES ON ME.
...UH...
WHAT...!!?

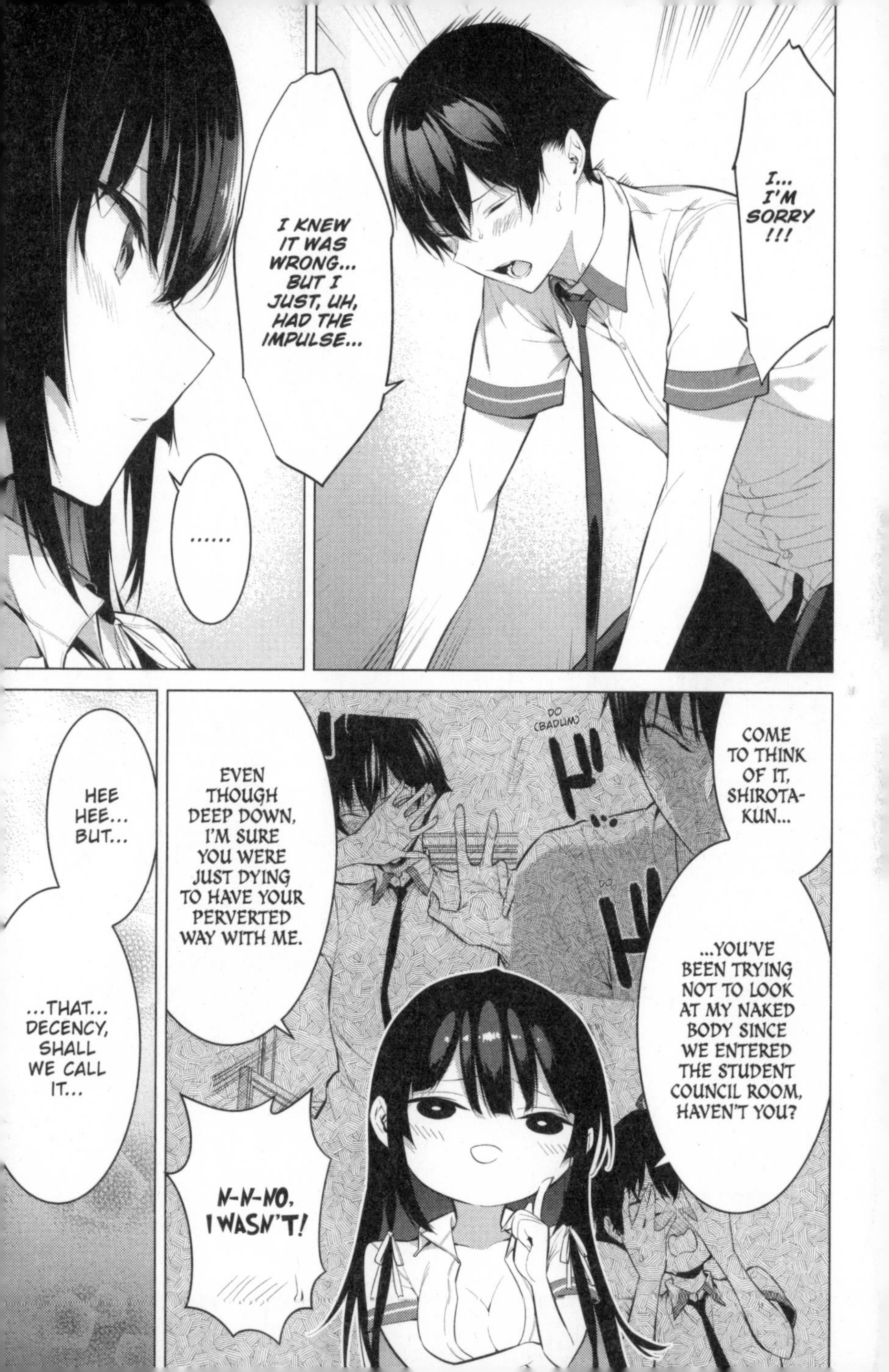
I... I'M SORRY!!!
I KNEW IT WAS WRONG... BUT I JUST, UH, HAD THE IMPULSE...
......
COME TO THINK OF IT, SHIROTA-KUN...
...YOU'VE BEEN TRYING NOT TO LOOK AT MY NAKED BODY SINCE WE ENTERED THE STUDENT COUNCIL ROOM, HAVEN'T YOU?
DO (BADUM)
DO
EVEN THOUGH DEEP DOWN, I'M SURE YOU WERE JUST DYING TO HAVE YOUR PERVERTED WAY WITH ME.
N-N-NO, I WASN'T!
HEE HEE... BUT...
...THAT... DECENCY, SHALL WE CALL IT...

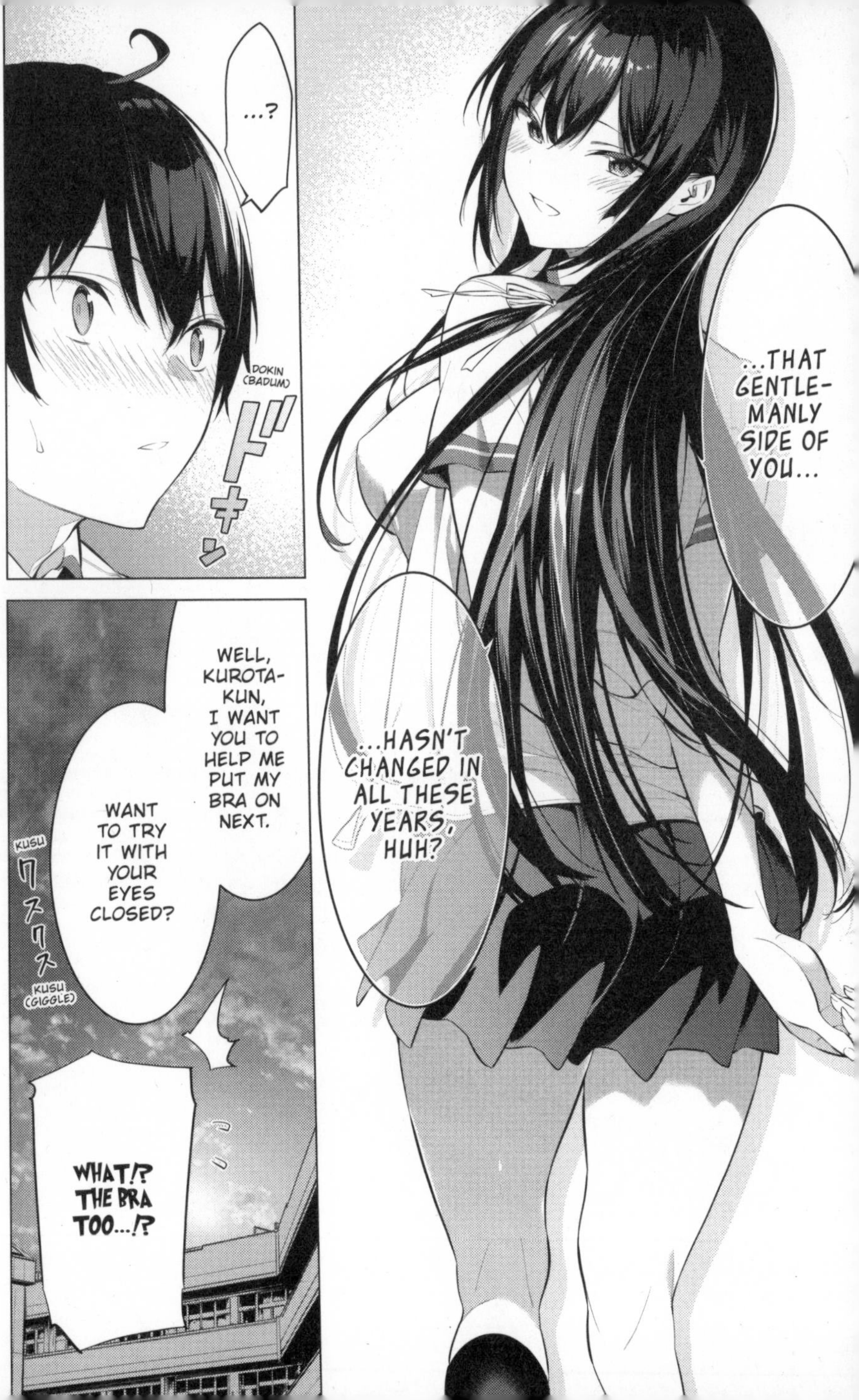
...THAT GENTLE-MANLY SIDE OF YOU...
...HASN'T CHANGED IN ALL THESE YEARS, HUH?
...?
DOKIN (BADUM)
ドキン
WELL, KUROTA-KUN, I WANT YOU TO HELP ME PUT MY BRA ON NEXT.
WANT TO TRY IT WITH YOUR EYES CLOSED?
KUSU KUSU (GIGGLE)
クスクス
WHAT!? THE BRA TOO...!?

Please
Put IT
Them On,
Takamine
♥San

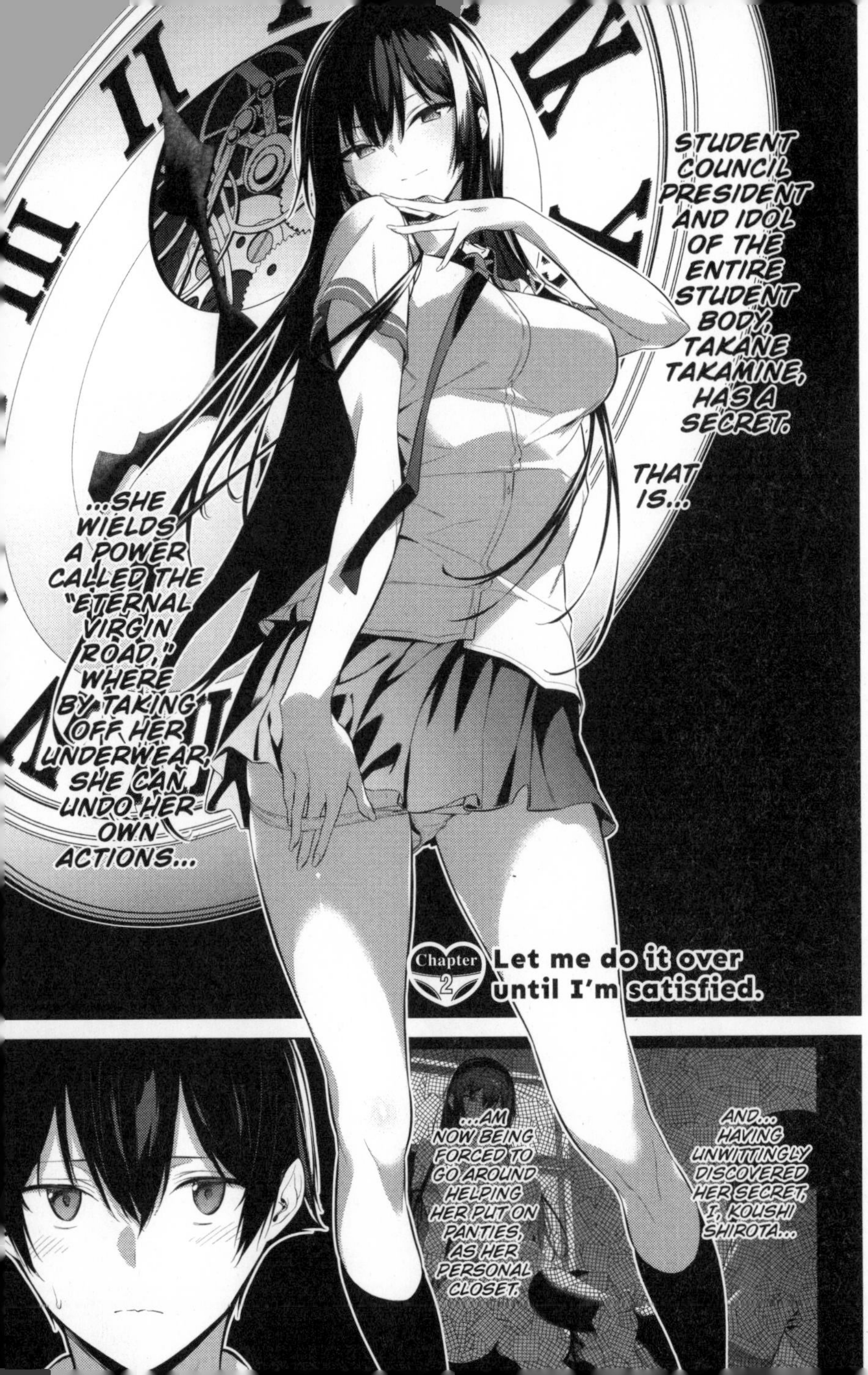

STUDENT COUNCIL PRESIDENT AND IDOL OF THE ENTIRE STUDENT BODY, TAKANE TAKAMINE, HAS A SECRET.
THAT IS...
...SHE WIELDS A POWER CALLED THE "ETERNAL VIRGIN ROAD," WHERE BY TAKING OFF HER UNDERWEAR, SHE CAN UNDO HER OWN ACTIONS...
Chapter 2 Let me do it over until I'm satisfied.
AND... HAVING UNWITTINGLY DISCOVERED HER SECRET, I, KOUSHI SHIROTA...
...AM NOW BEING FORCED TO GO AROUND HELPING HER PUT ON PANTIES, AS HER PERSONAL CLOSET.

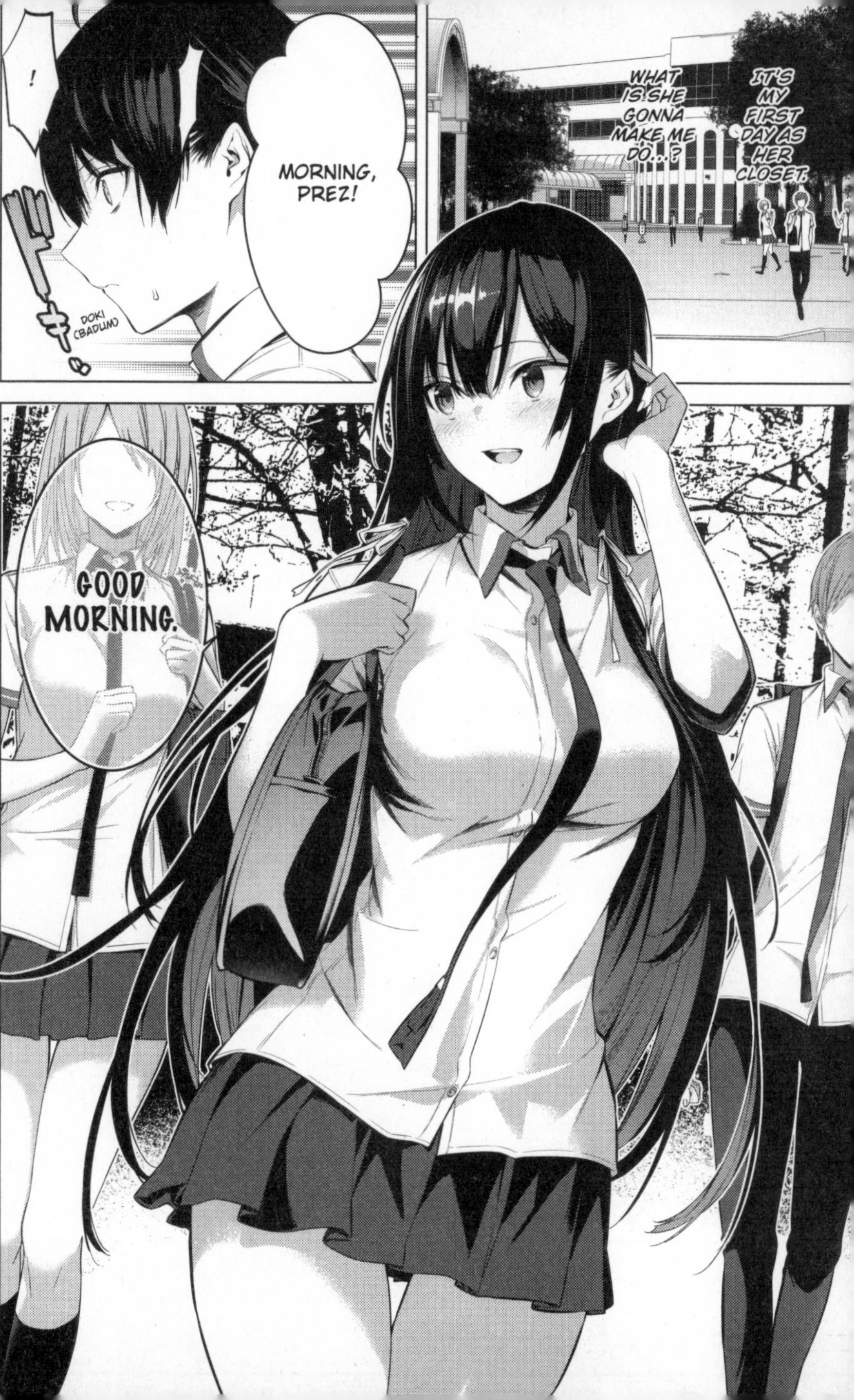
IT'S MY FIRST DAY AS HER CLOSET.
WHAT IS SHE GONNA MAKE ME DO...?
MORNING, PREZ!
!
DOKI (BADUM)
GOOD MORNING.

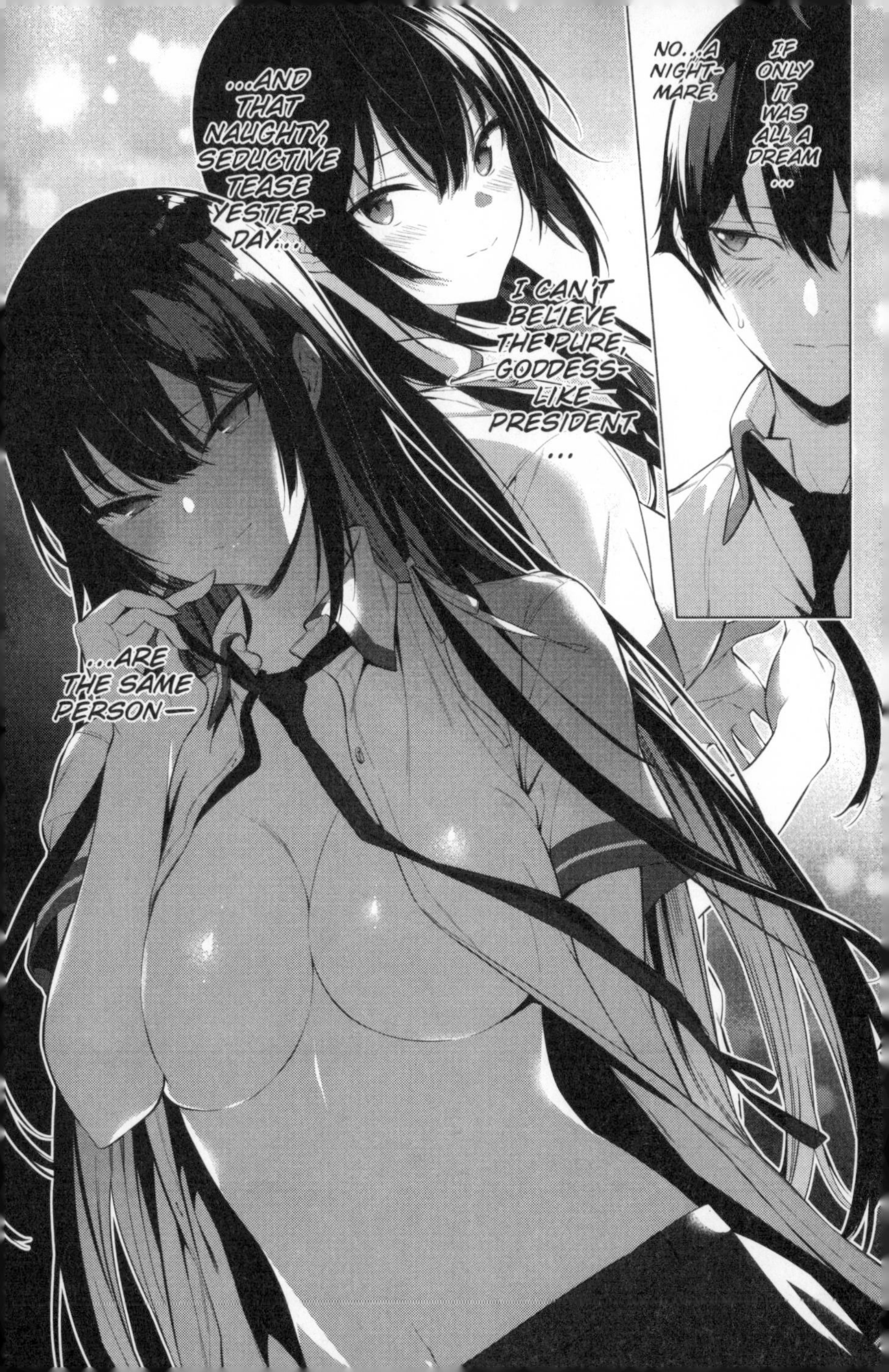
IF ONLY IT WAS ALL A DREAM...
NO...A NIGHT-MARE.
I CAN'T BELIEVE THE PURE, GODDESS-LIKE PRESIDENT...
...AND THAT NAUGHTY, SEDUCTIVE TEASE YESTER-DAY...
...ARE THE SAME PERSON—

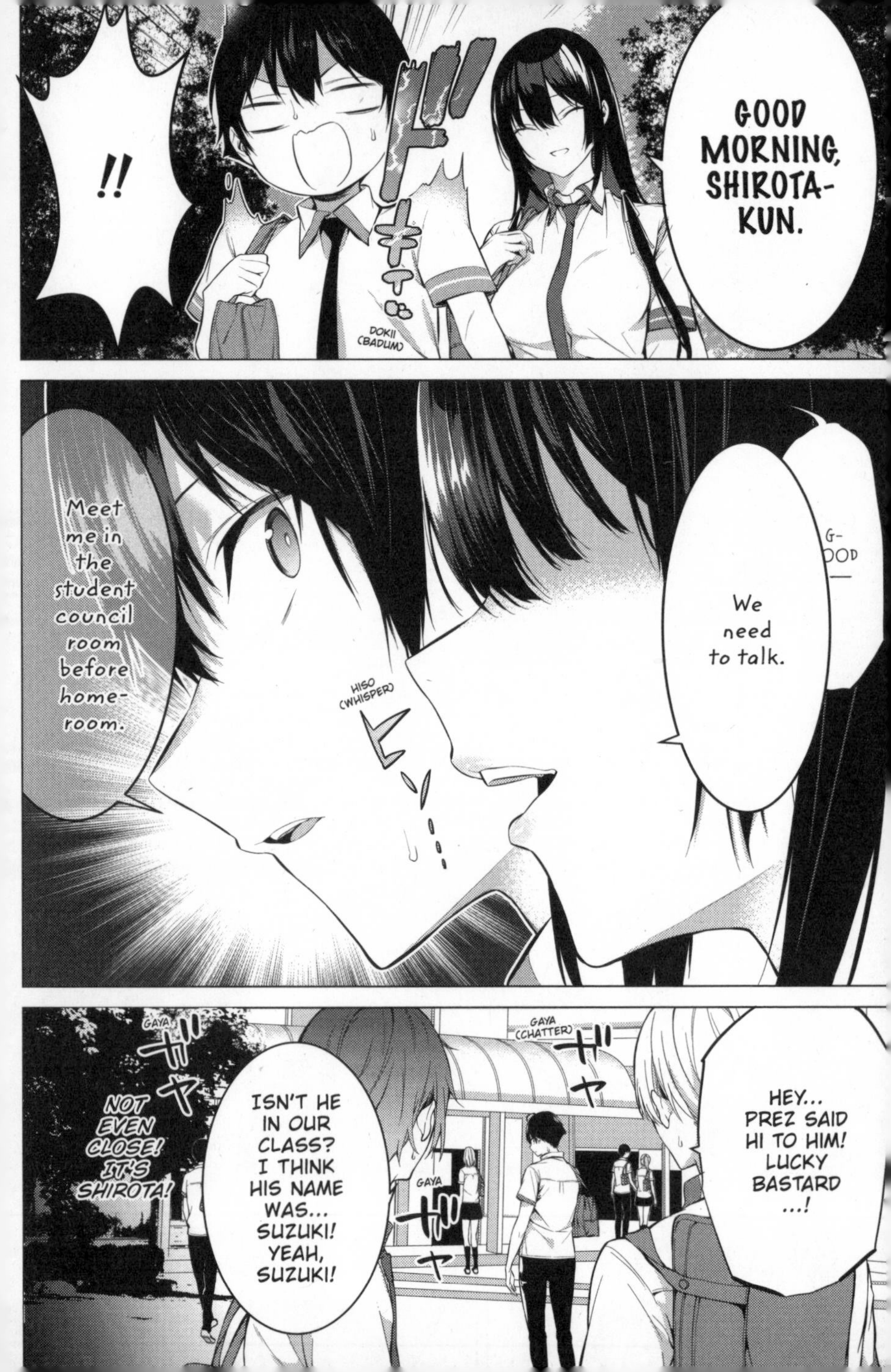
GOOD MORNING, SHIROTA-KUN.
DOKII (BADUM)
!!
G-OOD—
We need to talk.
HISO (WHISPER)
Meet me in the student council room before home-room.
HEY... PREZ SAID HI TO HIM! LUCKY BASTARD...!
GAYA (CHATTER)
ISN'T HE IN OUR CLASS? I THINK HIS NAME WAS... SUZUKI! YEAH, SUZUKI!
GAYA
NOT EVEN CLOSE! IT'S SHIROTA!
GAYA

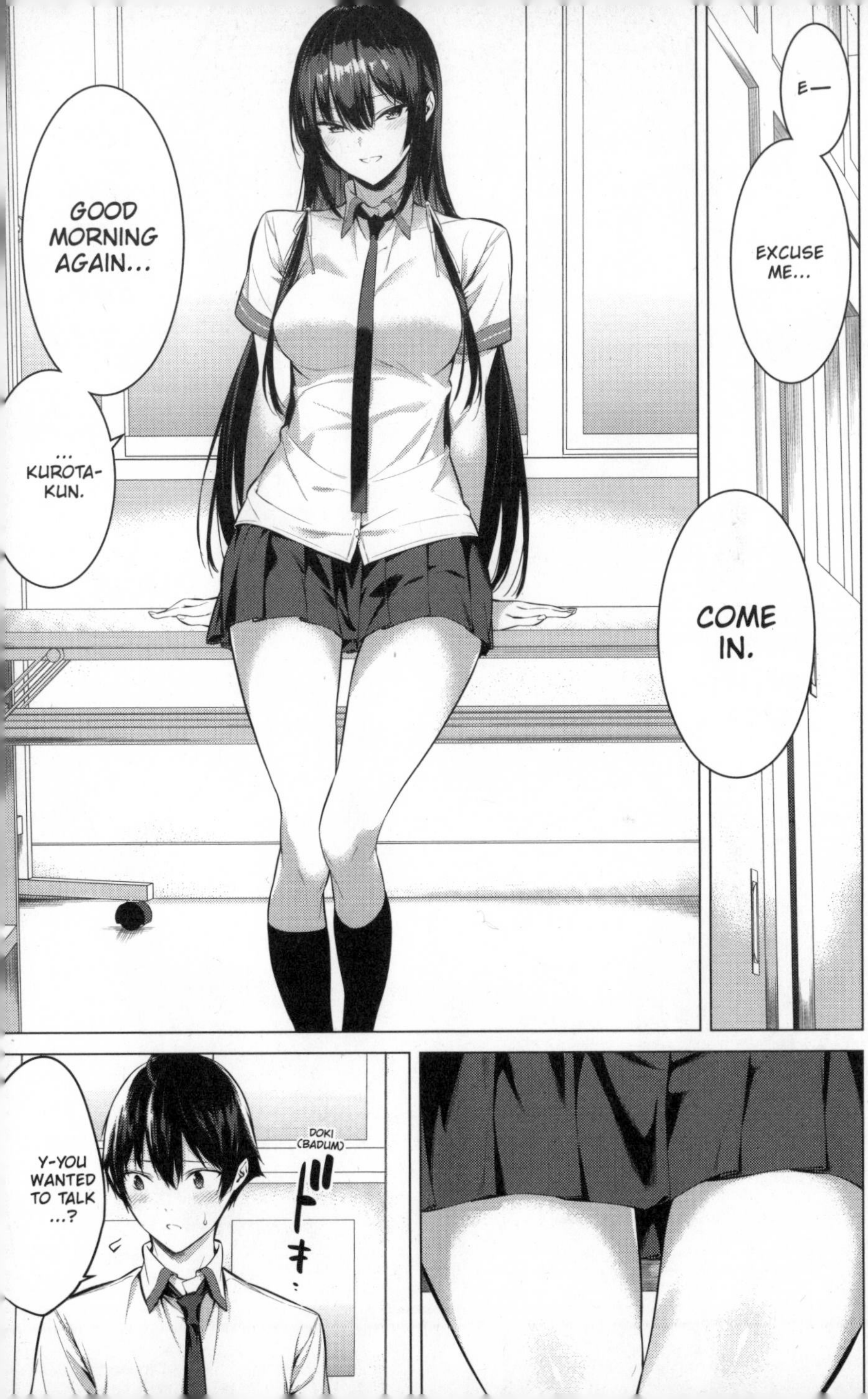
E—
EXCUSE ME...
COME IN.
GOOD MORNING AGAIN...
... KUROTA-KUN.
DOKI (BADUM)
ドキ
Y-YOU WANTED TO TALK ...?

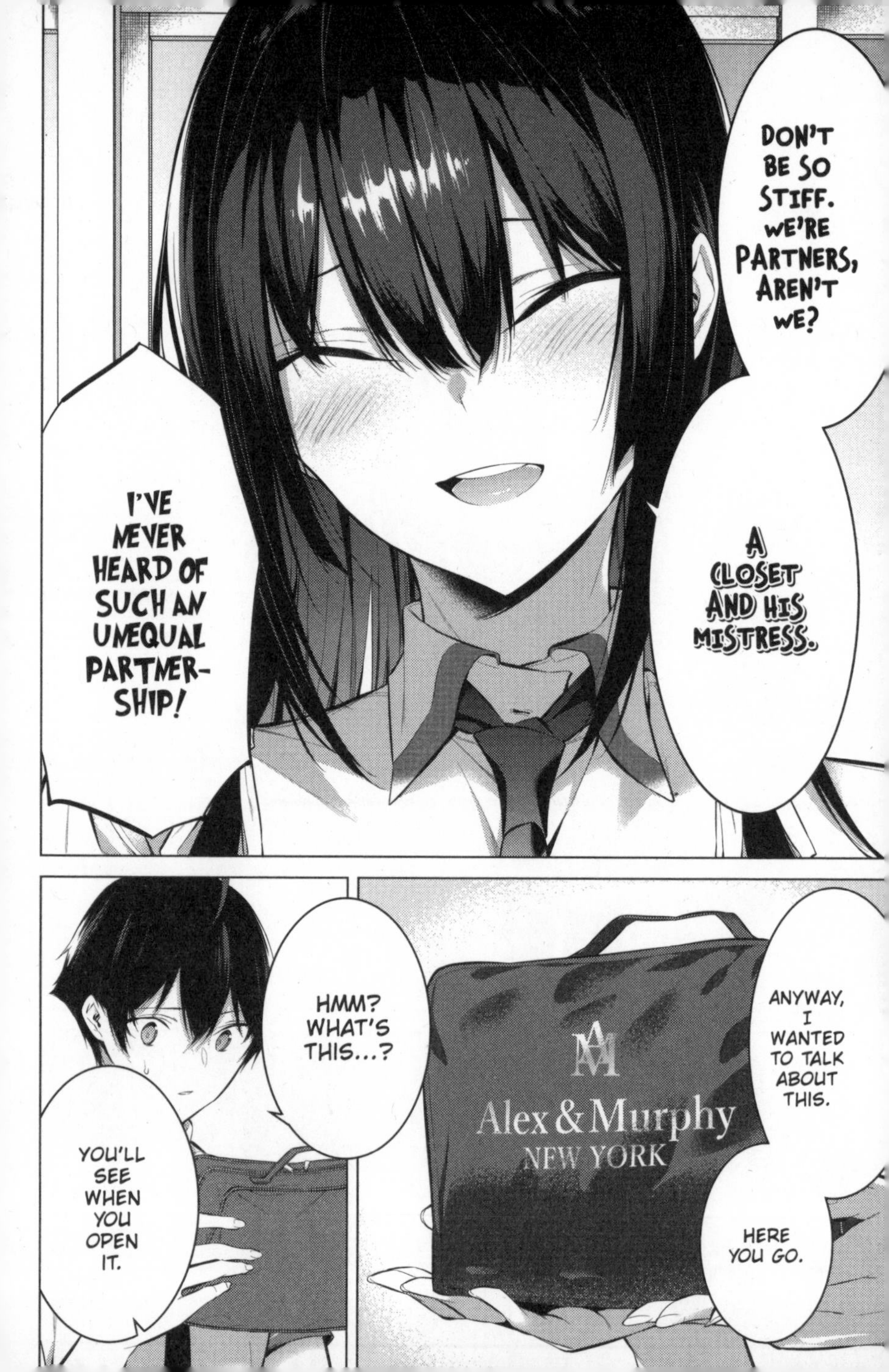
DON'T BE SO STIFF. WE'RE PARTNERS, AREN'T WE?
A CLOSET AND HIS MISTRESS.
I'VE NEVER HEARD OF SUCH AN UNEQUAL PARTNER-SHIP!
ANYWAY, I WANTED TO TALK ABOUT THIS.
Alex & Murphy
NEW YORK
HERE YOU GO.
HMM? WHAT'S THIS...?
YOU'LL SEE WHEN YOU OPEN IT.

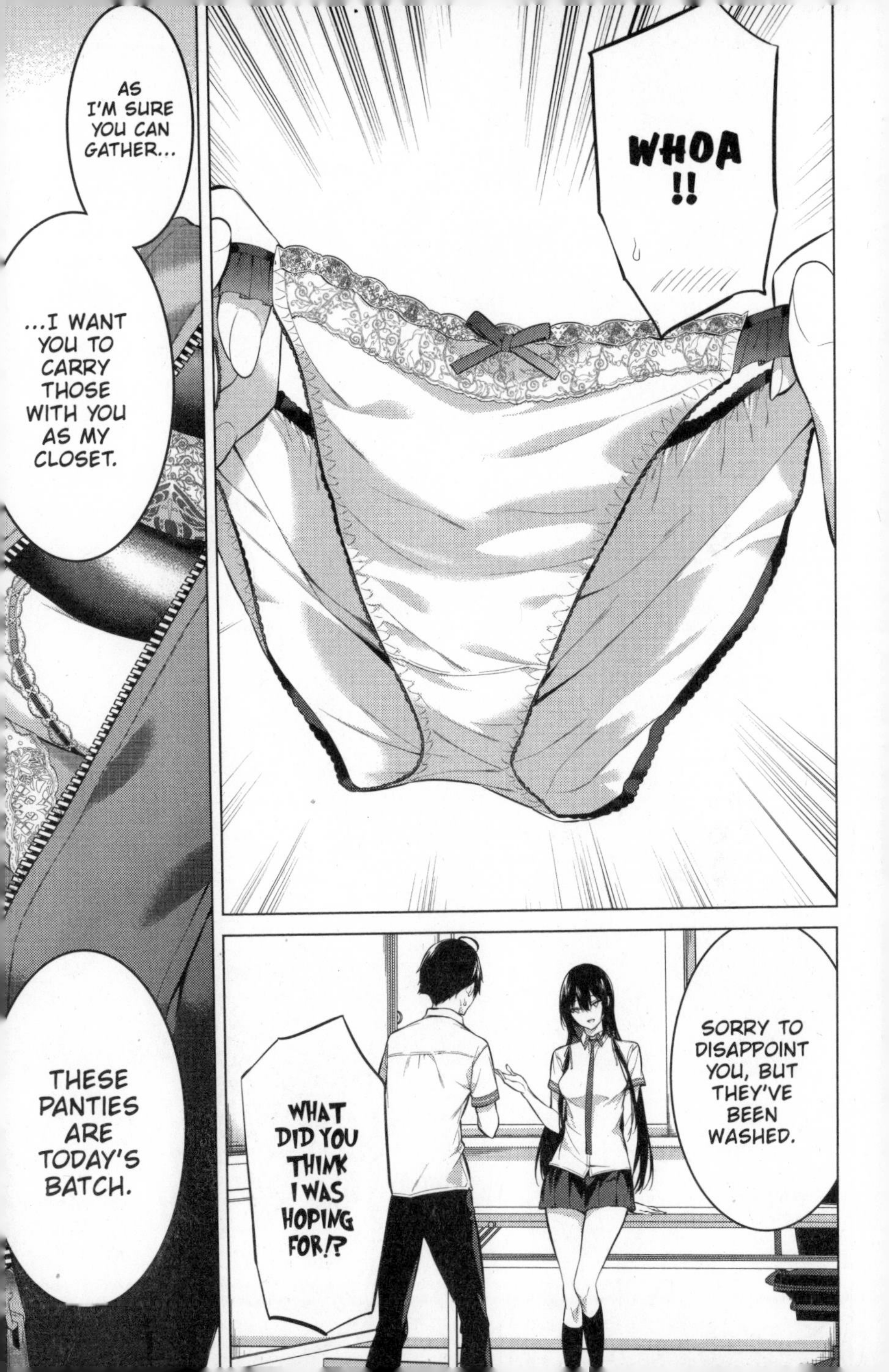
WHOA !!
SORRY TO DISAPPOINT YOU, BUT THEY'VE BEEN WASHED.
WHAT DID YOU THINK I WAS HOPING FOR!?
AS I'M SURE YOU CAN GATHER...
...I WANT YOU TO CARRY THOSE WITH YOU AS MY CLOSET.
THESE PANTIES ARE TODAY'S BATCH.

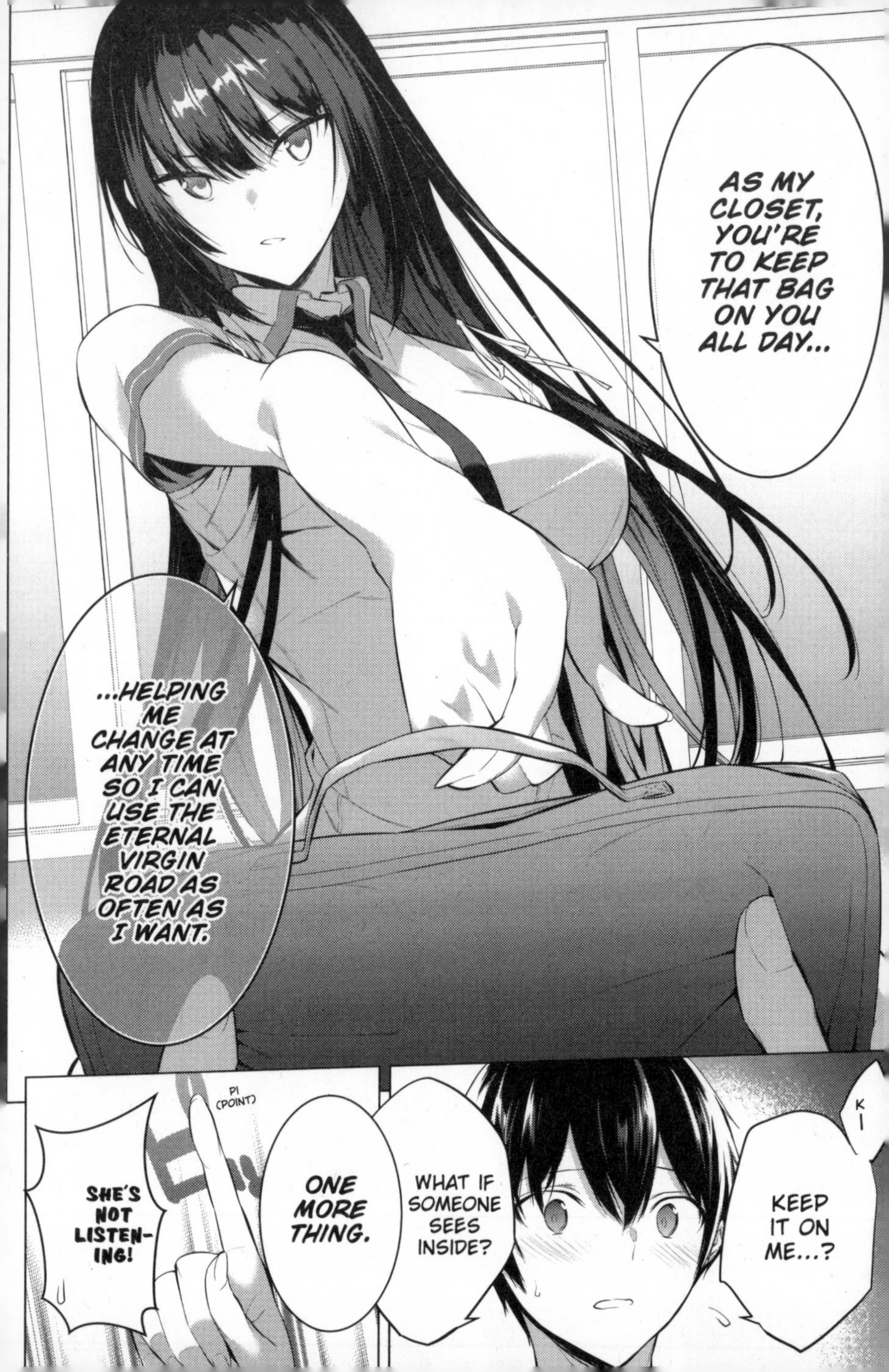
AS MY CLOSET, YOU'RE TO KEEP THAT BAG ON YOU ALL DAY...
...HELPING ME CHANGE AT ANY TIME SO I CAN USE THE ETERNAL VIRGIN ROAD AS OFTEN AS I WANT.
KI
KEEP IT ON ME...?
WHAT IF SOMEONE SEES INSIDE?
ONE MORE THING.
PI (POINT)
SHE'S NOT LISTEN-ING!

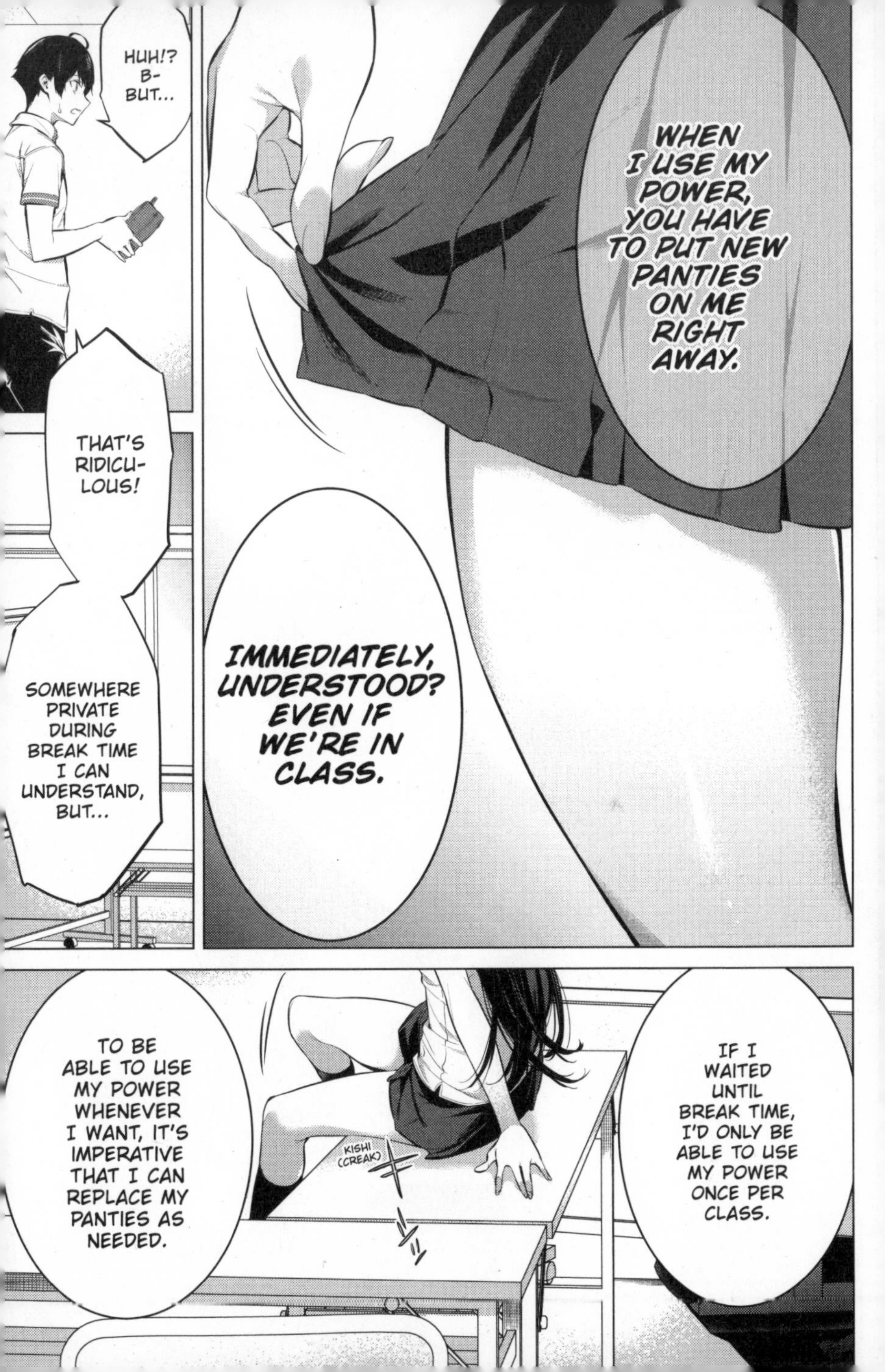
WHEN I USE MY POWER, YOU HAVE TO PUT NEW PANTIES ON ME RIGHT AWAY.
IMMEDIATELY, UNDERSTOOD? EVEN IF WE'RE IN CLASS.
HUH!? B-BUT...
THAT'S RIDICU-LOUS!
SOMEWHERE PRIVATE DURING BREAK TIME I CAN UNDERSTAND, BUT...
IF I WAITED UNTIL BREAK TIME, I'D ONLY BE ABLE TO USE MY POWER ONCE PER CLASS.
KISHI (CREAK)
TO BE ABLE TO USE MY POWER WHENEVER I WANT, IT'S IMPERATIVE THAT I CAN REPLACE MY PANTIES AS NEEDED.

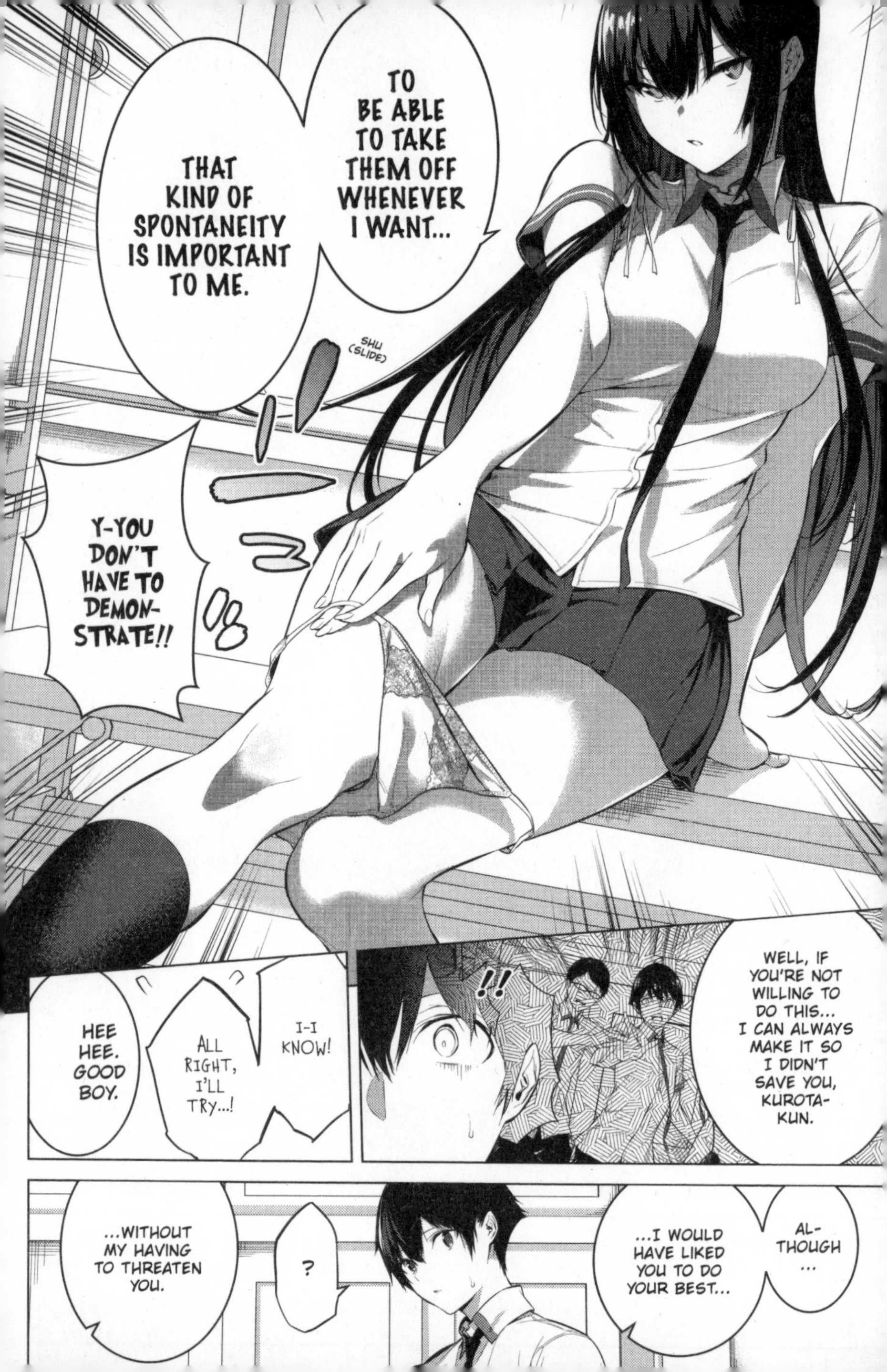
TO BE ABLE TO TAKE THEM OFF WHENEVER I WANT...
THAT KIND OF SPONTANEITY IS IMPORTANT TO ME.
SHU (SLIDE)
Y-YOU DON'T HAVE TO DEMON-STRATE!!
WELL, IF YOU'RE NOT WILLING TO DO THIS... I CAN ALWAYS MAKE IT SO I DIDN'T SAVE YOU, KUROTA-KUN.
!!
I-I KNOW!
ALL RIGHT, I'LL TRY...!
HEE HEE. GOOD BOY.
AL-THOUGH...
...I WOULD HAVE LIKED YOU TO DO YOUR BEST...
?
...WITHOUT MY HAVING TO THREATEN YOU.

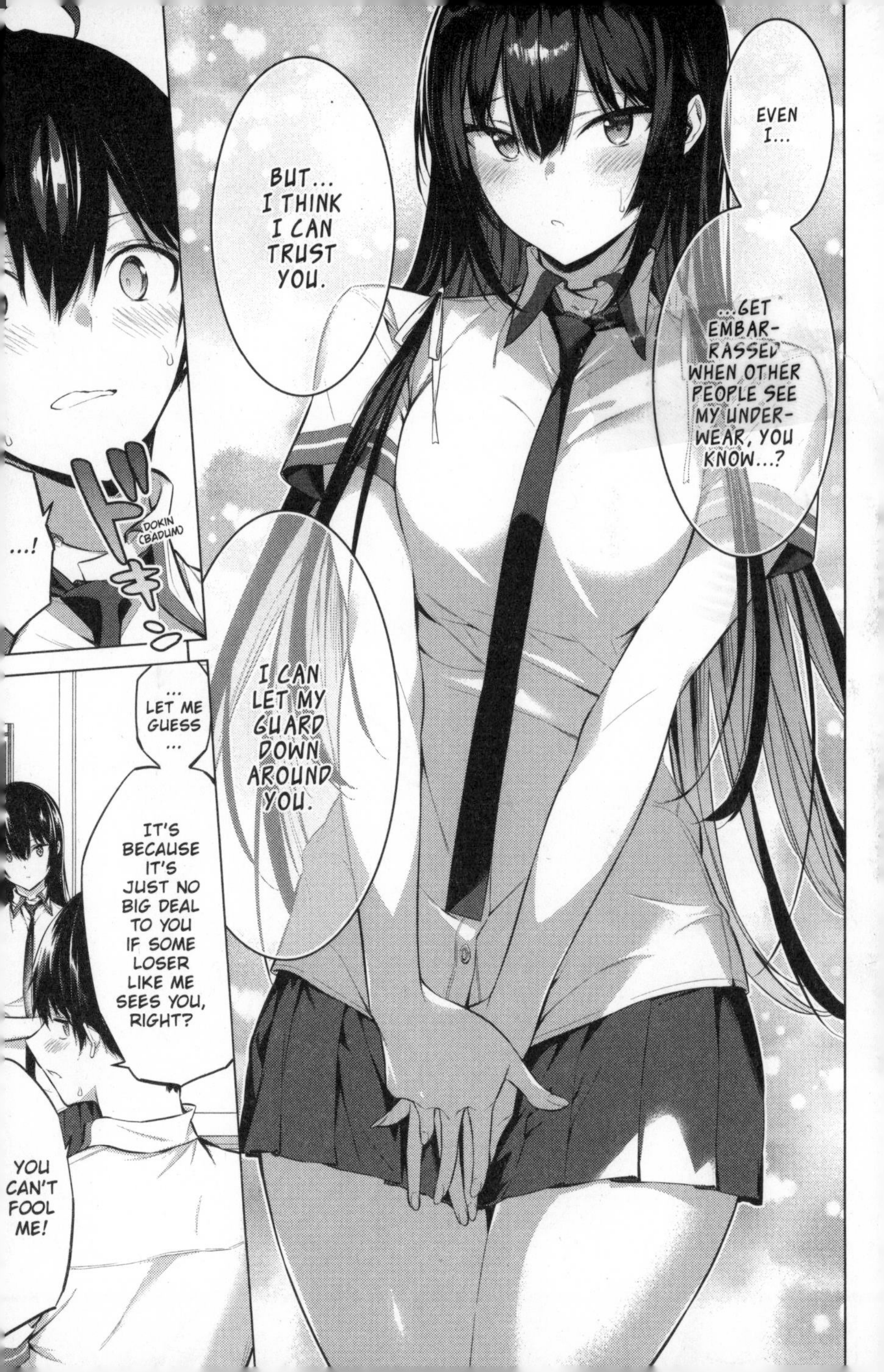
EVEN I...
...GET EMBARRASSED WHEN OTHER PEOPLE SEE MY UNDERWEAR, YOU KNOW...?
BUT... I THINK I CAN TRUST YOU.
I CAN LET MY GUARD DOWN AROUND YOU.
DOKIN (BADUM)
...!
... LET ME GUESS ...
IT'S BECAUSE IT'S JUST NO BIG DEAL TO YOU IF SOME LOSER LIKE ME SEES YOU, RIGHT?
YOU CAN'T FOOL ME!

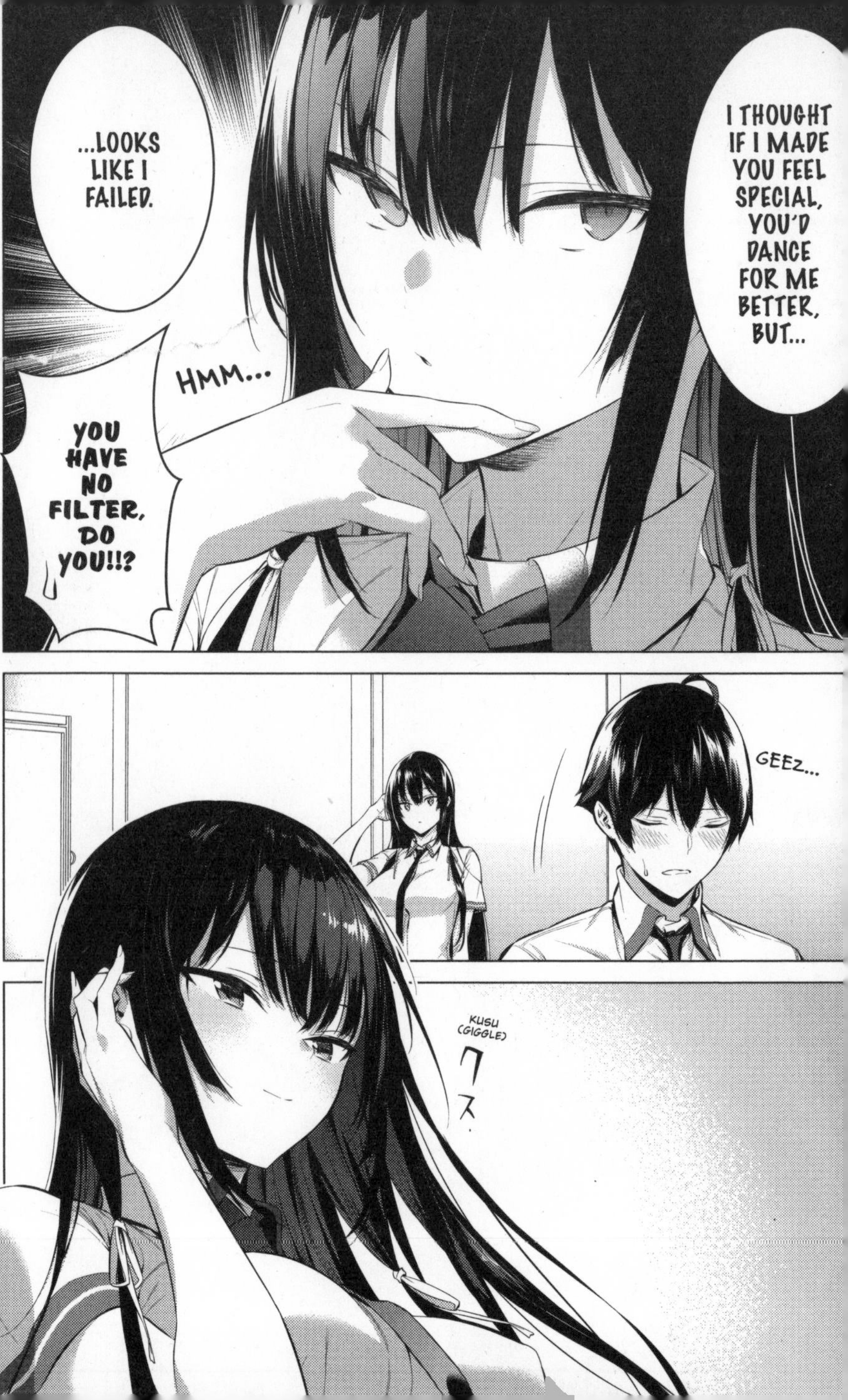
I THOUGHT IF I MADE YOU FEEL SPECIAL, YOU'D DANCE FOR ME BETTER, BUT...
...LOOKS LIKE I FAILED.
HMM...
YOU HAVE NO FILTER, DO YOU!!?
GEEZ...
クス
KUSU (GIGGLE)

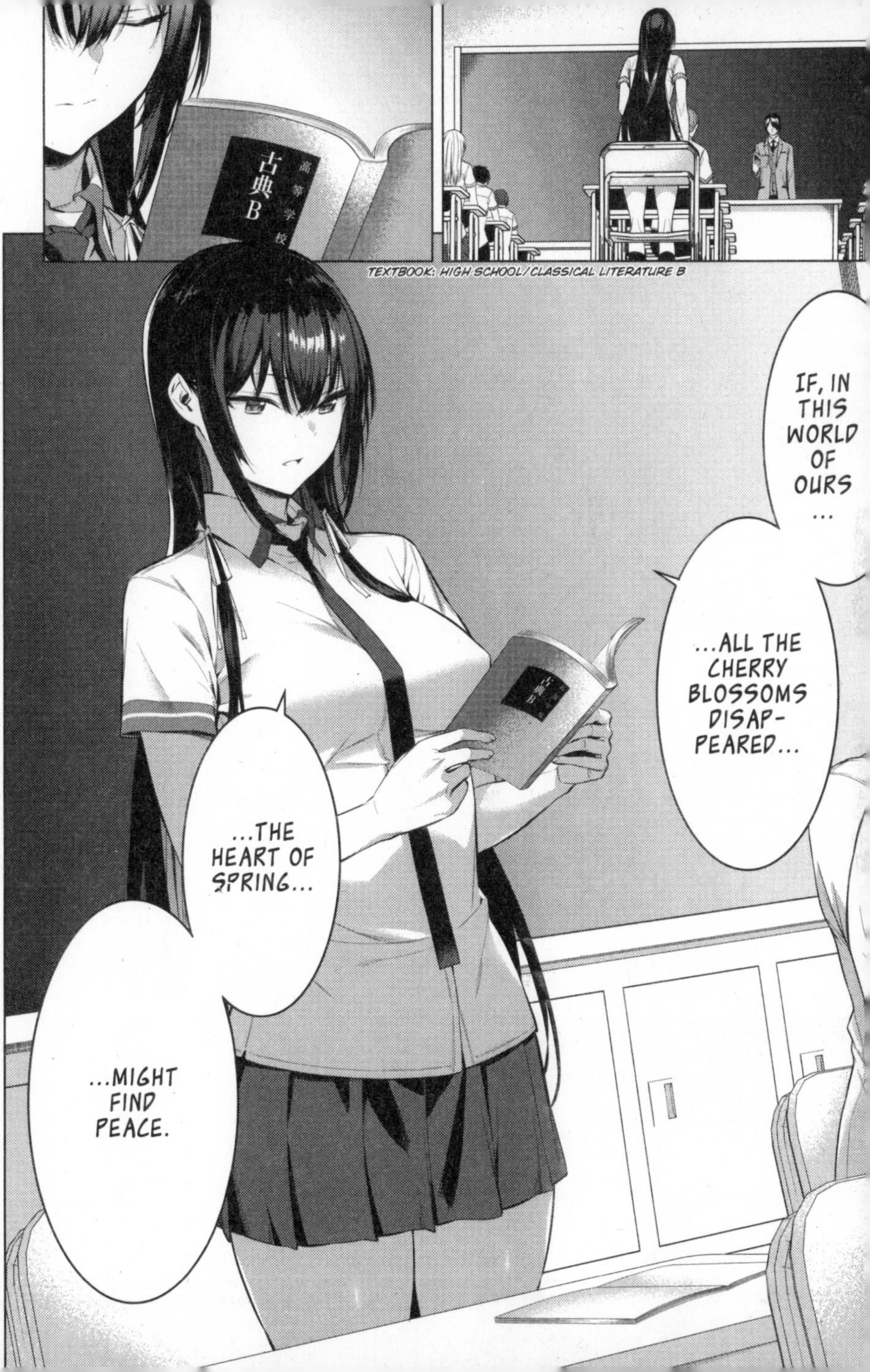
高等学校
古典B
TEXTBOOK: HIGH SCHOOL/CLASSICAL LITERATURE B
IF, IN THIS WORLD OF OURS...
...ALL THE CHERRY BLOSSOMS DISAPPEARED...
...THE HEART OF SPRING...
...MIGHT FIND PEACE.

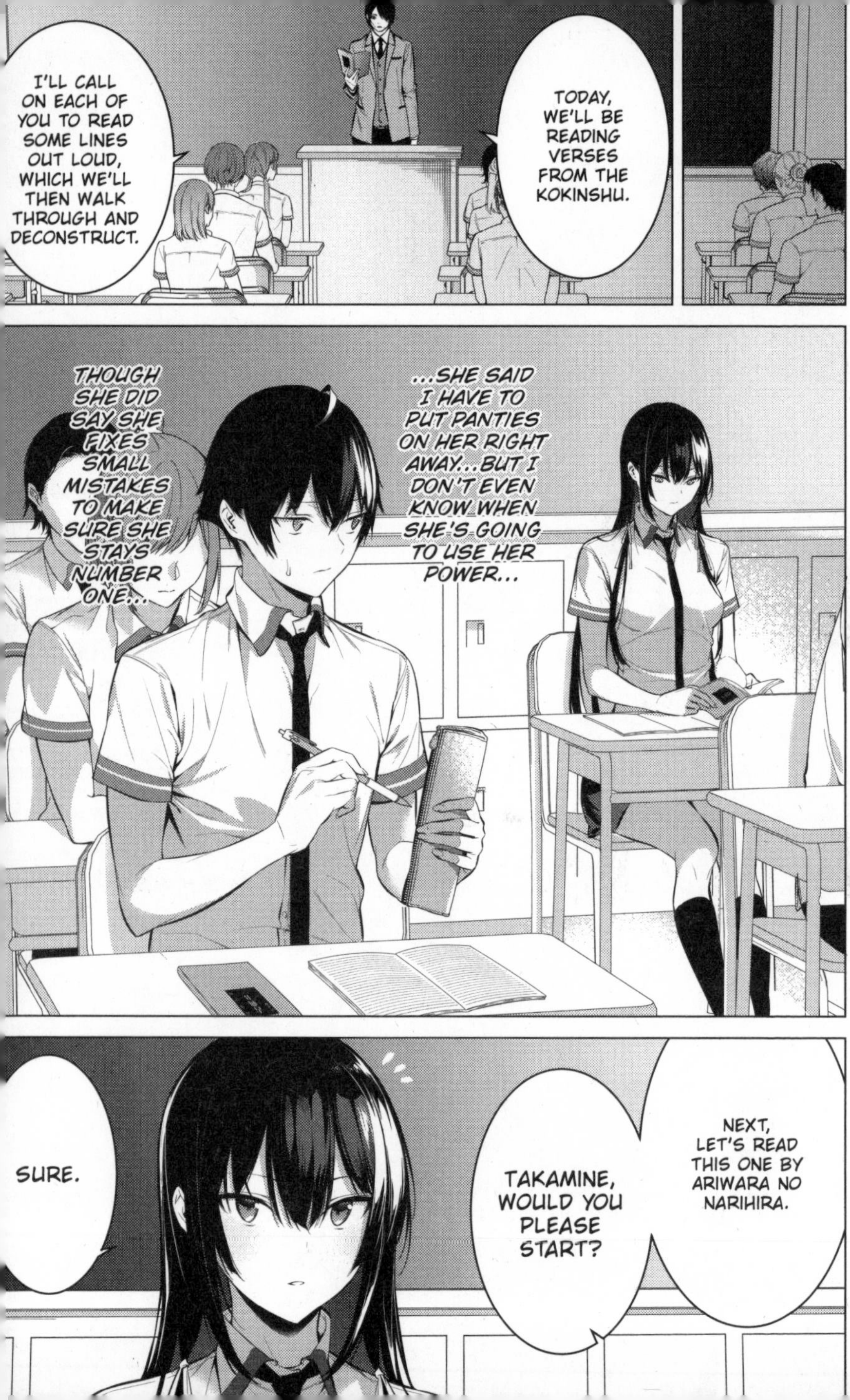
TODAY, WE'LL BE READING VERSES FROM THE KOKINSHU.
I'LL CALL ON EACH OF YOU TO READ SOME LINES OUT LOUD, WHICH WE'LL THEN WALK THROUGH AND DECONSTRUCT.
...SHE SAID I HAVE TO PUT PANTIES ON HER RIGHT AWAY...BUT I DON'T EVEN KNOW WHEN SHE'S GOING TO USE HER POWER...
THOUGH SHE DID SAY SHE FIXES SMALL MISTAKES TO MAKE SURE SHE STAYS NUMBER ONE...
NEXT, LET'S READ THIS ONE BY ARIWARA NO NARIHIRA.
TAKAMINE, WOULD YOU PLEASE START?
SURE.

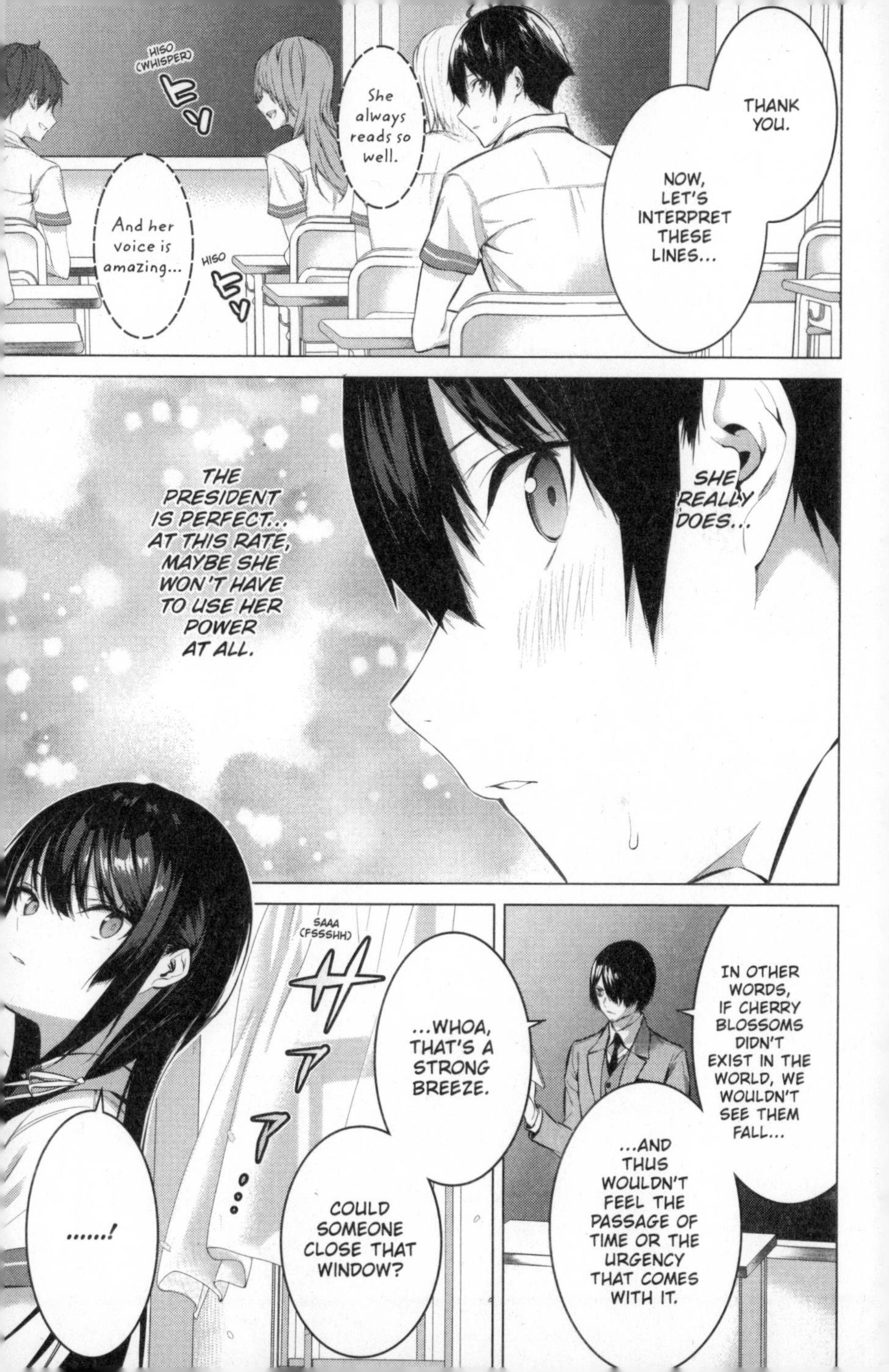
THANK YOU.
NOW, LET'S INTERPRET THESE LINES...
She always reads so well.
HISO (WHISPER)
And her voice is amazing...
HISO
SHE REALLY DOES...
THE PRESIDENT IS PERFECT... AT THIS RATE, MAYBE SHE WON'T HAVE TO USE HER POWER AT ALL.
IN OTHER WORDS, IF CHERRY BLOSSOMS DIDN'T EXIST IN THE WORLD, WE WOULDN'T SEE THEM FALL...
...AND THUS WOULDN'T FEEL THE PASSAGE OF TIME OR THE URGENCY THAT COMES WITH IT.
...WHOA, THAT'S A STRONG BREEZE.
SAAA (FSSSHH)
COULD SOMEONE CLOSE THAT WINDOW?
......!

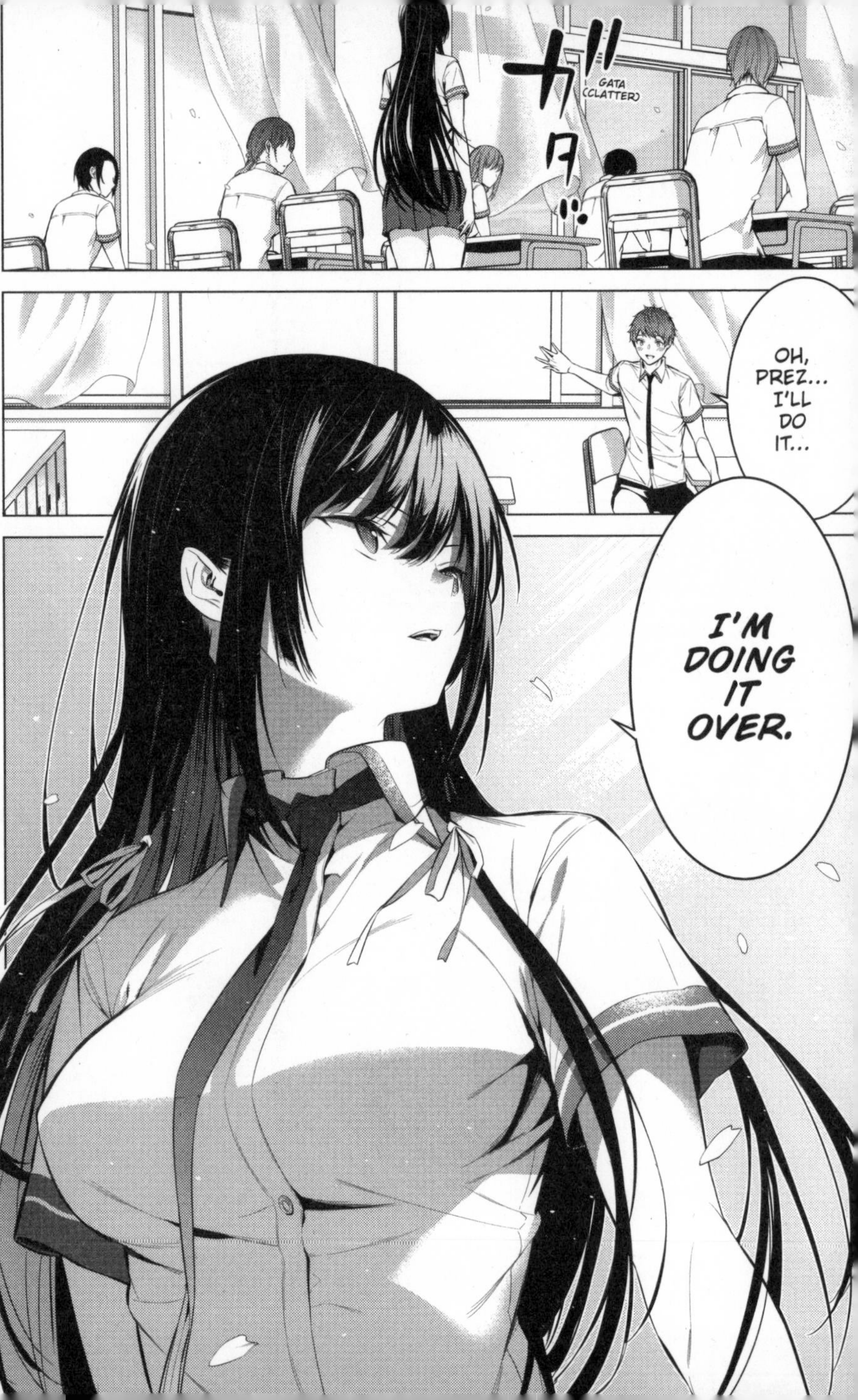
GATA (CLATTER)
OH, PREZ... I'LL DO IT...
I'M DOING IT OVER.

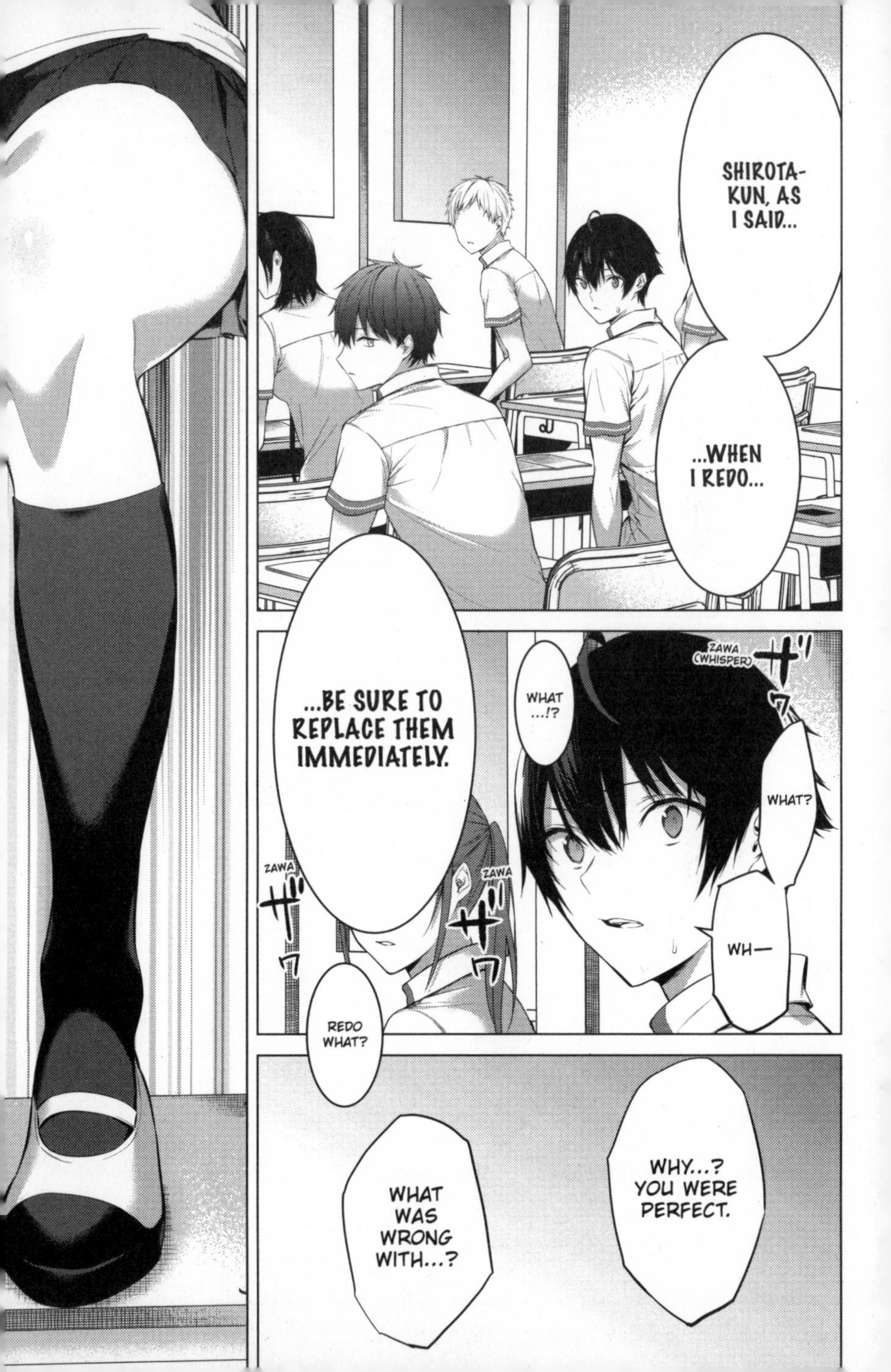
SHIROTA-KUN, AS I SAID...
...WHEN I REDO...
...BE SURE TO REPLACE THEM IMMEDIATELY.
ZAWA (WHISPER)
ザワ
WHAT ...!?
WHAT?
WH—
ZAWA
ザワ
ZAWA
ザワ
REDO WHAT?
WHY...? YOU WERE PERFECT.
WHAT WAS WRONG WITH...?

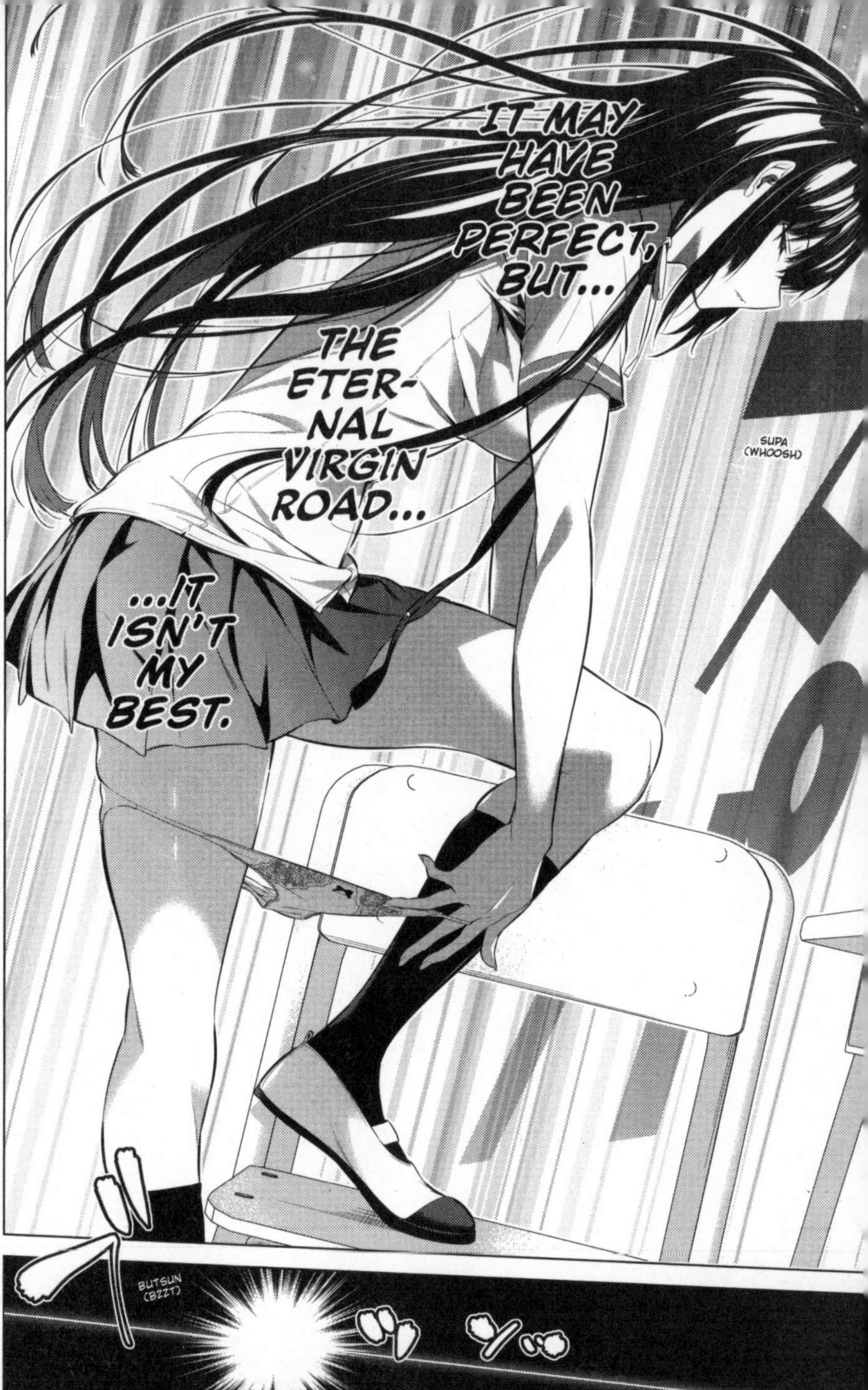
IT MAY HAVE BEEN PERFECT, BUT...
THE ETER-NAL VIRGIN ROAD...
SUPA (WHOOSH)
...IT ISN'T MY BEST.
BUTSUN (BZZT)

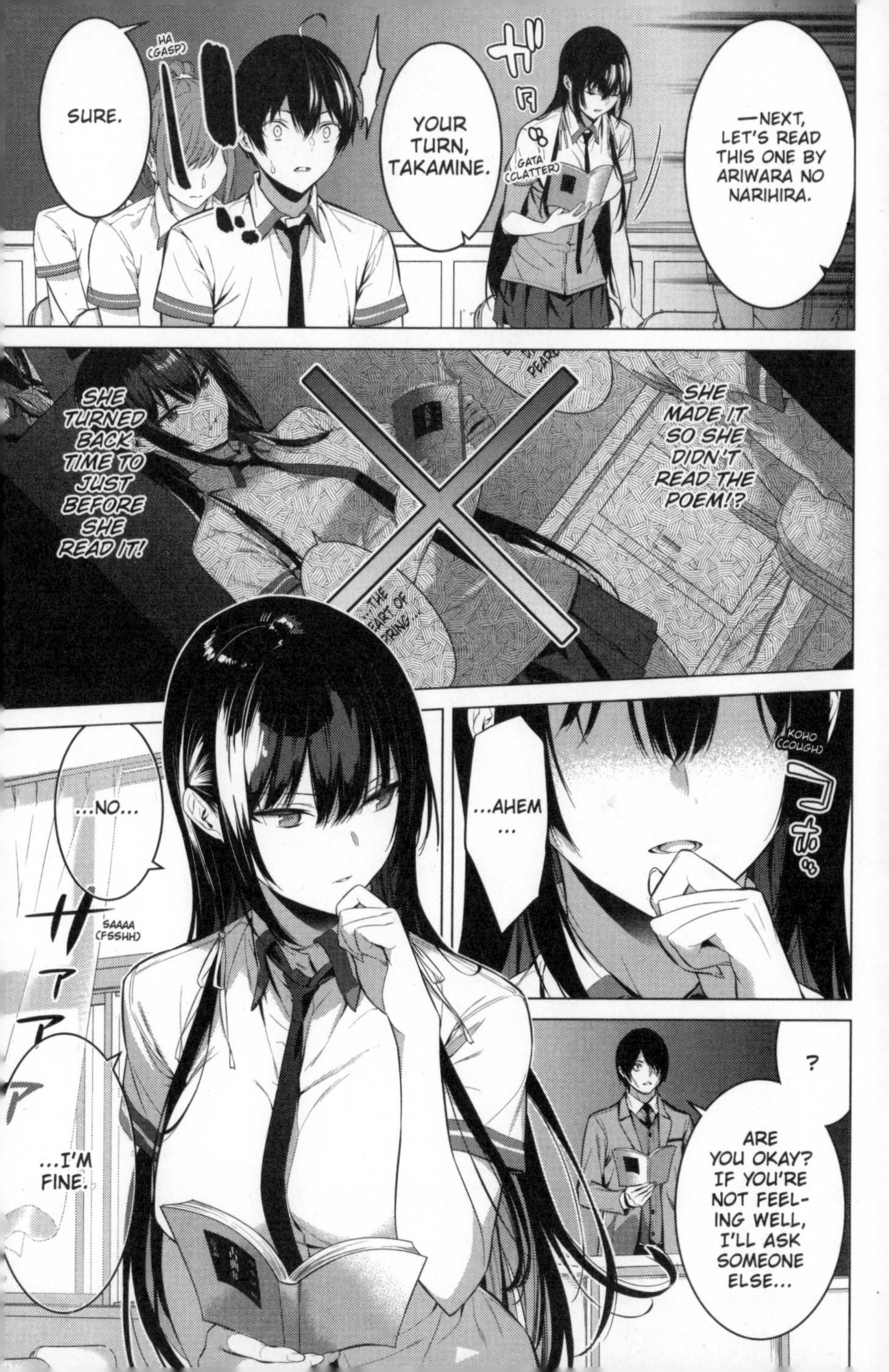
—NEXT, LET'S READ THIS ONE BY ARIWARA NO NARIHIRA.
GATA (CLATTER)
YOUR TURN, TAKAMINE.
HA (GASP)
SURE.
SHE MADE IT SO SHE DIDN'T READ THE POEM!?
SHE TURNED BACK TIME TO JUST BEFORE SHE READ IT!
KOHO (COUGH)
...AHEM ...
?
ARE YOU OKAY? IF YOU'RE NOT FEELING WELL, I'LL ASK SOMEONE ELSE...
...NO...
SAAAA (FSSHH)
...I'M FINE.

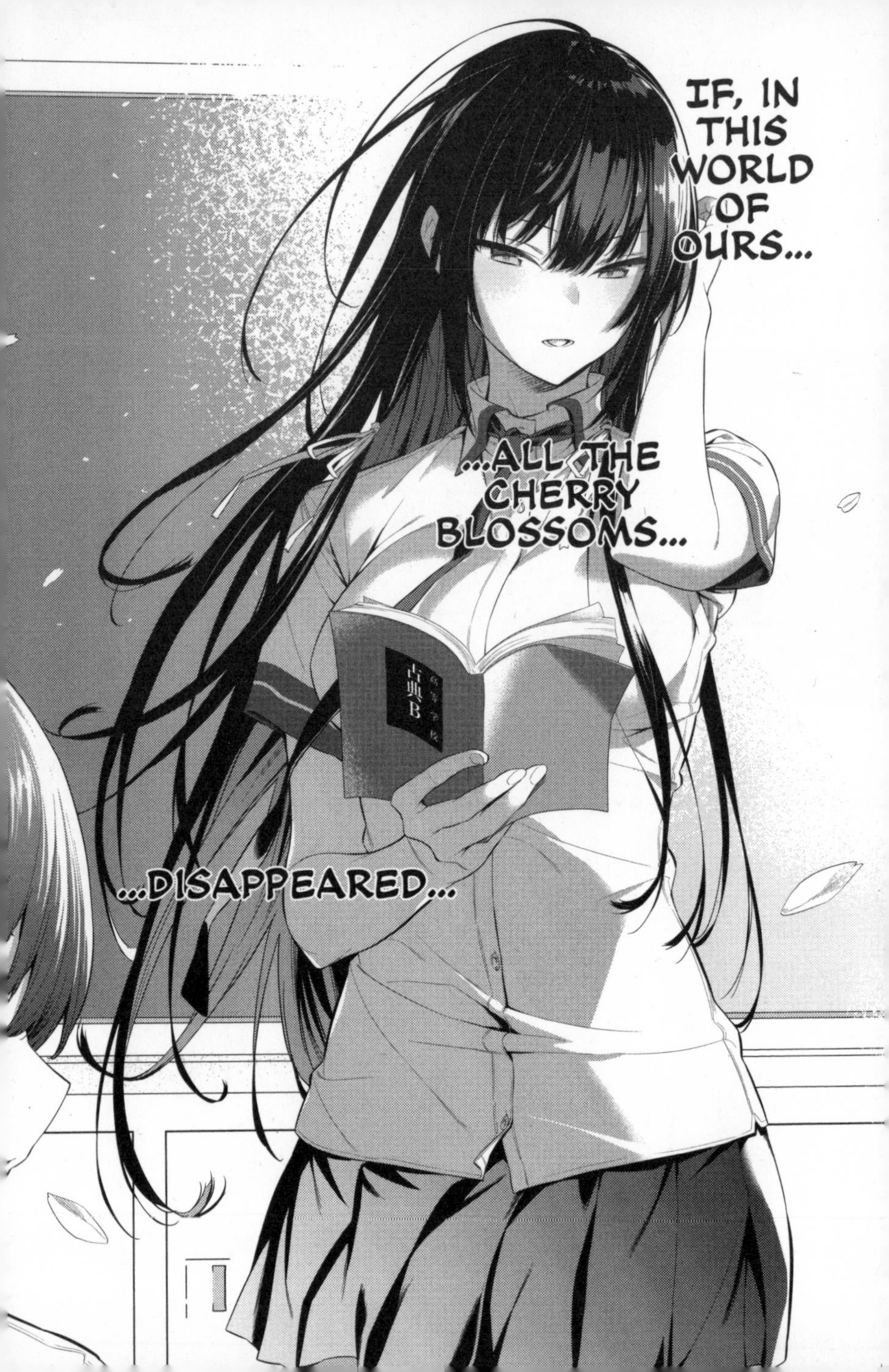
IF, IN THIS WORLD OF OURS...
...ALL THE CHERRY BLOSSOMS...
...DISAPPEARED...
古典B

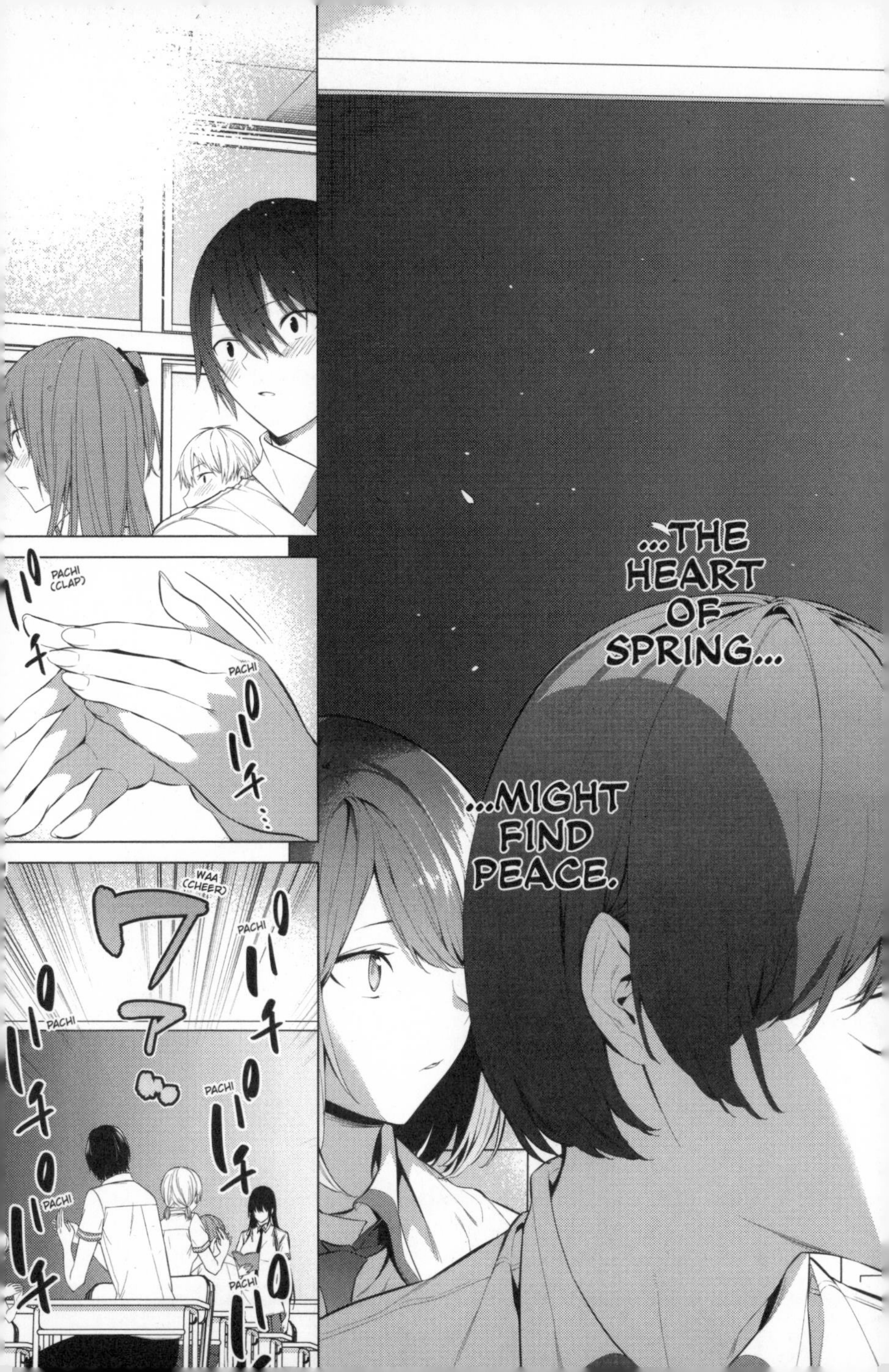
...THE HEART OF SPRING...
...MIGHT FIND PEACE.
PACHI (CLAP)
PACHI
WAA (CHEER)
PACHI
PACHI
PACHI
PACHI
PACHI

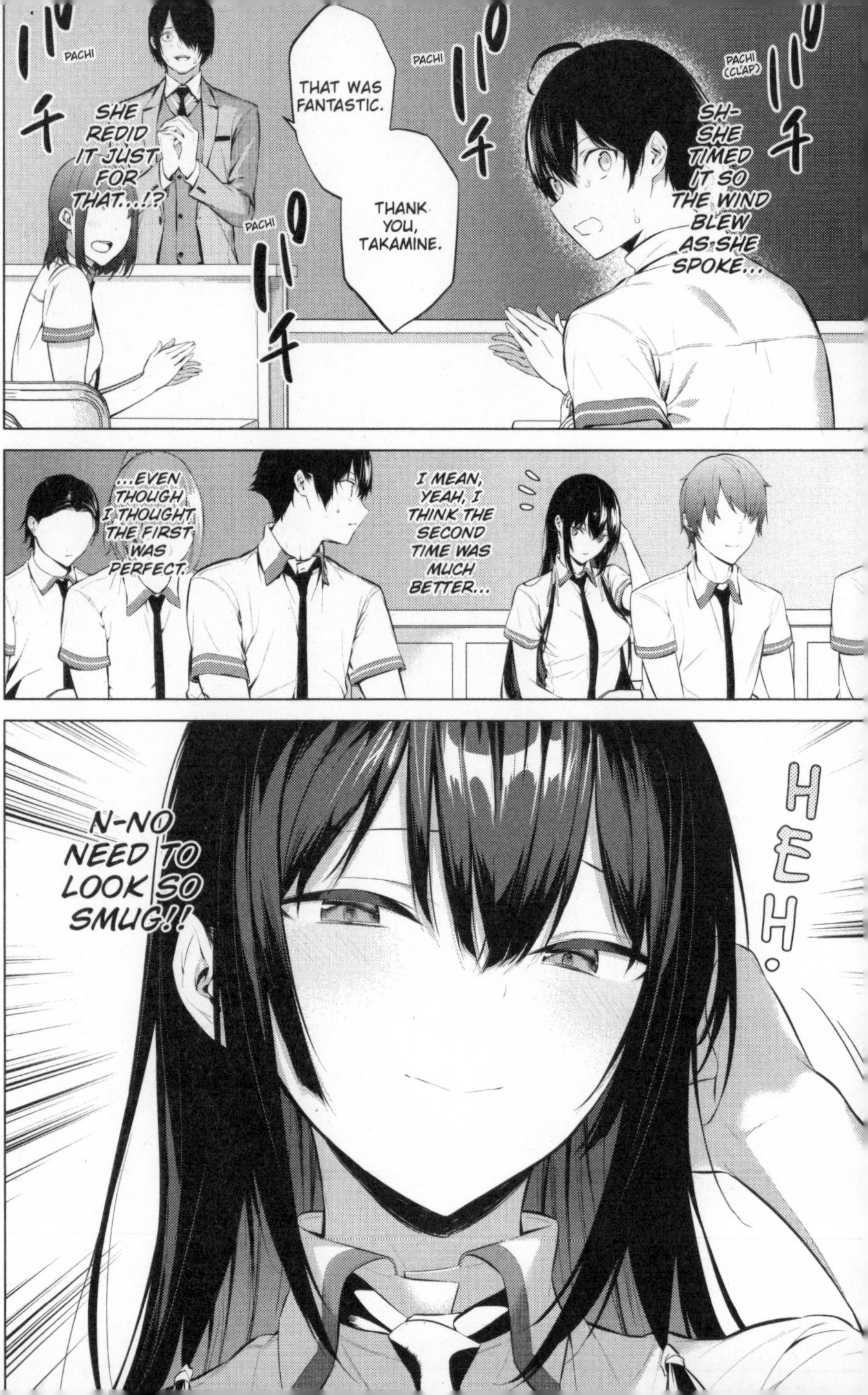
パチ
PACHI (CLAP)
SH-SHE TIMED IT SO THE WIND BLEW AS SHE SPOKE...
パチ
PACHI
THAT WAS FANTASTIC.
THANK YOU, TAKAMINE.
パチ
PACHI
SHE REDID IT JUST FOR THAT...!?
パチ
PACHI
I MEAN, YEAH, I THINK THE SECOND TIME WAS MUCH BETTER...
...EVEN THOUGH I THOUGHT THE FIRST WAS PERFECT.
HEH.
N-NO NEED TO LOOK SO SMUG!!

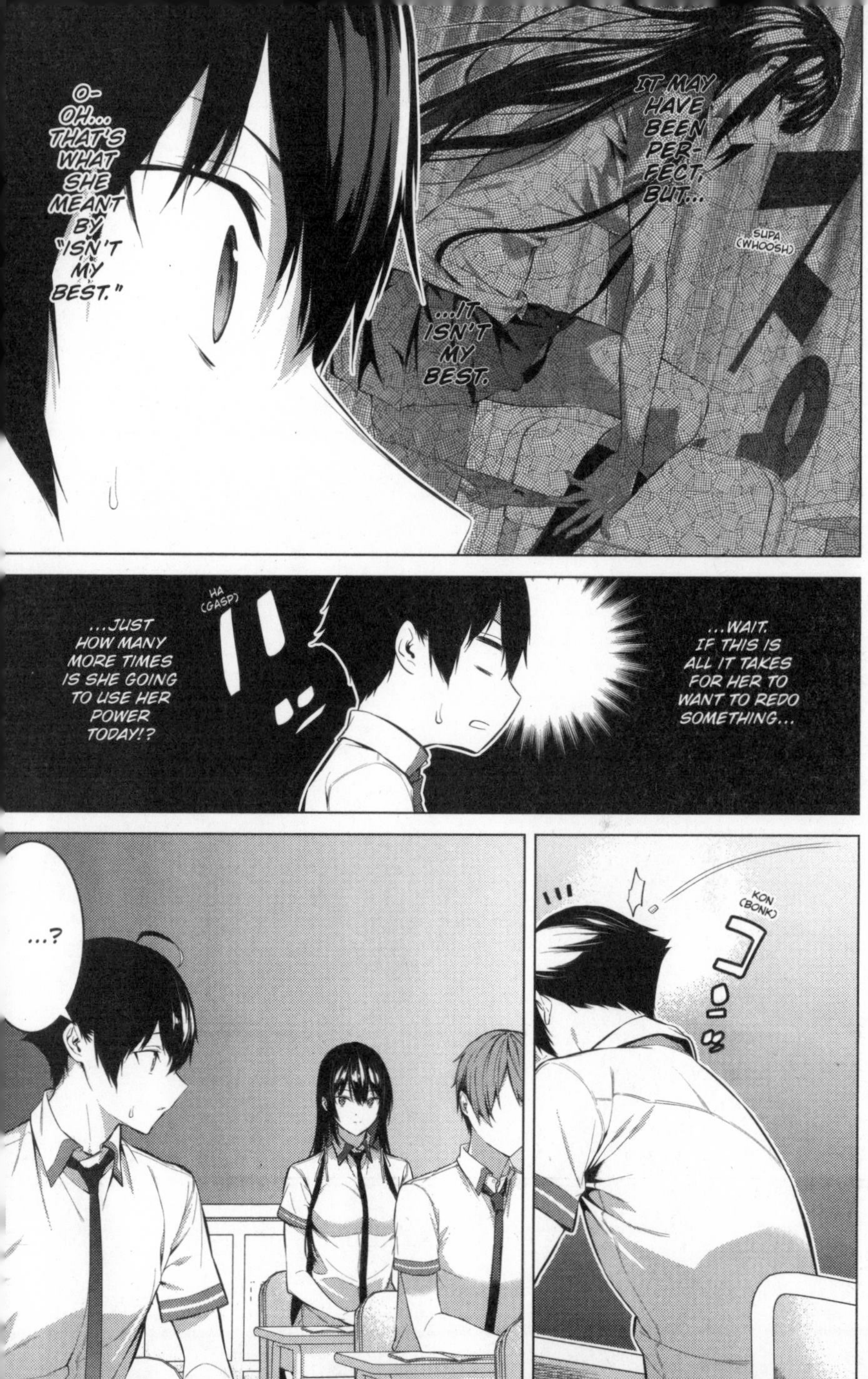
IT MAY HAVE BEEN PERFECT, BUT...
SUPA (WHOOSH)
...IT ISN'T MY BEST.
O-OH... THAT'S WHAT SHE MEANT BY "ISN'T MY BEST."
...WAIT. IF THIS IS ALL IT TAKES FOR HER TO WANT TO REDO SOMETHING...
HA (GASP)
...JUST HOW MANY MORE TIMES IS SHE GOING TO USE HER POWER TODAY!?
KON (BONK)
...?

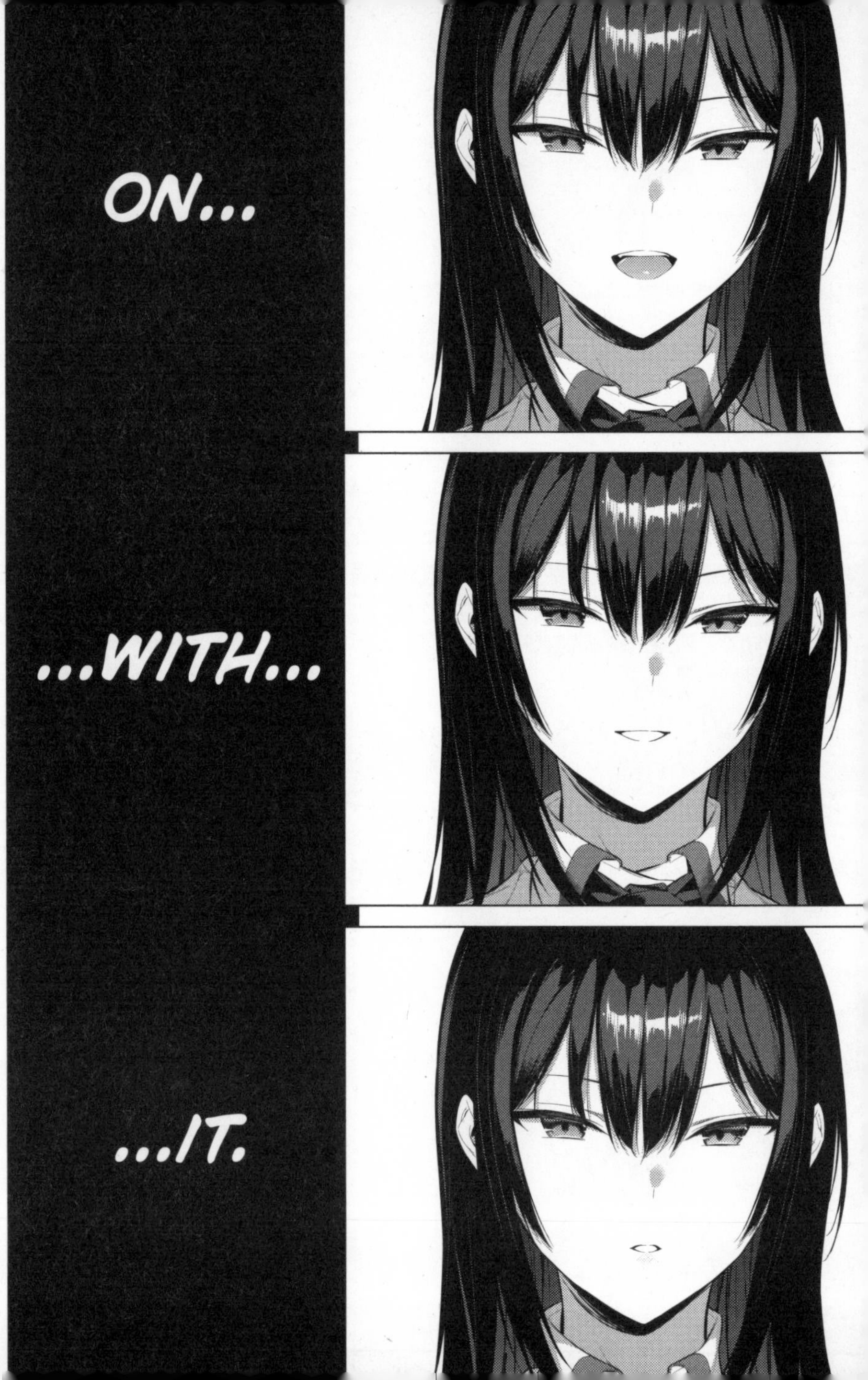
ON...
...WITH...
...IT.

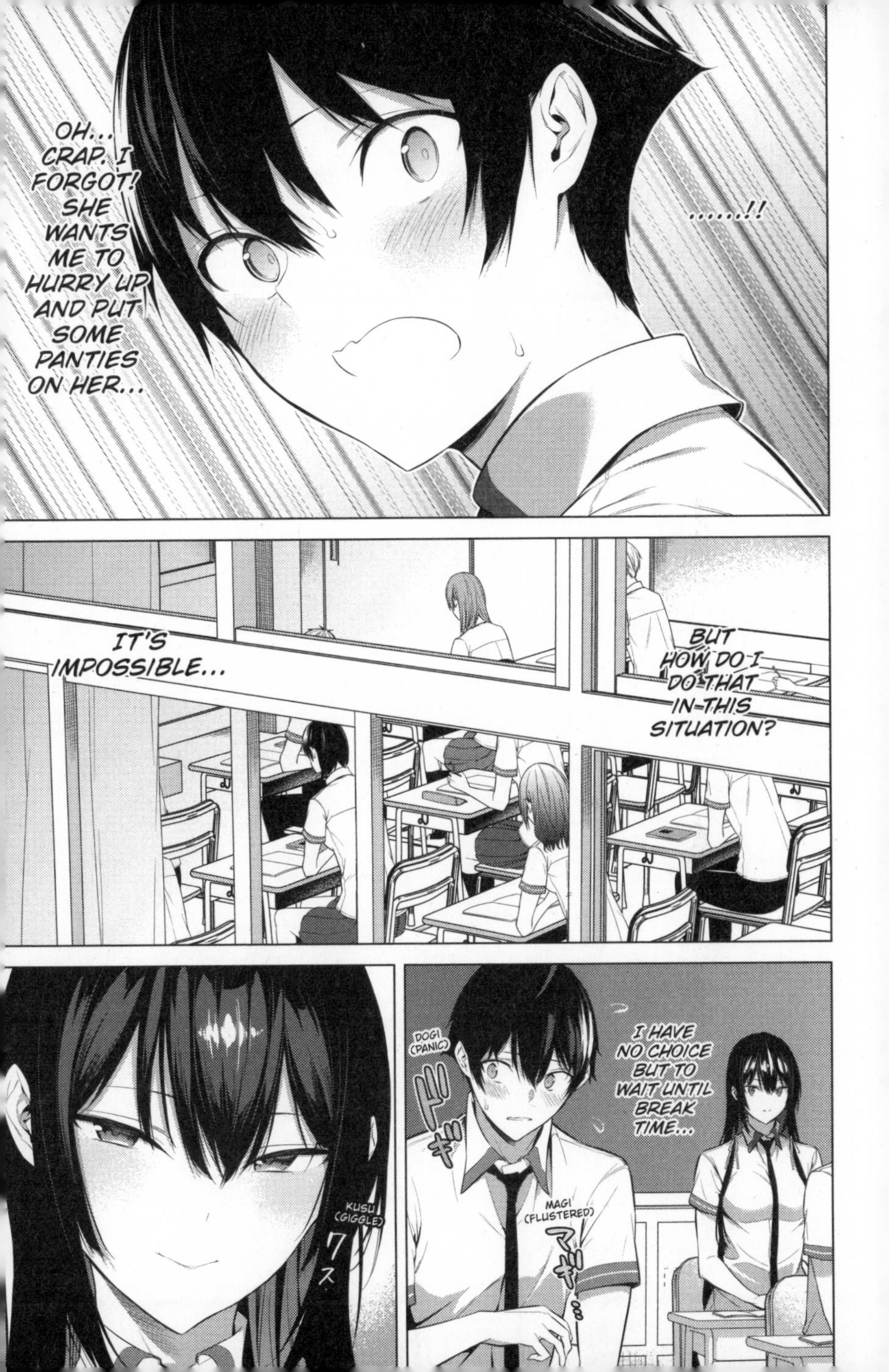
......!!
OH... CRAP. I FORGOT! SHE WANTS ME TO HURRY UP AND PUT SOME PANTIES ON HER...
BUT HOW DO I DO THAT IN THIS SITUATION?
IT'S IMPOSSIBLE...
I HAVE NO CHOICE BUT TO WAIT UNTIL BREAK TIME...
DOGI (PANIC)
ドギ
MAGI (FLUSTERED)
マギ...
KUSU (GIGGLE)
クス

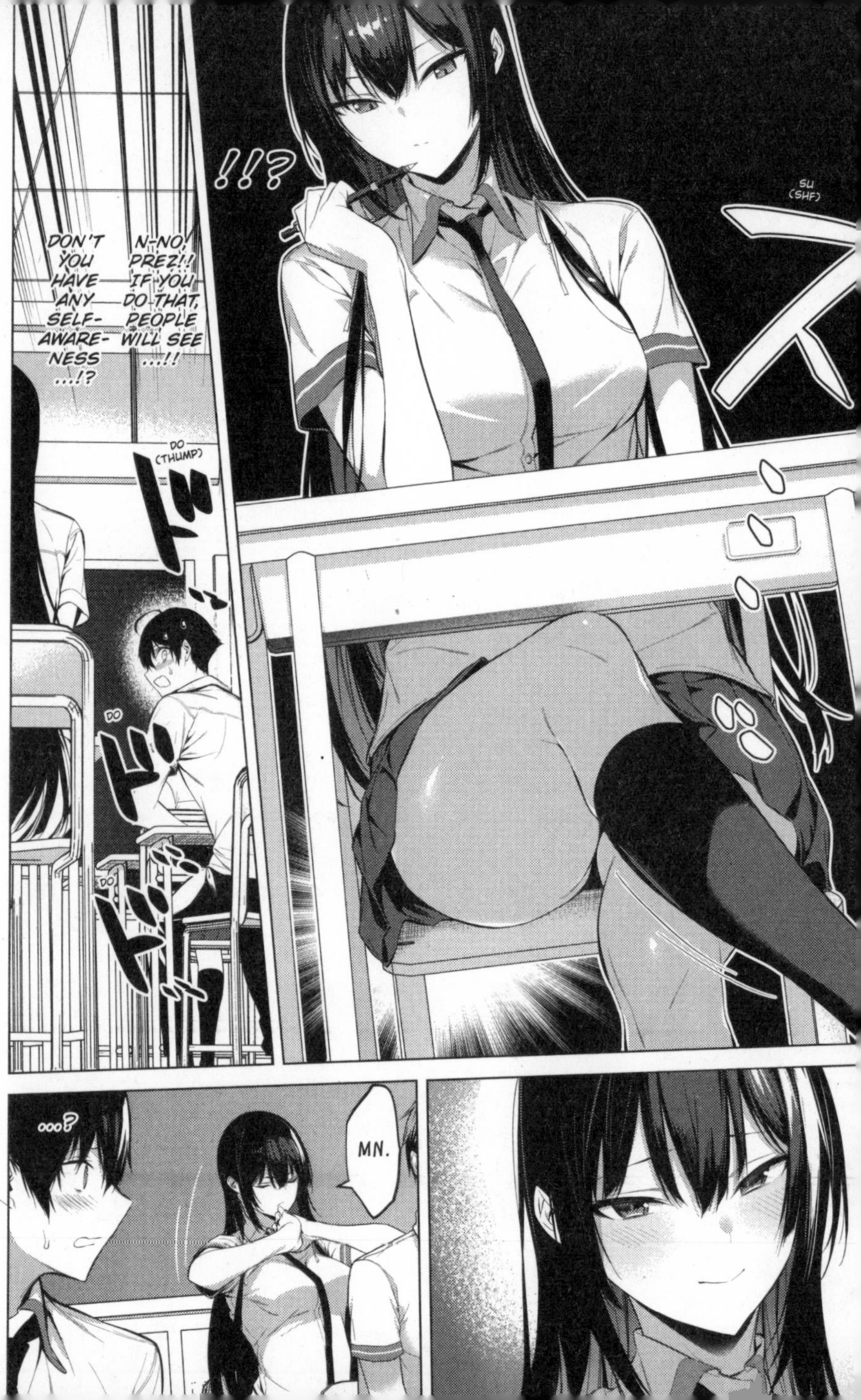

SU (SHF)
!!?
N-NO! PREZ!! IF YOU DO THAT, PEOPLE WILL SEE ...!!
DON'T YOU HAVE ANY SELF-AWARENESS ...!?
DO (THUMP)
DO
DO
MN.
...?

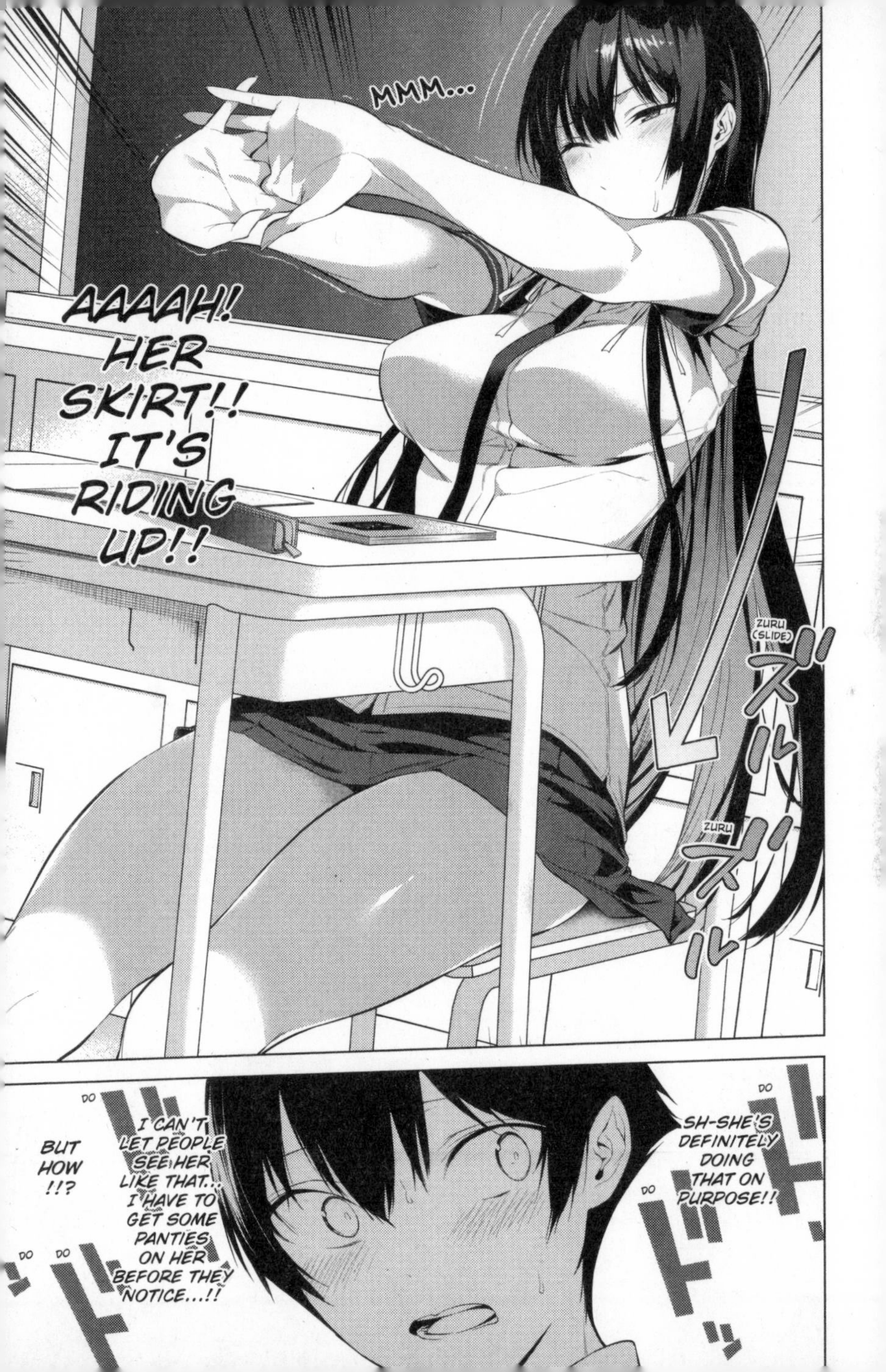
MMM...
AAAAH! HER SKIRT!! IT'S RIDING UP!!
ZURU (SLIDE)
ZURU
DO
SH-SHE'S DEFINITELY DOING THAT ON PURPOSE!!
DO
I CAN'T LET PEOPLE SEE HER LIKE THAT... I HAVE TO GET SOME PANTIES ON HER BEFORE THEY NOTICE...!!
BUT HOW!!?
DO DO

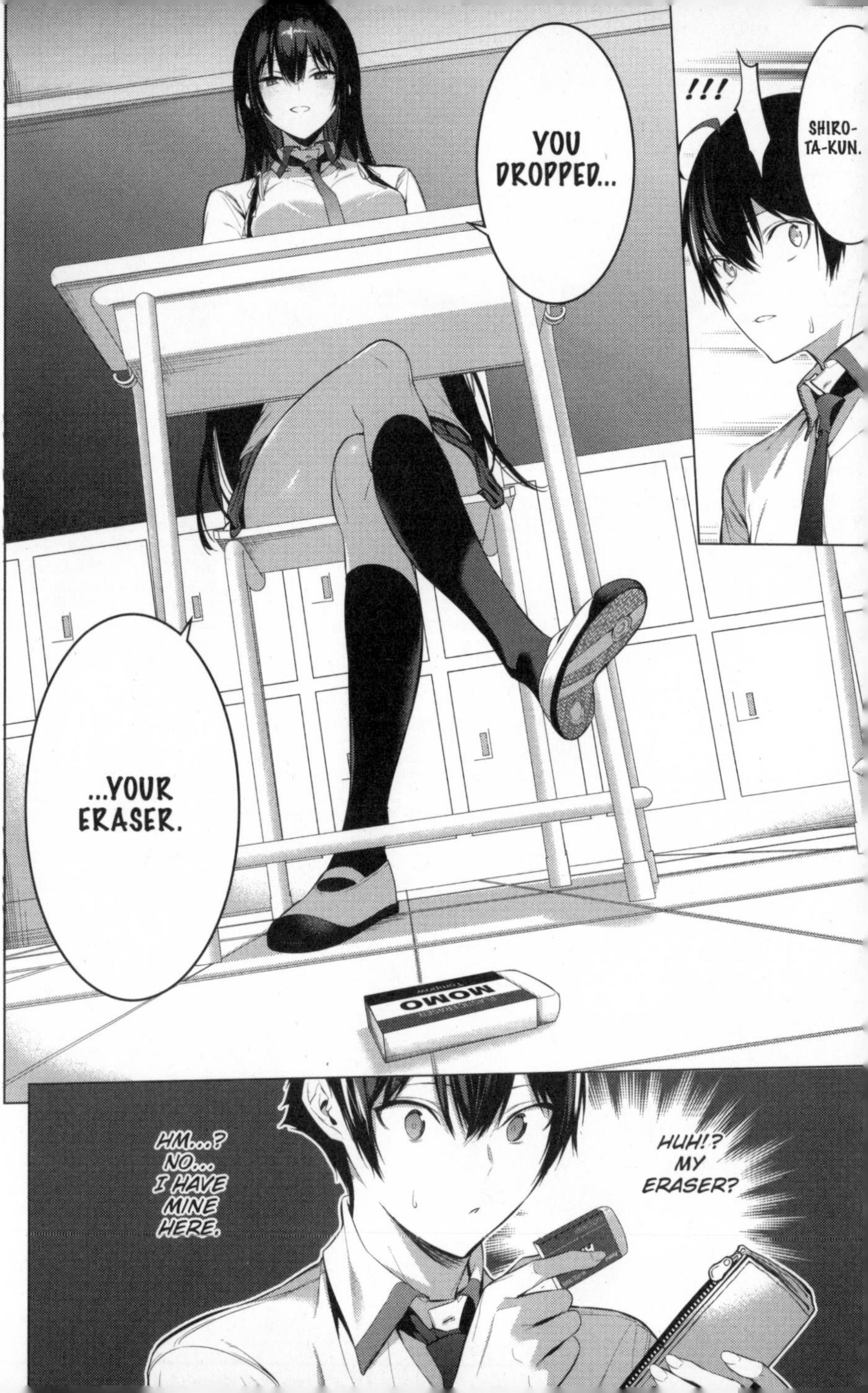
SHIRO-TA-KUN.
!!!
YOU DROPPED...
...YOUR ERASER.
HUH!? MY ERASER?
HM...? NO... I HAVE MINE HERE.

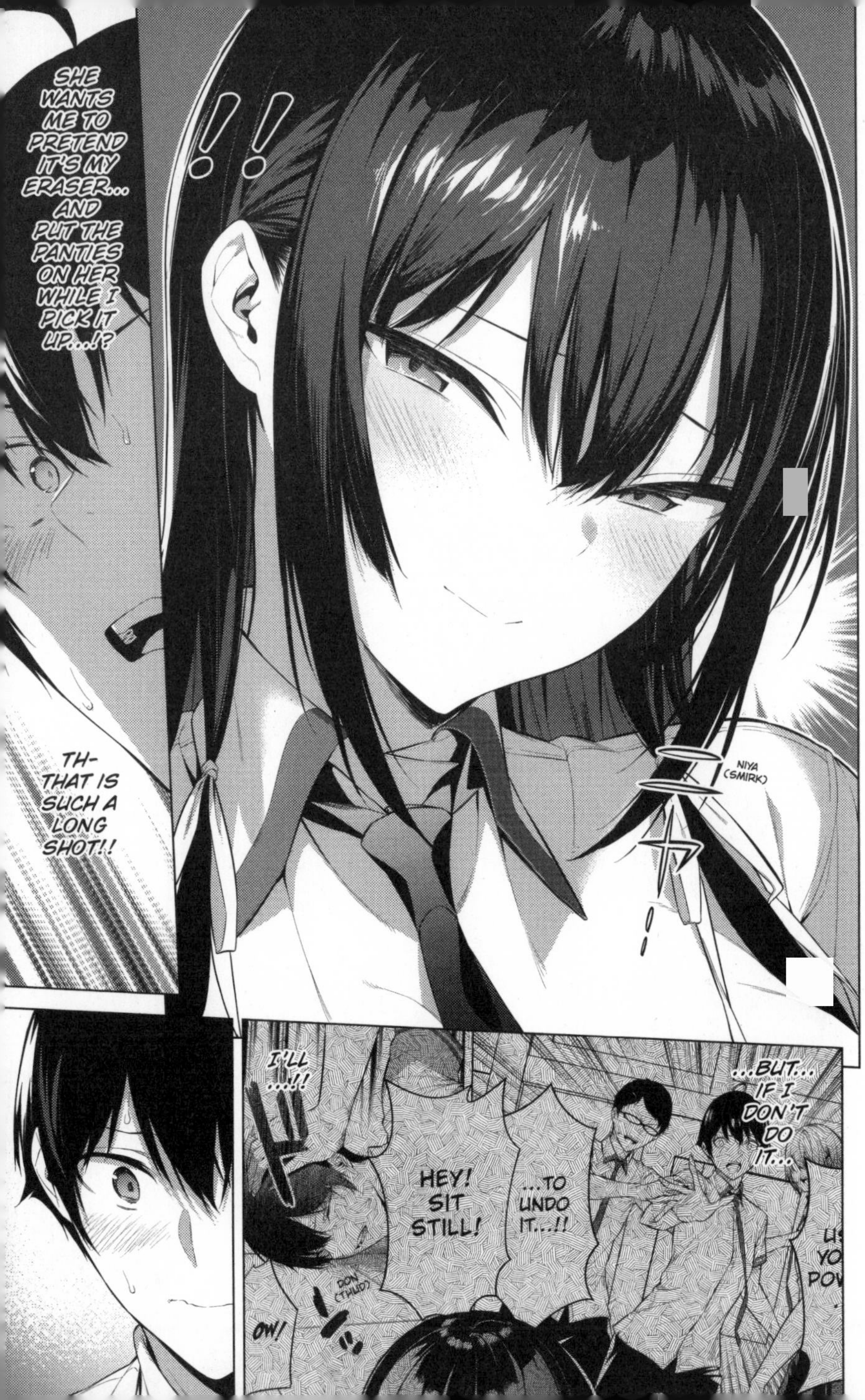
!!
NIYA (SMIRK)
SHE WANTS ME TO PRETEND IT'S MY ERASER... AND PUT THE PANTIES ON HER WHILE I PICK IT UP...!?
TH-THAT IS SUCH A LONG SHOT!!
...BUT... IF I DON'T DO IT...
...TO UNDO IT...!!
HEY! SIT STILL!
I'LL ...!!
DON (THUD)
OW!

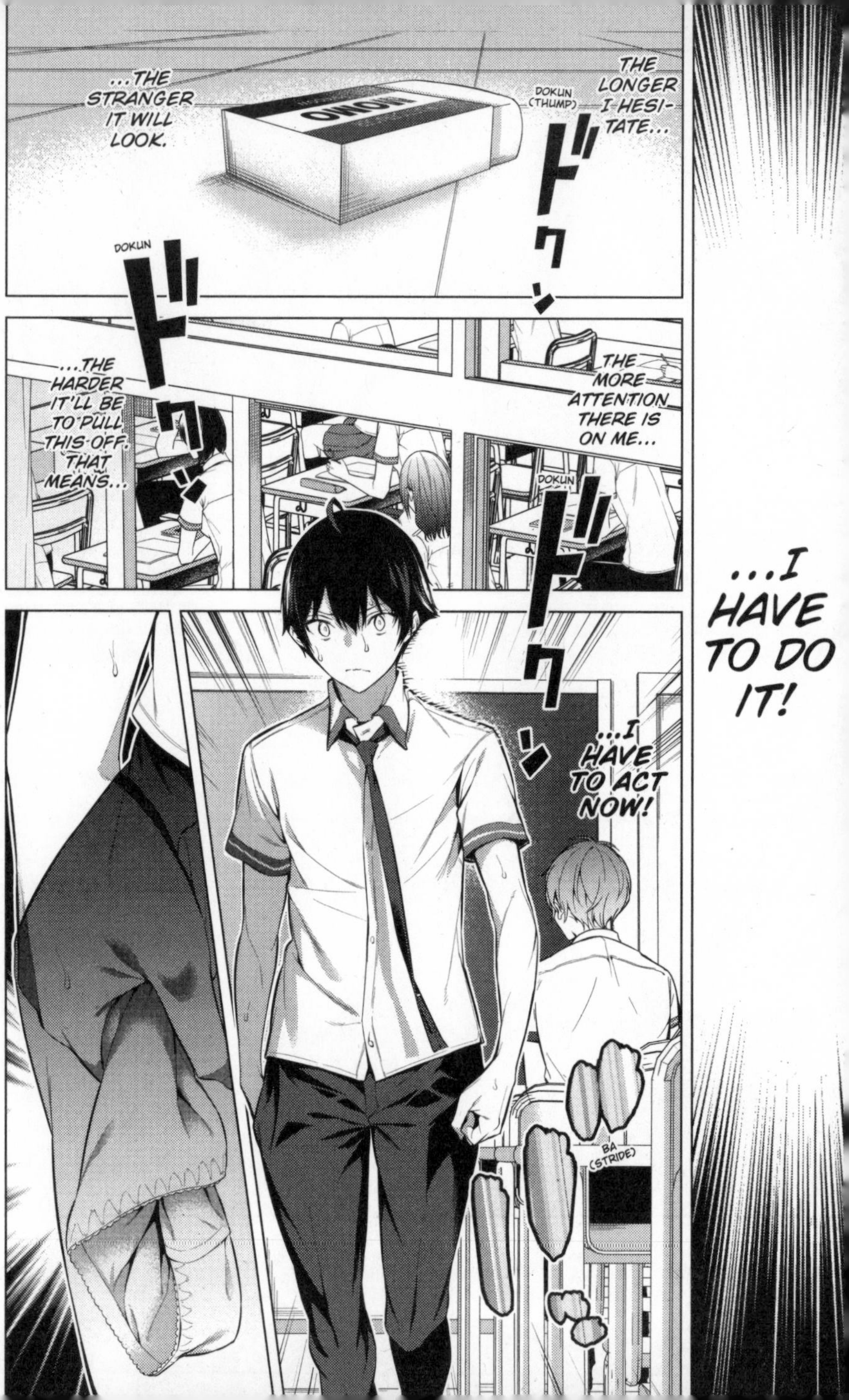
THE LONGER I HESI-TATE...
DOKUN (THUMP)
...THE STRANGER IT WILL LOOK.
DOKUN
THE MORE ATTENTION THERE IS ON ME...
DOKUN
...THE HARDER IT'LL BE TO PULL THIS OFF. THAT MEANS...
...I HAVE TO DO IT!
...I HAVE TO ACT NOW!
BA (STRIDE)

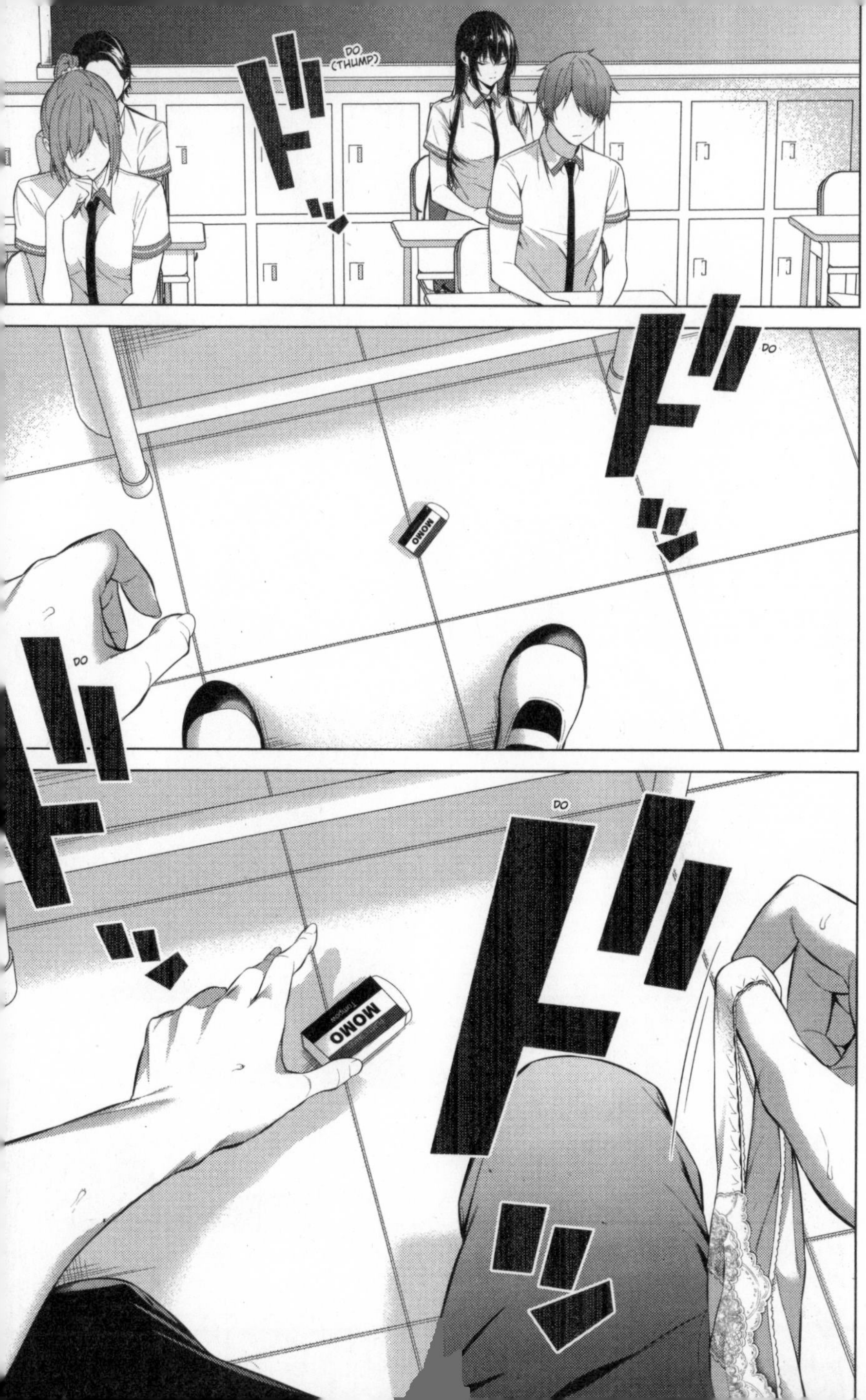
DO
(THUMP)
DO
MOMO
DO
DO
MOMO

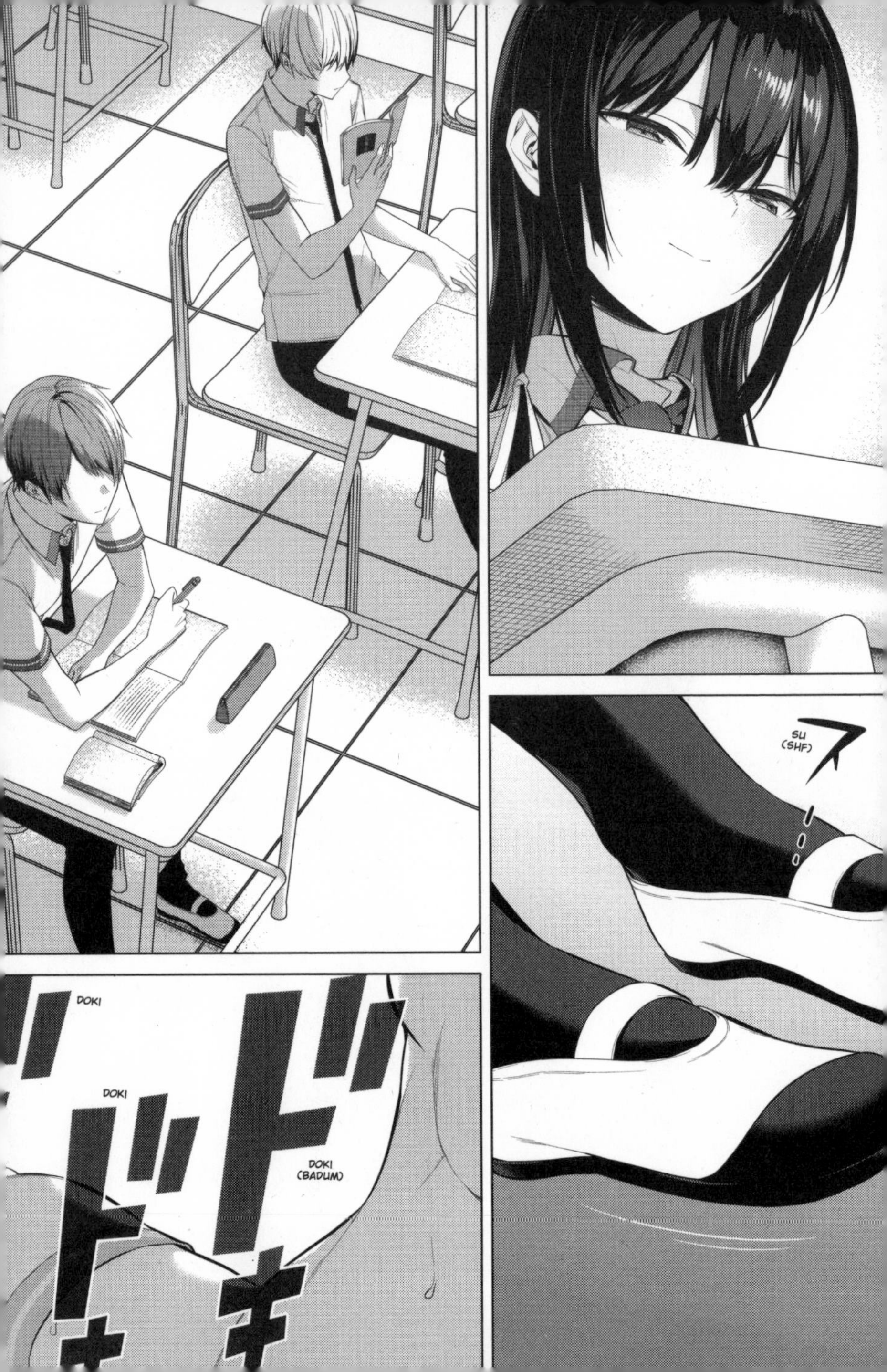
SU
(SHF)
DOKI
DOKI
DOKI
(BADUM)

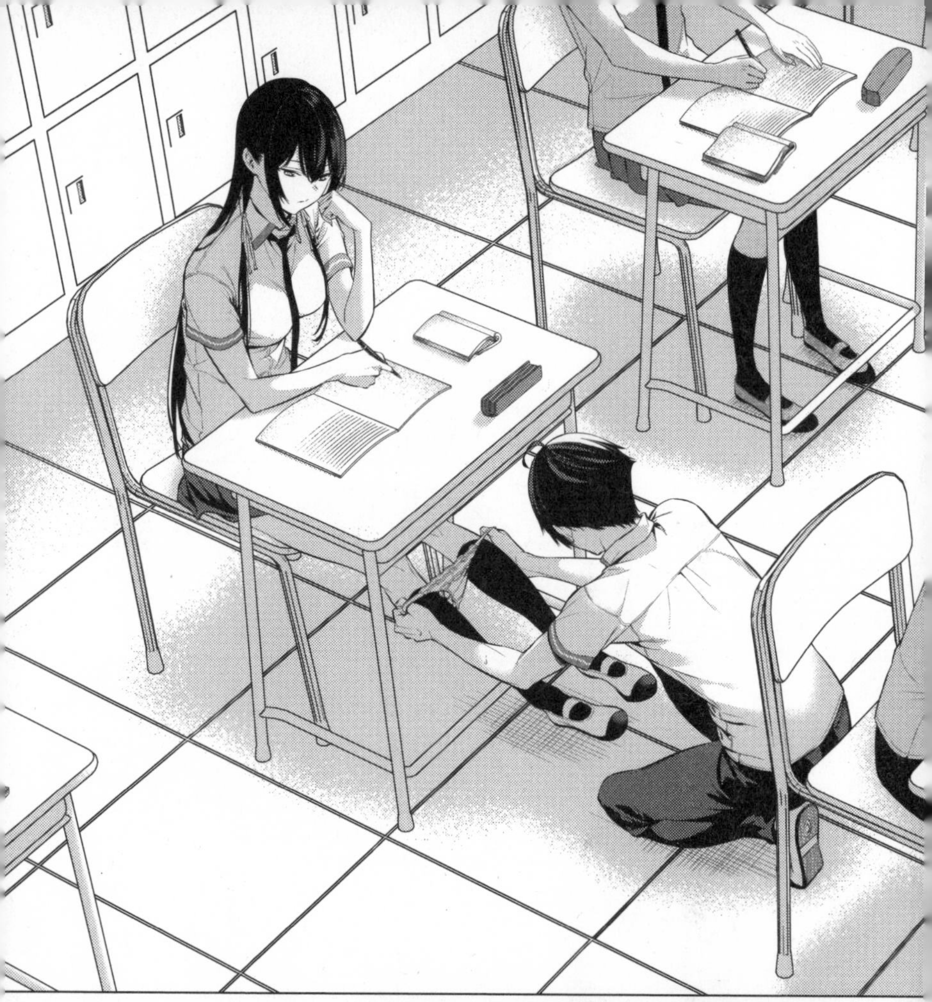

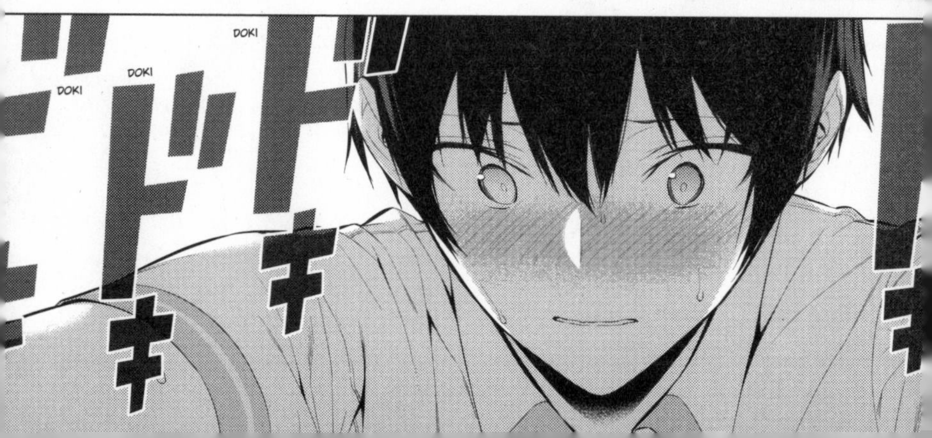
DOKI
DOKI
DOKI

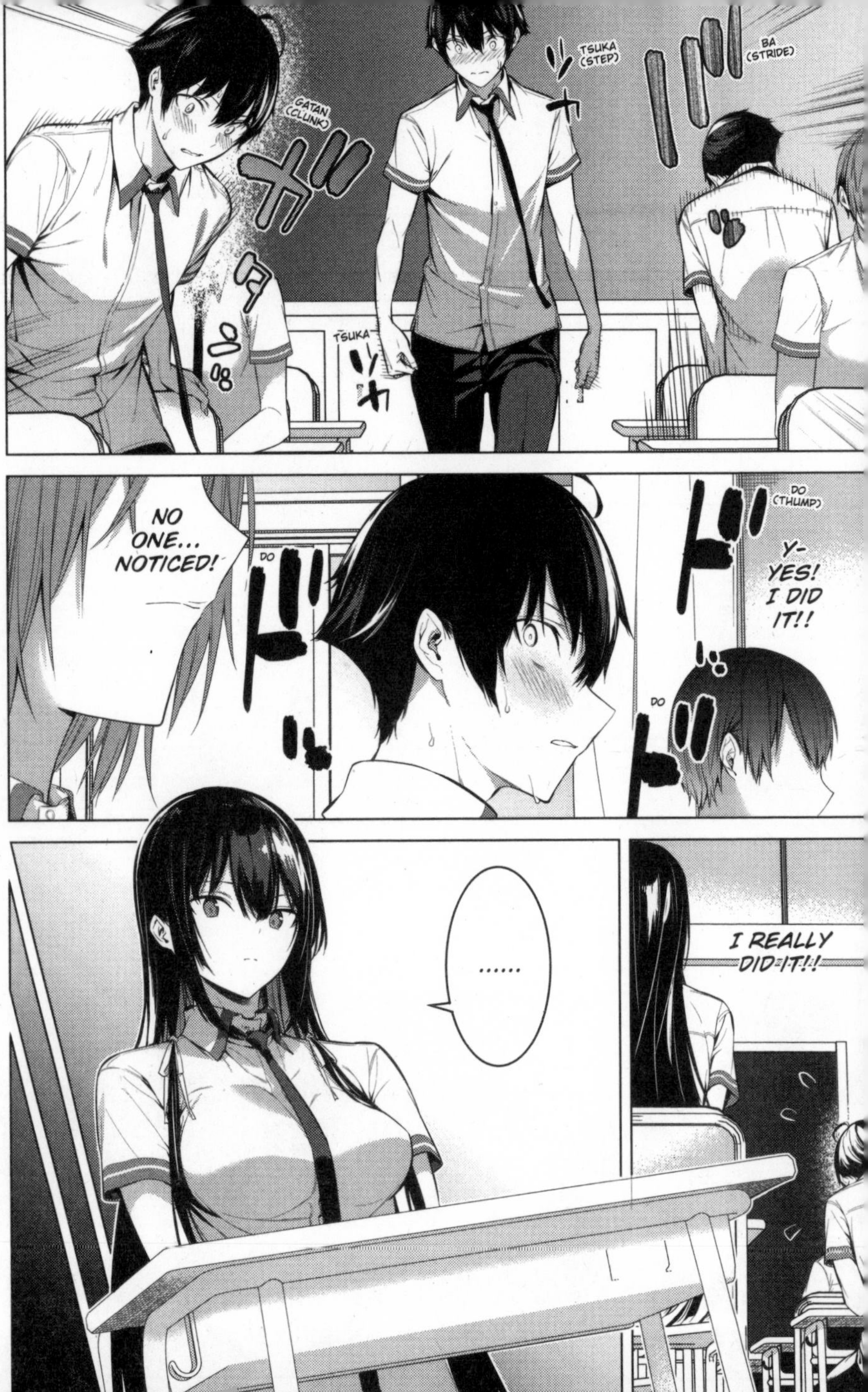
BA (STRIDE)
TSUKA (STEP)
GATAN (CLUNK)
TSUKA
DO (THUMP)
Y- YES! I DID IT!!
DO
DO
NO ONE... NOTICED!
I REALLY DID IT!!
......

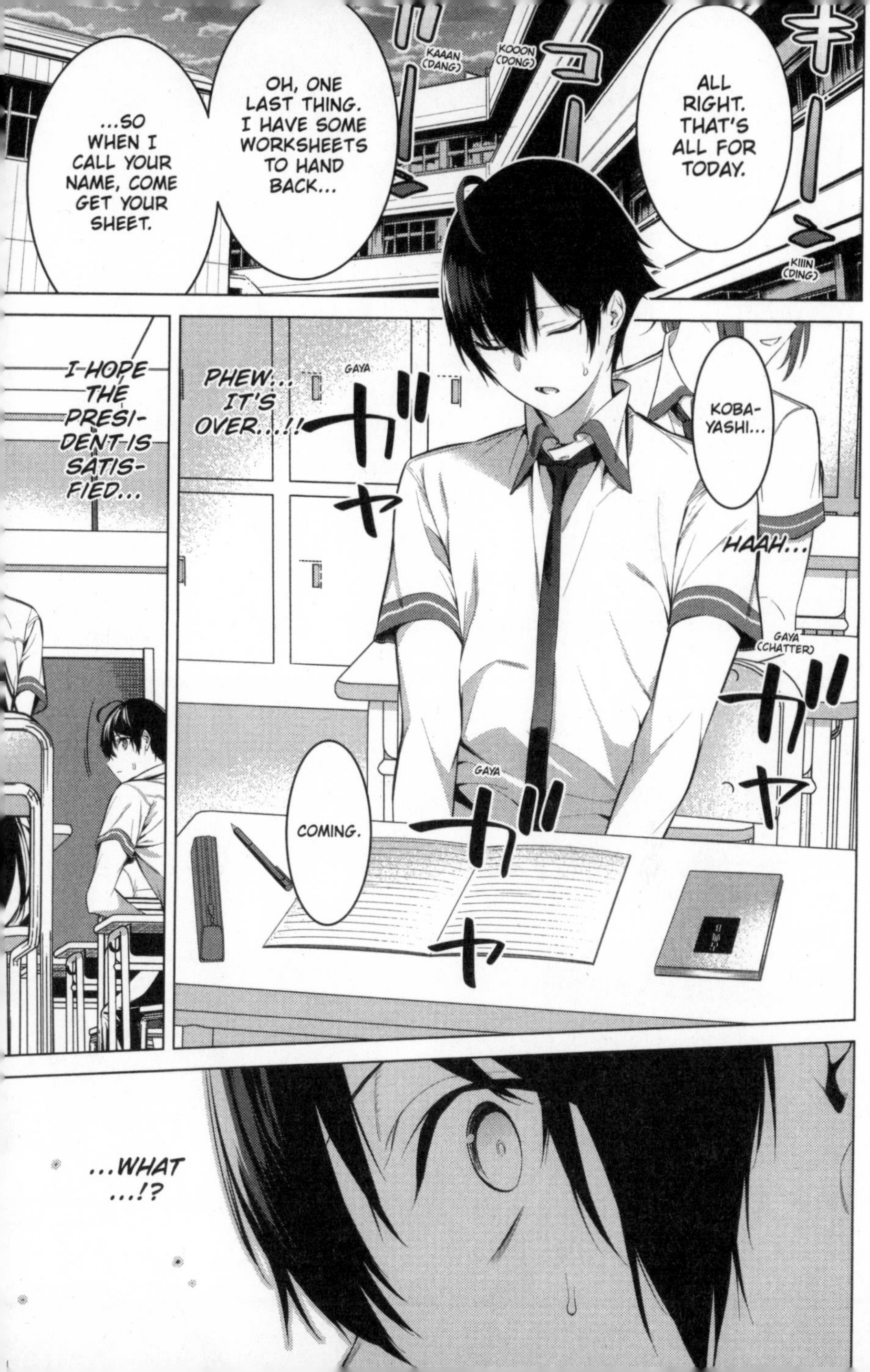

KIIN (DING)
ALL RIGHT. THAT'S ALL FOR TODAY.
KOOON (DONG)
KAAAN (DANG)
OH, ONE LAST THING. I HAVE SOME WORKSHEETS TO HAND BACK...
...SO WHEN I CALL YOUR NAME, COME GET YOUR SHEET.
KOBA-YASHI...
HAAH...
GAYA (CHATTER)
COMING.
GAYA
PHEW... IT'S OVER...!!
GAYA
I HOPE THE PRESI-DENT IS SATIS-FIED...
...WHAT ...!?

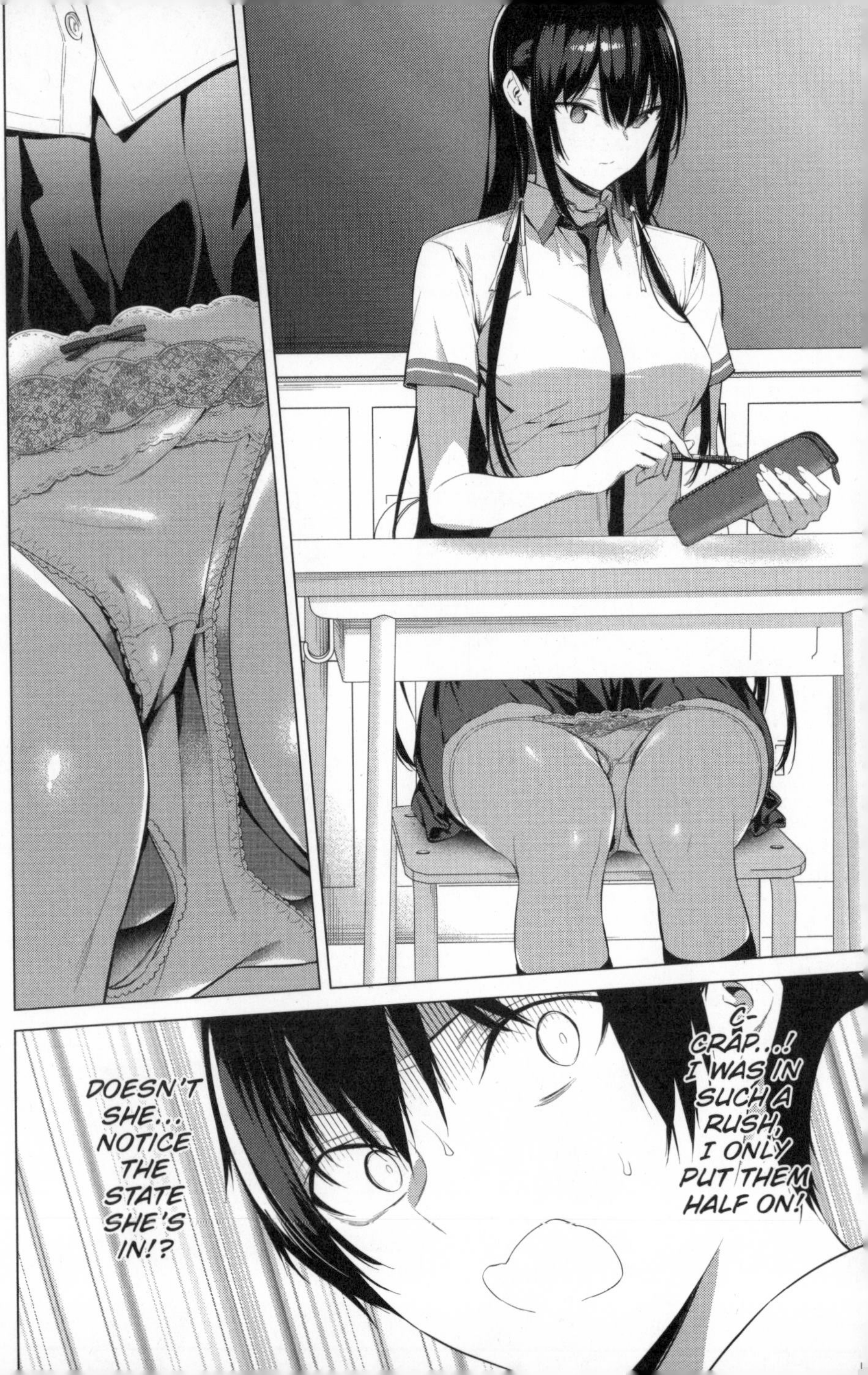
C-CRAP..! I WAS IN SUCH A RUSH, I ONLY PUT THEM HALF ON!
DOESN'T SHE... NOTICE THE STATE SHE'S IN!?

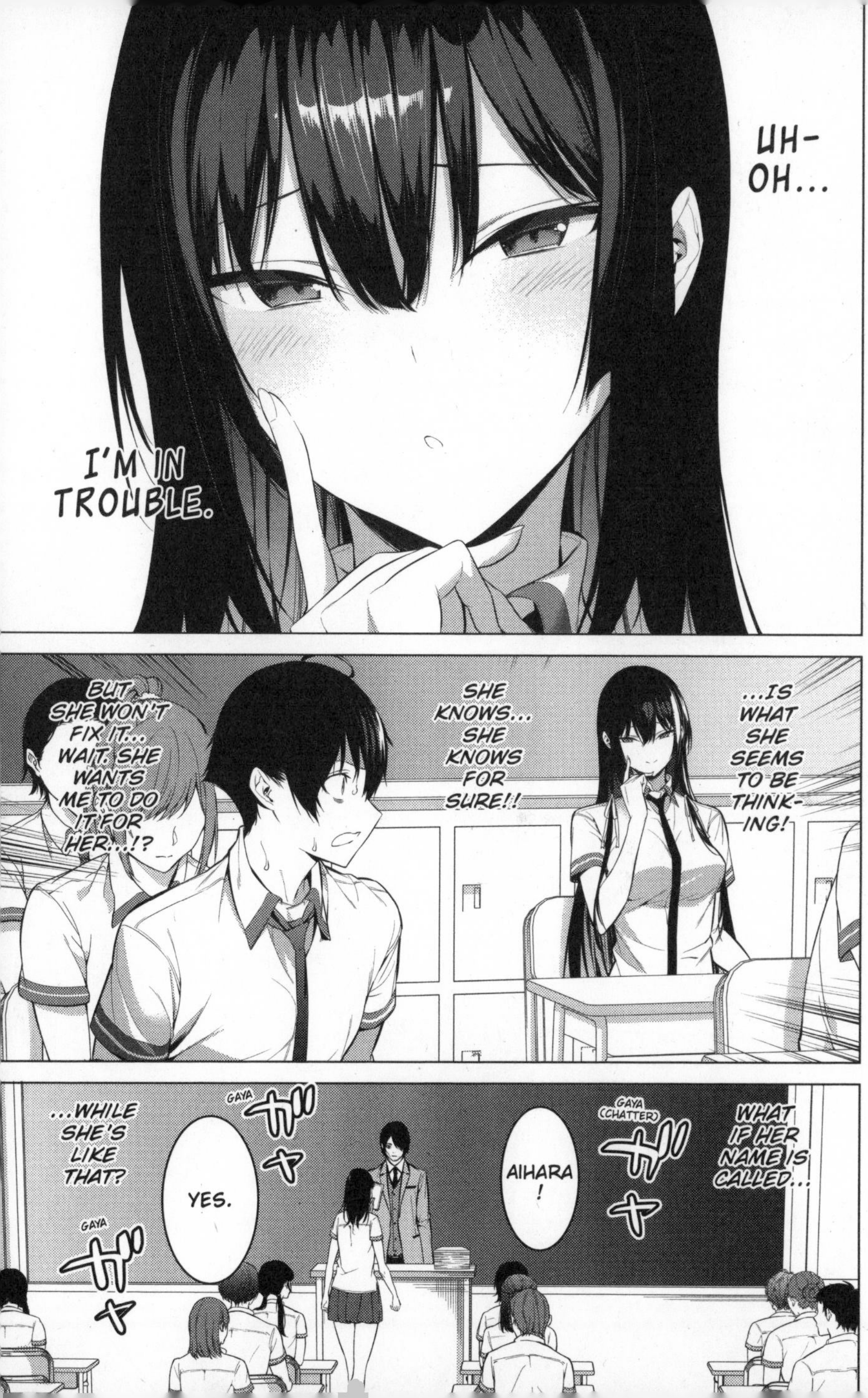
UH-OH...
I'M IN TROUBLE.
...IS WHAT SHE SEEMS TO BE THINKING!
SHE KNOWS... SHE KNOWS FOR SURE!!
BUT SHE WON'T FIX IT... WAIT. SHE WANTS ME TO DO IT FOR HER...!?
WHAT IF HER NAME IS CALLED...
GAYA (CHATTER)
AIHARA!
YES.
GAYA
...WHILE SHE'S LIKE THAT?
GAYA

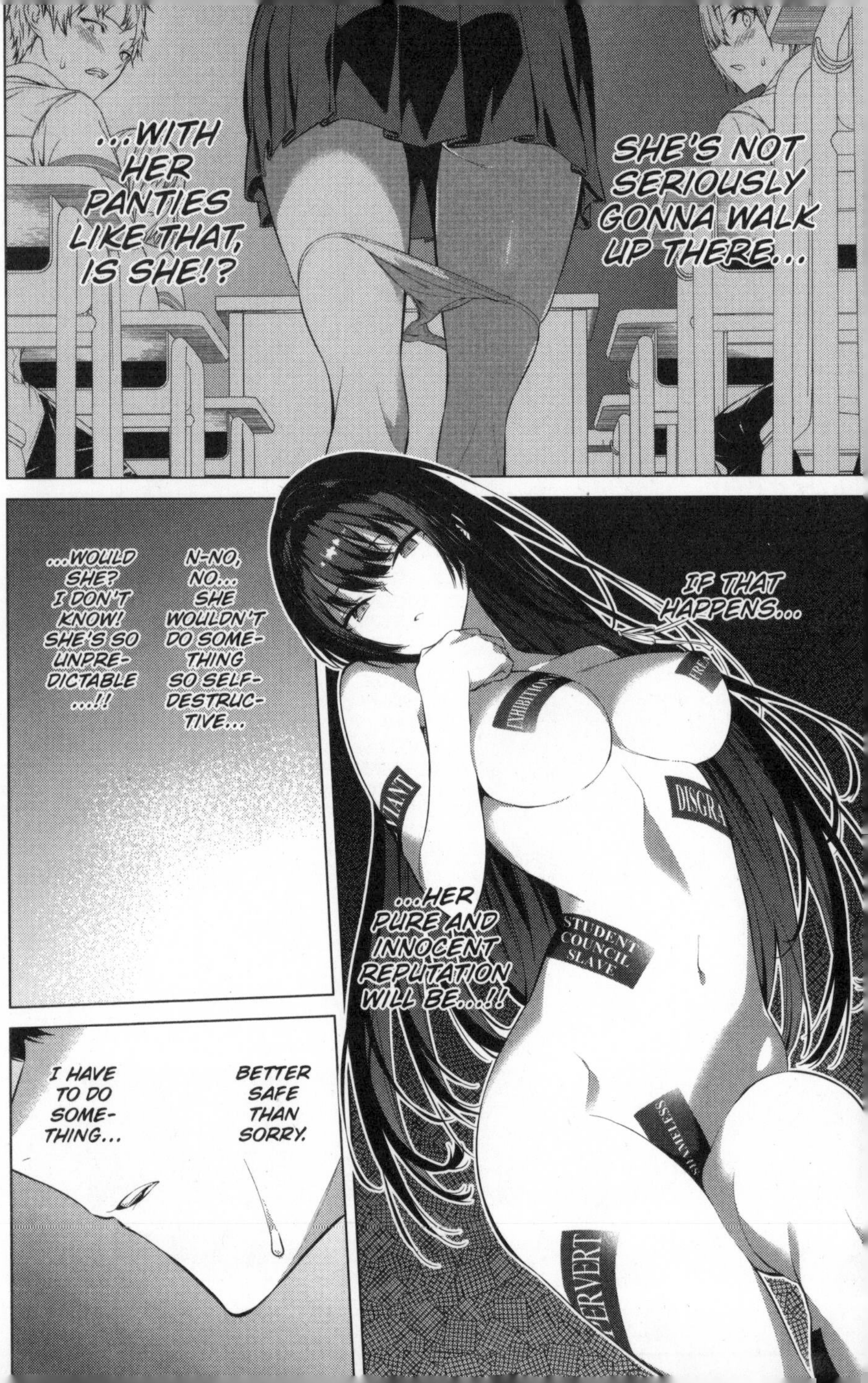
SHE'S NOT SERIOUSLY GONNA WALK UP THERE...
...WITH HER PANTIES LIKE THAT, IS SHE!?
IF THAT HAPPENS...
...HER PURE AND INNOCENT REPUTATION WILL BE...!!
STUDENT COUNCIL SLAVE
N-NO, NO... SHE WOULDN'T DO SOME-THING SO SELF-DESTRUC-TIVE...
...WOULD SHE? I DON'T KNOW! SHE'S SO UNPRE-DICTABLE ...!!
BETTER SAFE THAN SORRY.
I HAVE TO DO SOME-THING...

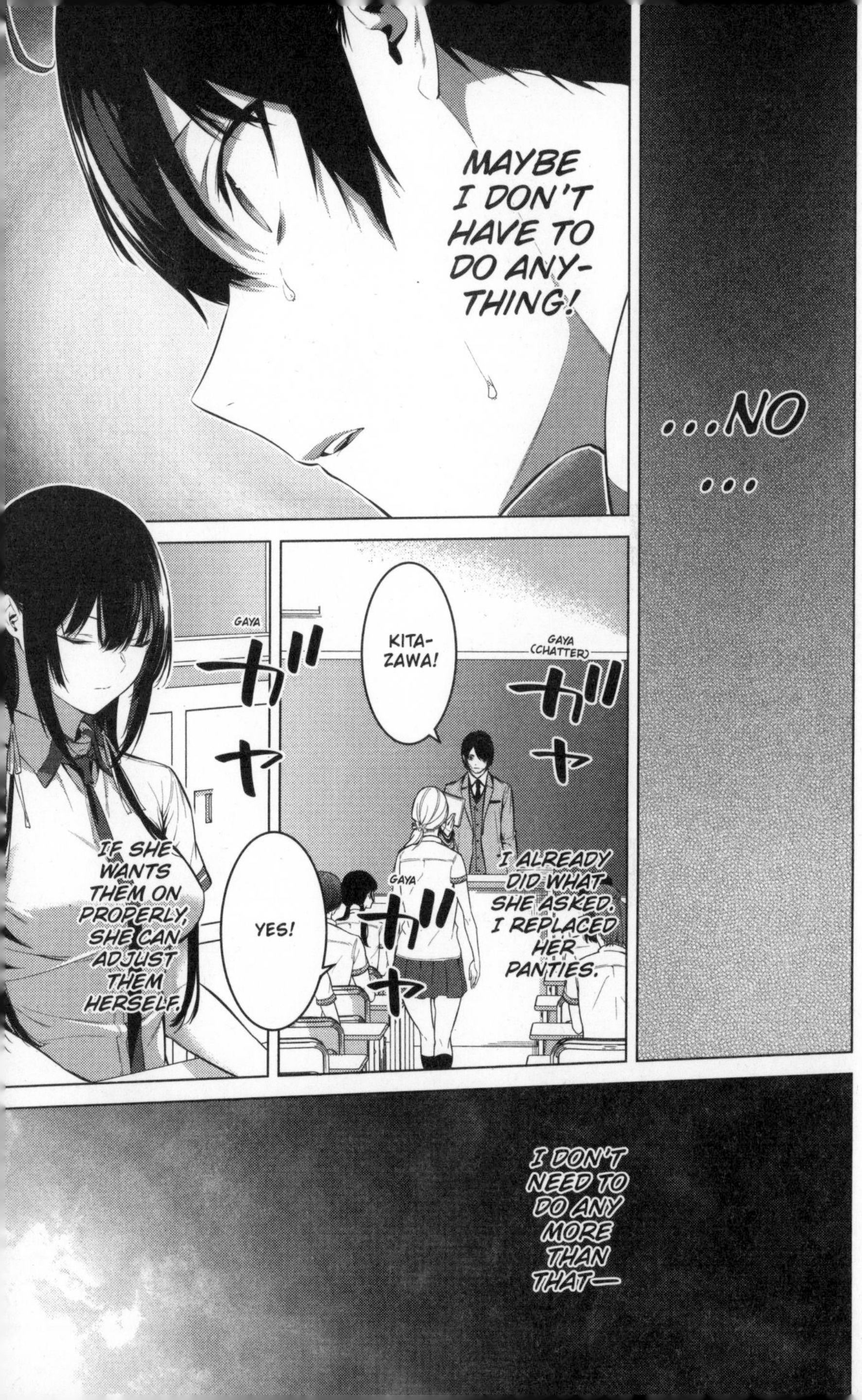
...NO ...
MAYBE I DON'T HAVE TO DO ANY-THING!
GAYA (CHATTER)
KITA-ZAWA!
I ALREADY DID WHAT SHE ASKED. I REPLACED HER PANTIES.
GAYA
YES!
GAYA
IF SHE WANTS THEM ON PROPERLY, SHE CAN ADJUST THEM HERSELF.
I DON'T NEED TO DO ANY MORE THAN THAT—

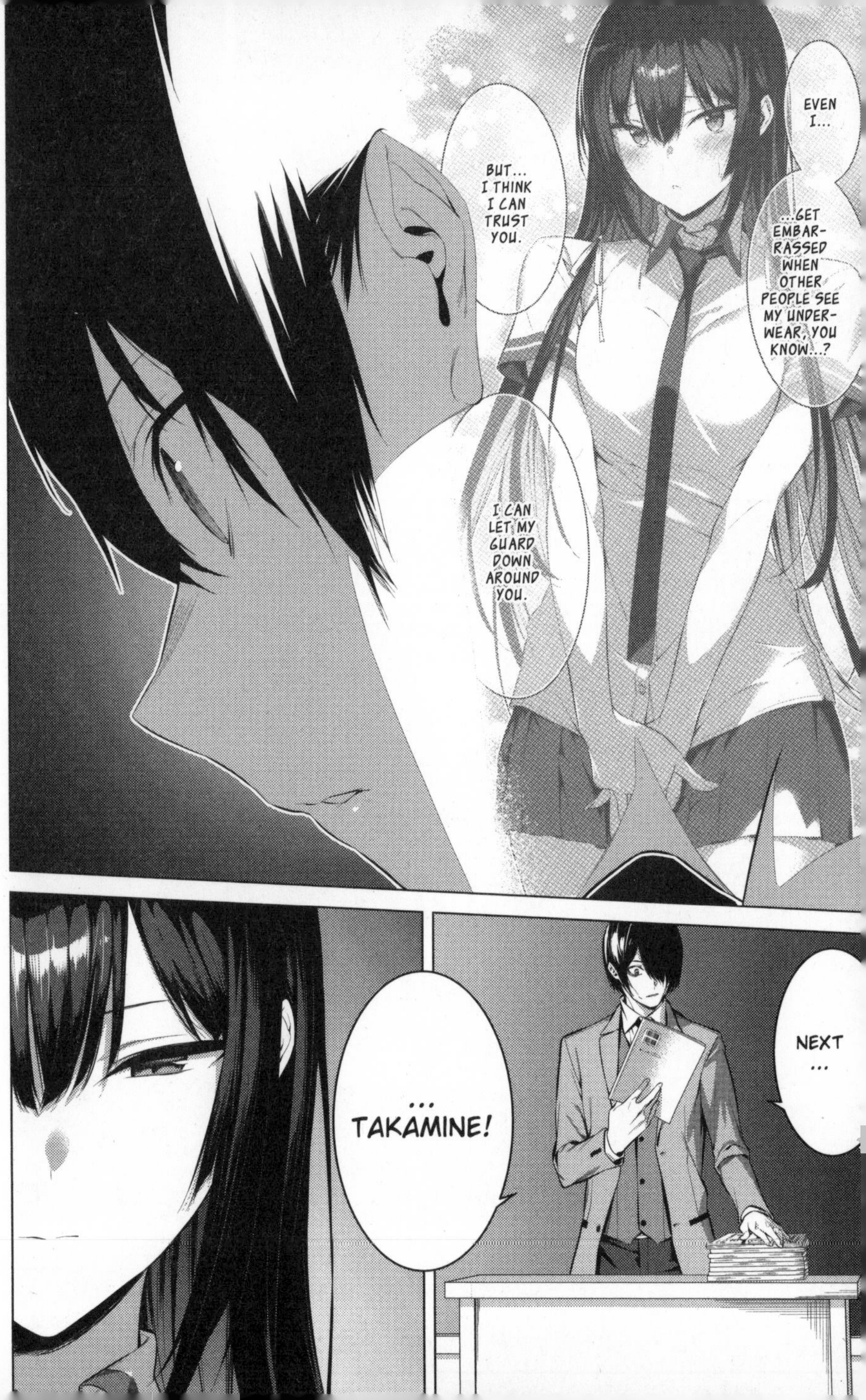
EVEN I...
...GET EMBAR-RASSED WHEN OTHER PEOPLE SEE MY UNDER-WEAR, YOU KNOW...?
BUT... I THINK I CAN TRUST YOU.
I CAN LET MY GUARD DOWN AROUND YOU.
NEXT...
...TAKAMINE!

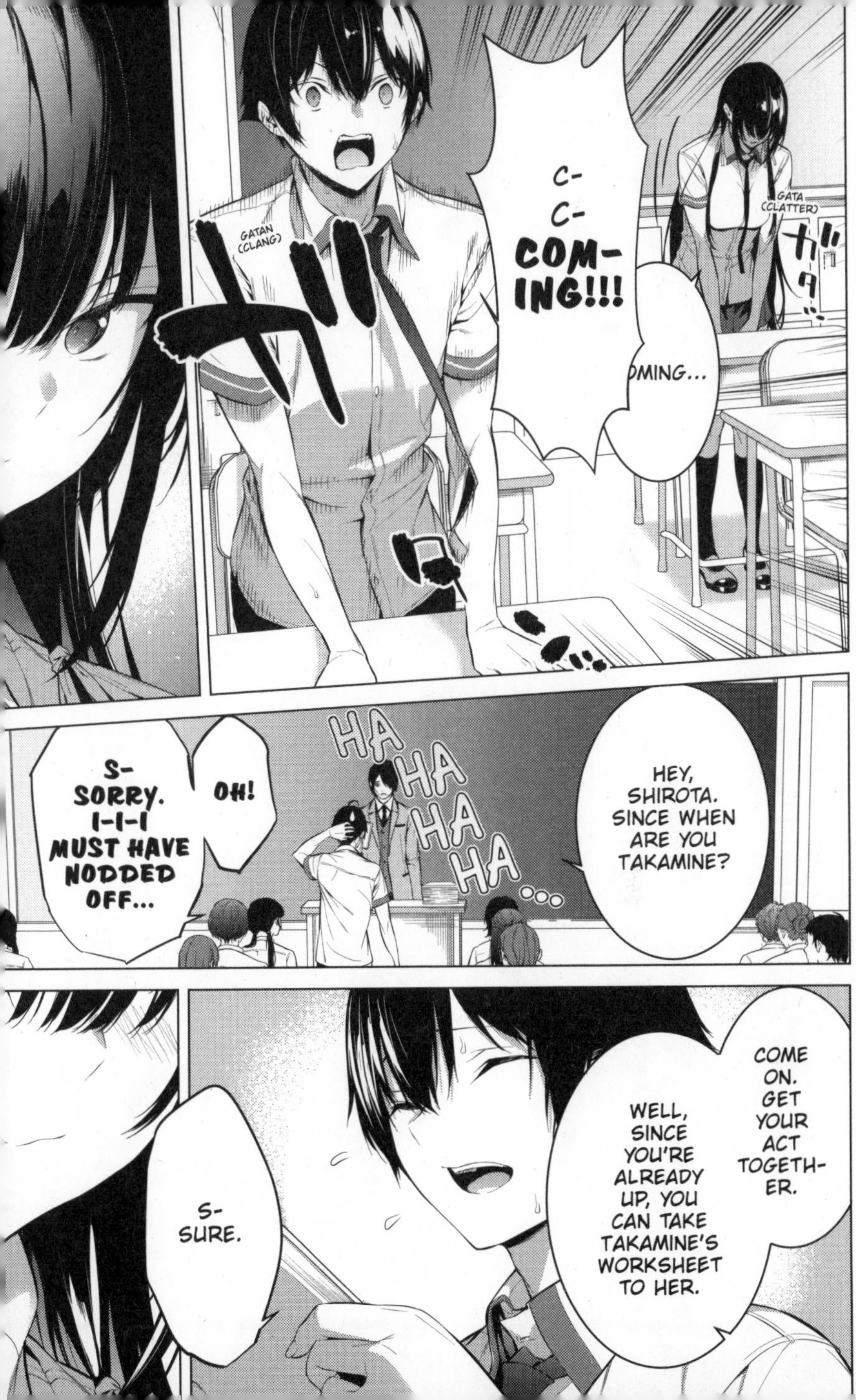
GATA (CLATTER)
C- C- COMING!!!
OMING...
GATAN (CLANG)
HEY, SHIROTA. SINCE WHEN ARE YOU TAKAMINE?
HA HA HA HA...
OH!
S-SORRY. I-I-I MUST HAVE NODDED OFF...
COME ON. GET YOUR ACT TOGETHER.
WELL, SINCE YOU'RE ALREADY UP, YOU CAN TAKE TAKAMINE'S WORKSHEET TO HER.
S-SURE.

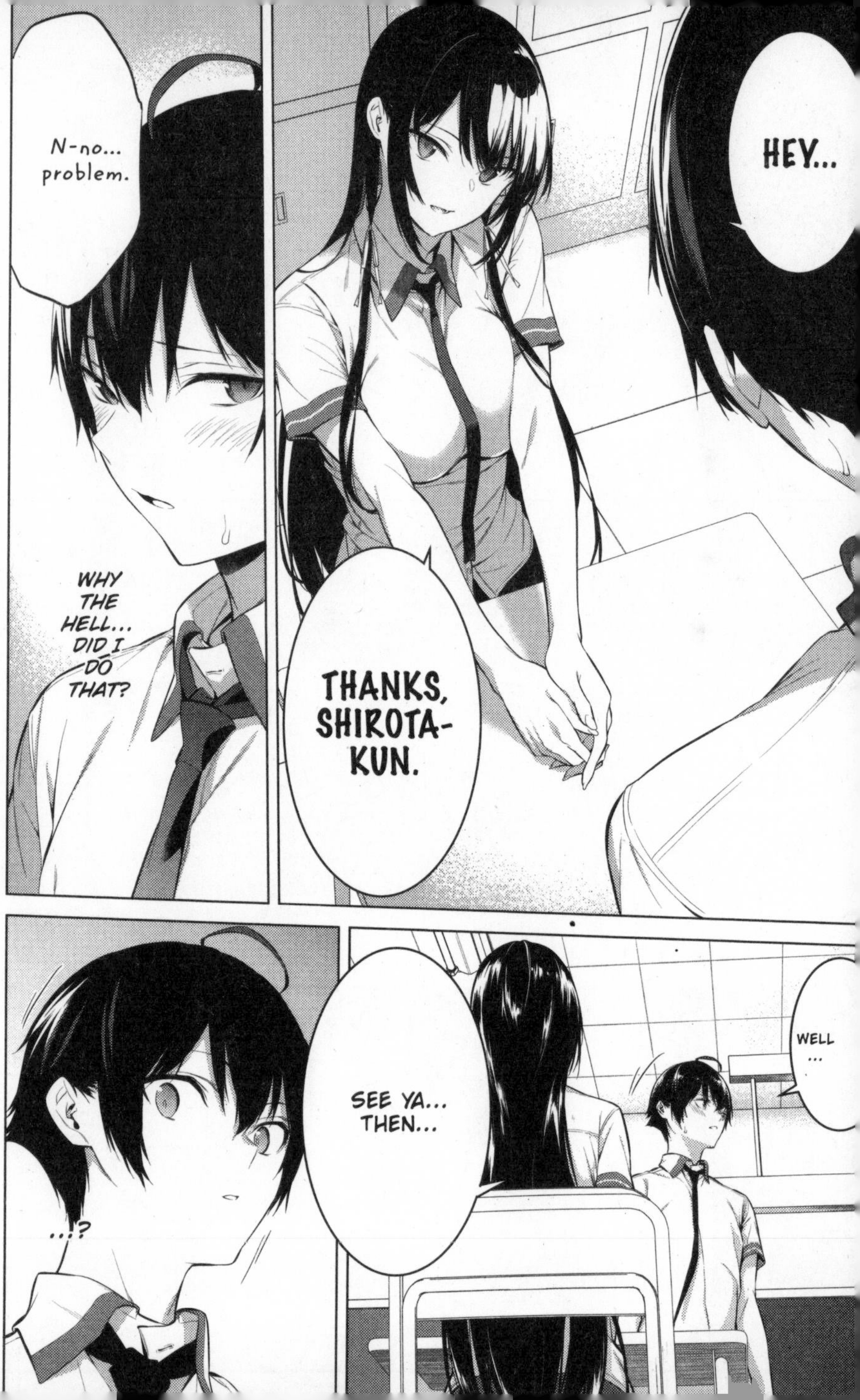
HEY...
THANKS, SHIROTA-KUN.
N-no... problem.
WHY THE HELL... DID I DO THAT?
WELL ...
SEE YA... THEN...
...?

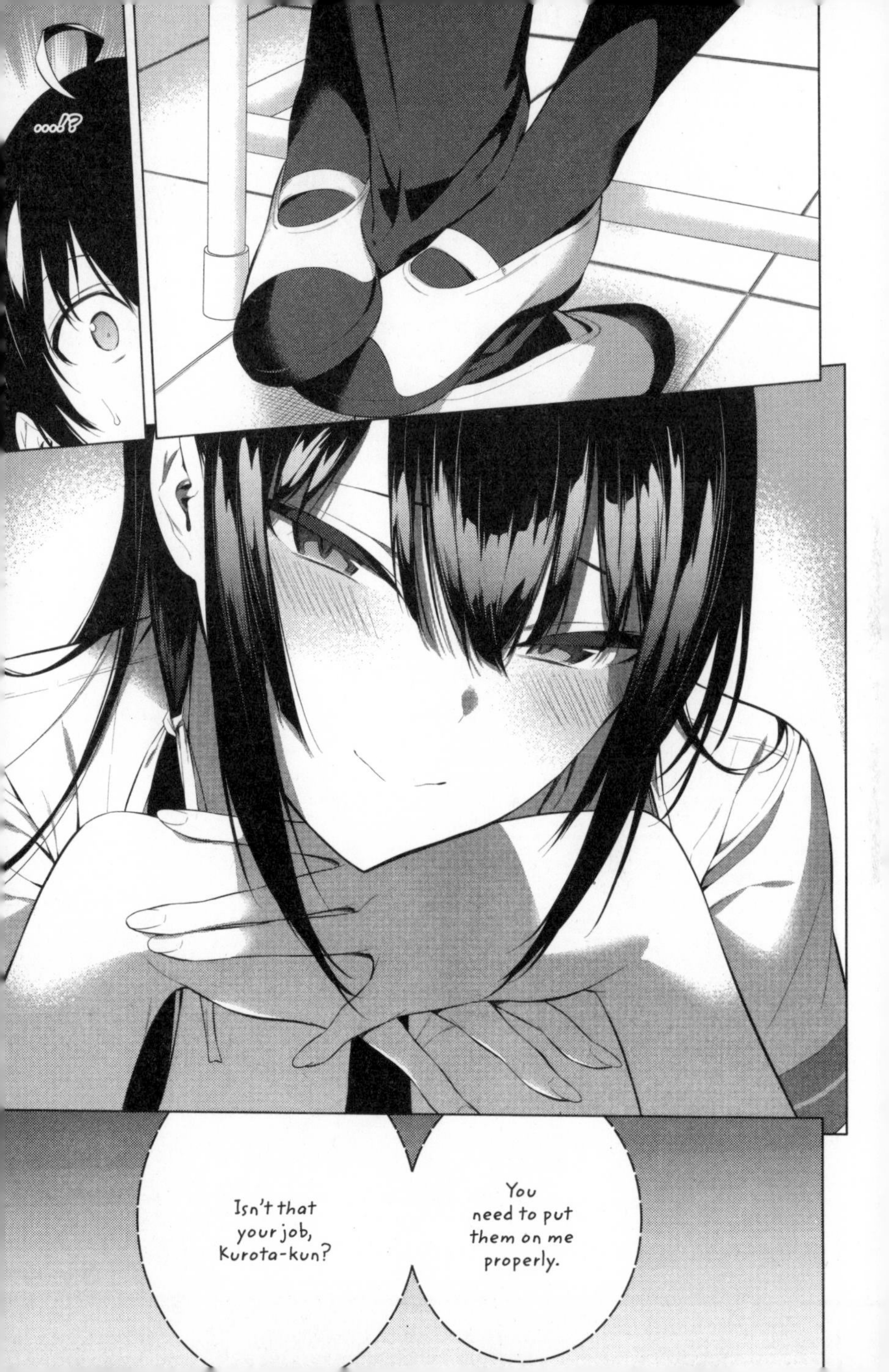
...!?
You need to put them on me properly.
Isn't that your job, Kurota-kun?

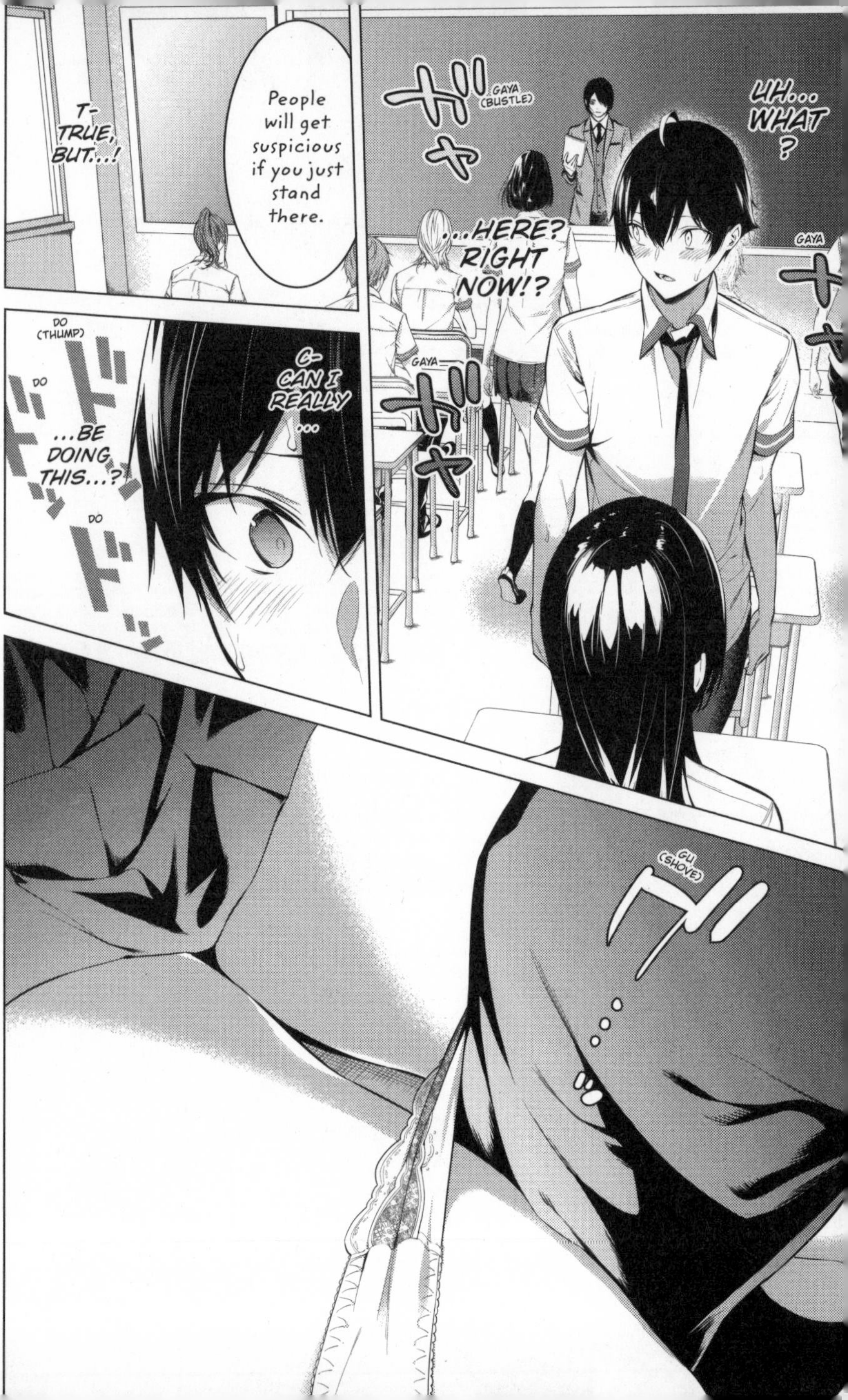
GAYA (BUSTLE)
UH... WHAT?
...HERE? RIGHT NOW!?
GAYA
GAYA
People will get suspicious if you just stand there.
T-TRUE, BUT...!
DO (THUMP)
DO
C-CAN I REALLY...
...BE DOING THIS...?
DO
GU (SHOVE)

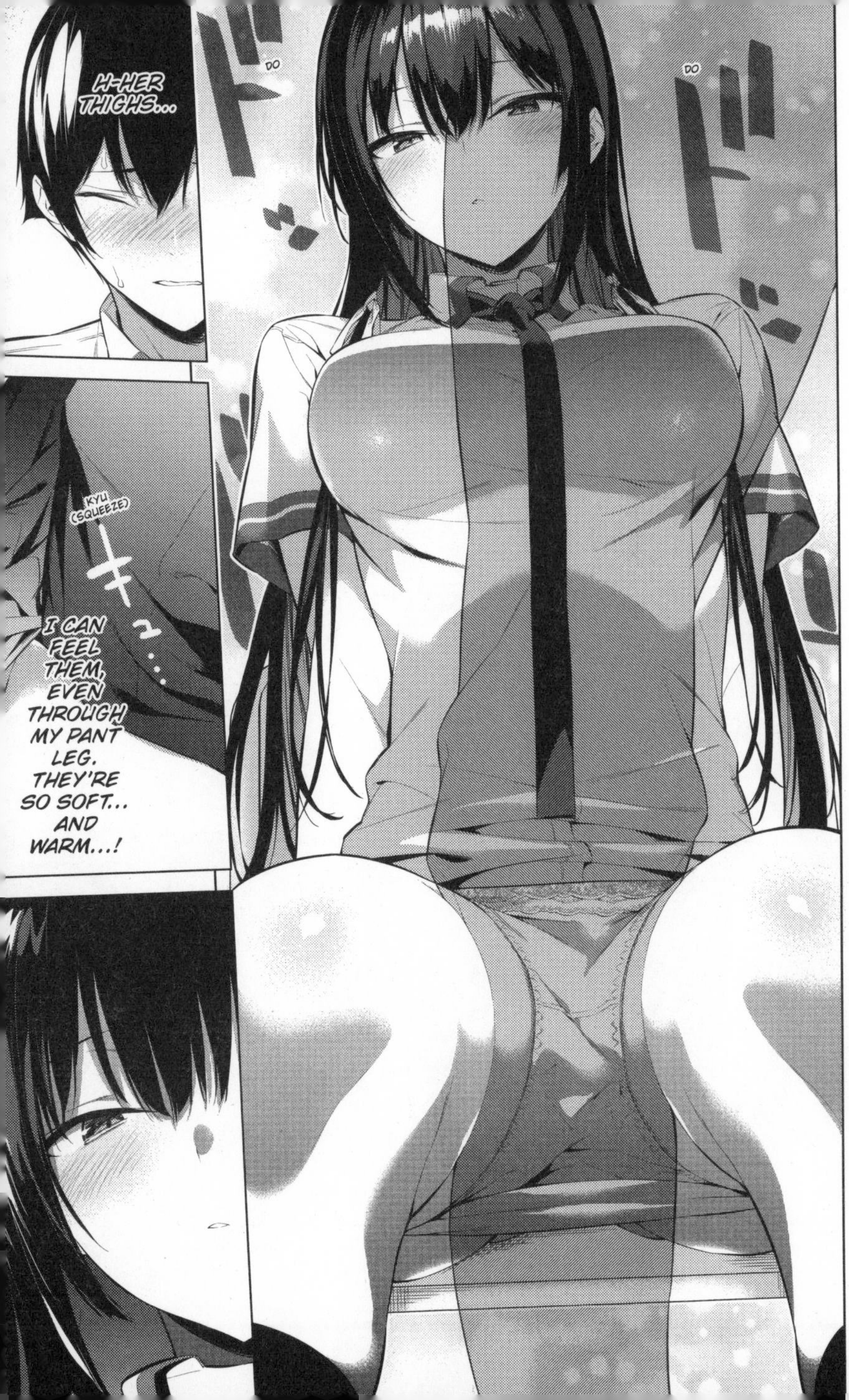
DO
DO
H-HER THIGHS...
KYU (SQUEEZE)
I CAN FEEL THEM, EVEN THROUGH MY PANT LEG. THEY'RE SO SOFT... AND WARM...!

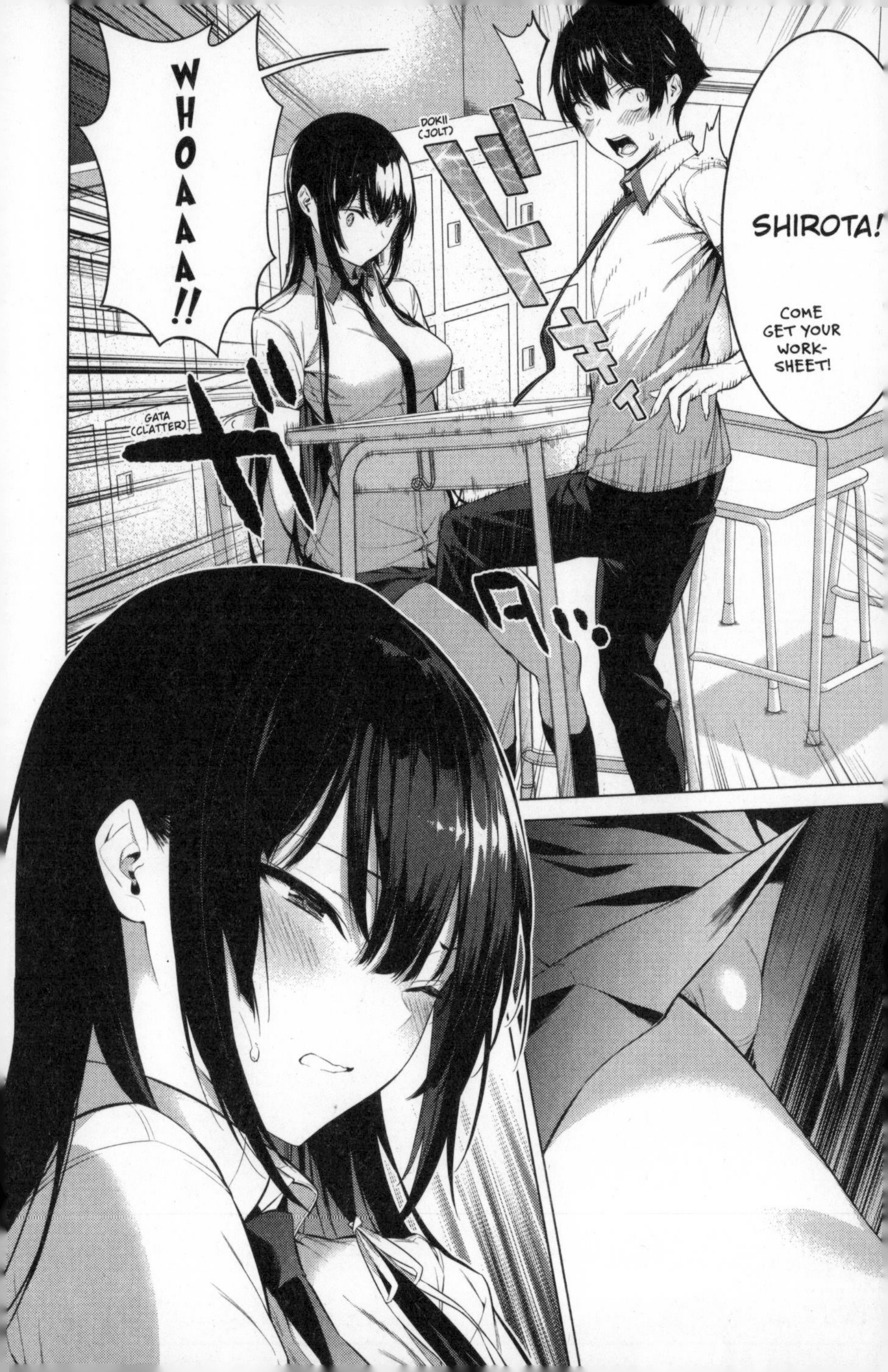
SHIROTA!
COME GET YOUR WORK-SHEET!
DOKII (JOLT)
WHOAAAA!!
GATA (CLATTER)

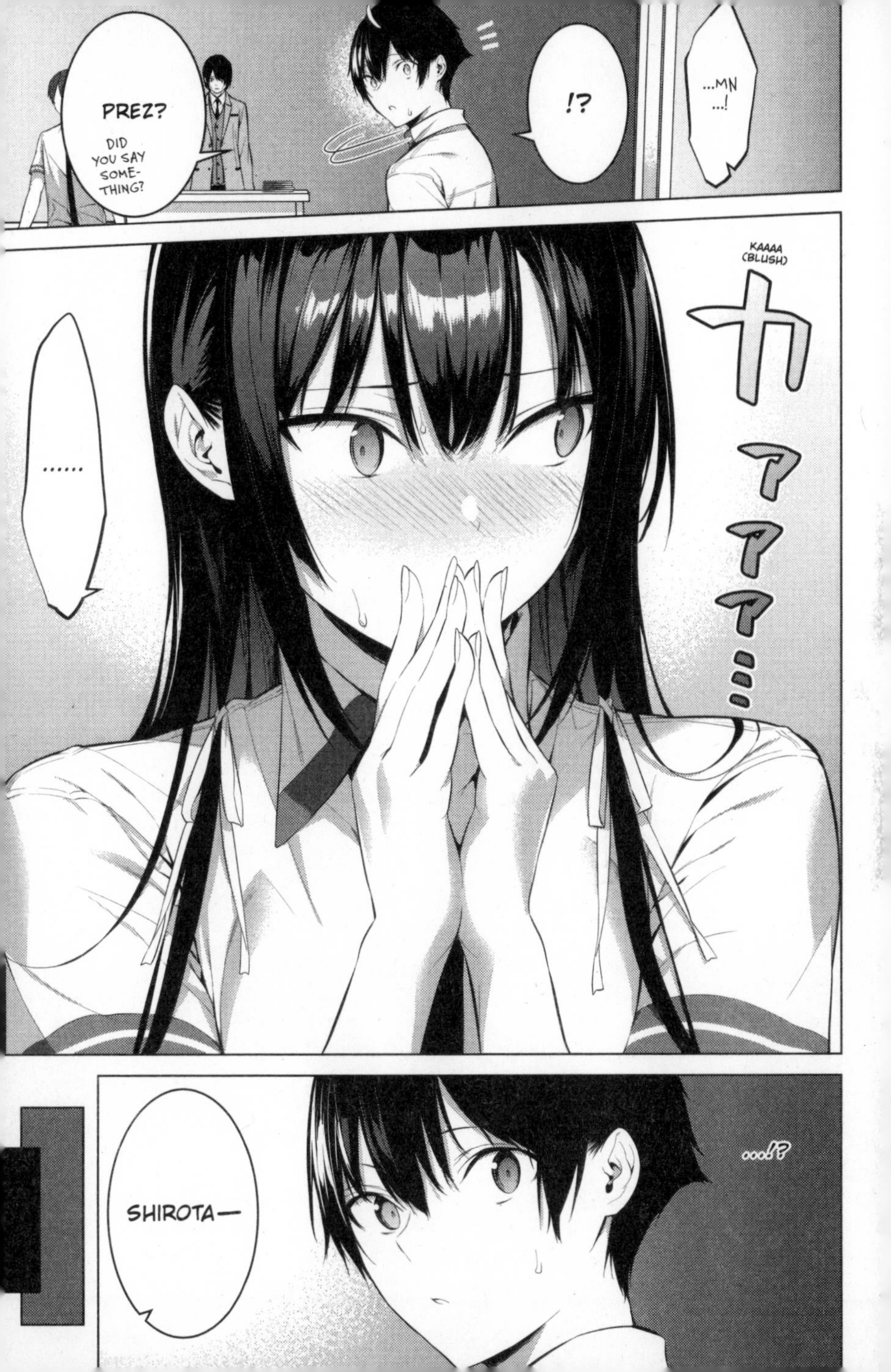
...MN ...!
!?
PREZ?
DID YOU SAY SOME-THING?
KAAAA (BLUSH)
......
ooo!?
SHIROTA—

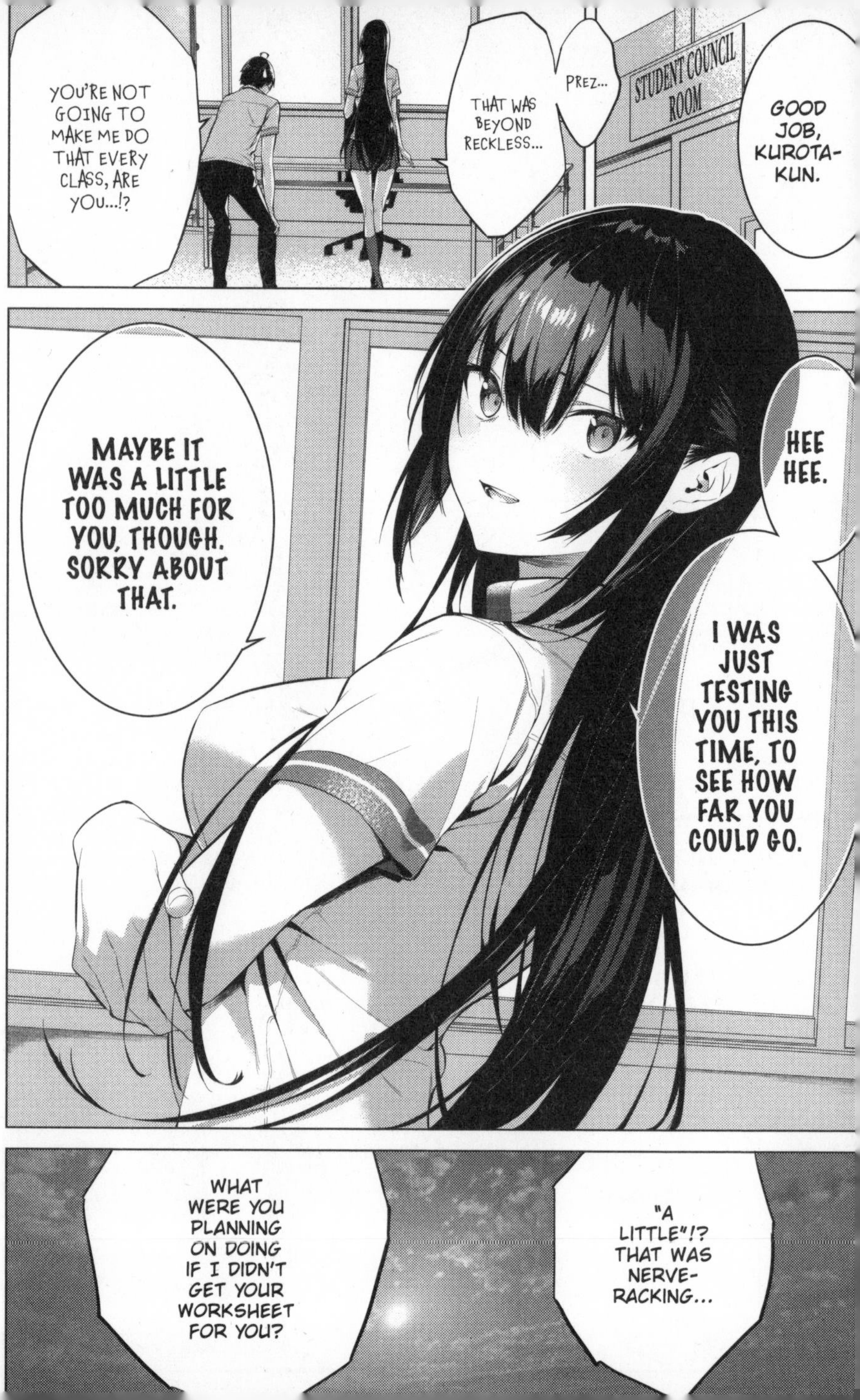
STUDENT COUNCIL ROOM
GOOD JOB, KUROTA-KUN.
PREZ...
THAT WAS BEYOND RECKLESS...
YOU'RE NOT GOING TO MAKE ME DO THAT EVERY CLASS, ARE YOU...!?
HEE HEE.
I WAS JUST TESTING YOU THIS TIME, TO SEE HOW FAR YOU COULD GO.
MAYBE IT WAS A LITTLE TOO MUCH FOR YOU, THOUGH. SORRY ABOUT THAT.
"A LITTLE"!? THAT WAS NERVE-RACKING...
WHAT WERE YOU PLANNING ON DOING IF I DIDN'T GET YOUR WORKSHEET FOR YOU?

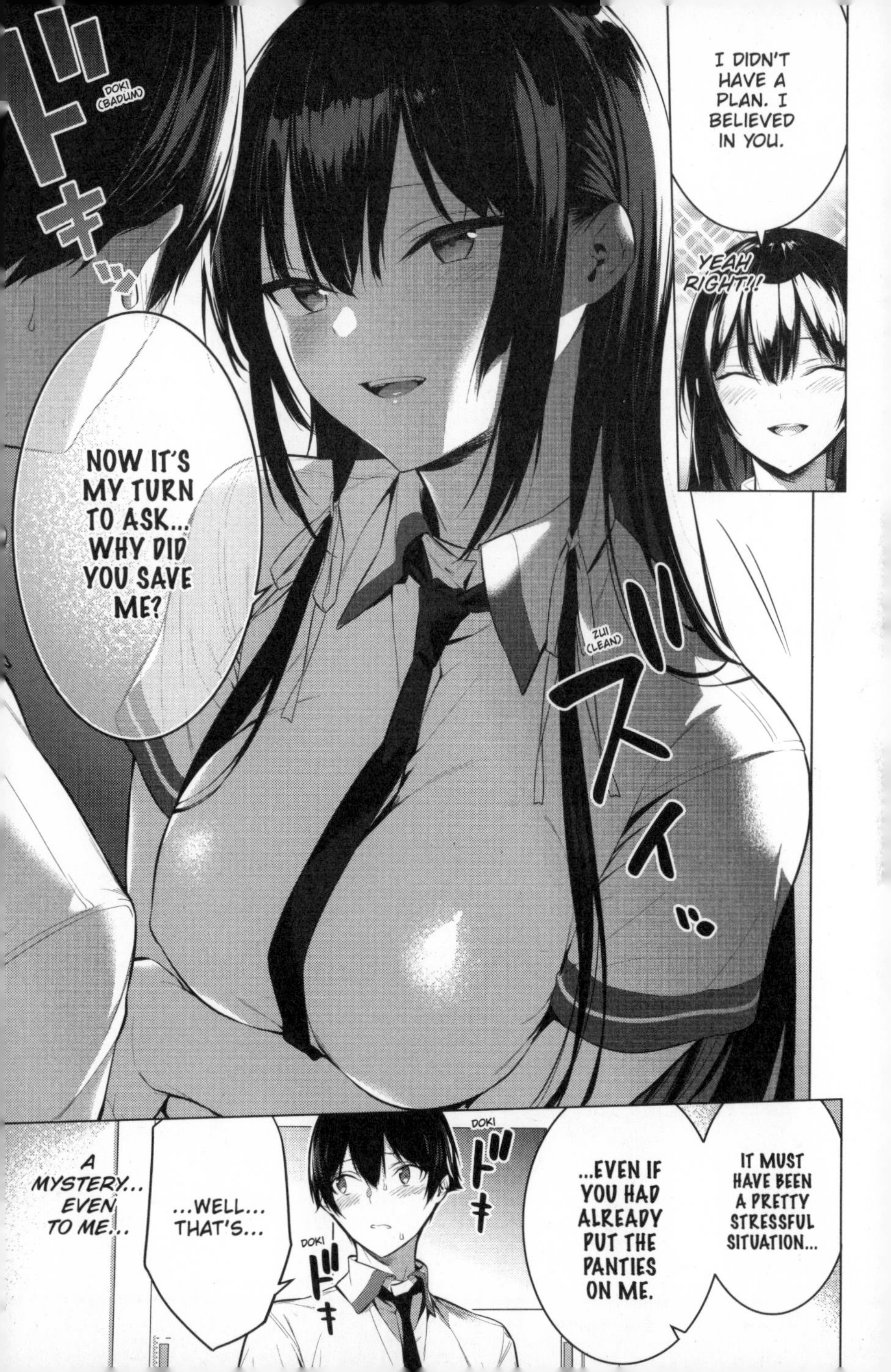
I DIDN'T HAVE A PLAN. I BELIEVED IN YOU.
YEAH RIGHT!!
DOKI (BADUM)
NOW IT'S MY TURN TO ASK... WHY DID YOU SAVE ME?
ZUI (CLEAN)
IT MUST HAVE BEEN A PRETTY STRESSFUL SITUATION...
...EVEN IF YOU HAD ALREADY PUT THE PANTIES ON ME.
DOKI
DOKI
...WELL... THAT'S...
A MYSTERY... EVEN TO ME...

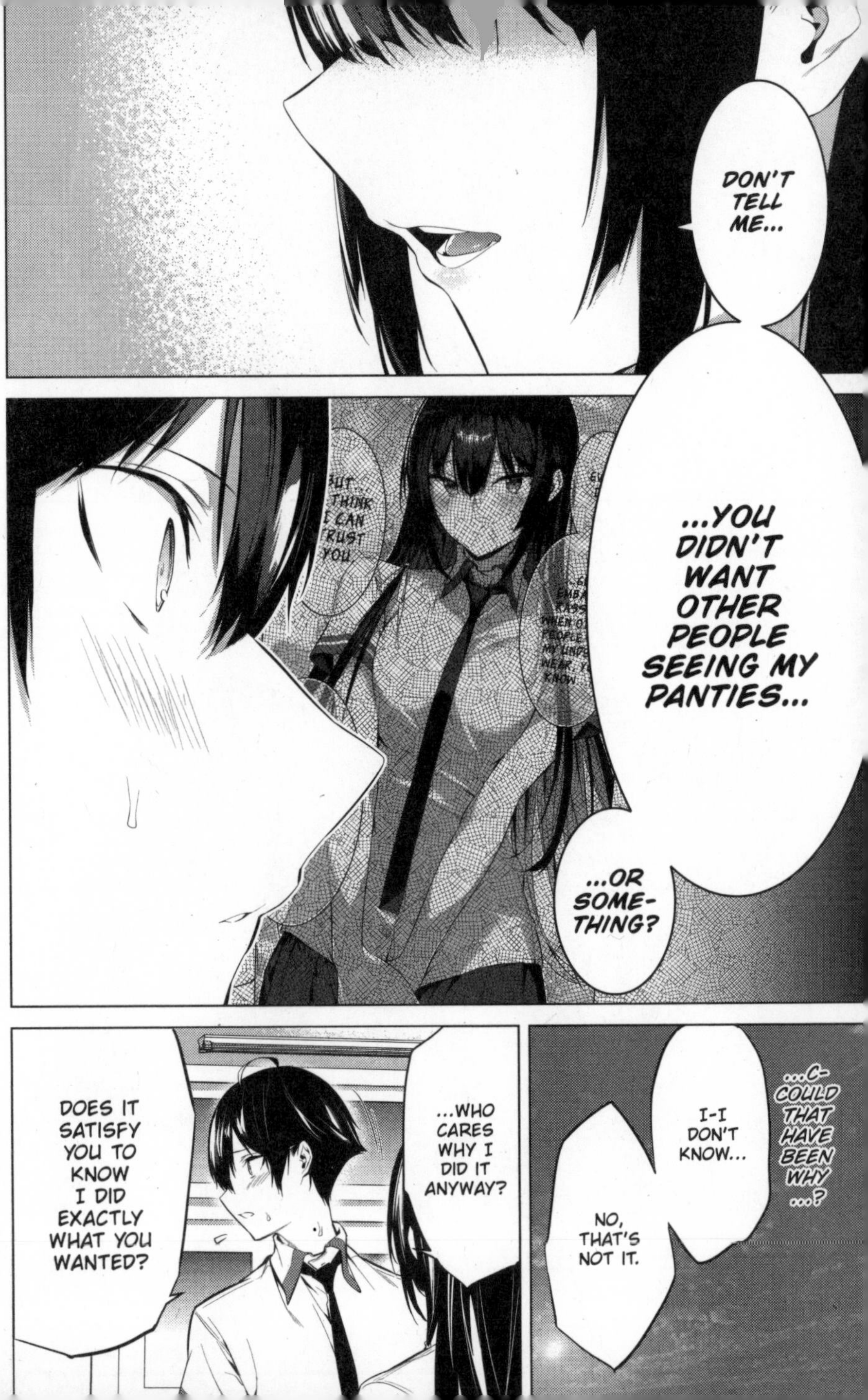
DON'T TELL ME...
...YOU DIDN'T WANT OTHER PEOPLE SEEING MY PANTIES...
...OR SOME-THING?
...C-COULD THAT HAVE BEEN WHY...?
I-I DON'T KNOW...
NO, THAT'S NOT IT.
...WHO CARES WHY I DID IT ANYWAY?
DOES IT SATISFY YOU TO KNOW I DID EXACTLY WHAT YOU WANTED?

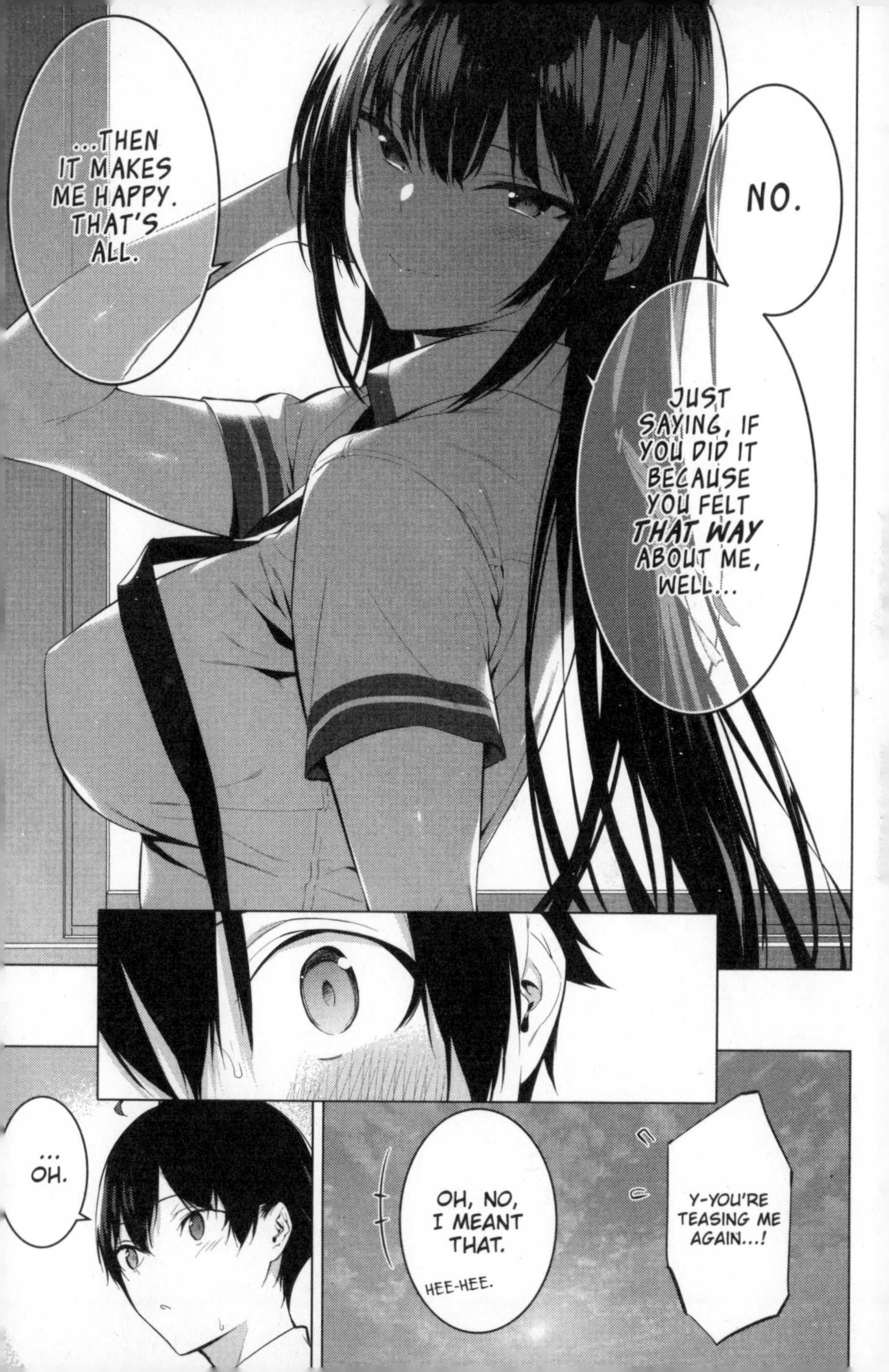
NO.
JUST SAYING, IF YOU DID IT BECAUSE YOU FELT THAT WAY ABOUT ME, WELL...
...THEN IT MAKES ME HAPPY. THAT'S ALL.
Y-YOU'RE TEASING ME AGAIN...!
OH, NO, I MEANT THAT.
HEE-HEE.
... OH.

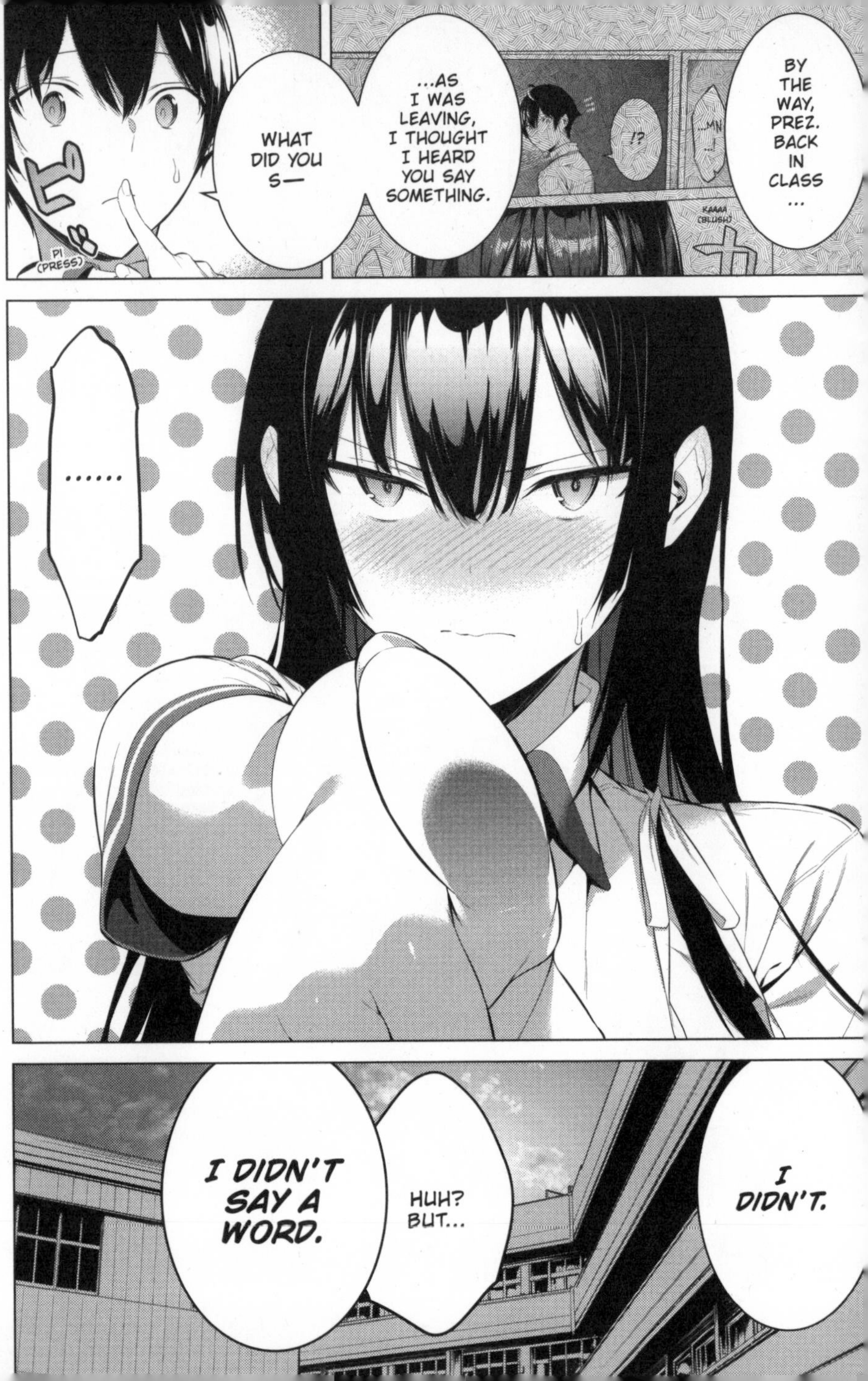
BY THE WAY, PREZ. BACK IN CLASS...
...MN...!
KAAAA (BLUSH)
!?
...AS I WAS LEAVING, I THOUGHT I HEARD YOU SAY SOMETHING.
WHAT DID YOU S—
PI (PRESS)
......
I DIDN'T.
HUH? BUT...
I DIDN'T SAY A WORD.

Please
Put
Them On,
Takamine
♥San

Chapter 3 Do you want to look or not?

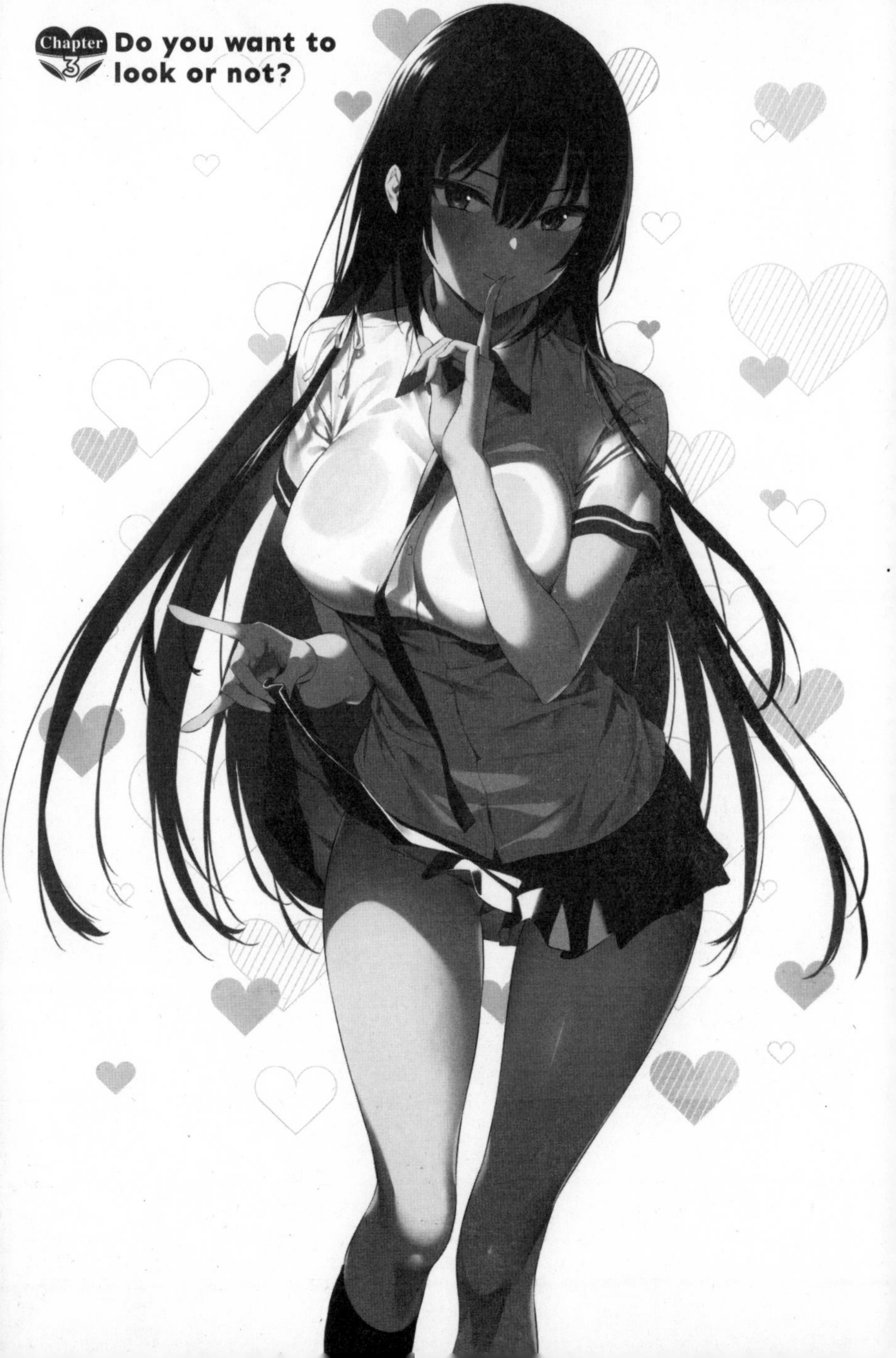

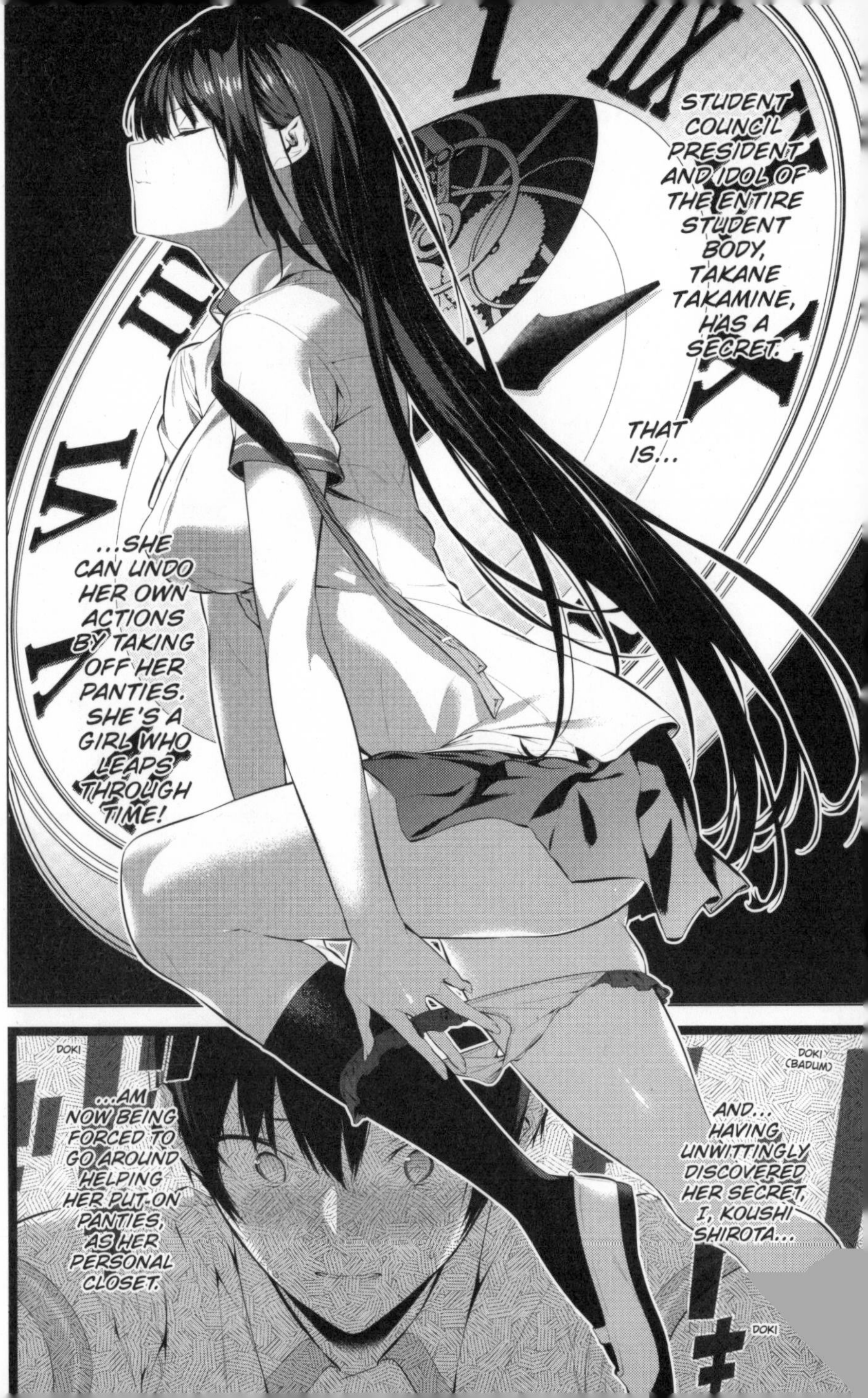
STUDENT COUNCIL PRESIDENT AND IDOL OF THE ENTIRE STUDENT BODY, TAKANE TAKAMINE, HAS A SECRET.
THAT IS...
...SHE CAN UNDO HER OWN ACTIONS BY TAKING OFF HER PANTIES. SHE'S A GIRL WHO LEAPS THROUGH TIME!
DOKI (BADUM)
DOKI
AND... HAVING UNWITTINGLY DISCOVERED HER SECRET, I, KOUSHI SHIROTA...
...AM NOW BEING FORCED TO GO AROUND HELPING HER PUT ON PANTIES, AS HER PERSONAL CLOSET.
DOKI

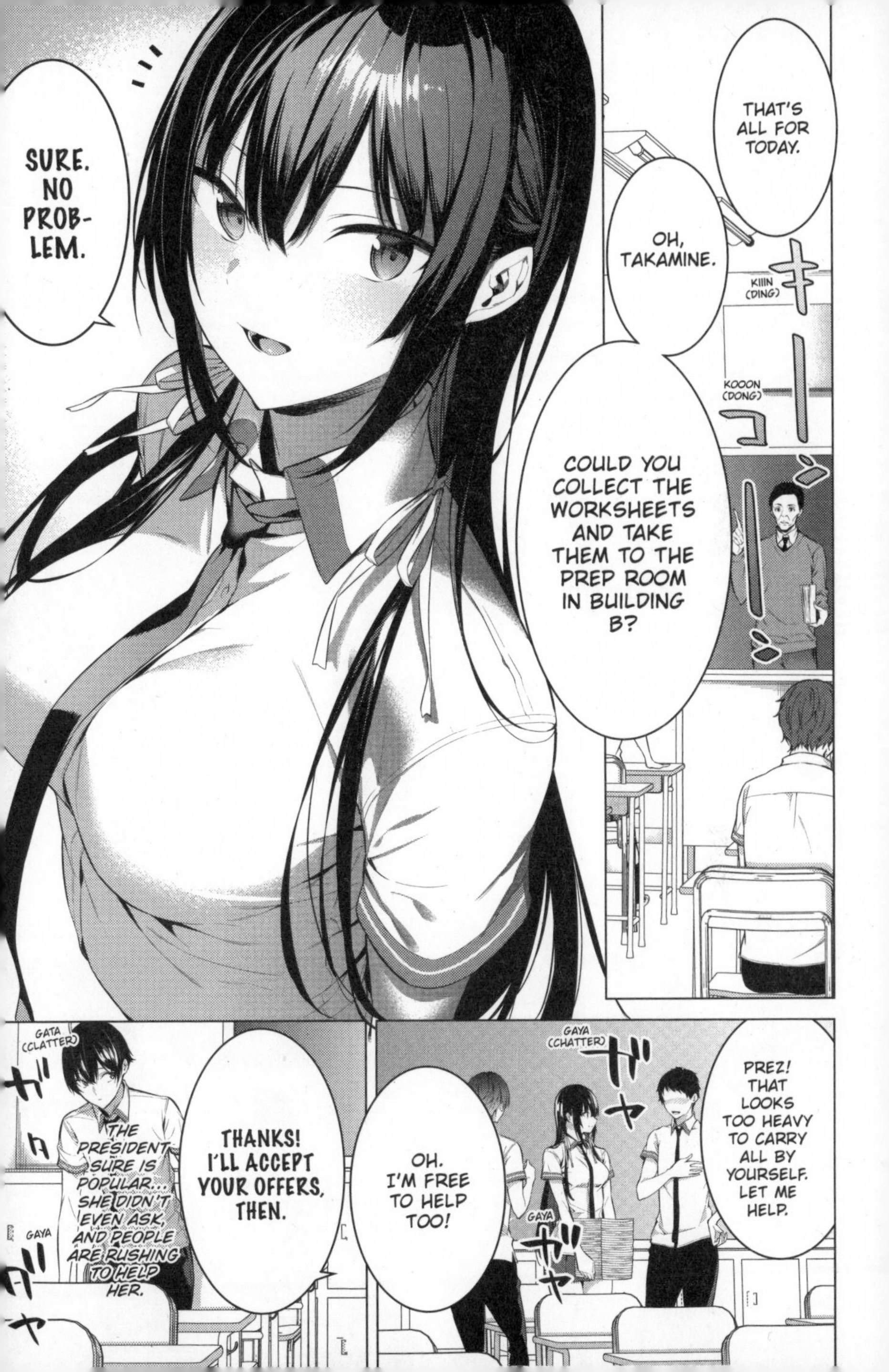
THAT'S ALL FOR TODAY.
OH, TAKAMINE.
KIIN (DING)
KOOON (DONG)
COULD YOU COLLECT THE WORKSHEETS AND TAKE THEM TO THE PREP ROOM IN BUILDING B?
SURE. NO PROB-LEM.
GAYA (CHATTER)
PREZ! THAT LOOKS TOO HEAVY TO CARRY ALL BY YOURSELF. LET ME HELP.
OH. I'M FREE TO HELP TOO!
GAYA
GATA (CLATTER)
THANKS! I'LL ACCEPT YOUR OFFERS, THEN.
THE PRESIDENT SURE IS POPULAR... SHE DIDN'T EVEN ASK, AND PEOPLE ARE RUSHING TO HELP HER.
GAYA

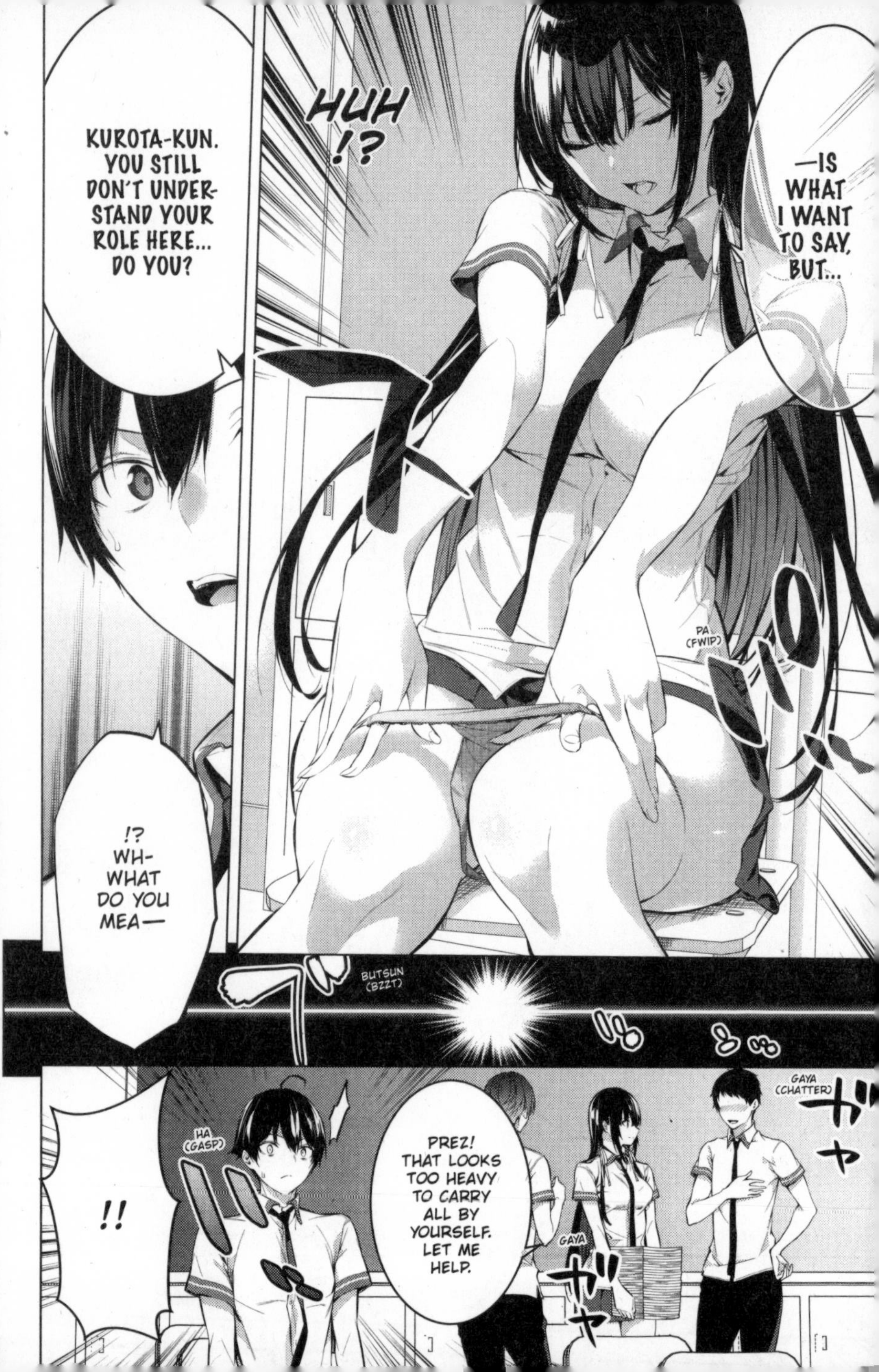
—IS WHAT I WANT TO SAY, BUT...
HUH!?
KUROTA-KUN. YOU STILL DON'T UNDER-STAND YOUR ROLE HERE... DO YOU?
PA (FWIP)
!? WH-WHAT DO YOU MEA—
BUTSUN (BZZT)
GAYA (CHATTER)
GAYA
PREZ! THAT LOOKS TOO HEAVY TO CARRY ALL BY YOURSELF. LET ME HELP.
HA (GASP)
!!

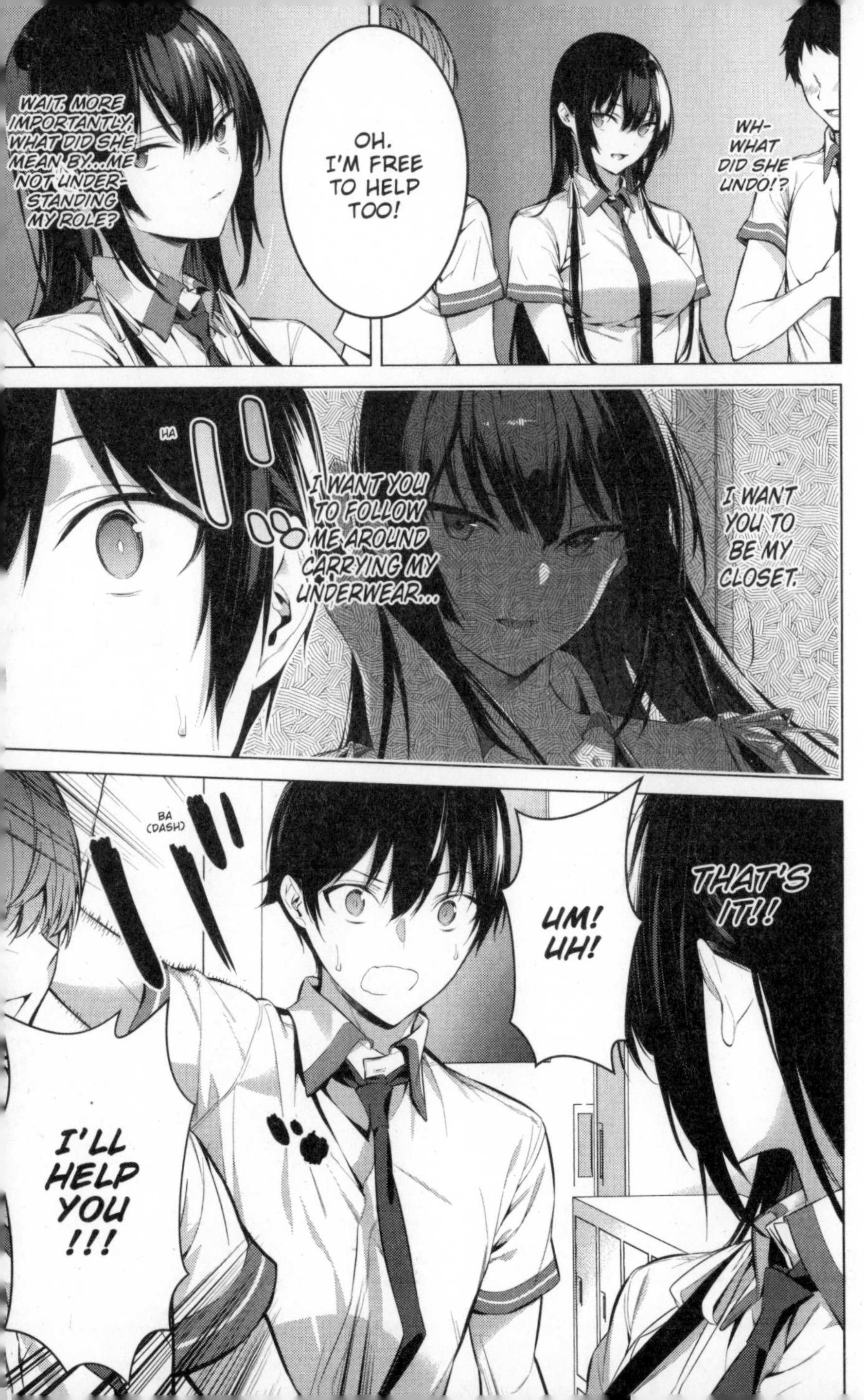

WH- WHAT DID SHE UNDO!?
OH. I'M FREE TO HELP TOO!
WAIT. MORE IMPORTANTLY, WHAT DID SHE MEAN BY...ME NOT UNDERSTANDING MY ROLE?
I WANT YOU TO BE MY CLOSET.
I WANT YOU TO FOLLOW ME AROUND CARRYING MY UNDERWEAR...
HA
THAT'S IT!!
UM! UH!
BA (DASH)
I'LL HELP YOU!!!

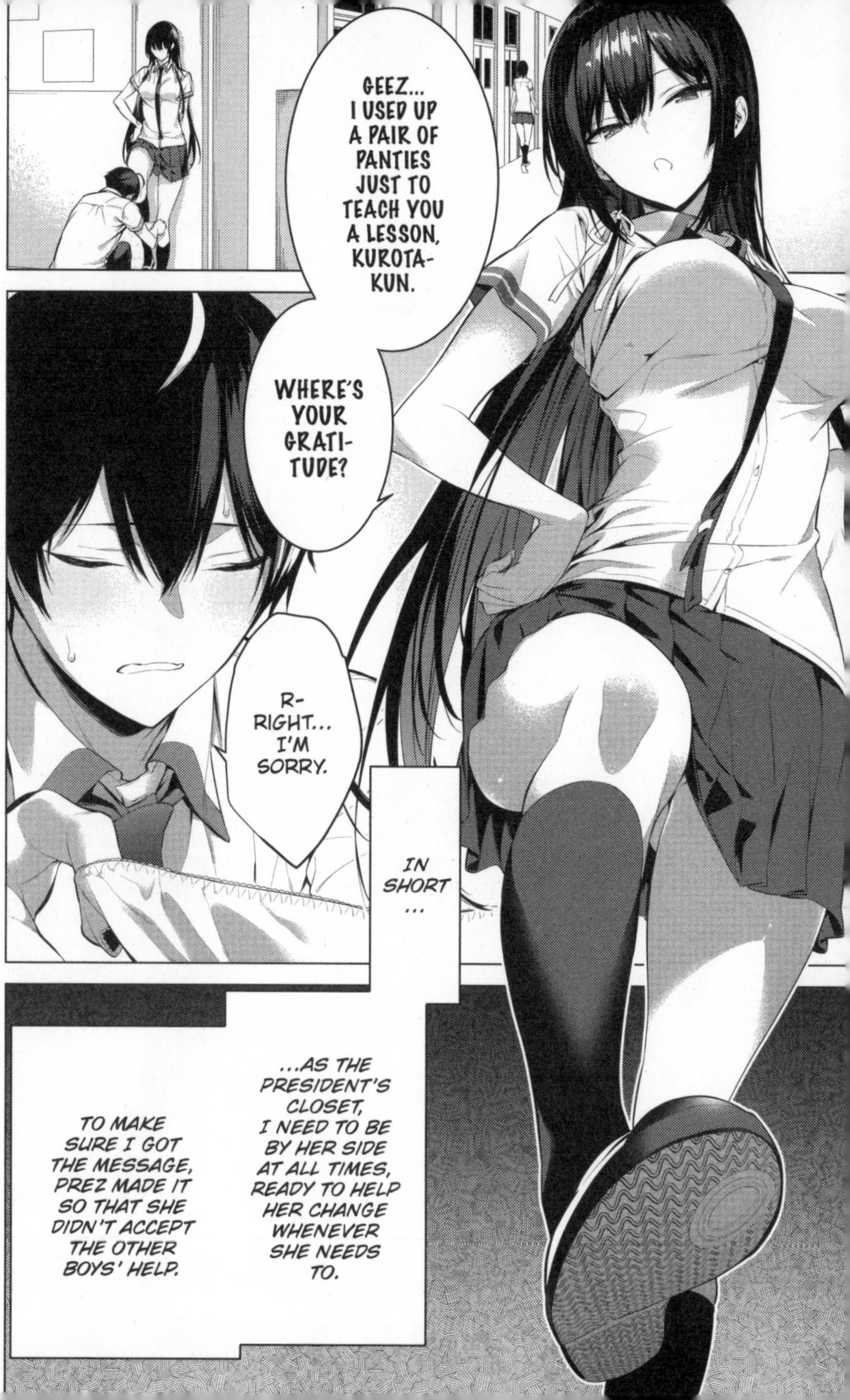
GEEZ... I USED UP A PAIR OF PANTIES JUST TO TEACH YOU A LESSON, KUROTA-KUN.
WHERE'S YOUR GRATI-TUDE?
R-RIGHT... I'M SORRY.
IN SHORT...
...AS THE PRESIDENT'S CLOSET, I NEED TO BE BY HER SIDE AT ALL TIMES, READY TO HELP HER CHANGE WHENEVER SHE NEEDS TO.
TO MAKE SURE I GOT THE MESSAGE, PREZ MADE IT SO THAT SHE DIDN'T ACCEPT THE OTHER BOYS' HELP.

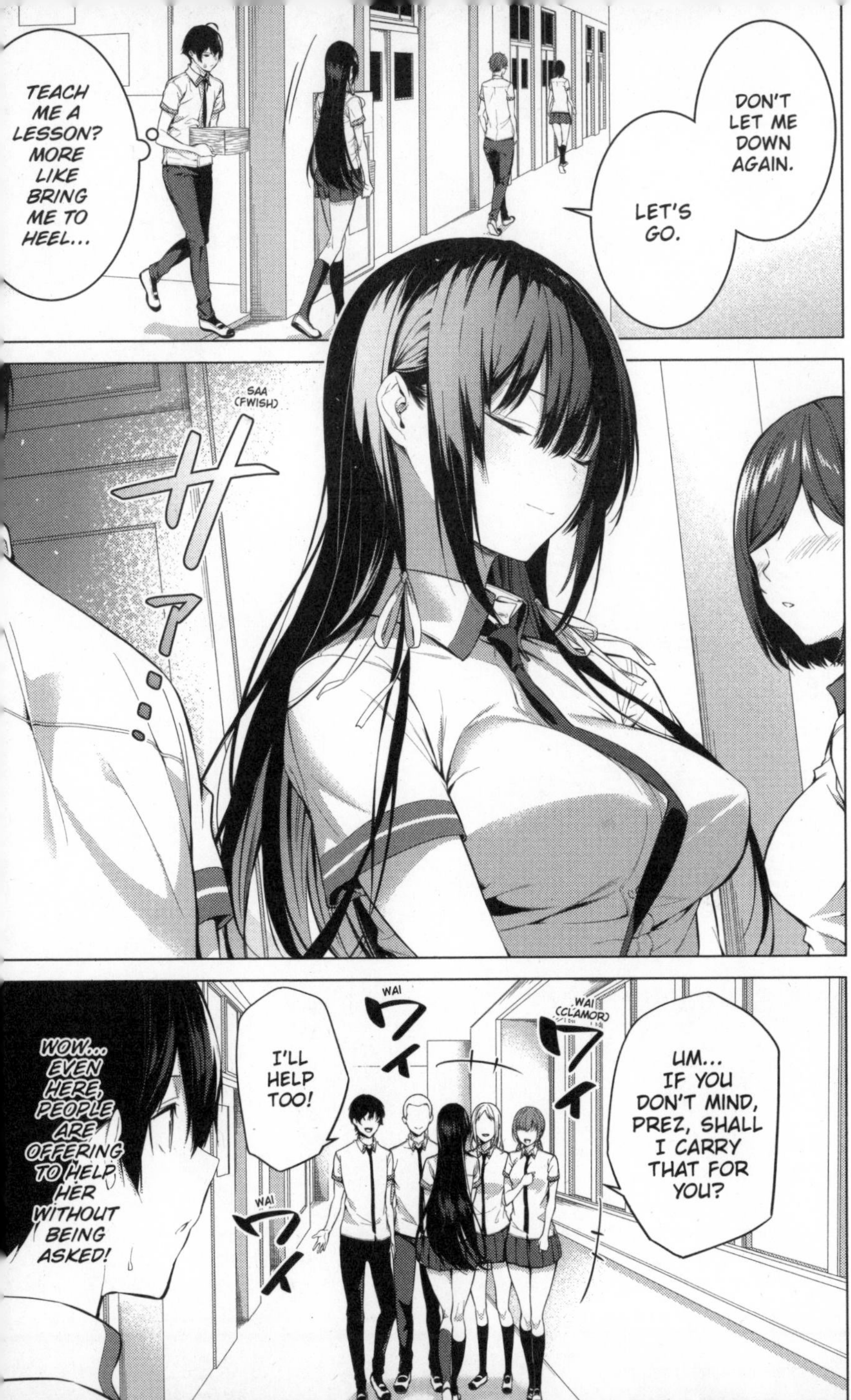
DON'T LET ME DOWN AGAIN.
LET'S GO.
TEACH ME A LESSON? MORE LIKE BRING ME TO HEEL...
SAA (FWISH)
UM... IF YOU DON'T MIND, PREZ, SHALL I CARRY THAT FOR YOU?
WAI (CLAMOR)
WAI
I'LL HELP TOO!
WAI
WOW... EVEN HERE, PEOPLE ARE OFFERING TO HELP HER WITHOUT BEING ASKED!

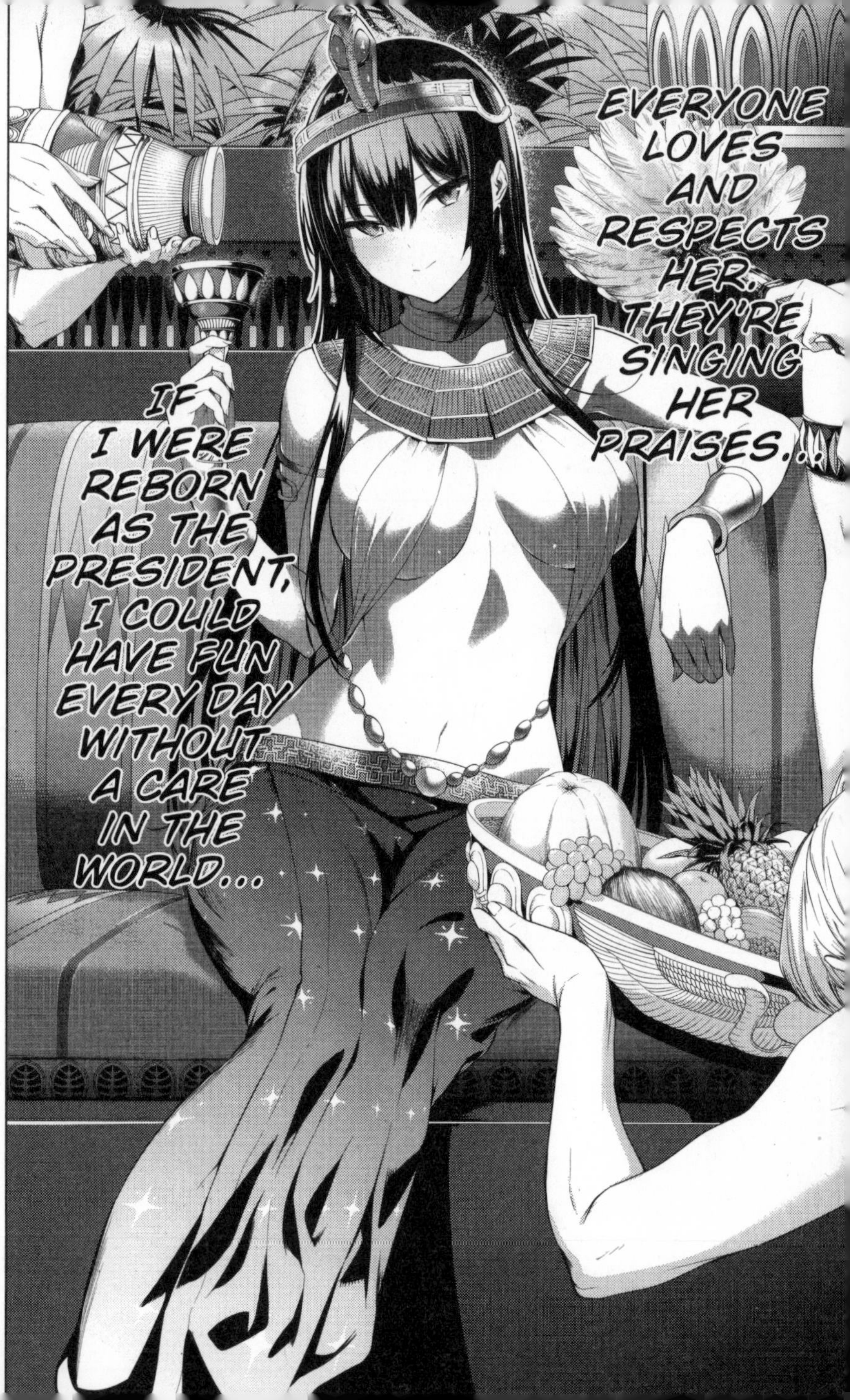
EVERYONE LOVES AND RESPECTS HER. THEY'RE SINGING HER PRAISES...!
IF I WERE REBORN AS THE PRESIDENT, I COULD HAVE FUN EVERY DAY WITHOUT A CARE IN THE WORLD...

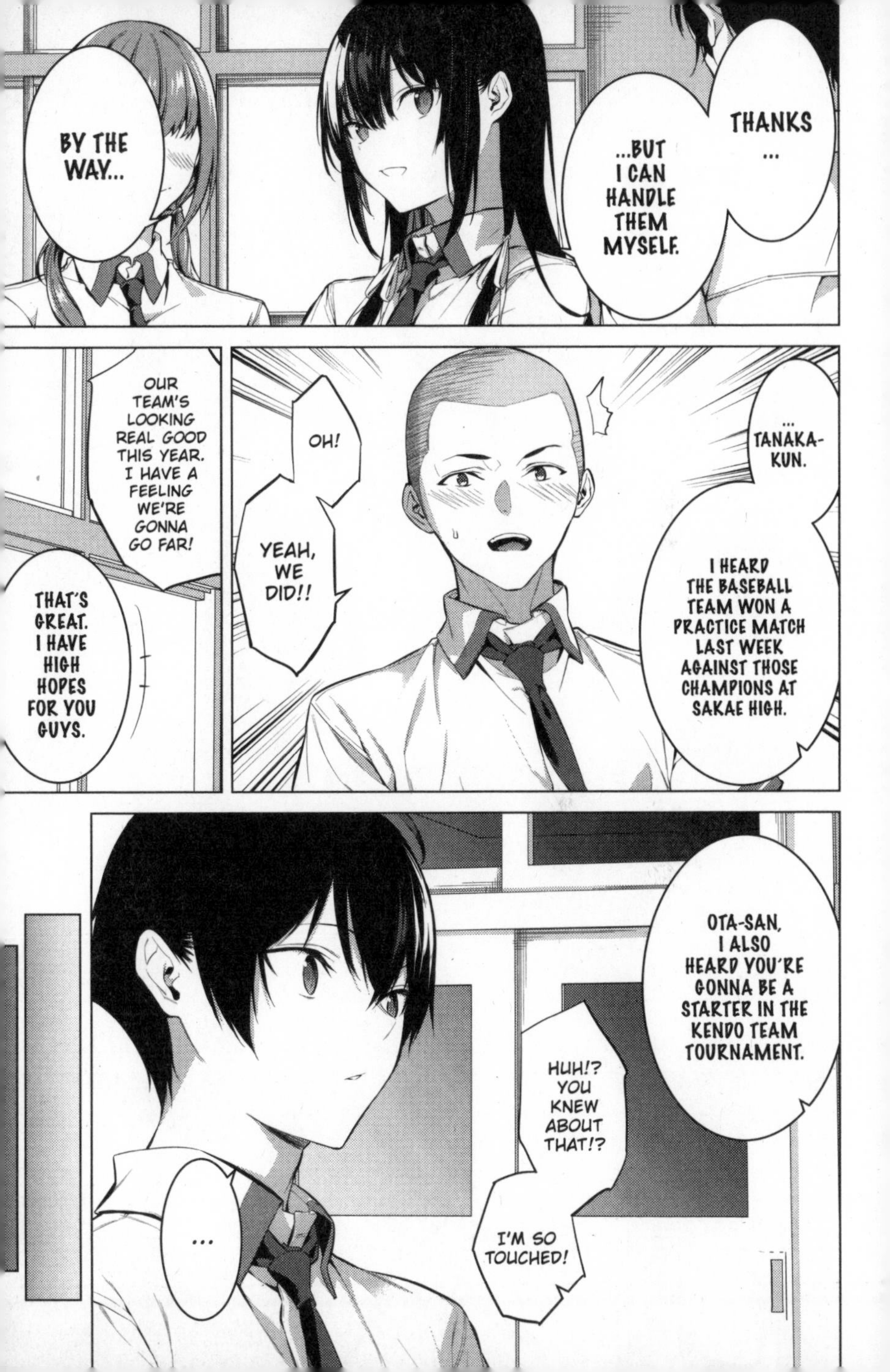
THANKS...
...BUT I CAN HANDLE THEM MYSELF.
BY THE WAY...
...TANAKA-KUN.
I HEARD THE BASEBALL TEAM WON A PRACTICE MATCH LAST WEEK AGAINST THOSE CHAMPIONS AT SAKAE HIGH.
OH!
YEAH, WE DID!!
OUR TEAM'S LOOKING REAL GOOD THIS YEAR. I HAVE A FEELING WE'RE GONNA GO FAR!
THAT'S GREAT. I HAVE HIGH HOPES FOR YOU GUYS.
OTA-SAN, I ALSO HEARD YOU'RE GONNA BE A STARTER IN THE KENDO TEAM TOURNAMENT.
HUH!? YOU KNEW ABOUT THAT!?
I'M SO TOUCHED!
...

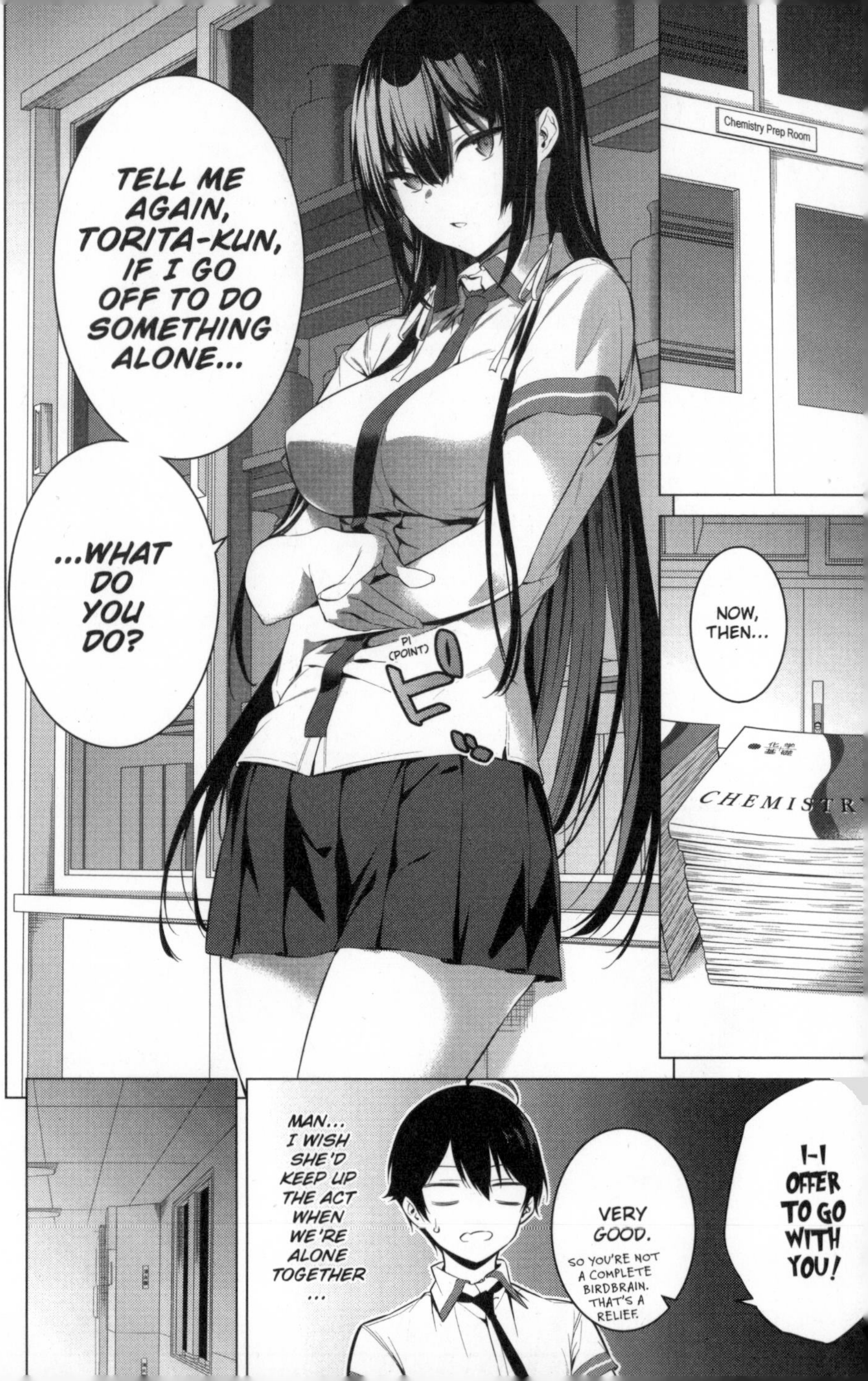

Chemistry Prep Room
NOW, THEN...
CHEMISTRY
TELL ME AGAIN, TORITA-KUN, IF I GO OFF TO DO SOMETHING ALONE...
...WHAT DO YOU DO?
PI (POINT)
I-I OFFER TO GO WITH YOU!
VERY GOOD.
SO YOU'RE NOT A COMPLETE BIRDBRAIN. THAT'S A RELIEF.
MAN... I WISH SHE'D KEEP UP THE ACT WHEN WE'RE ALONE TOGETHER...

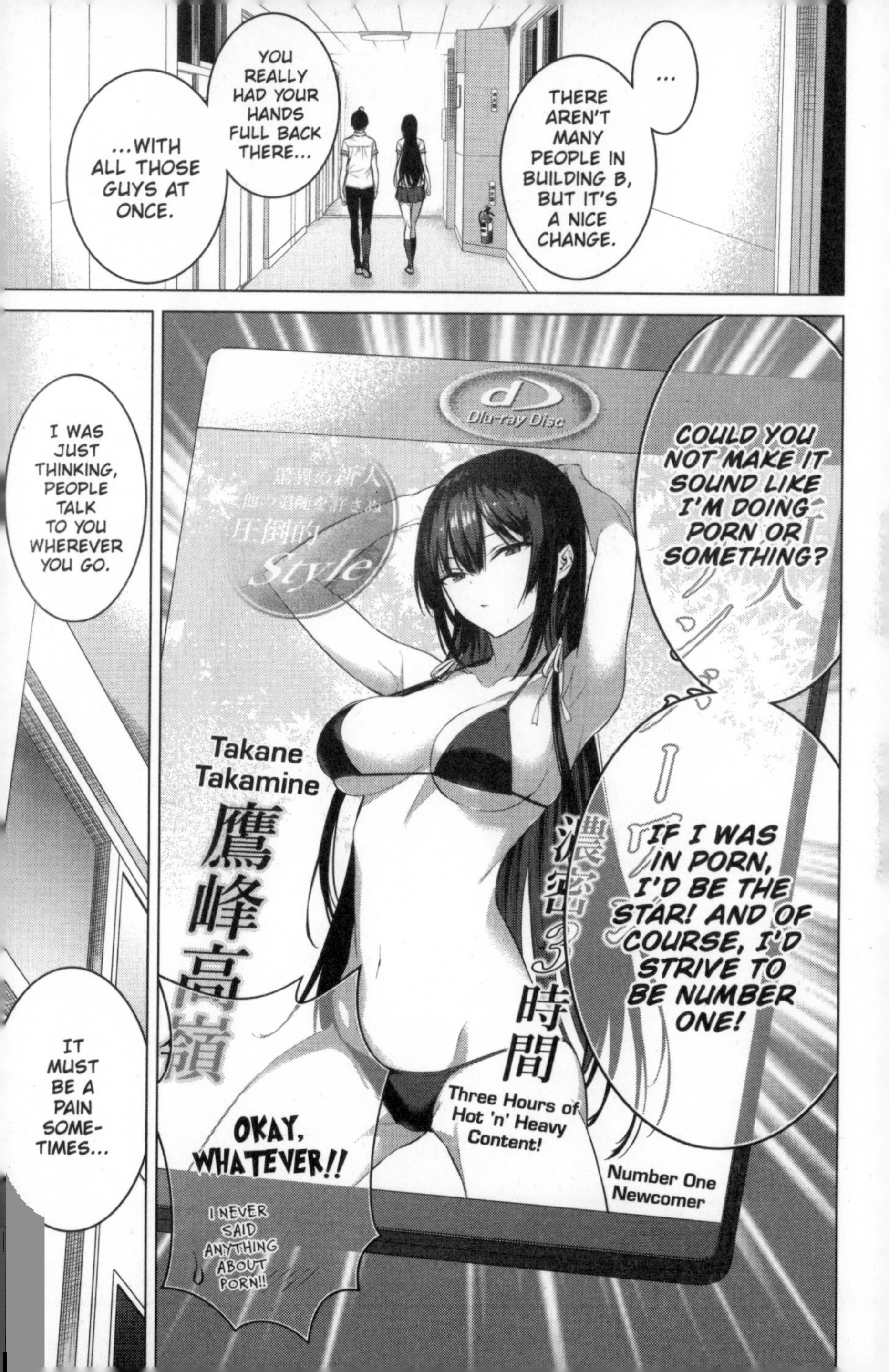
...
THERE AREN'T MANY PEOPLE IN BUILDING B, BUT IT'S A NICE CHANGE.
YOU REALLY HAD YOUR HANDS FULL BACK THERE...
...WITH ALL THOSE GUYS AT ONCE.
COULD YOU NOT MAKE IT SOUND LIKE I'M DOING PORN OR SOMETHING?
IF I WAS IN PORN, I'D BE THE STAR! AND OF COURSE, I'D STRIVE TO BE NUMBER ONE!
Diu-ray Disc
圧倒的
Style
濃密3時間
Three Hours of Hot 'n' Heavy Content!
Takane Takamine
鷹峰高嶺
Number One Newcomer
OKAY, WHATEVER!!
I NEVER SAID ANYTHING ABOUT PORN!!
I WAS JUST THINKING, PEOPLE TALK TO YOU WHEREVER YOU GO.
IT MUST BE A PAIN SOMETIMES...

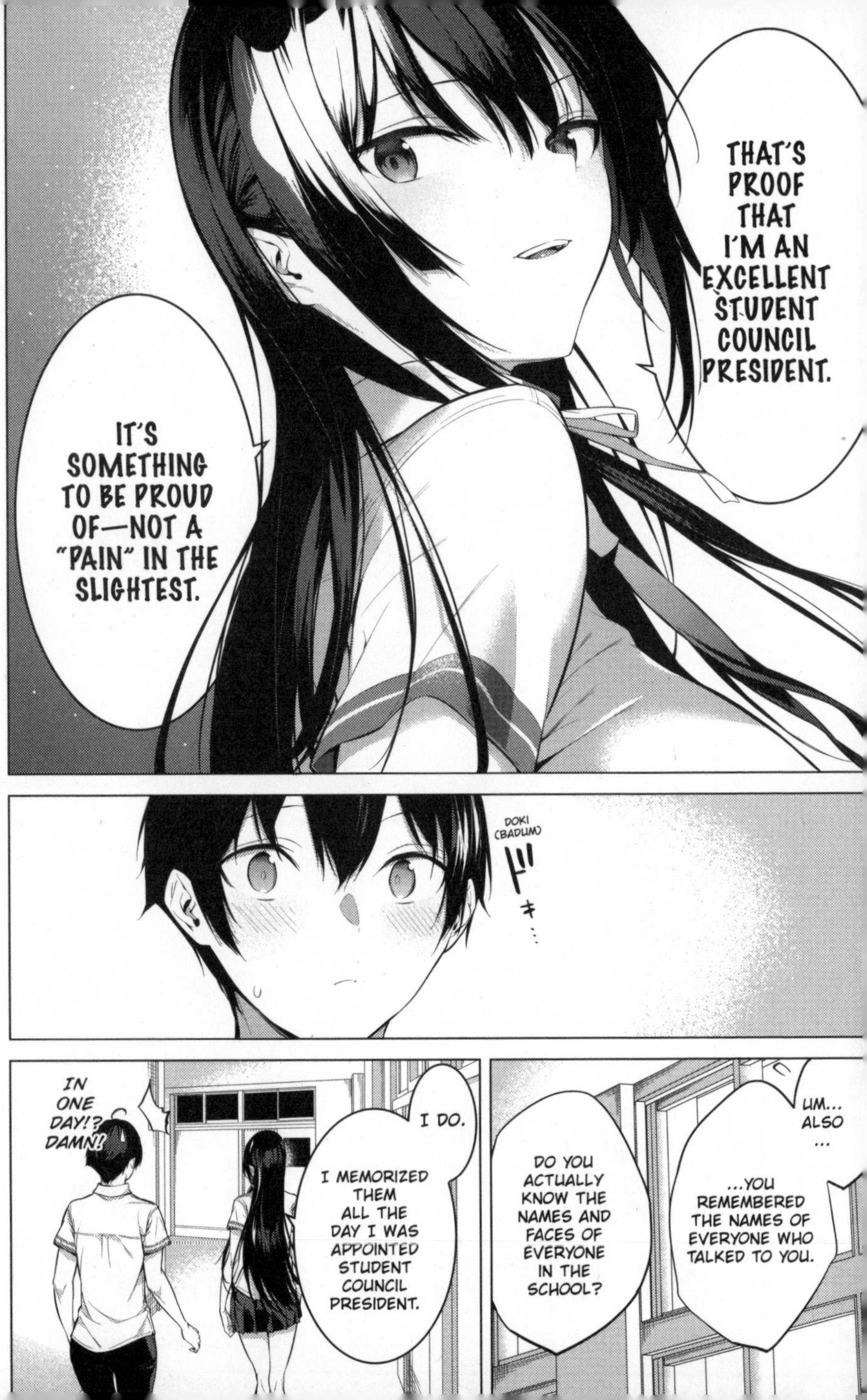
THAT'S PROOF THAT I'M AN EXCELLENT STUDENT COUNCIL PRESIDENT.
IT'S SOMETHING TO BE PROUD OF—NOT A "PAIN" IN THE SLIGHTEST.
DOKI (BADUM)
UM... ALSO ...
...YOU REMEMBERED THE NAMES OF EVERYONE WHO TALKED TO YOU.
DO YOU ACTUALLY KNOW THE NAMES AND FACES OF EVERYONE IN THE SCHOOL?
I DO.
I MEMORIZED THEM ALL THE DAY I WAS APPOINTED STUDENT COUNCIL PRESIDENT.
IN ONE DAY!? DAMN!

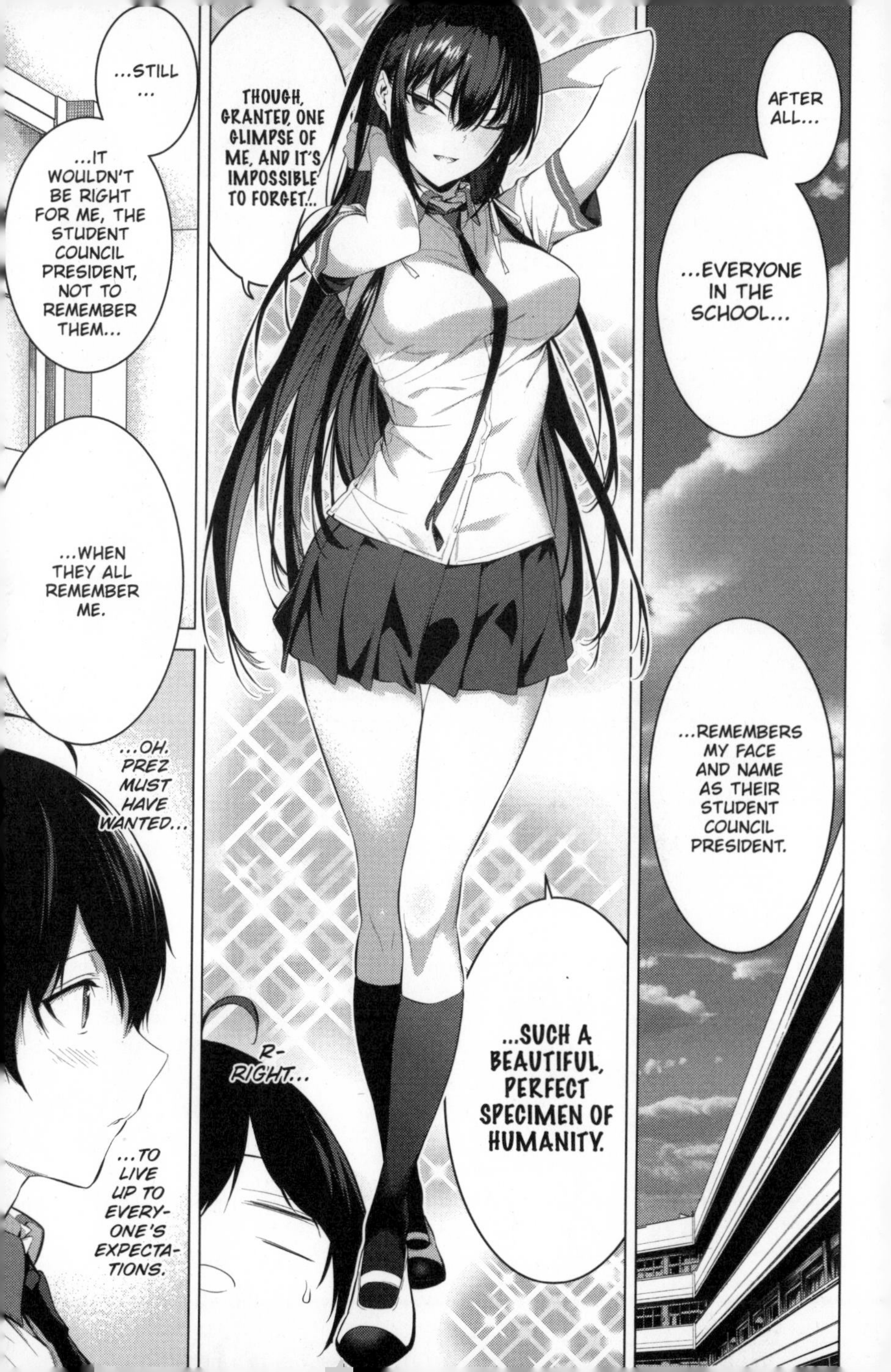
AFTER ALL...
...EVERYONE IN THE SCHOOL...
...REMEMBERS MY FACE AND NAME AS THEIR STUDENT COUNCIL PRESIDENT.
THOUGH, GRANTED, ONE GLIMPSE OF ME, AND IT'S IMPOSSIBLE TO FORGET!...
...SUCH A BEAUTIFUL, PERFECT SPECIMEN OF HUMANITY.
R-RIGHT...
...STILL ...
...IT WOULDN'T BE RIGHT FOR ME, THE STUDENT COUNCIL PRESIDENT, NOT TO REMEMBER THEM...
...WHEN THEY ALL REMEMBER ME.
...OH. PREZ MUST HAVE WANTED...
...TO LIVE UP TO EVERY-ONE'S EXPECTA-TIONS.

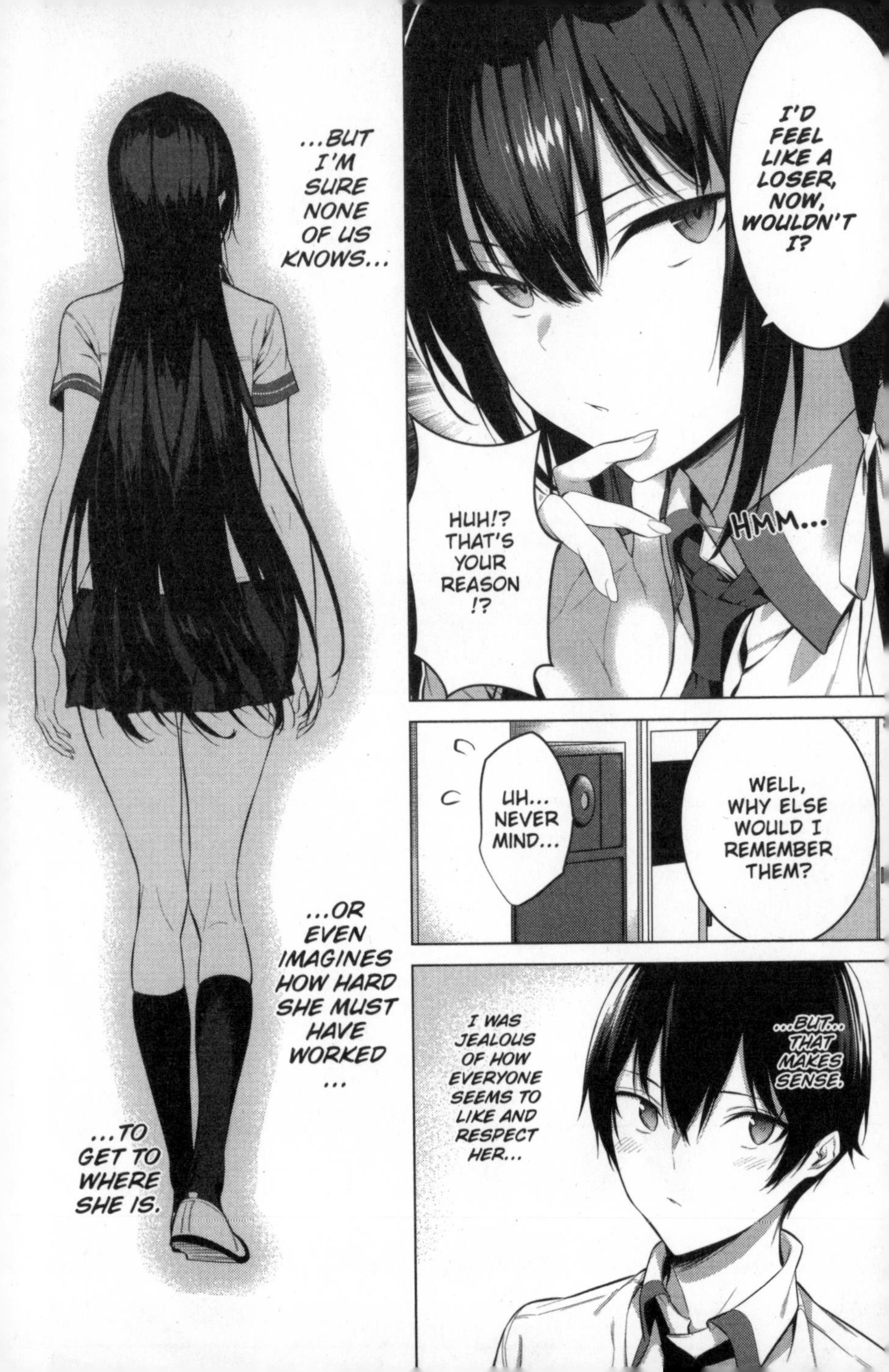
I'D FEEL LIKE A LOSER, NOW, WOULDN'T I?
HMM...
HUH!? THAT'S YOUR REASON !?
WELL, WHY ELSE WOULD I REMEMBER THEM?
UH... NEVER MIND...
...BUT... THAT MAKES SENSE.
I WAS JEALOUS OF HOW EVERYONE SEEMS TO LIKE AND RESPECT HER...
...BUT I'M SURE NONE OF US KNOWS...
...OR EVEN IMAGINES HOW HARD SHE MUST HAVE WORKED ...
...TO GET TO WHERE SHE IS.

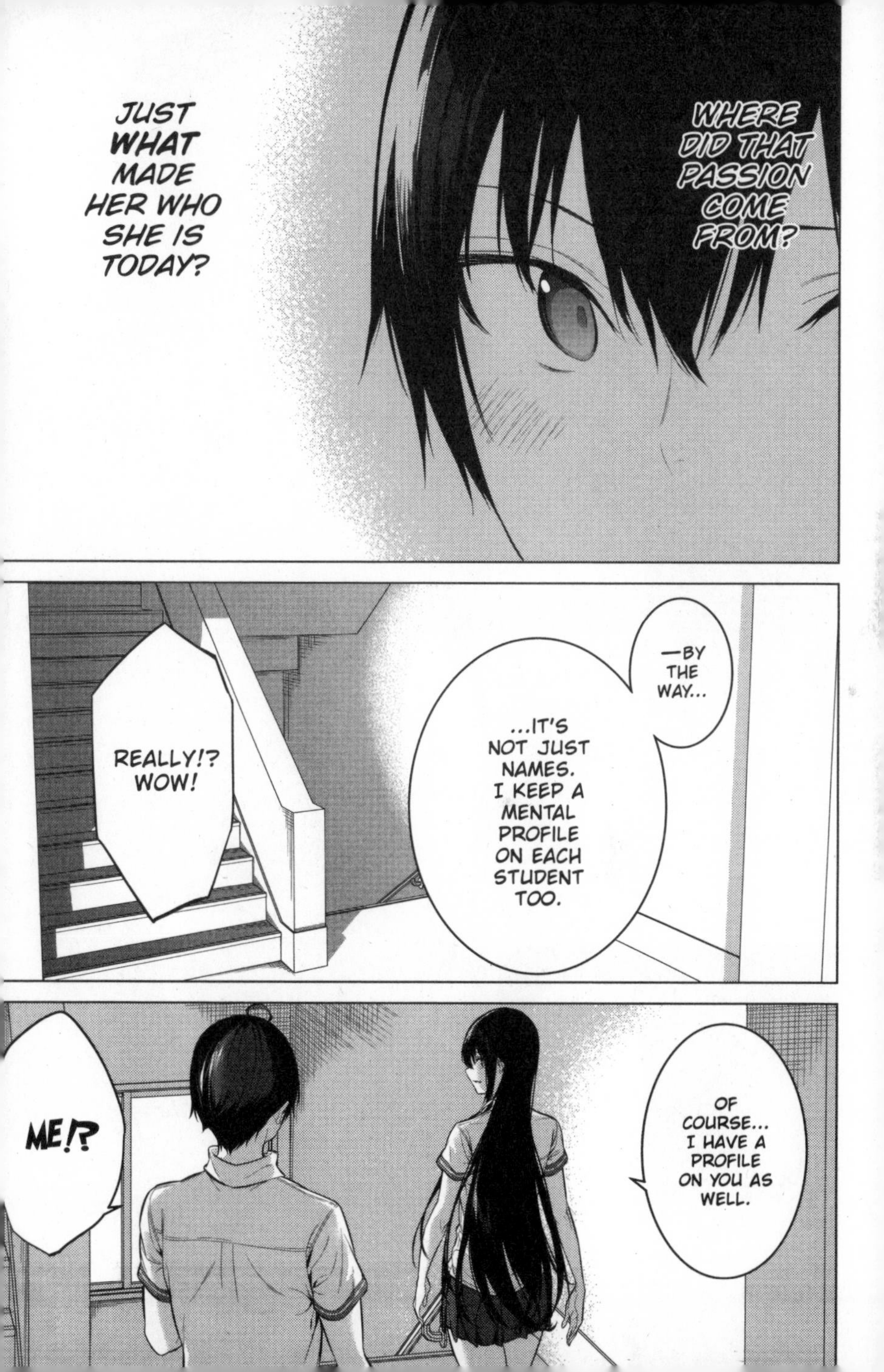
WHERE DID THAT PASSION COME FROM?
JUST WHAT MADE HER WHO SHE IS TODAY?
—BY THE WAY...
...IT'S NOT JUST NAMES. I KEEP A MENTAL PROFILE ON EACH STUDENT TOO.
REALLY!? WOW!
OF COURSE... I HAVE A PROFILE ON YOU AS WELL.
ME!?

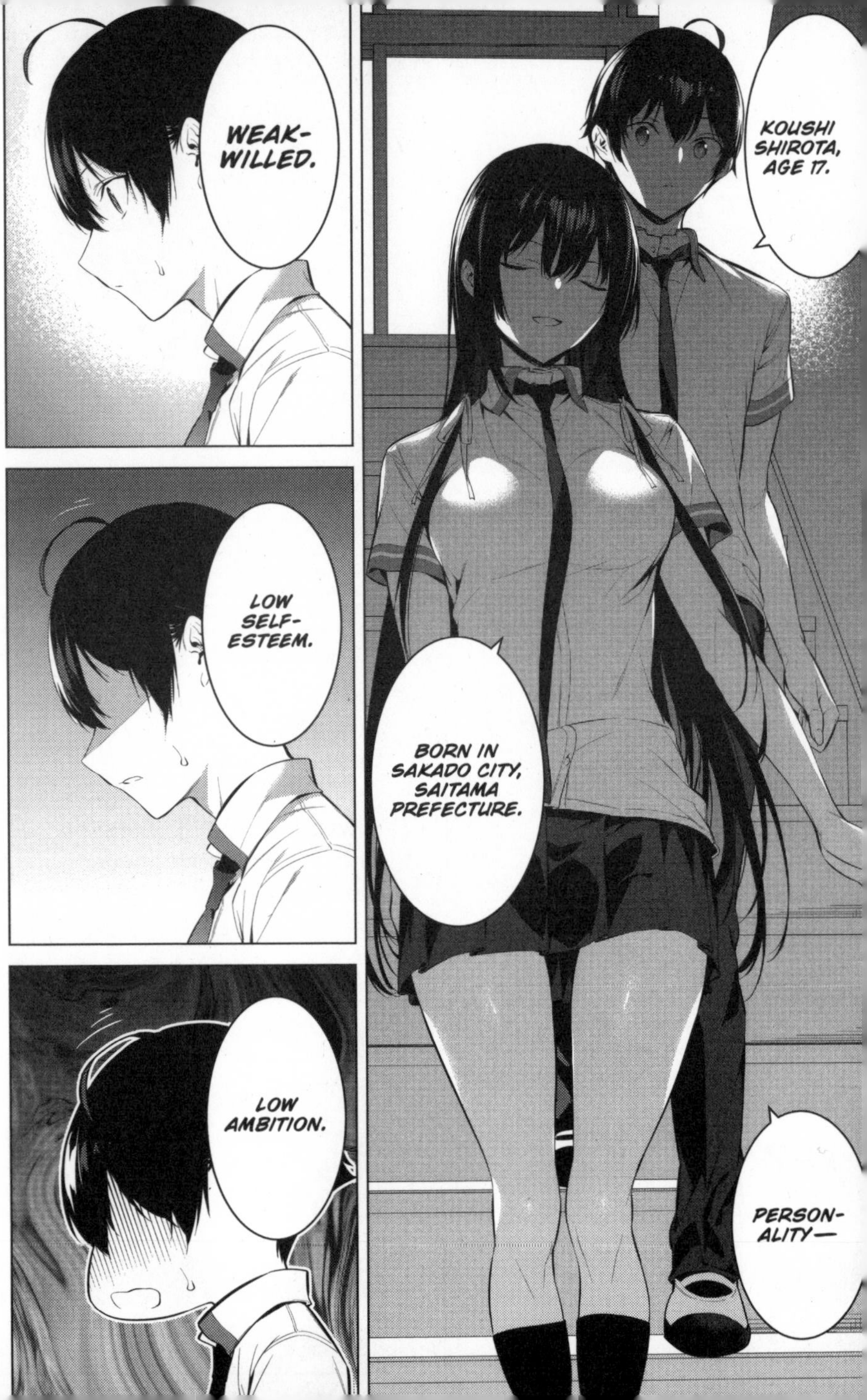
KOUSHI SHIROTA, AGE 17.
BORN IN SAKADO CITY, SAITAMA PREFECTURE.
PERSONALITY—
WEAK-WILLED.
LOW SELF-ESTEEM.
LOW AMBITION.

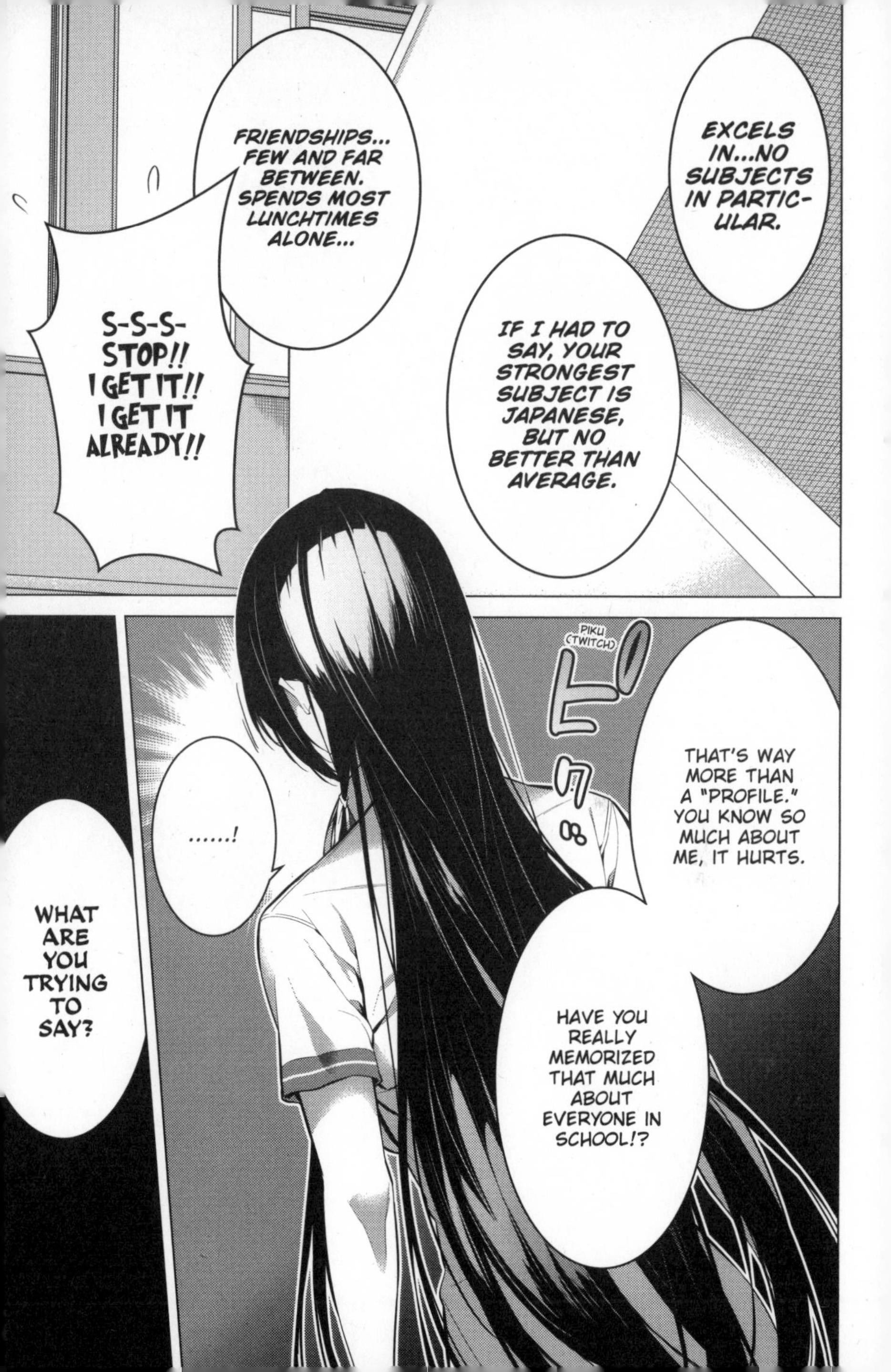
EXCELS IN...NO SUBJECTS IN PARTICULAR.
IF I HAD TO SAY, YOUR STRONGEST SUBJECT IS JAPANESE, BUT NO BETTER THAN AVERAGE.
FRIENDSHIPS... FEW AND FAR BETWEEN. SPENDS MOST LUNCHTIMES ALONE...
S-S-S-STOP!! I GET IT!! I GET IT ALREADY!!
PIKU (TWITCH)
THAT'S WAY MORE THAN A "PROFILE." YOU KNOW SO MUCH ABOUT ME, IT HURTS.
HAVE YOU REALLY MEMORIZED THAT MUCH ABOUT EVERYONE IN SCHOOL!?
......!
WHAT ARE YOU TRYING TO SAY?

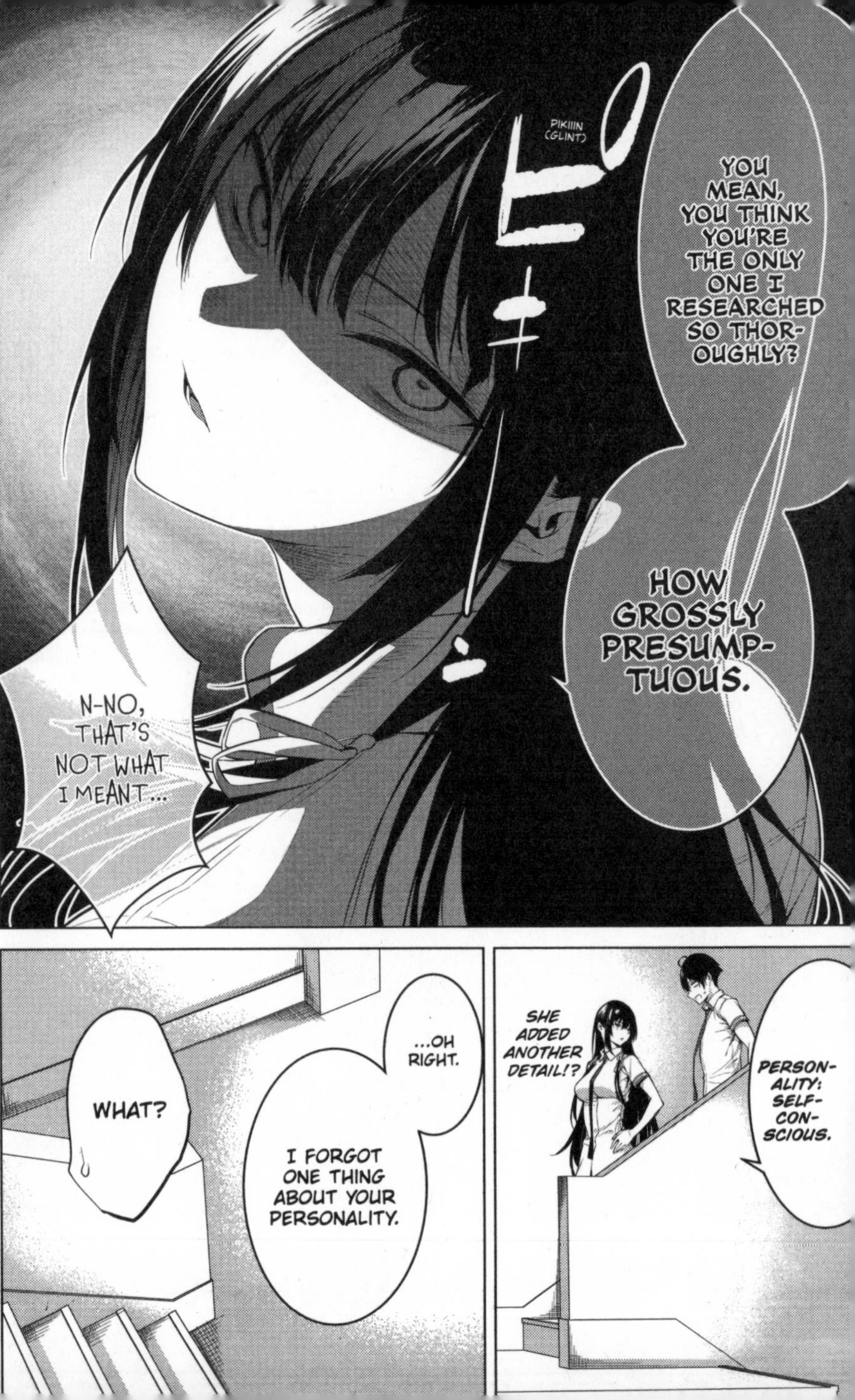
YOU MEAN, YOU THINK YOU'RE THE ONLY ONE I RESEARCHED SO THOROUGHLY?
HOW GROSSLY PRESUMPTUOUS.
PIKIIIN (GLINT)
N-NO, THAT'S NOT WHAT I MEANT...
PERSONALITY: SELF-CONSCIOUS.
SHE ADDED ANOTHER DETAIL!?
...OH RIGHT.
I FORGOT ONE THING ABOUT YOUR PERSONALITY.
WHAT?

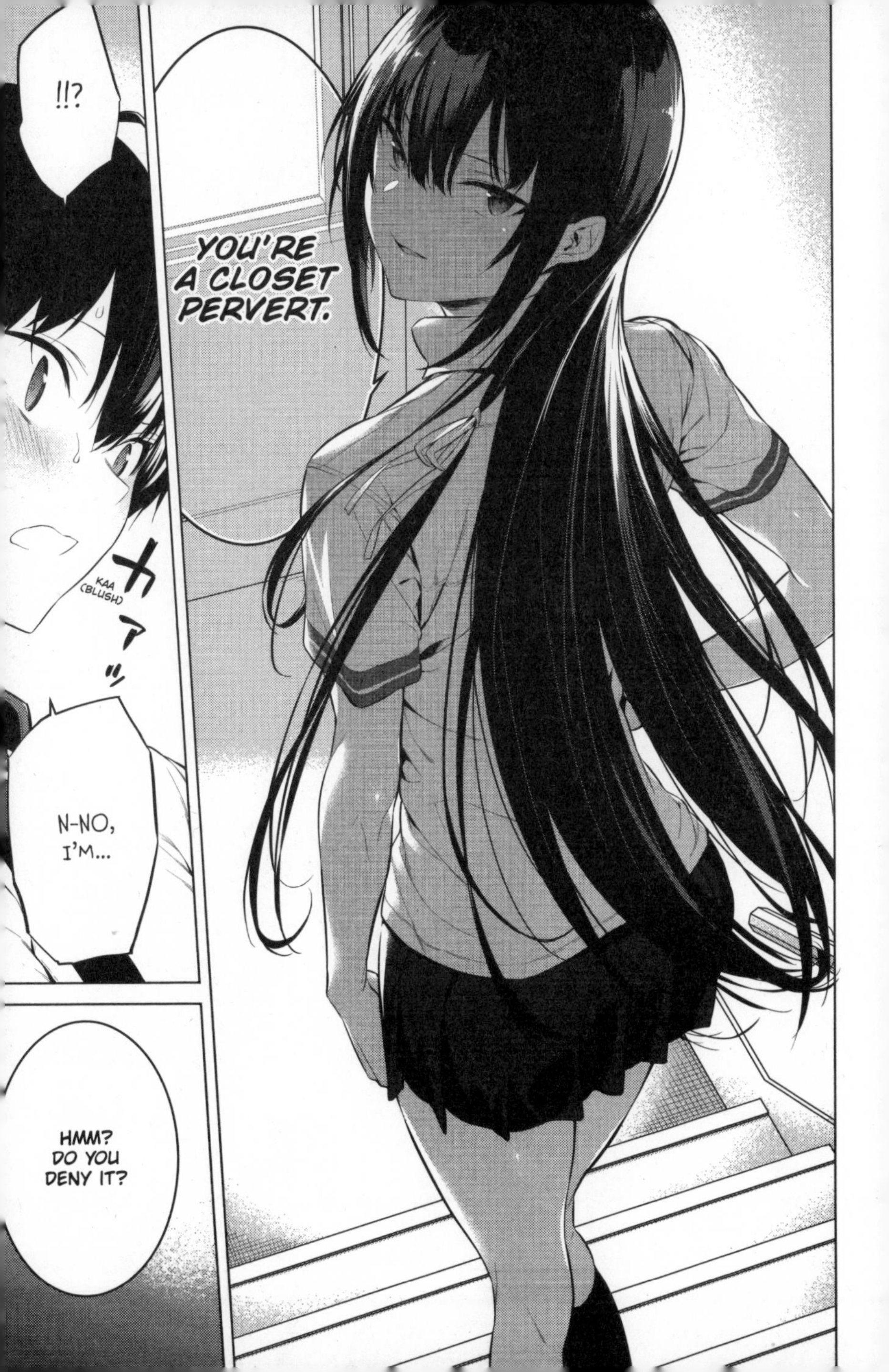
YOU'RE A CLOSET PERVERT.
!!?
KAA (BLUSH)
N-NO, I'M...
HMM? DO YOU DENY IT?

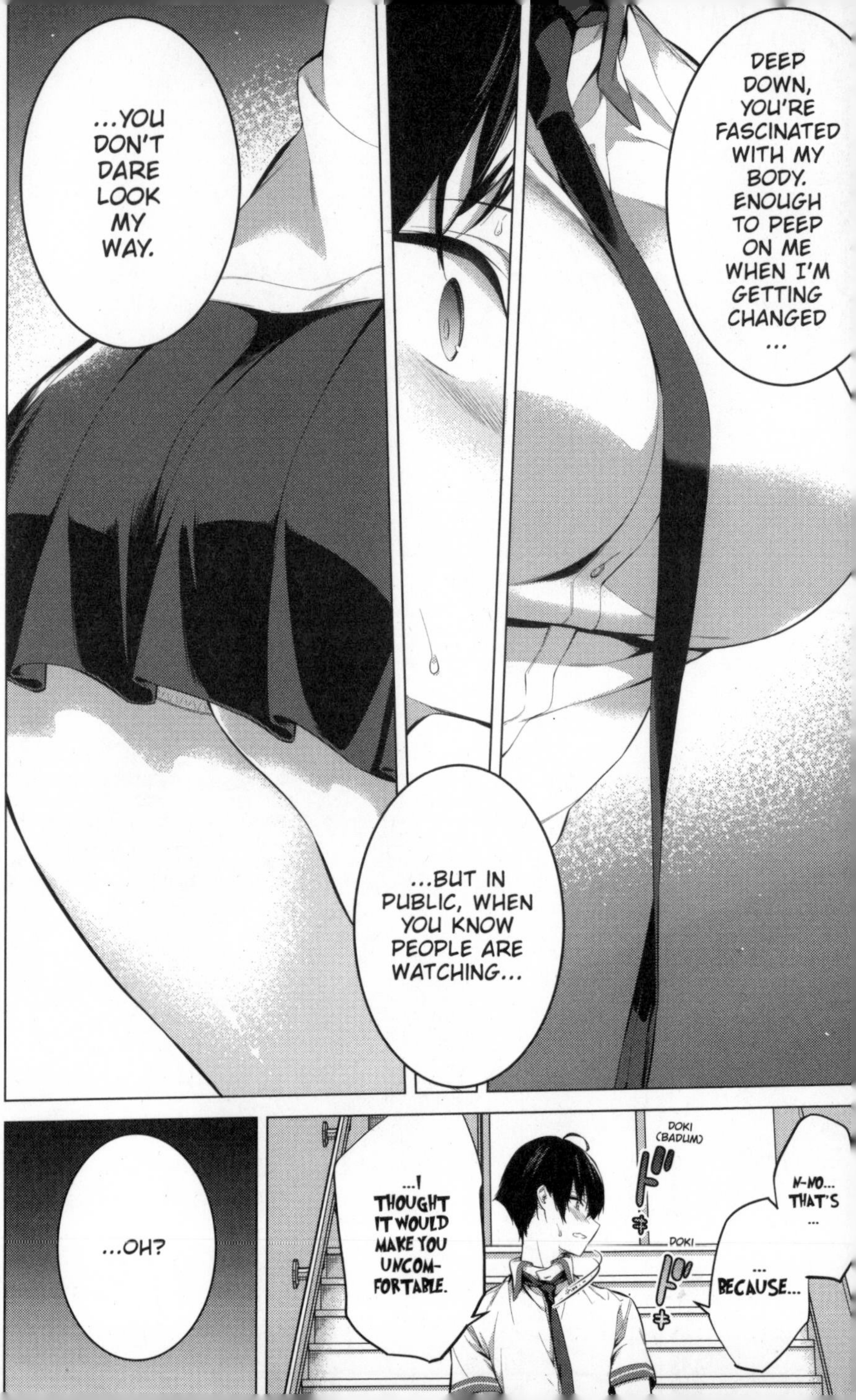
DEEP DOWN, YOU'RE FASCINATED WITH MY BODY. ENOUGH TO PEEP ON ME WHEN I'M GETTING CHANGED ...
...YOU DON'T DARE LOOK MY WAY.
...BUT IN PUBLIC, WHEN YOU KNOW PEOPLE ARE WATCHING...
N-NO... THAT'S ...
DOKI (BADUM)
DOKI
... BECAUSE...
...I THOUGHT IT WOULD MAKE YOU UNCOM-FORTABLE.
...OH?

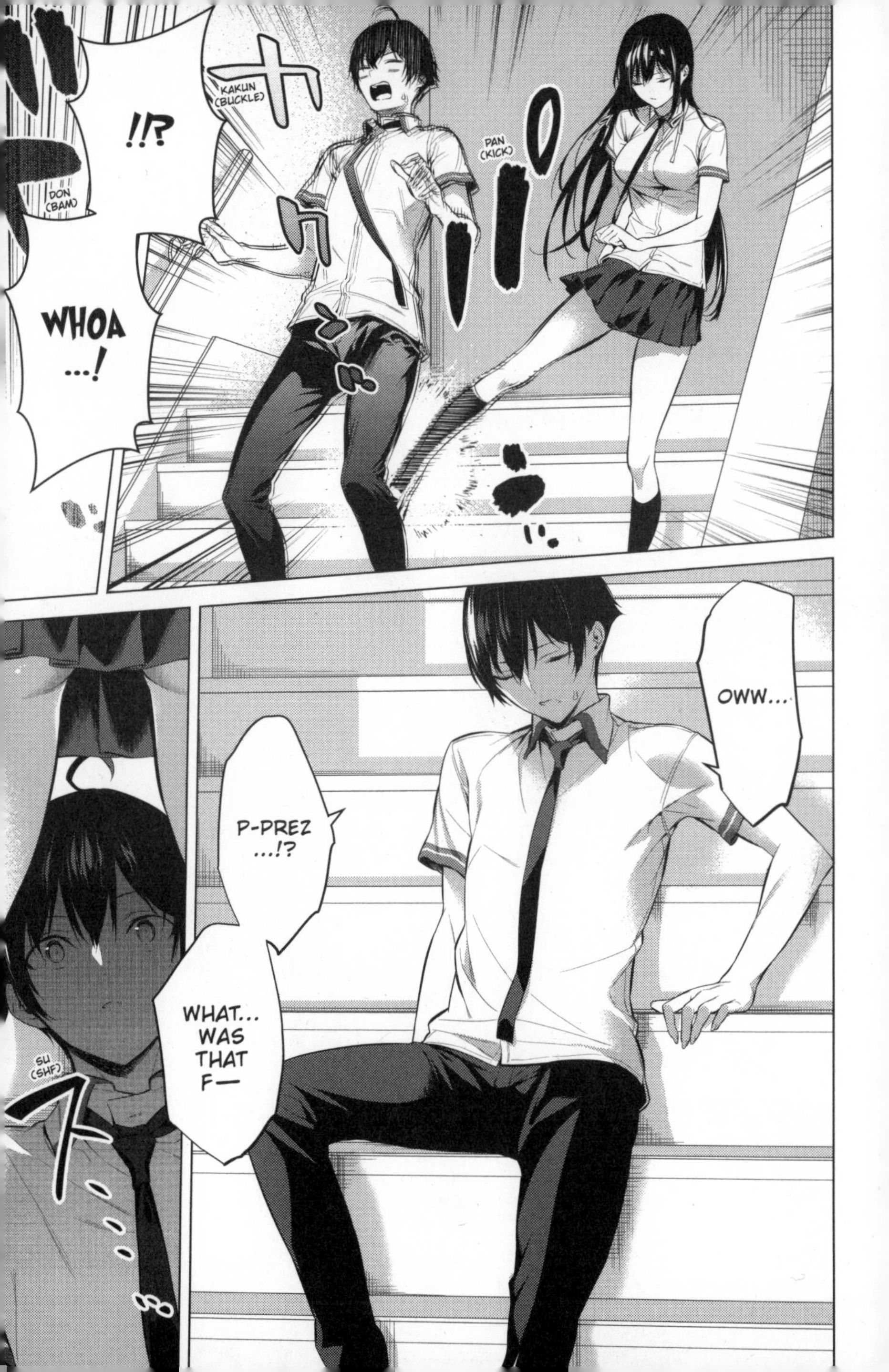
PAN (KICK)
KAKUN (BUCKLE)
!!?
DON (BAM)
WHOA ...!
OWW...
P-PREZ ...!?
WHAT... WAS THAT F—
SU (SHF)

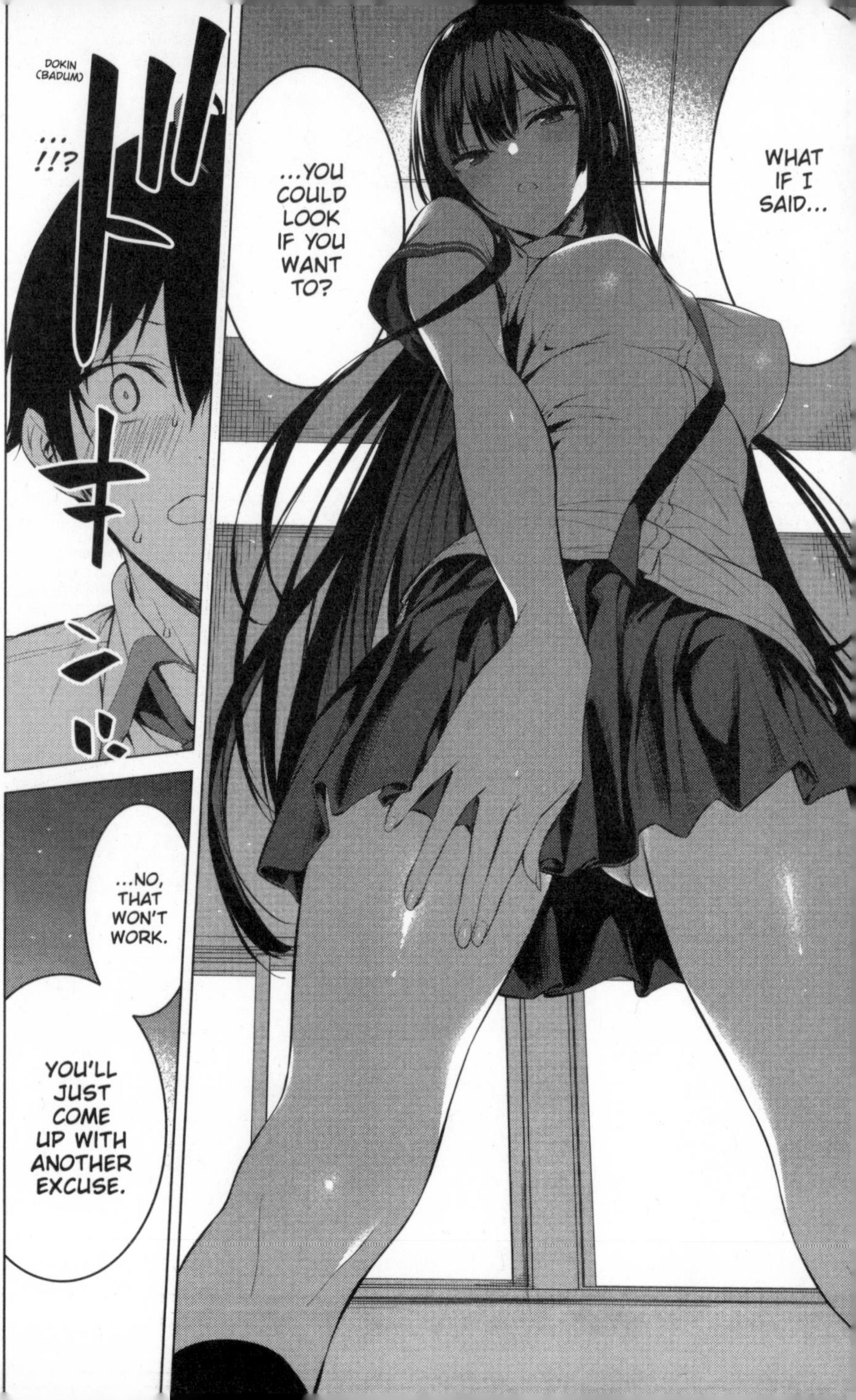
WHAT IF I SAID...
...YOU COULD LOOK IF YOU WANT TO?
DOKIN (BADUM)
...!!?
...NO, THAT WON'T WORK.
YOU'LL JUST COME UP WITH ANOTHER EXCUSE.

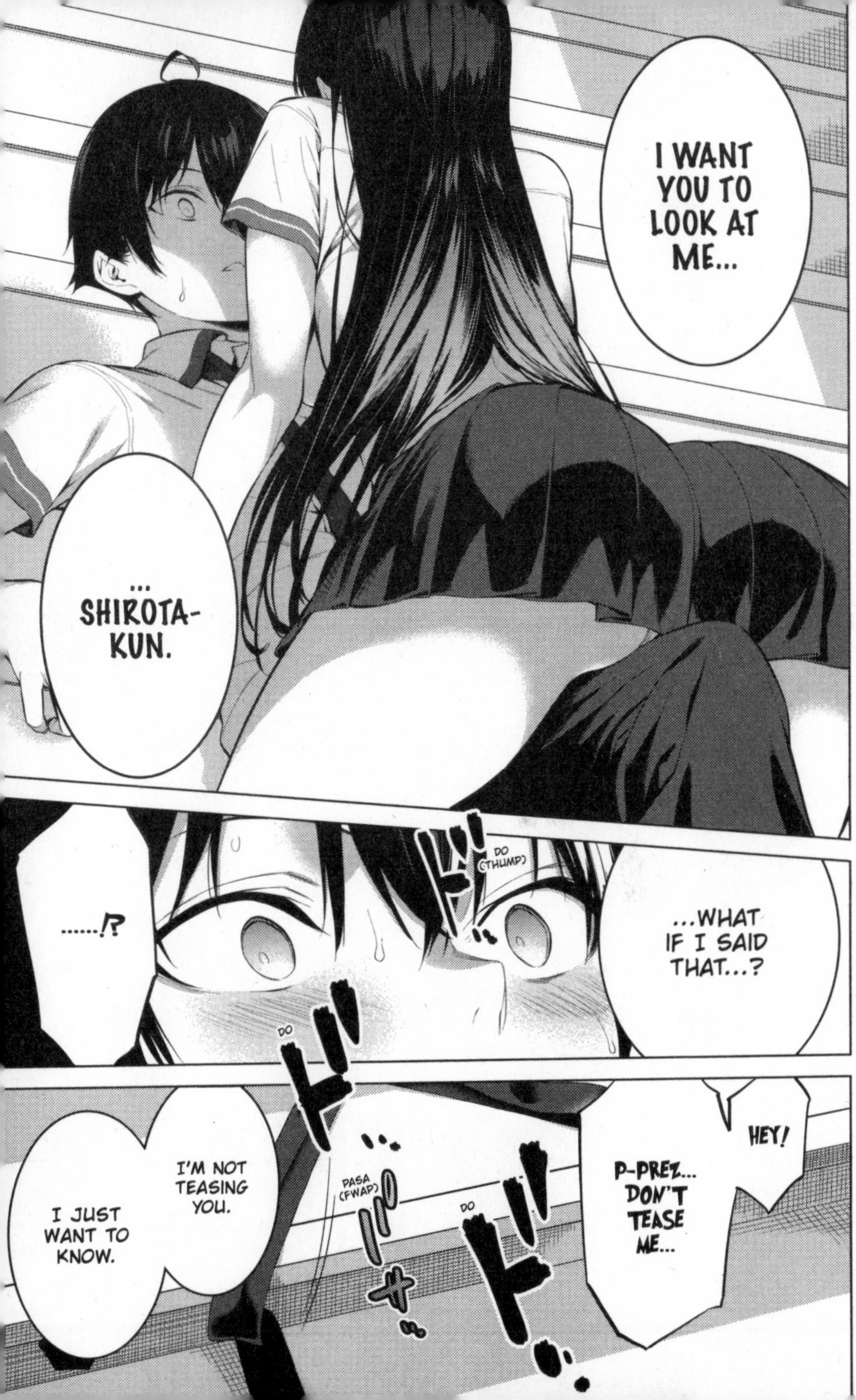
I WANT YOU TO LOOK AT ME...
... SHIROTA-KUN.
...WHAT IF I SAID THAT...?
DO (THUMP)
......!?
DO
HEY!
P-PREZ... DON'T TEASE ME...
DO
PASA (FWAP)
I'M NOT TEASING YOU.
I JUST WANT TO KNOW.

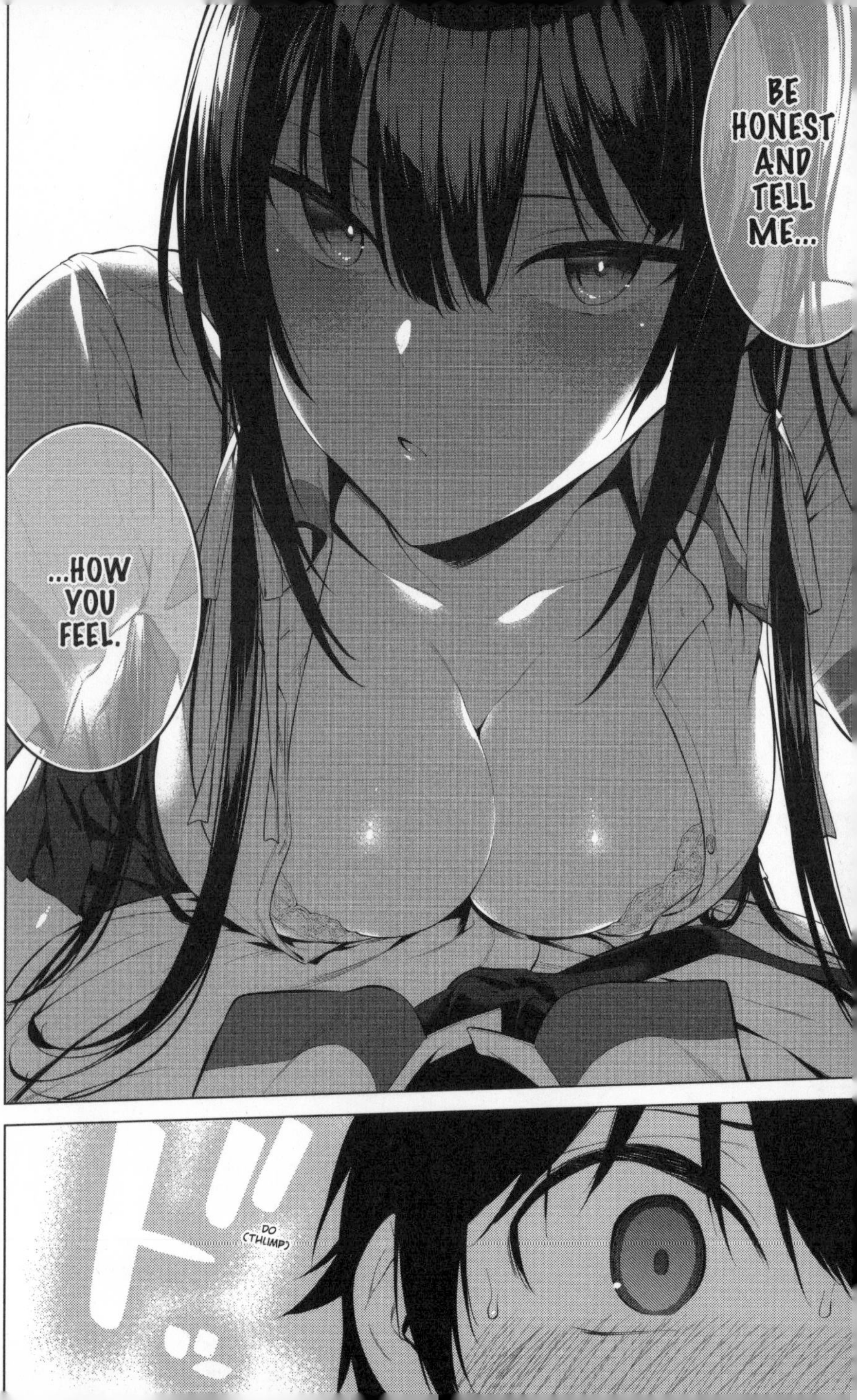
BE HONEST AND TELL ME...
...HOW YOU FEEL.
DO (THUMP)

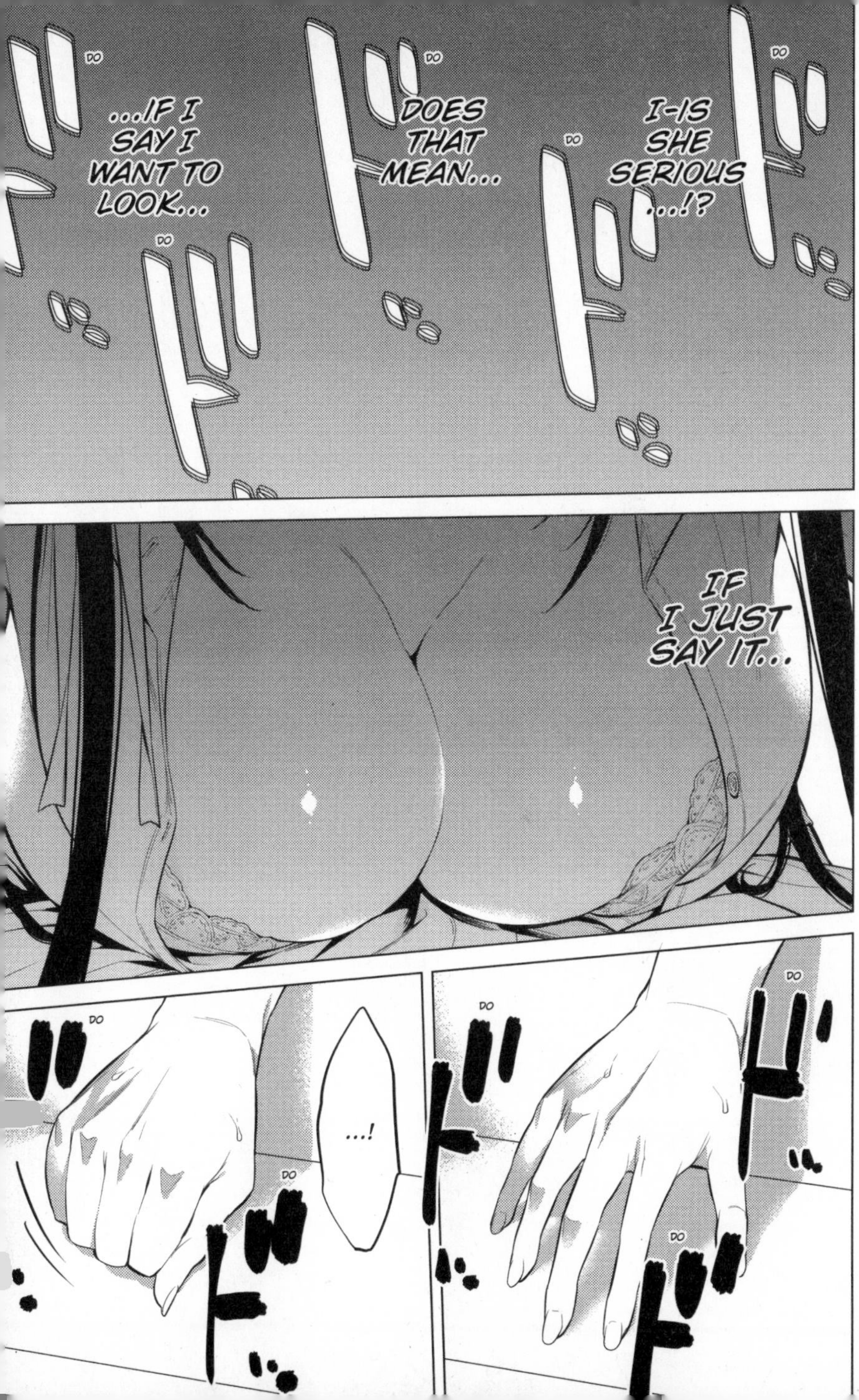
DO
DO
I-IS SHE SERIOUS ...!?
DO
DOES THAT MEAN...
DO
...IF I SAY I WANT TO LOOK...
DO
IF I JUST SAY IT...
DO
DO
DO
...!
DO
DO

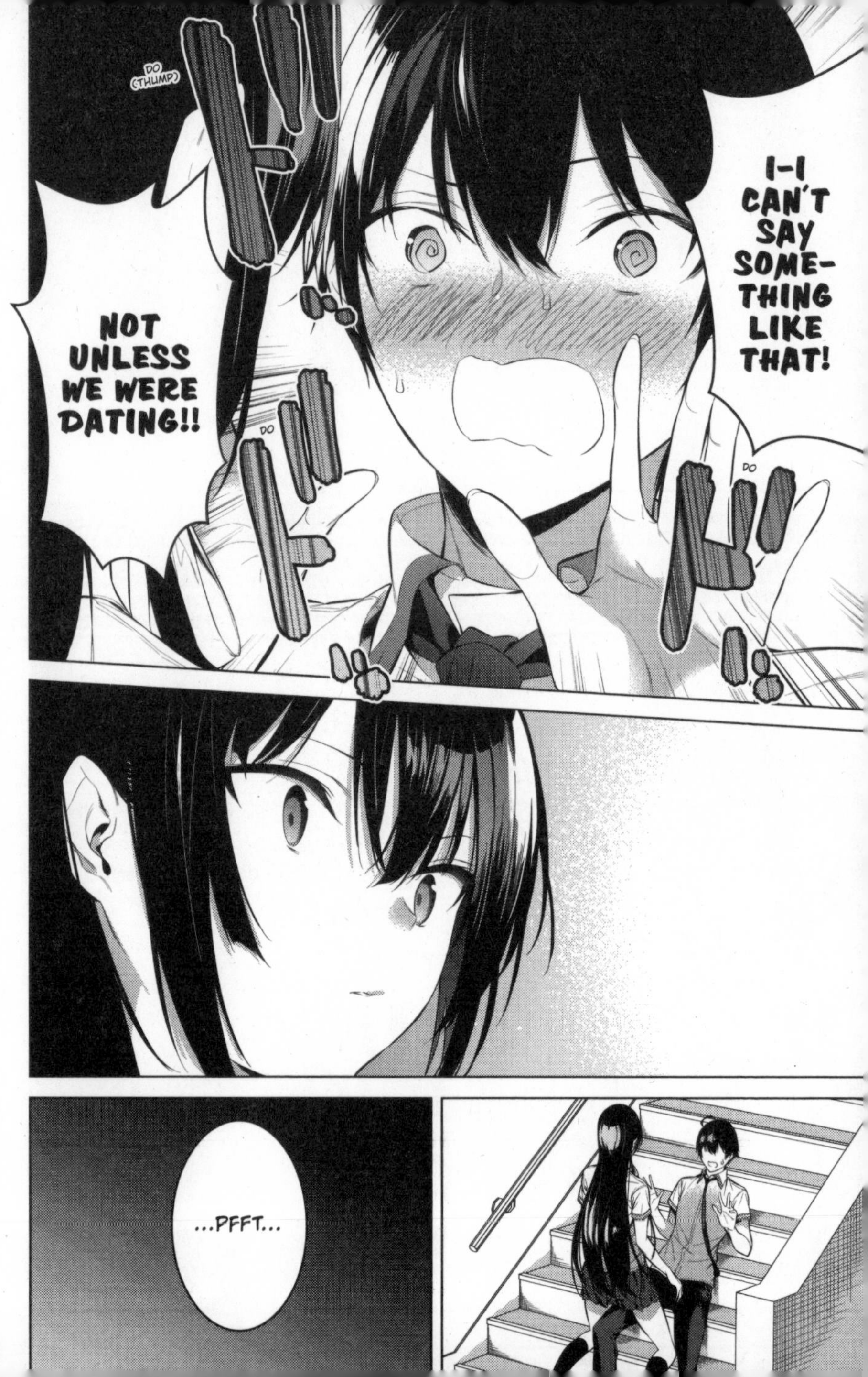
DO (THUMP)
I-I CAN'T SAY SOME-THING LIKE THAT!
NOT UNLESS WE WERE DATING!!
DO
DO
...PFFT...

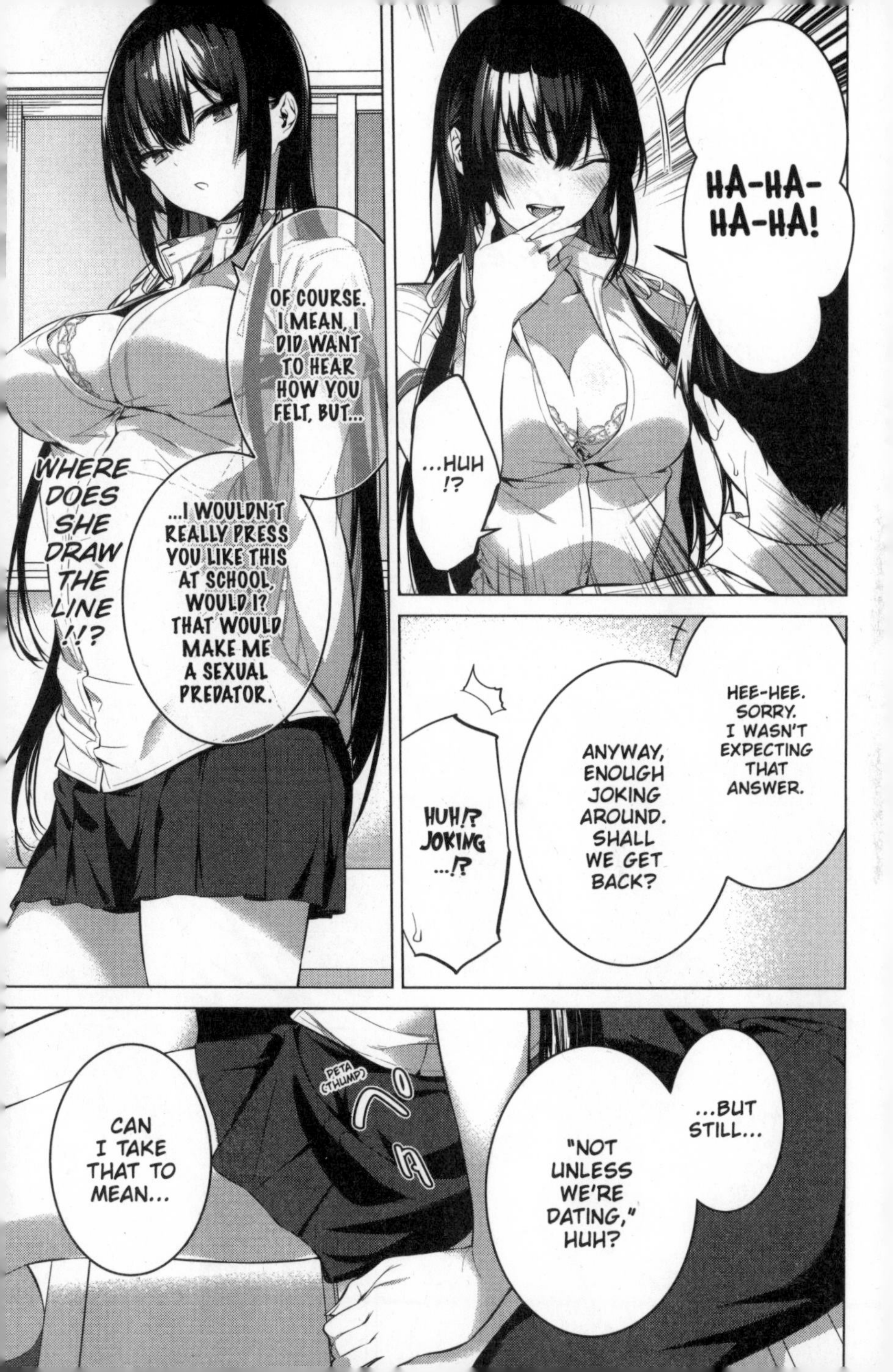
HA-HA-HA-HA!
...HUH!?
HEE-HEE. SORRY. I WASN'T EXPECTING THAT ANSWER.
ANYWAY, ENOUGH JOKING AROUND. SHALL WE GET BACK?
HUH!? JOKING...!?
OF COURSE. I MEAN, I DID WANT TO HEAR HOW YOU FELT, BUT...
...I WOULDN'T REALLY PRESS YOU LIKE THIS AT SCHOOL, WOULD I? THAT WOULD MAKE ME A SEXUAL PREDATOR.
WHERE DOES SHE DRAW THE LINE!!?
...BUT STILL...
"NOT UNLESS WE'RE DATING," HUH?
PETA (THUMP)
CAN I TAKE THAT TO MEAN...

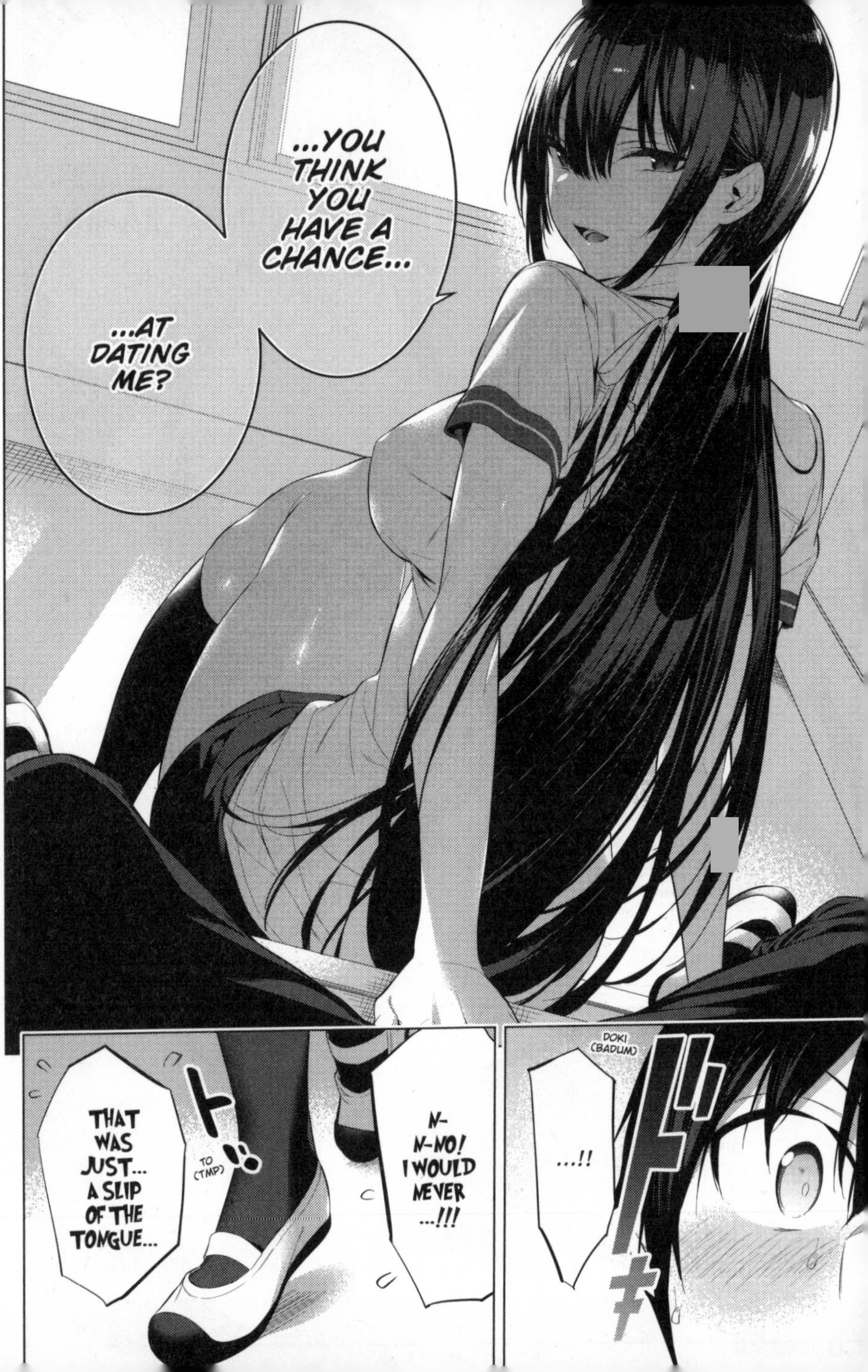

...YOU THINK YOU HAVE A CHANCE...
...AT DATING ME?
DOKI (BADUM)
...!!
N-N-NO! I WOULD NEVER ...!!!
TO (TMP)
THAT WAS JUST... A SLIP OF THE TONGUE...

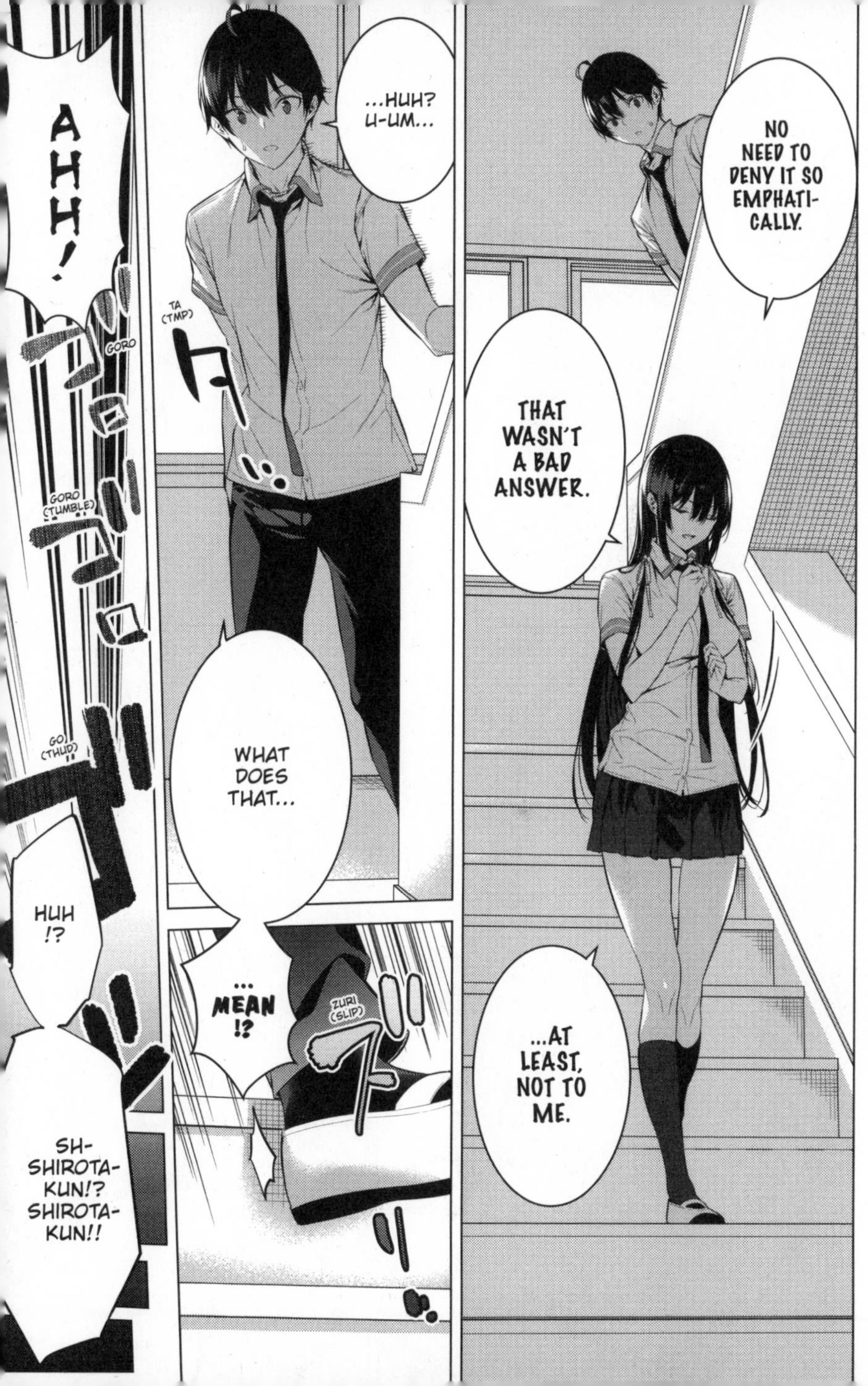
NO NEED TO DENY IT SO EMPHATI-CALLY.
THAT WASN'T A BAD ANSWER.
...AT LEAST, NOT TO ME.
...HUH? U-UM...
TA (TMP)
WHAT DOES THAT...
...MEAN!?
ZURI (SLIP)
AHH!
GORO
GORO (TUMBLE)
GO (THUD)
HUH!?
SH-SHIROTA-KUN!? SHIROTA-KUN!!

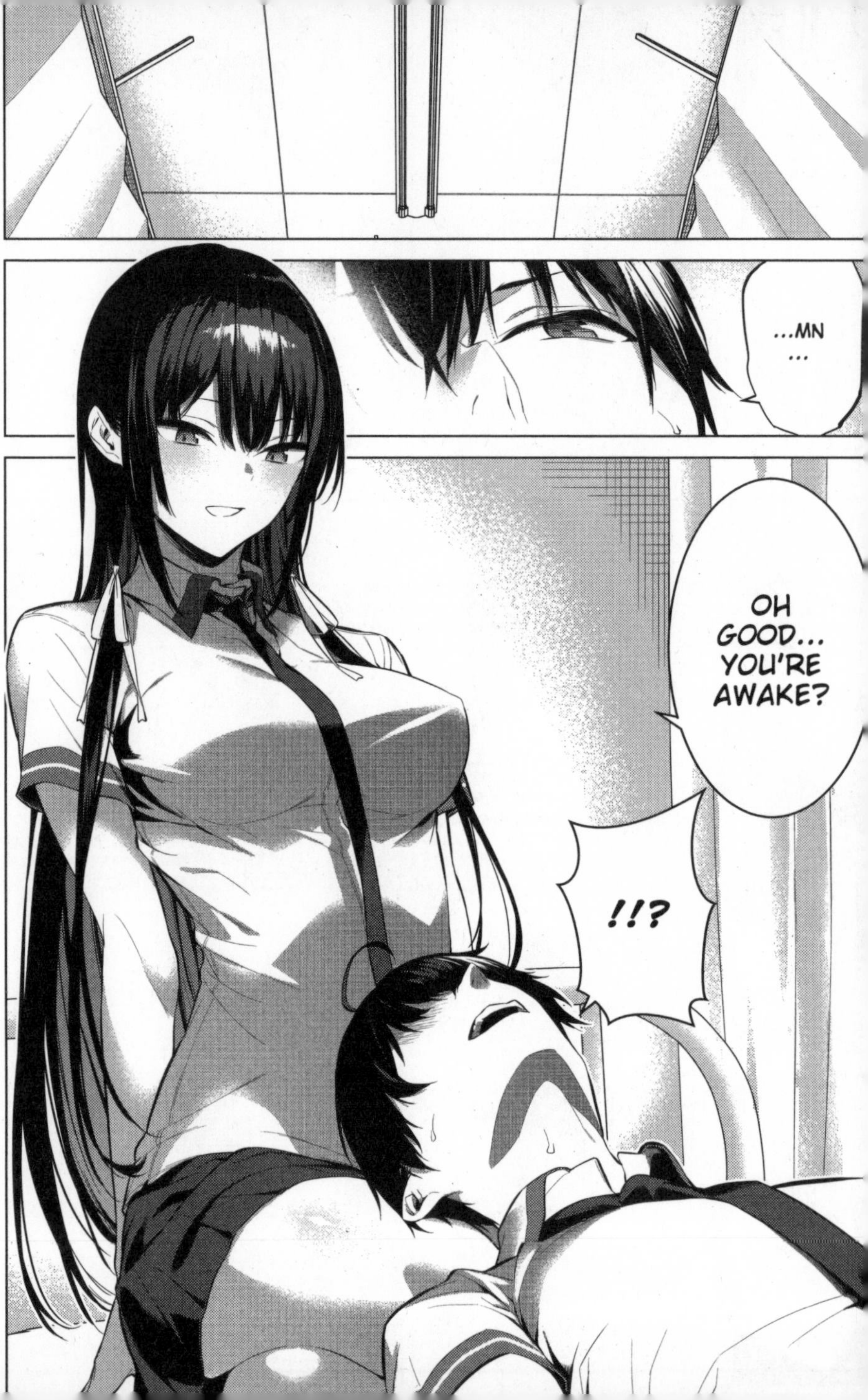
...MN
...
OH GOOD... YOU'RE AWAKE?
!!?

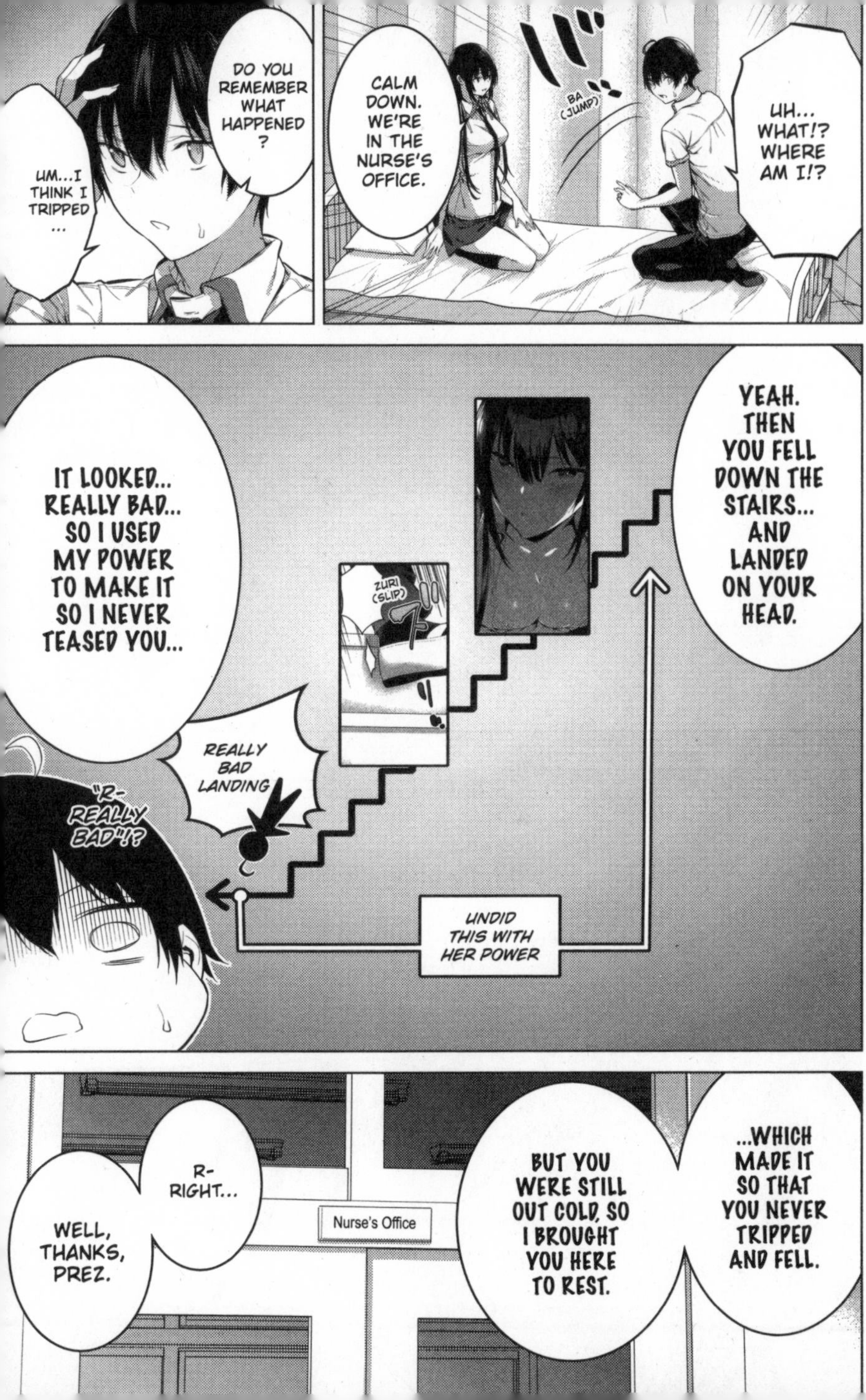

UH... WHAT!? WHERE AM I!?
BA (JUMP)
CALM DOWN. WE'RE IN THE NURSE'S OFFICE.
DO YOU REMEMBER WHAT HAPPENED?
UM...I THINK I TRIPPED...
YEAH. THEN YOU FELL DOWN THE STAIRS... AND LANDED ON YOUR HEAD.
ZURI (SLIP)
UNDID THIS WITH HER POWER
IT LOOKED... REALLY BAD... SO I USED MY POWER TO MAKE IT SO I NEVER TEASED YOU...
REALLY BAD LANDING
"R-REALLY BAD"!?
...WHICH MADE IT SO THAT YOU NEVER TRIPPED AND FELL.
BUT YOU WERE STILL OUT COLD, SO I BROUGHT YOU HERE TO REST.
Nurse's Office
R-RIGHT...
WELL, THANKS, PREZ.

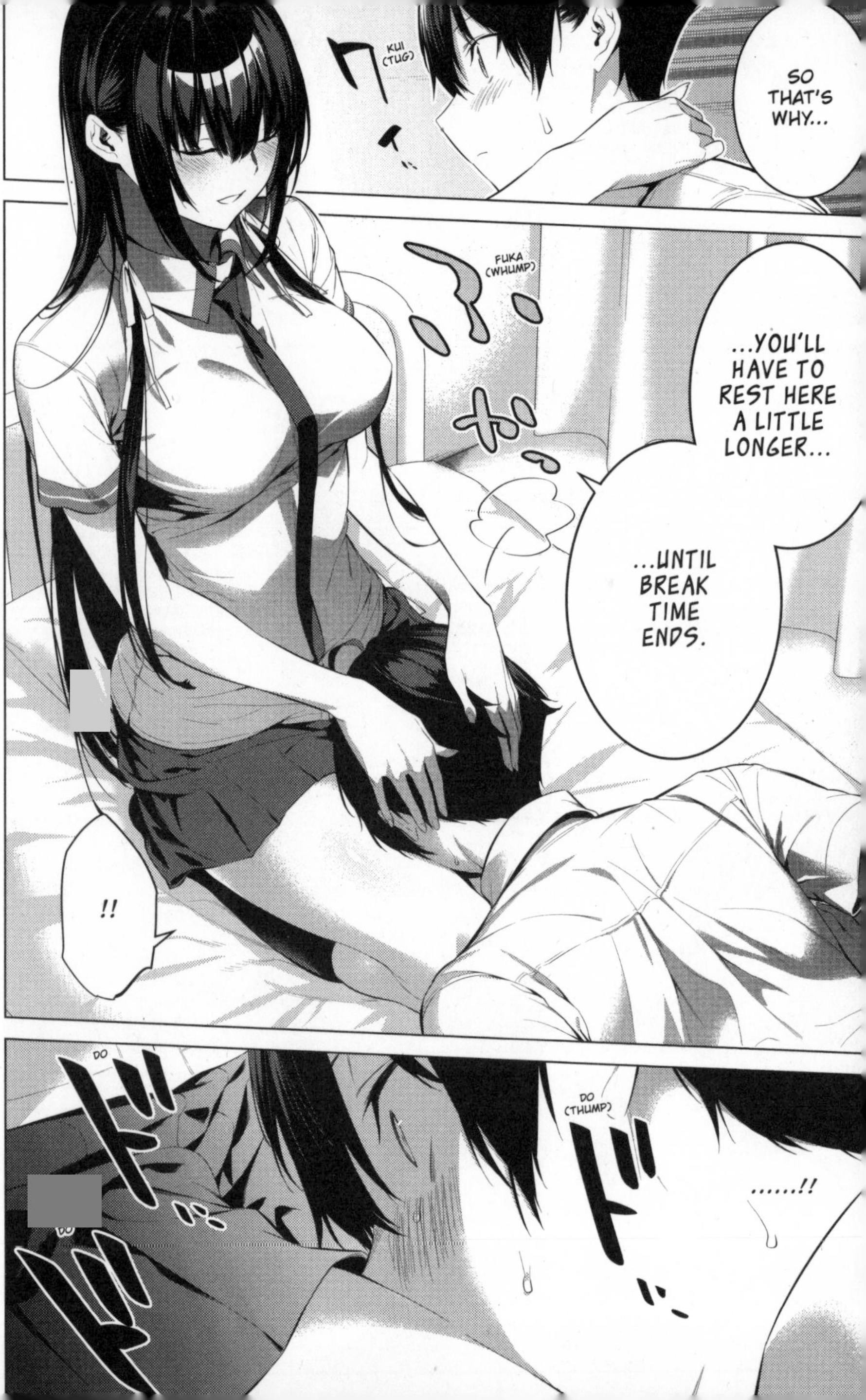
SO THAT'S WHY...
KUI (TUG)
...YOU'LL HAVE TO REST HERE A LITTLE LONGER...
...UNTIL BREAK TIME ENDS.
FUKA (WHUMP)
!!
DO (THUMP)
......!!
DO
DO

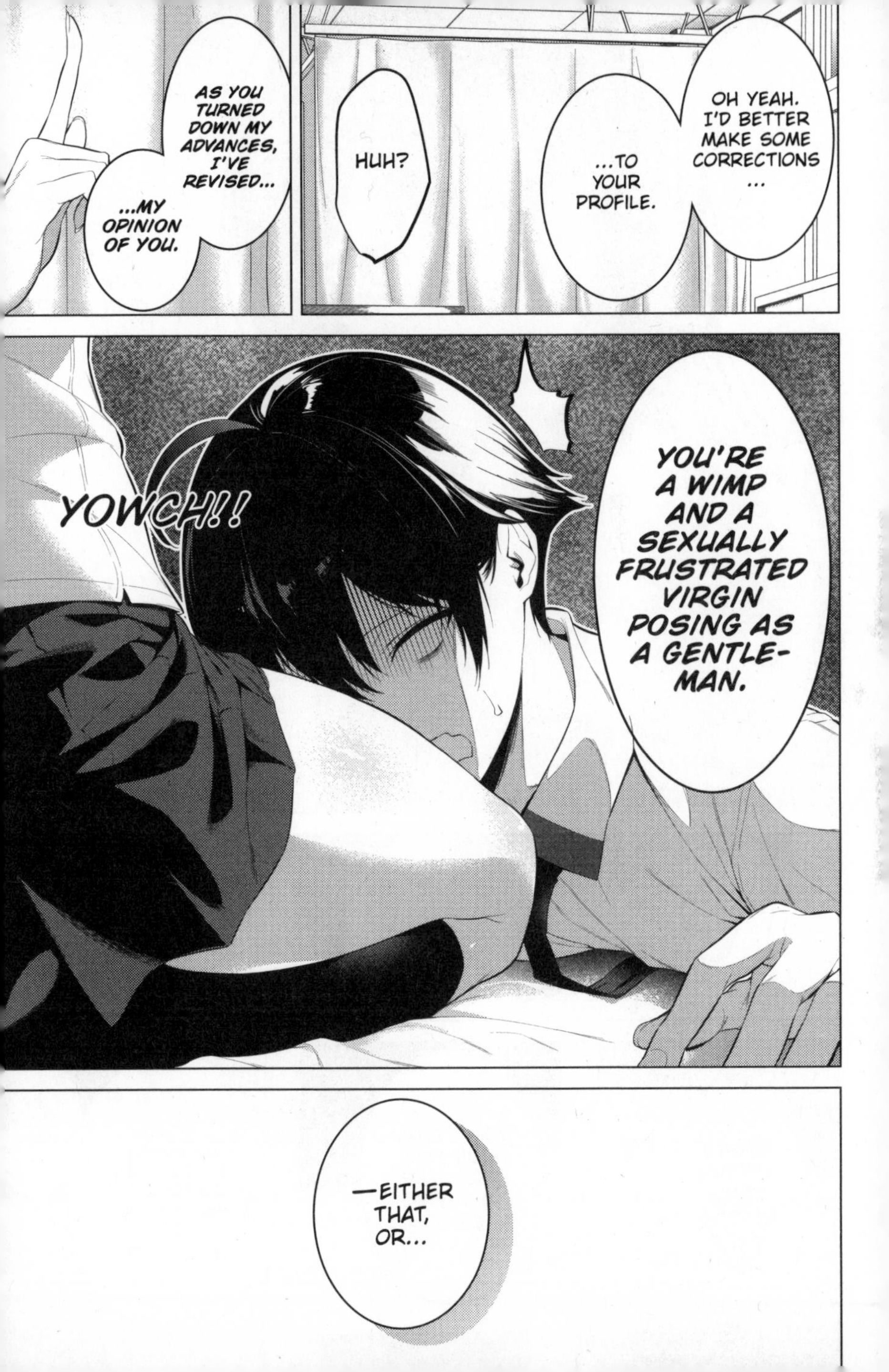

OH YEAH. I'D BETTER MAKE SOME CORRECTIONS ...
...TO YOUR PROFILE.
HUH?
AS YOU TURNED DOWN MY ADVANCES, I'VE REVISED...
...MY OPINION OF YOU.
YOU'RE A WIMP AND A SEXUALLY FRUSTRATED VIRGIN POSING AS A GENTLE-MAN.
YOWCH!!
—EITHER THAT, OR...

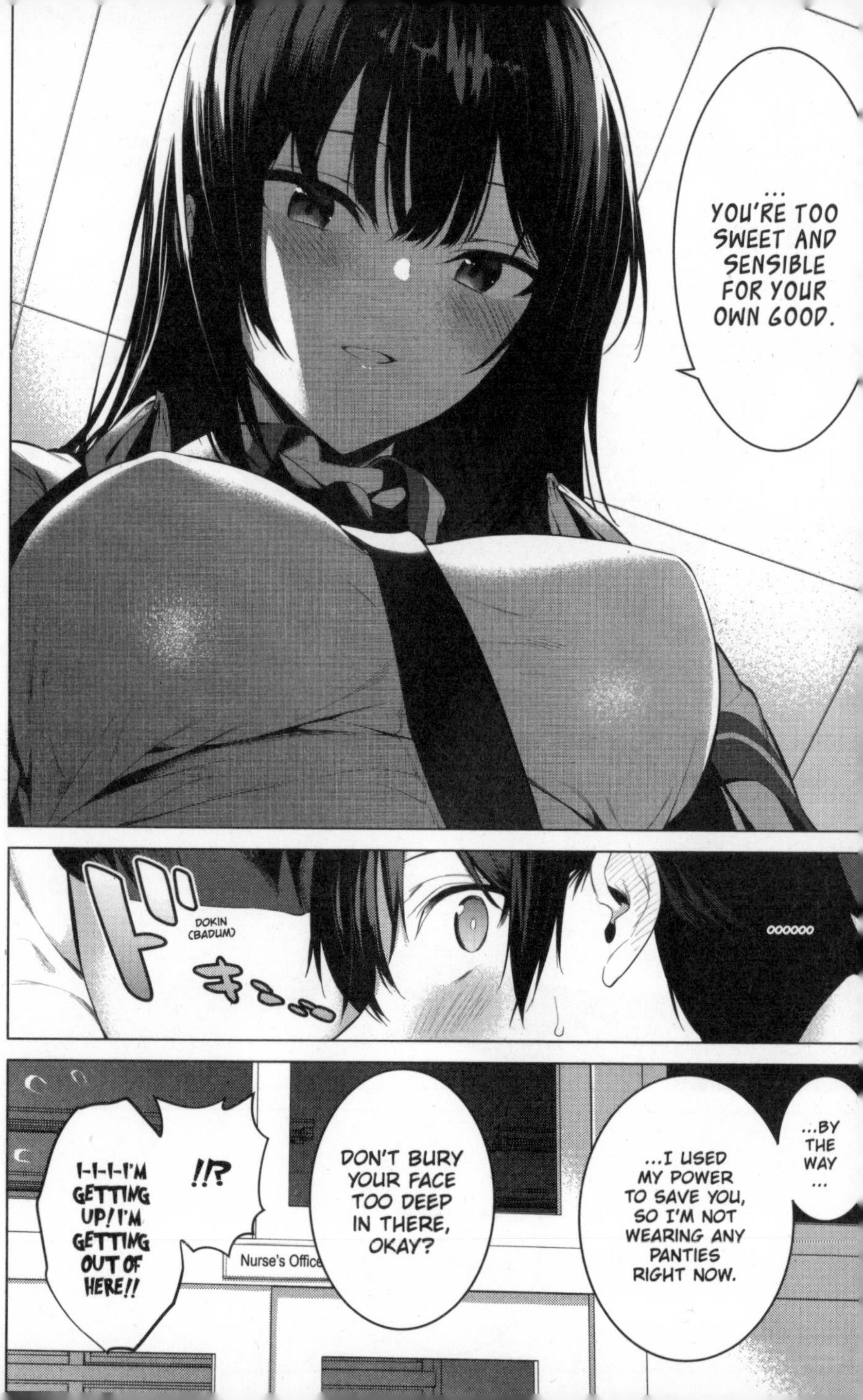
... YOU'RE TOO SWEET AND SENSIBLE FOR YOUR OWN GOOD.
oooooo
DOKIN (BADUM)
...BY THE WAY ...
...I USED MY POWER TO SAVE YOU, SO I'M NOT WEARING ANY PANTIES RIGHT NOW.
DON'T BURY YOUR FACE TOO DEEP IN THERE, OKAY?
Nurse's Office
!!?
I-I-I-I'M GETTING UP! I'M GETTING OUT OF HERE!!

Please
Put
Them On,
Takamine
♥San

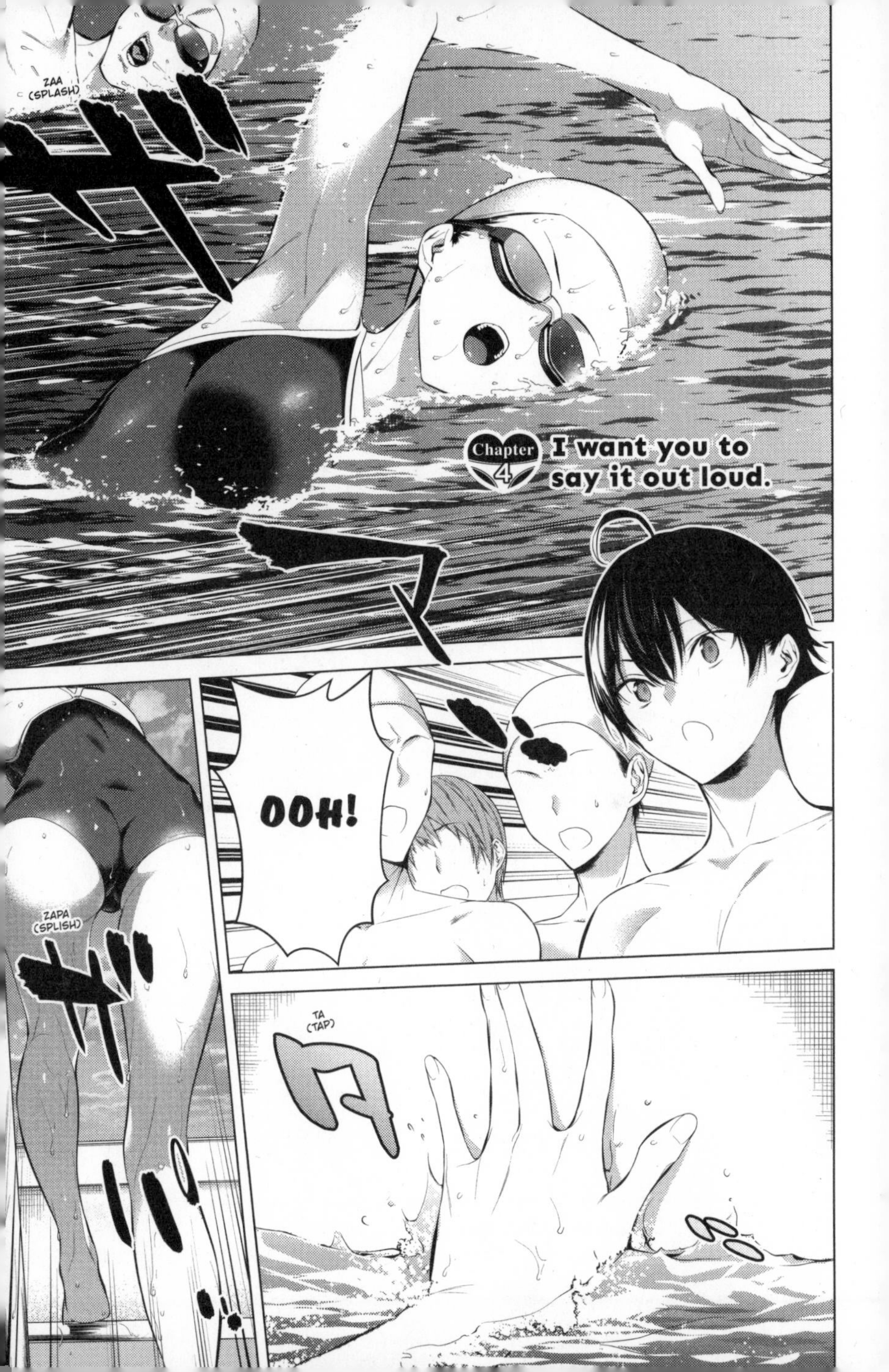
ZAA (SPLASH)
Chapter 4
I want you to say it out loud.
OOH!
TA (TAP)
ZAPA (SPLISH)

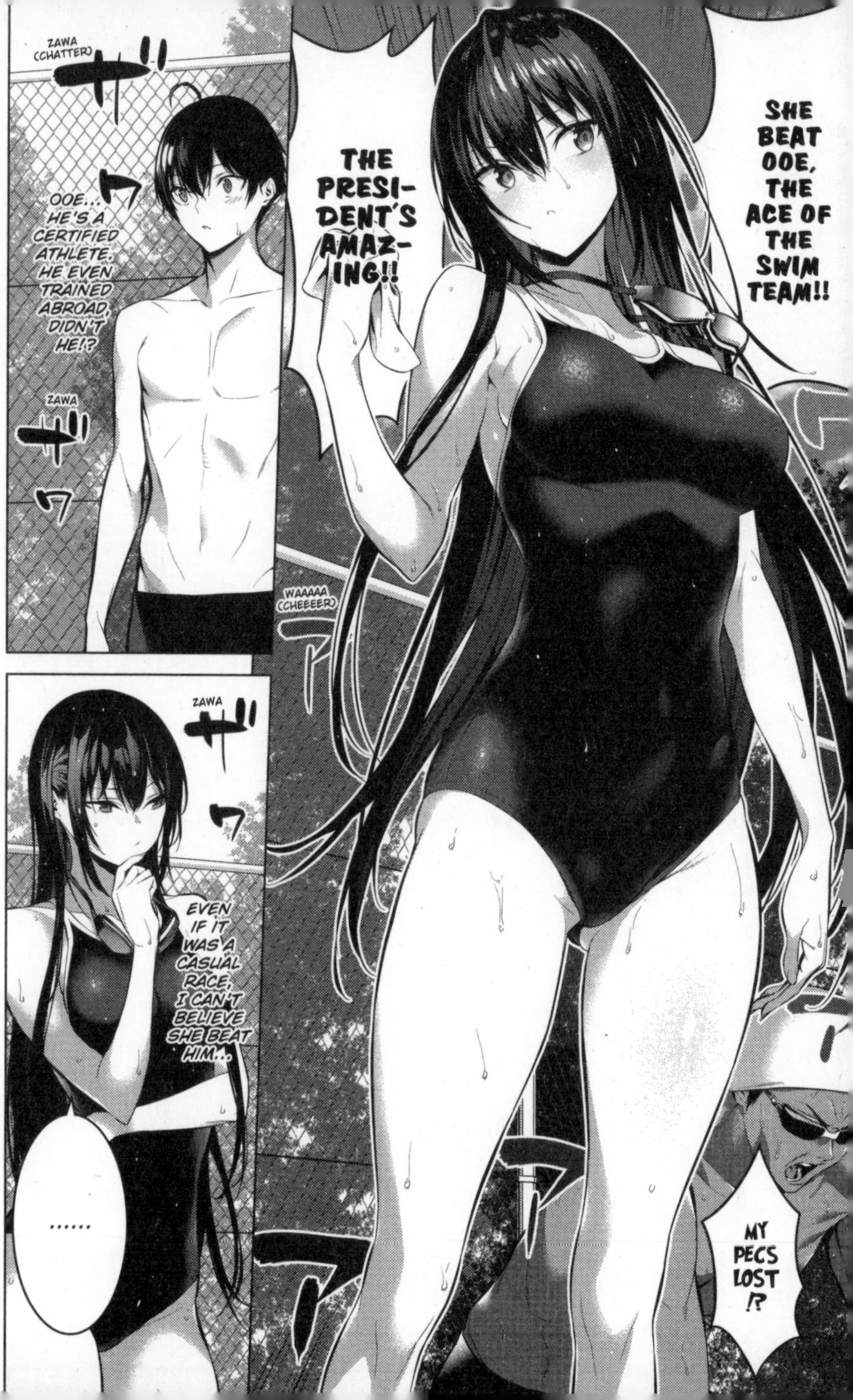
SHE BEAT OOE, THE ACE OF THE SWIM TEAM!!
THE PRESIDENT'S AMAZING!!
WAAAAA (CHEEEER)
MY PECS LOST!?
ZAWA (CHATTER)
OOE... HE'S A CERTIFIED ATHLETE. HE EVEN TRAINED ABROAD, DIDN'T HE!?
ZAWA
ZAWA
EVEN IF IT WAS A CASUAL RACE, I CAN'T BELIEVE SHE BEAT HIM...
......

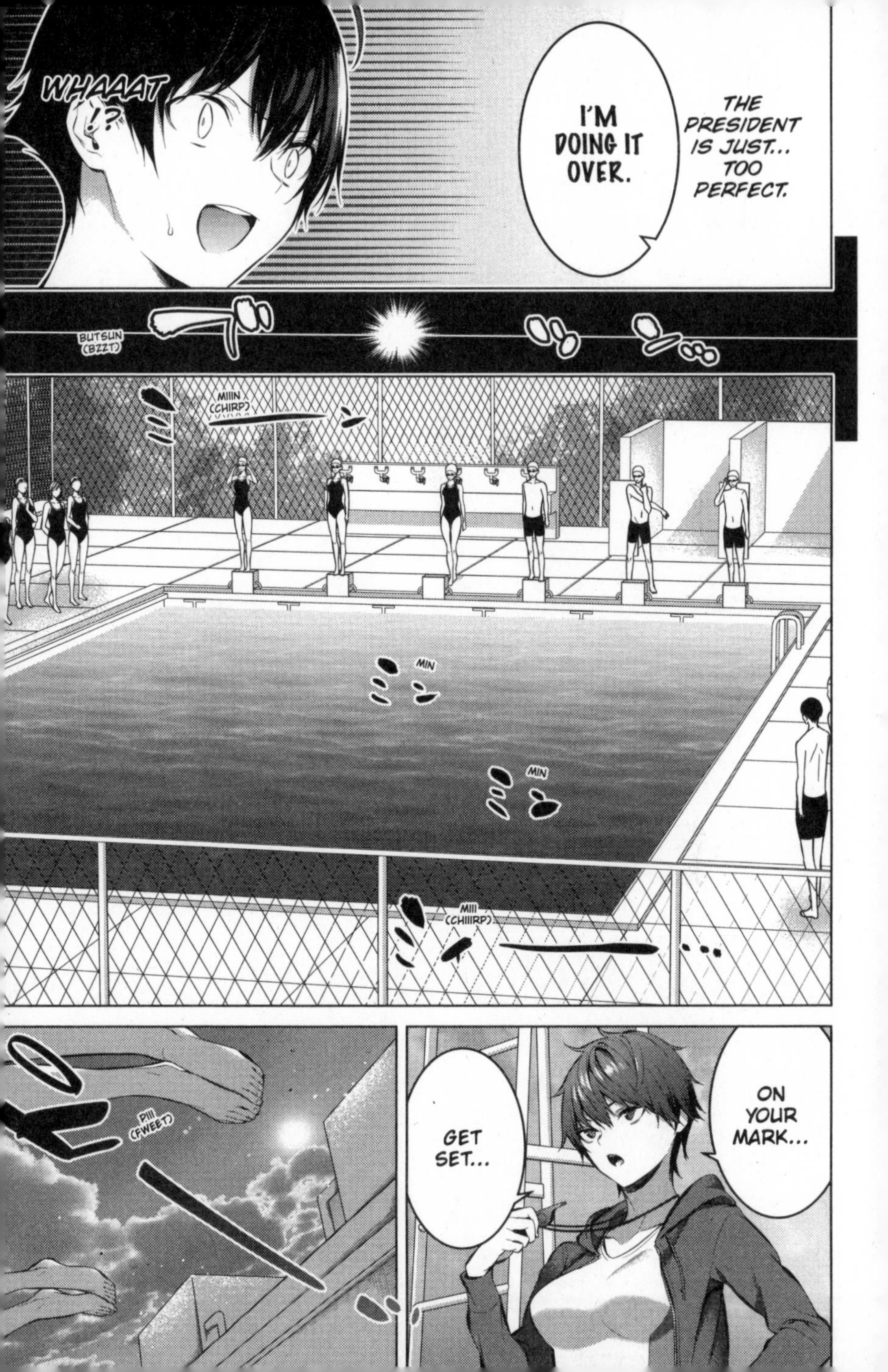
THE PRESIDENT IS JUST... TOO PERFECT.
I'M DOING IT OVER.
WHAAAT !?
BUTSUN (BZZT)
MIIIN (CHIRP)
MIN
MIN
MIII (CHIIIRP)
ON YOUR MARK...
GET SET...
PIII (FWEET)

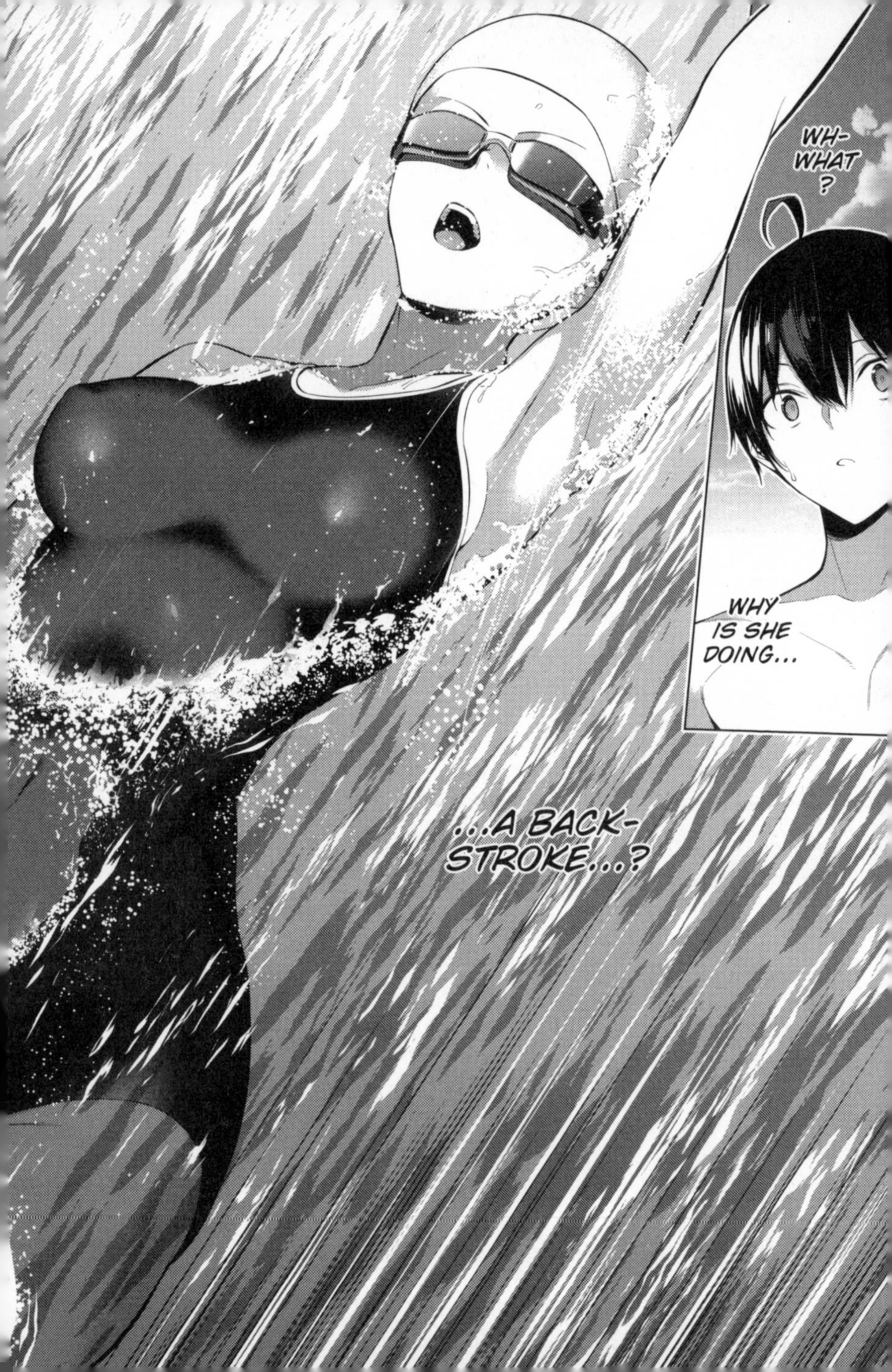
WH- WHAT?
WHY IS SHE DOING...
...A BACK-STROKE...?

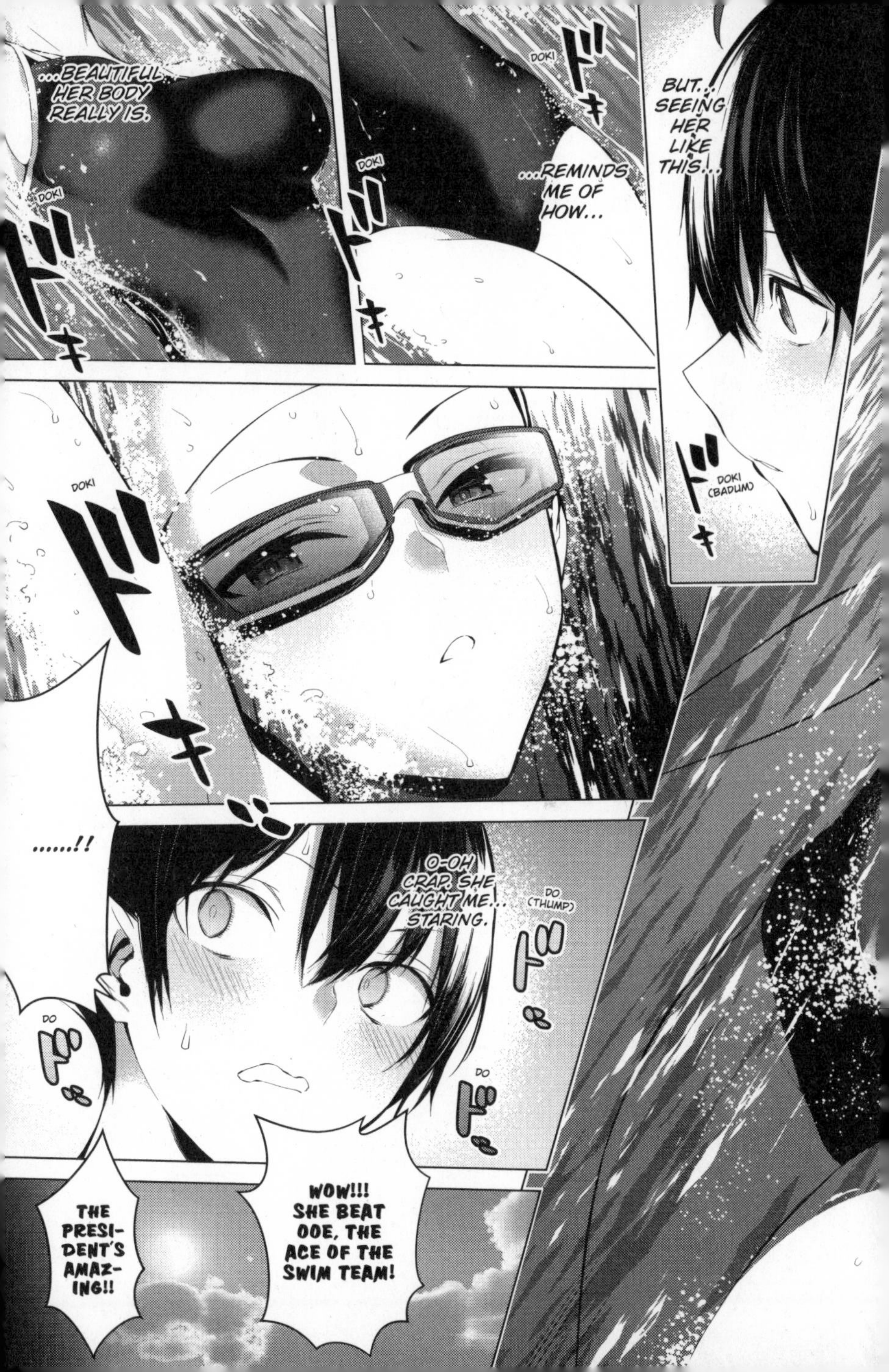
BUT... SEEING HER LIKE THIS...
DOKI (BADUM)
...REMINDS ME OF HOW...
DOKI
...BEAUTIFUL HER BODY REALLY IS.
DOKI
DOKI
DOKI
O-OH CRAP. SHE CAUGHT ME... STARING.
DO (THUMP)
......!!
DO
DO
WOW!!! SHE BEAT OOE, THE ACE OF THE SWIM TEAM!
THE PRESI-DENT'S AMAZ-ING!!

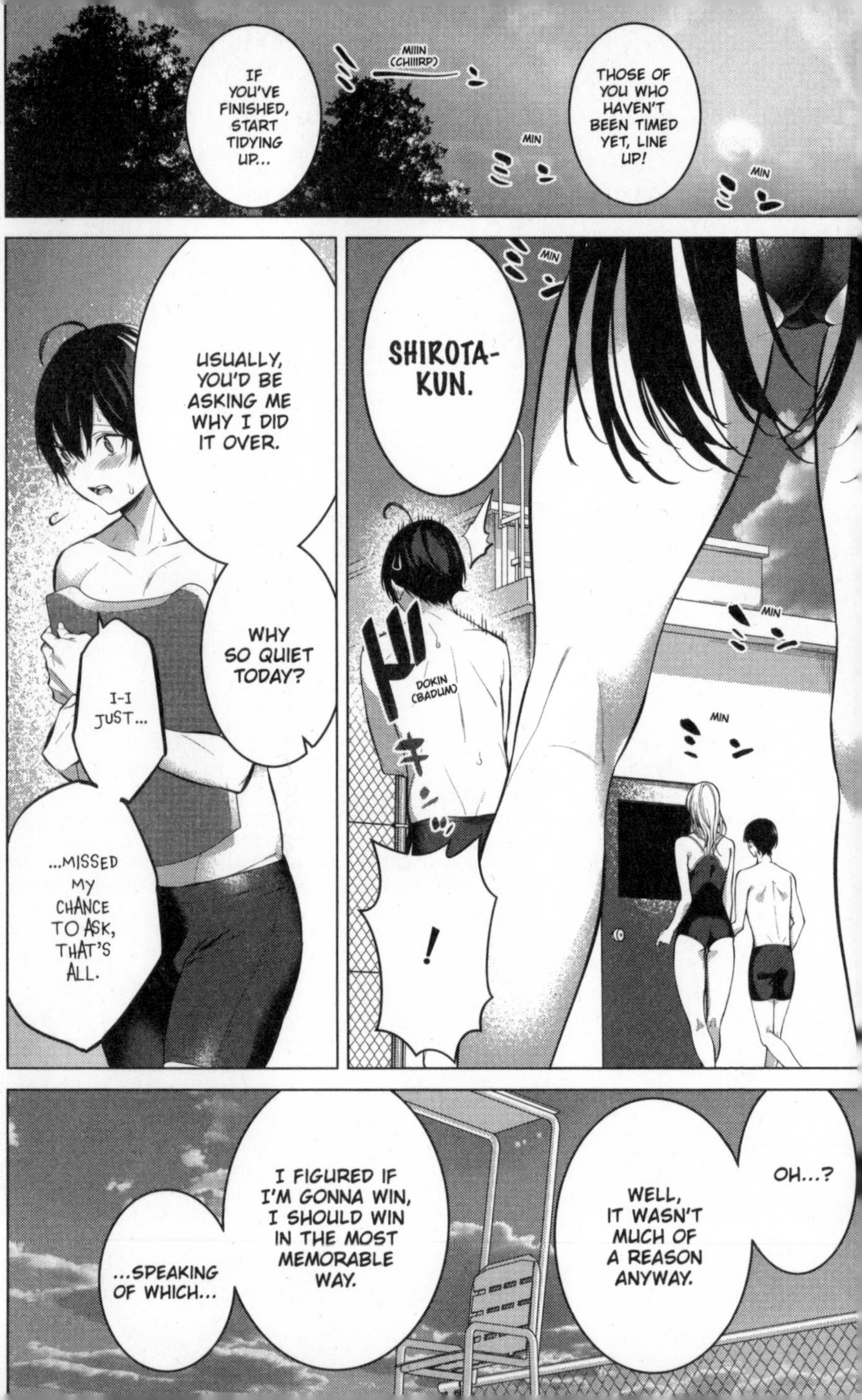
MIN
THOSE OF YOU WHO HAVEN'T BEEN TIMED YET, LINE UP!
MIN
MIIN (CHIIIRP)
IF YOU'VE FINISHED, START TIDYING UP...
MIN
SHIROTA-KUN.
MIN
MIN
DOKIN (BADUM)
!
USUALLY, YOU'D BE ASKING ME WHY I DID IT OVER.
WHY SO QUIET TODAY?
I-I JUST...
...MISSED MY CHANCE TO ASK, THAT'S ALL.
OH...?
WELL, IT WASN'T MUCH OF A REASON ANYWAY.
I FIGURED IF I'M GONNA WIN, I SHOULD WIN IN THE MOST MEMORABLE WAY.
...SPEAKING OF WHICH...

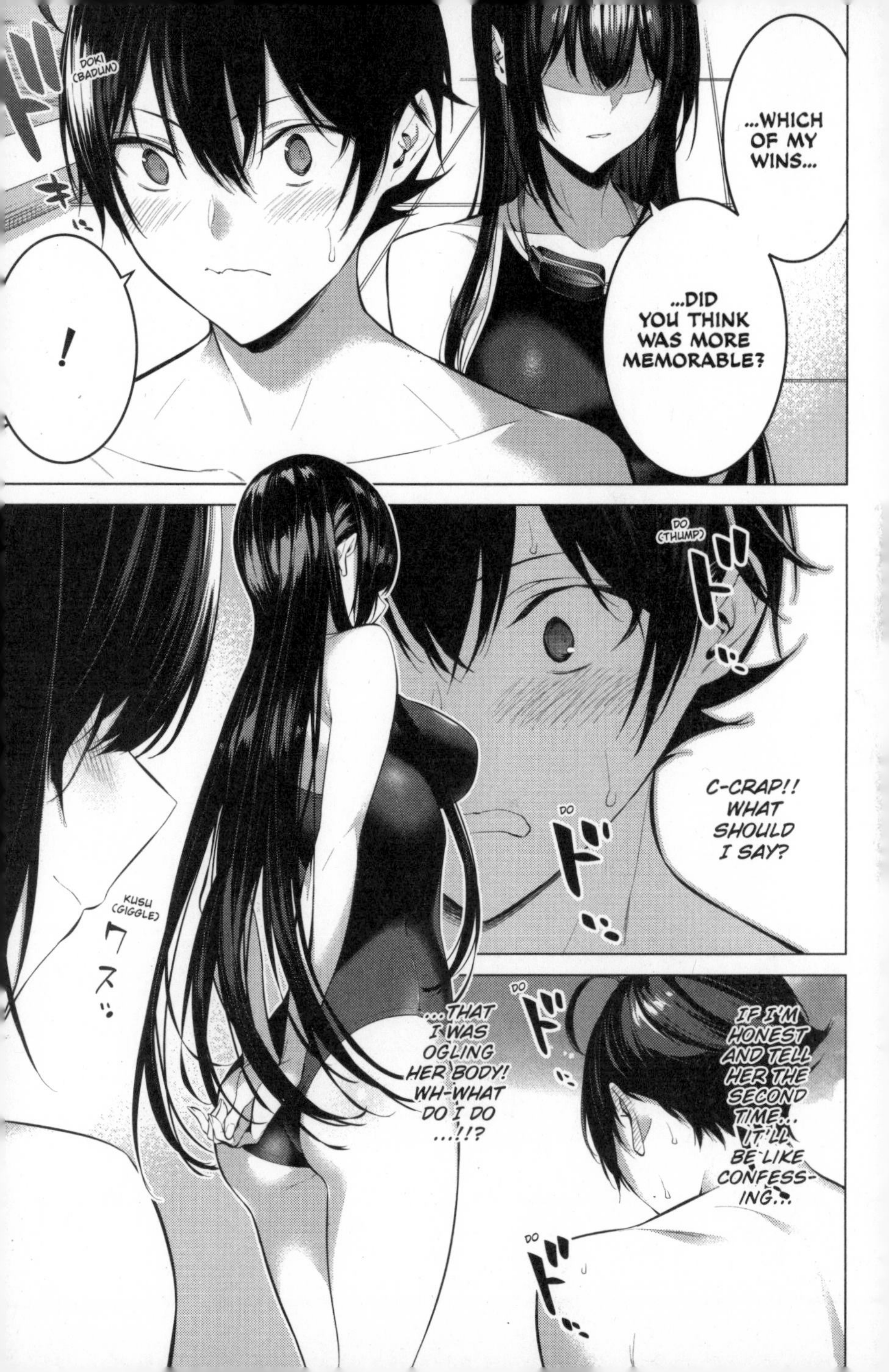
...WHICH OF MY WINS...
...DID YOU THINK WAS MORE MEMORABLE?
DOKI (BADUM)
!
DO (THUMP)
C-CRAP!! WHAT SHOULD I SAY?
DO
IF I'M HONEST AND TELL HER THE SECOND TIME... IT'LL BE LIKE CONFESSING...
...THAT I WAS OGLING HER BODY! WH-WHAT DO I DO ...!!?
DO
DO
KUSU (GIGGLE)

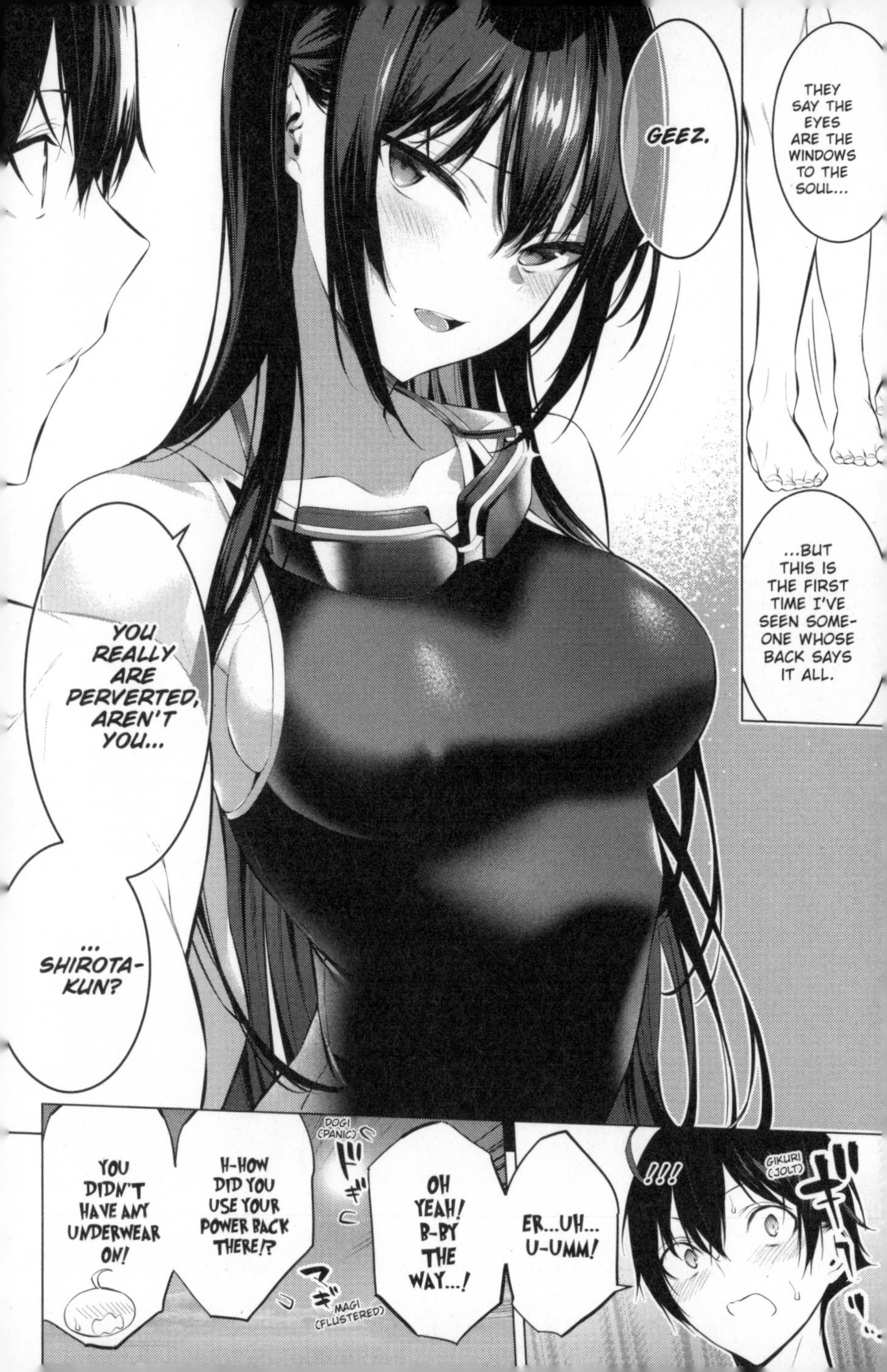
THEY SAY THE EYES ARE THE WINDOWS TO THE SOUL...
...BUT THIS IS THE FIRST TIME I'VE SEEN SOME-ONE WHOSE BACK SAYS IT ALL.
GEEZ.
YOU REALLY ARE PERVERTED, AREN'T YOU...
...SHIROTA-KUN?
GIKURI (JOLT)
!!!
ER...UH... U-UMM!
OH YEAH! B-BY THE WAY...!
DOGI (PANIC)
H-HOW DID YOU USE YOUR POWER BACK THERE!?
MAGI (FLUSTERED)
YOU DIDN'T HAVE ANY UNDERWEAR ON!

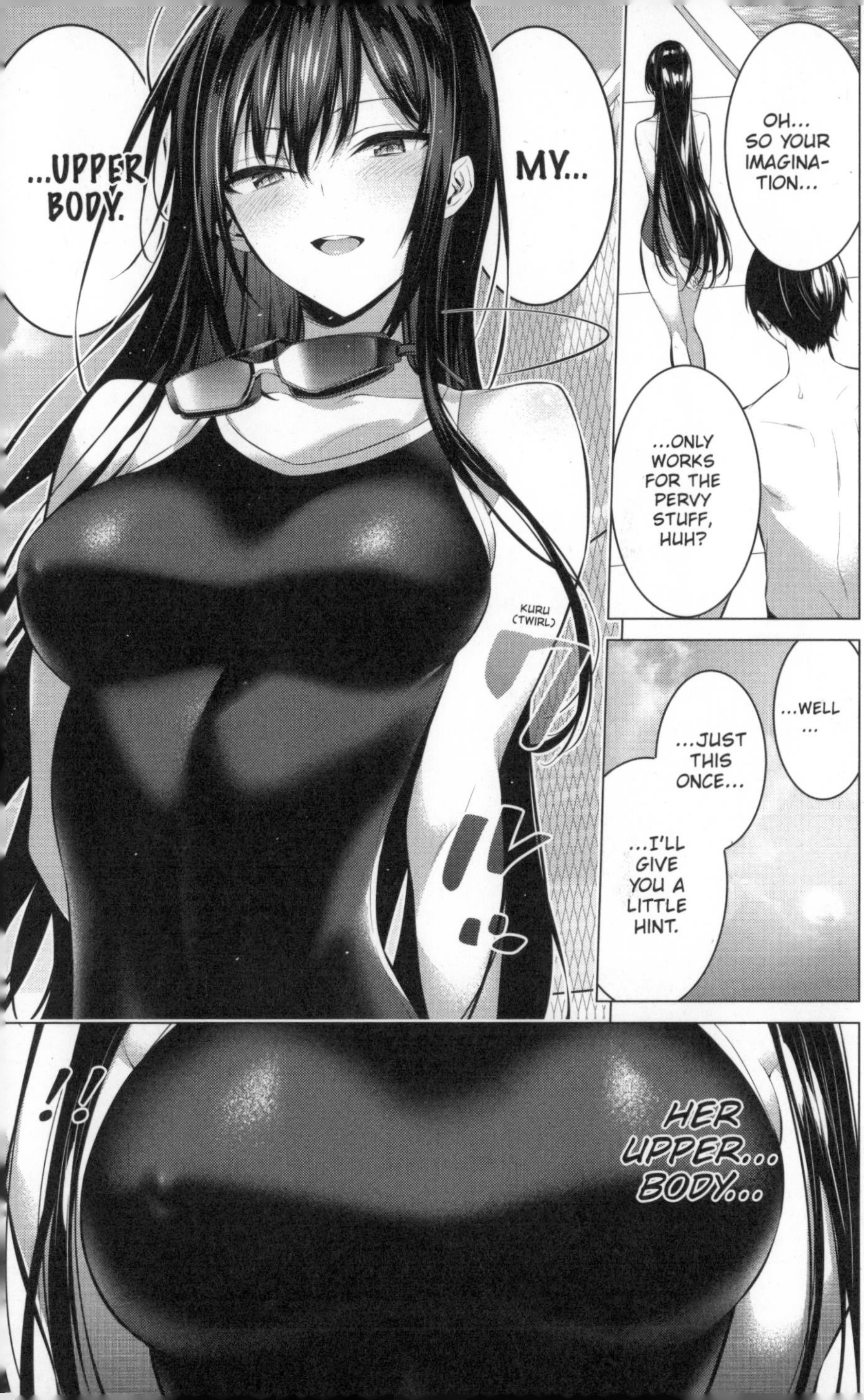
OH... SO YOUR IMAGINATION...
...ONLY WORKS FOR THE PERVY STUFF, HUH?
...WELL...
...JUST THIS ONCE...
...I'LL GIVE YOU A LITTLE HINT.
MY...
...UPPER BODY.
KURU (TWIRL)
!!
HER UPPER... BODY...

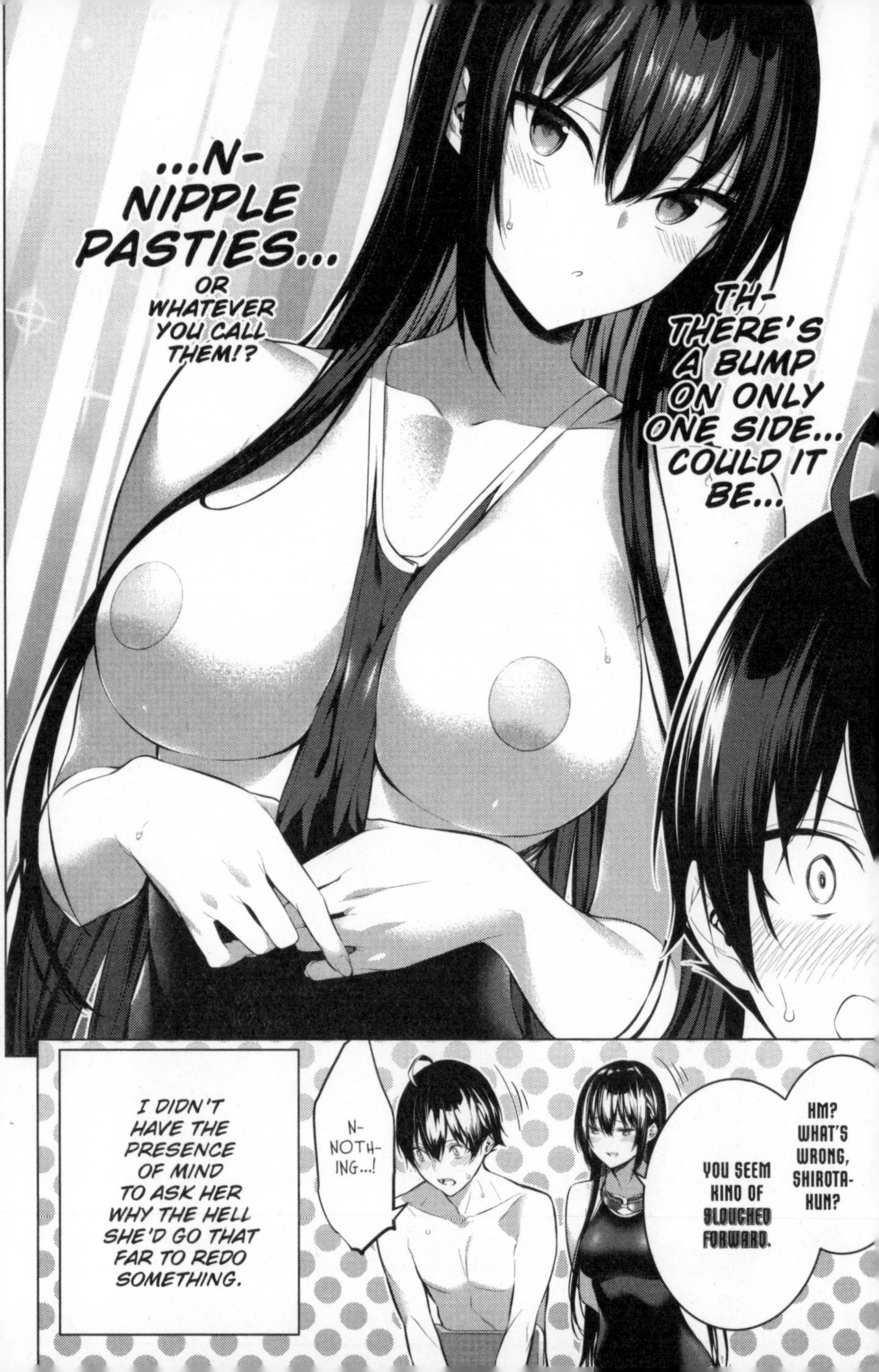
TH-THERE'S A BUMP ON ONLY ONE SIDE... COULD IT BE...
...N-NIPPLE PASTIES...
OR WHATEVER YOU CALL THEM!?
HM? WHAT'S WRONG, SHIROTA-KUN?
YOU SEEM KIND OF SLOUCHED FORWARD.
N-NOTHING...!
I DIDN'T HAVE THE PRESENCE OF MIND TO ASK HER WHY THE HELL SHE'D GO THAT FAR TO REDO SOMETHING.

Please
Put
Them On,
Takamine
♥San

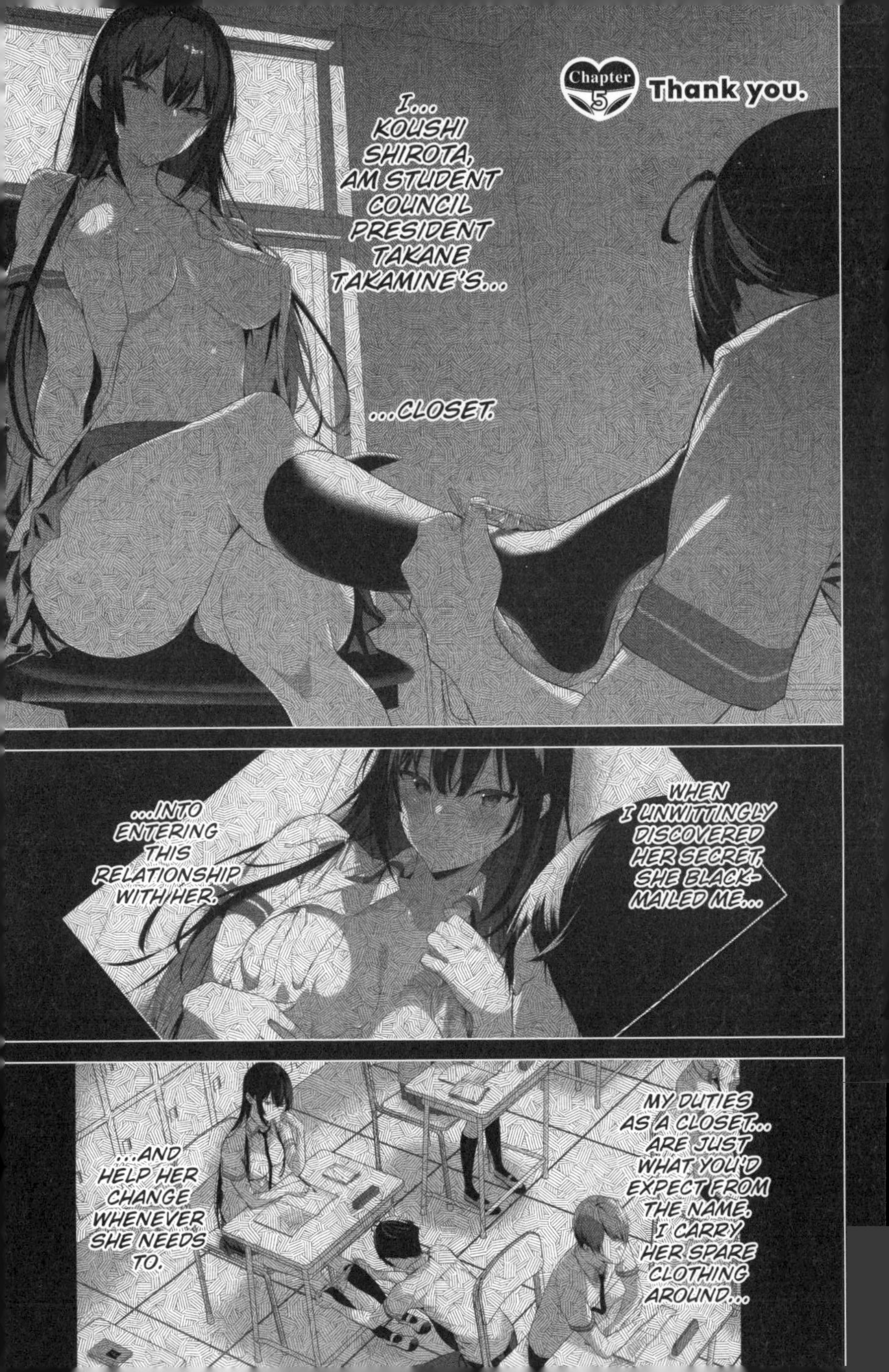
Chapter 5 Thank you.
I... KOUSHI SHIROTA, AM STUDENT COUNCIL PRESIDENT TAKANE TAKAMINE'S...
...CLOSET.
WHEN I UNWITTINGLY DISCOVERED HER SECRET, SHE BLACK-MAILED ME...
...INTO ENTERING THIS RELATIONSHIP WITH HER.
MY DUTIES AS A CLOSET... ARE JUST WHAT YOU'D EXPECT FROM THE NAME. I CARRY HER SPARE CLOTHING AROUND...
...AND HELP HER CHANGE WHENEVER SHE NEEDS TO.

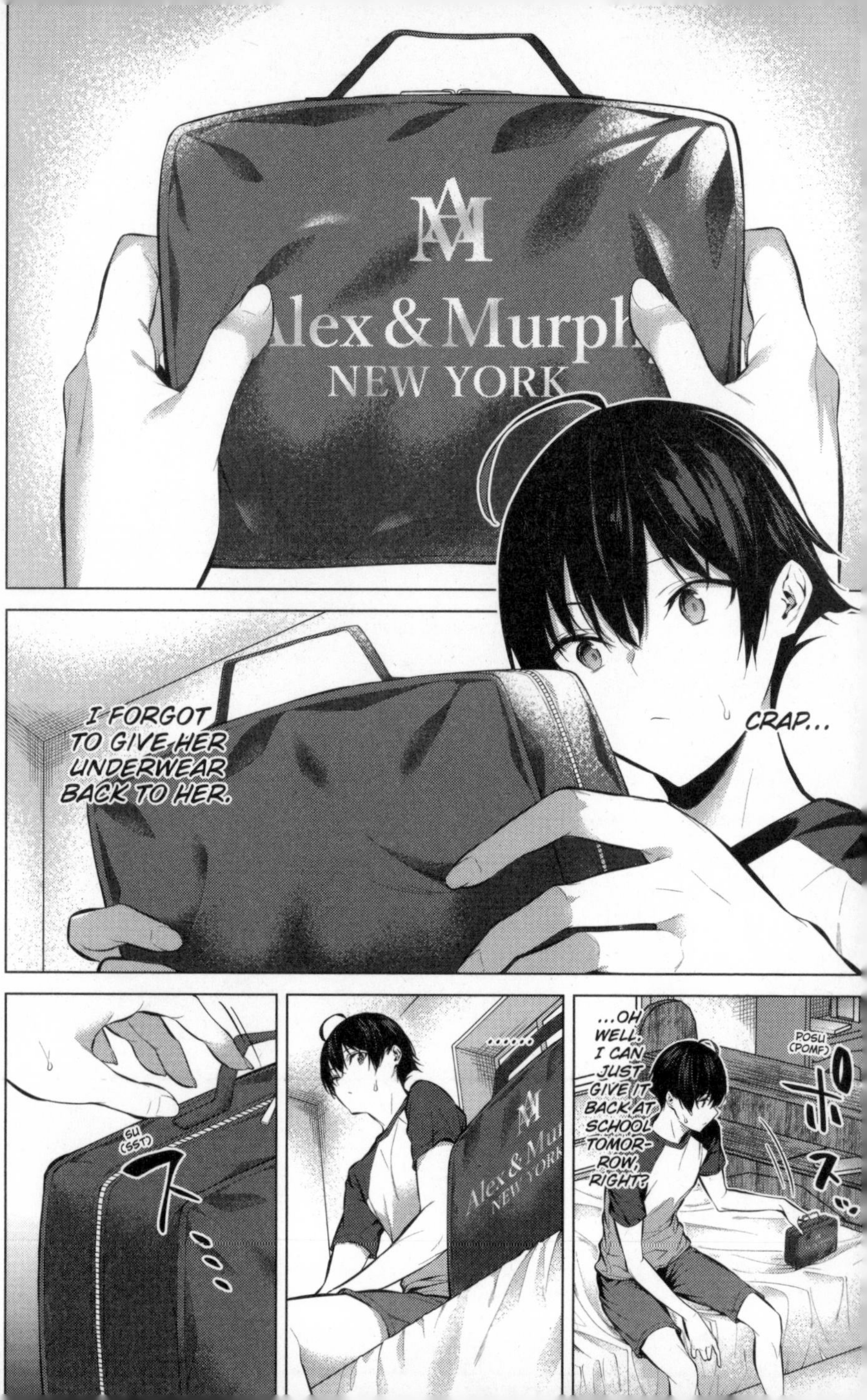
NEW YORK
CRAP...
I FORGOT TO GIVE HER UNDERWEAR BACK TO HER.
...OH WELL, I CAN JUST GIVE IT BACK AT SCHOOL TOMOR-ROW, RIGHT?
POSU (POMF)
ポスッ
......
SU (SST)
ス…

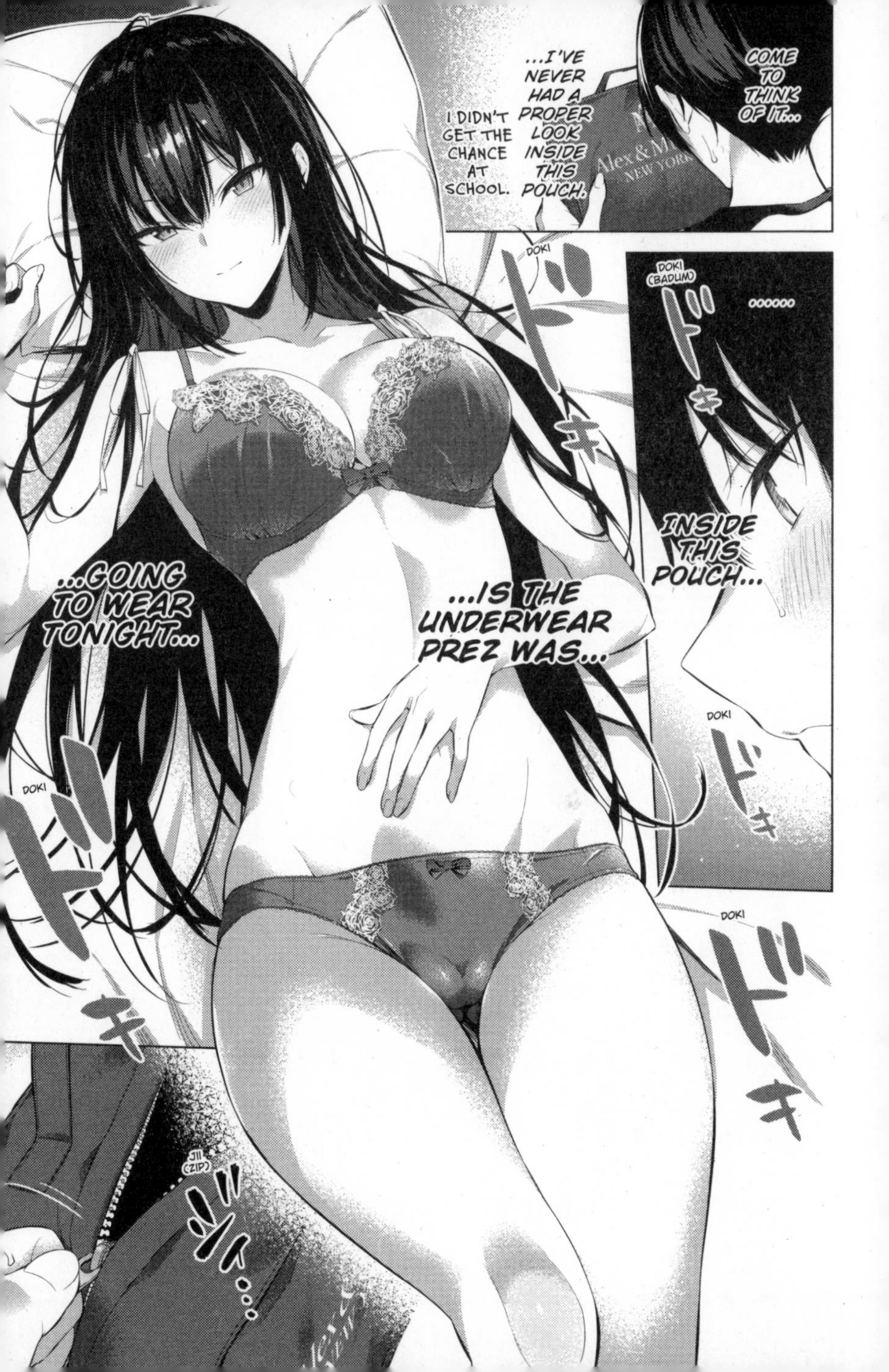
COME TO THINK OF IT...
...I'VE NEVER HAD A PROPER LOOK INSIDE THIS POUCH.
I DIDN'T GET THE CHANCE AT SCHOOL.
DOKI
DOKI (BADUM)
......
INSIDE THIS POUCH...
DOKI
...IS THE UNDERWEAR PREZ WAS...
...GOING TO WEAR TONIGHT...
DOKI
DOKI
JII (ZIP)

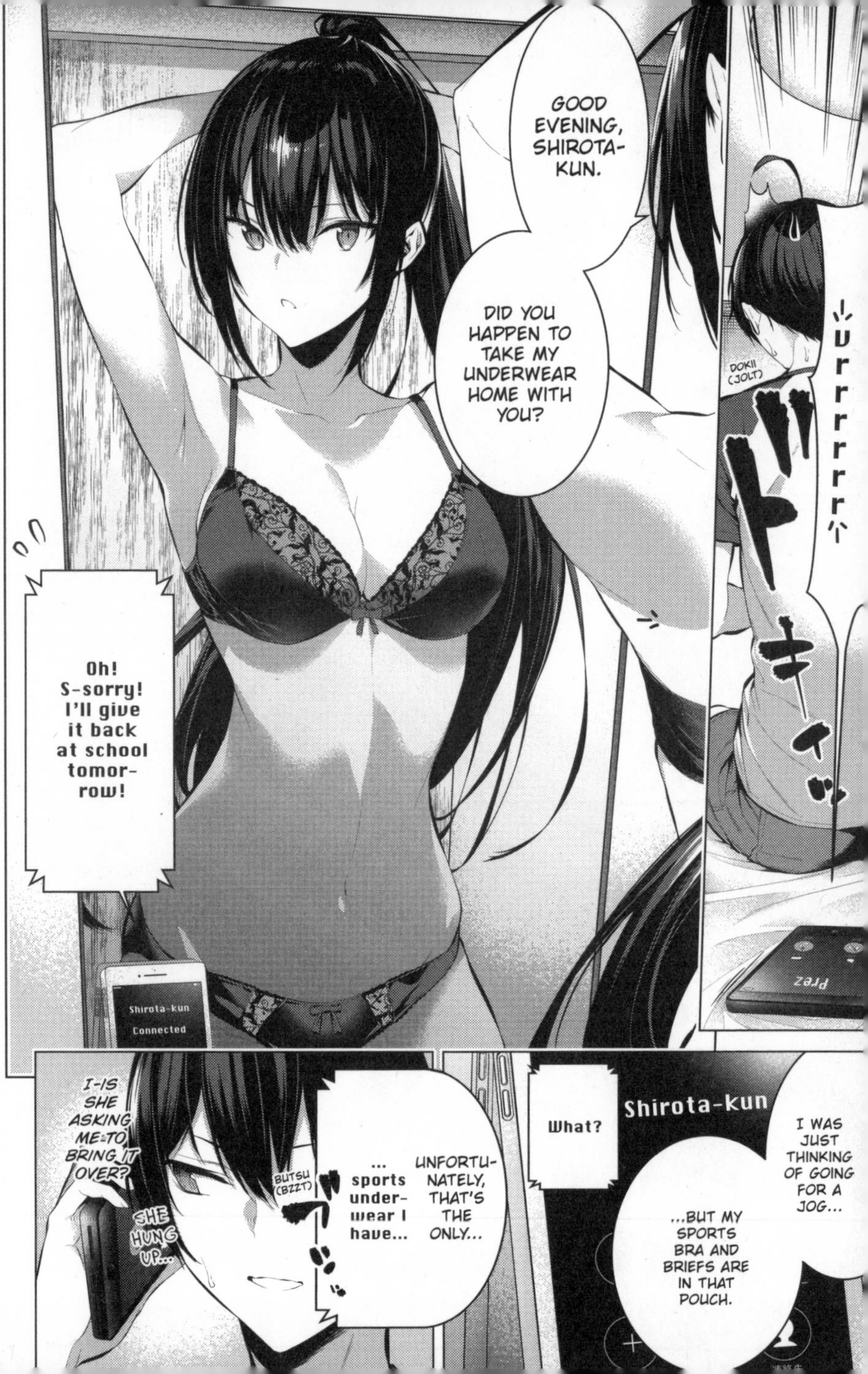
Vrrrrrrr
DOKII (JOLT)
Prez
GOOD EVENING, SHIROTA-KUN.
DID YOU HAPPEN TO TAKE MY UNDERWEAR HOME WITH YOU?
Oh! S-sorry! I'll give it back at school tomor-row!
Shirota-kun
Connected
I WAS JUST THINKING OF GOING FOR A JOG...
Shirota-kun
What?
...BUT MY SPORTS BRA AND BRIEFS ARE IN THAT POUCH.
UNFORTU-NATELY, THAT'S THE ONLY...
... sports under-wear I have...
BUTSU (BZZT)
I-IS SHE ASKING ME TO BRING IT OVER?
SHE HUNG UP...

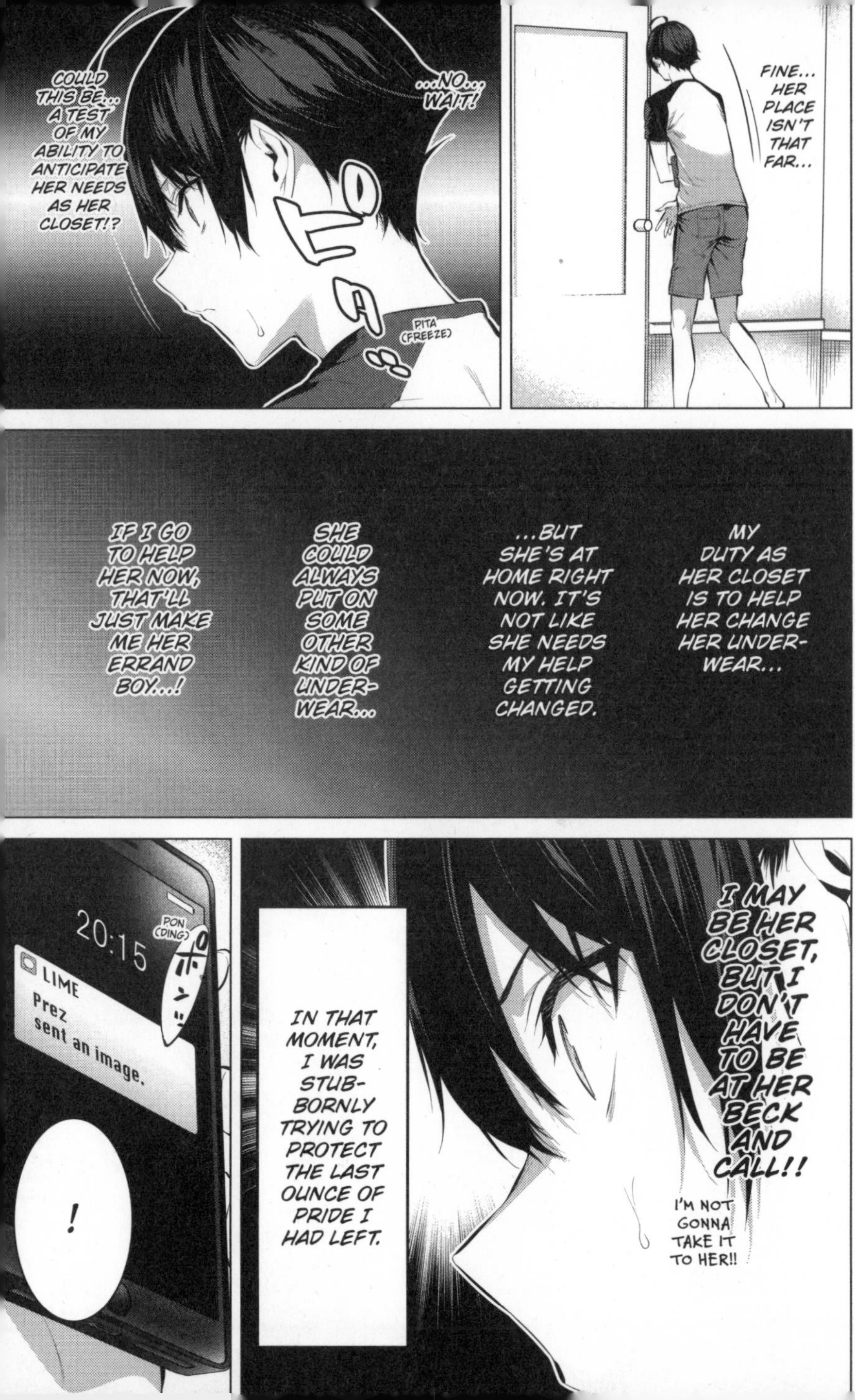
FINE... HER PLACE ISN'T THAT FAR...
...NO... WAIT!
COULD THIS BE... A TEST OF MY ABILITY TO ANTICIPATE HER NEEDS AS HER CLOSET!?
PITA (FREEZE)
MY DUTY AS HER CLOSET IS TO HELP HER CHANGE HER UNDER-WEAR...
...BUT SHE'S AT HOME RIGHT NOW. IT'S NOT LIKE SHE NEEDS MY HELP GETTING CHANGED.
SHE COULD ALWAYS PUT ON SOME OTHER KIND OF UNDER-WEAR...
IF I GO TO HELP HER NOW, THAT'LL JUST MAKE ME HER ERRAND BOY...!
I MAY BE HER CLOSET, BUT I DON'T HAVE TO BE AT HER BECK AND CALL!!
I'M NOT GONNA TAKE IT TO HER!!
IN THAT MOMENT, I WAS STUB-BORNLY TRYING TO PROTECT THE LAST OUNCE OF PRIDE I HAD LEFT.
PON (DING)
20:15
LIME
Prez sent an image.
!

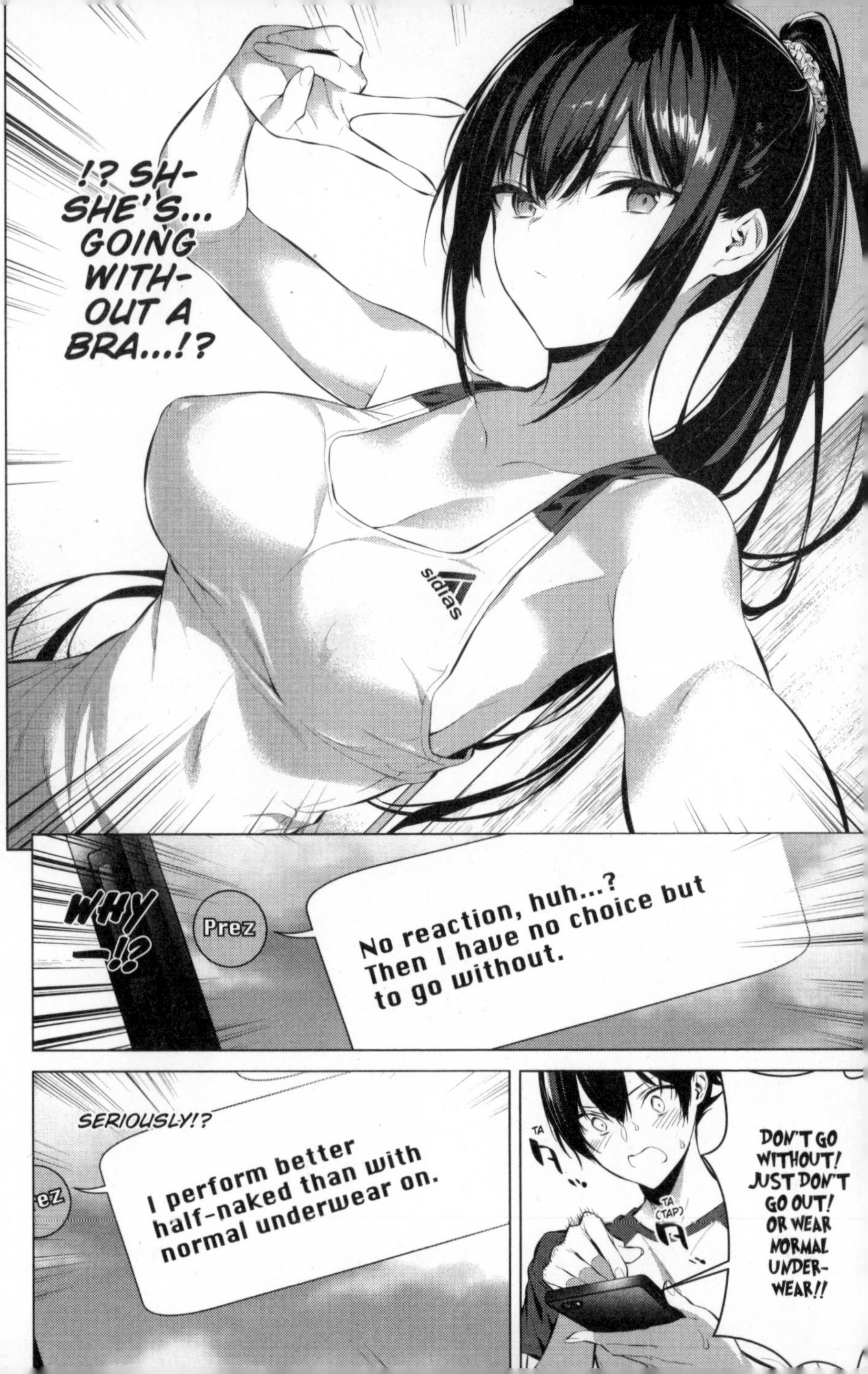
!? SH-SHE'S... GOING WITHOUT A BRA...!?
sidias
Prez
No reaction, huh...? Then I have no choice but to go without.
WHY—!?
TA
TA (TAP)
DON'T GO WITHOUT! JUST DON'T GO OUT! OR WEAR NORMAL UNDERWEAR!!
SERIOUSLY!?
I perform better half-naked than with normal underwear on.

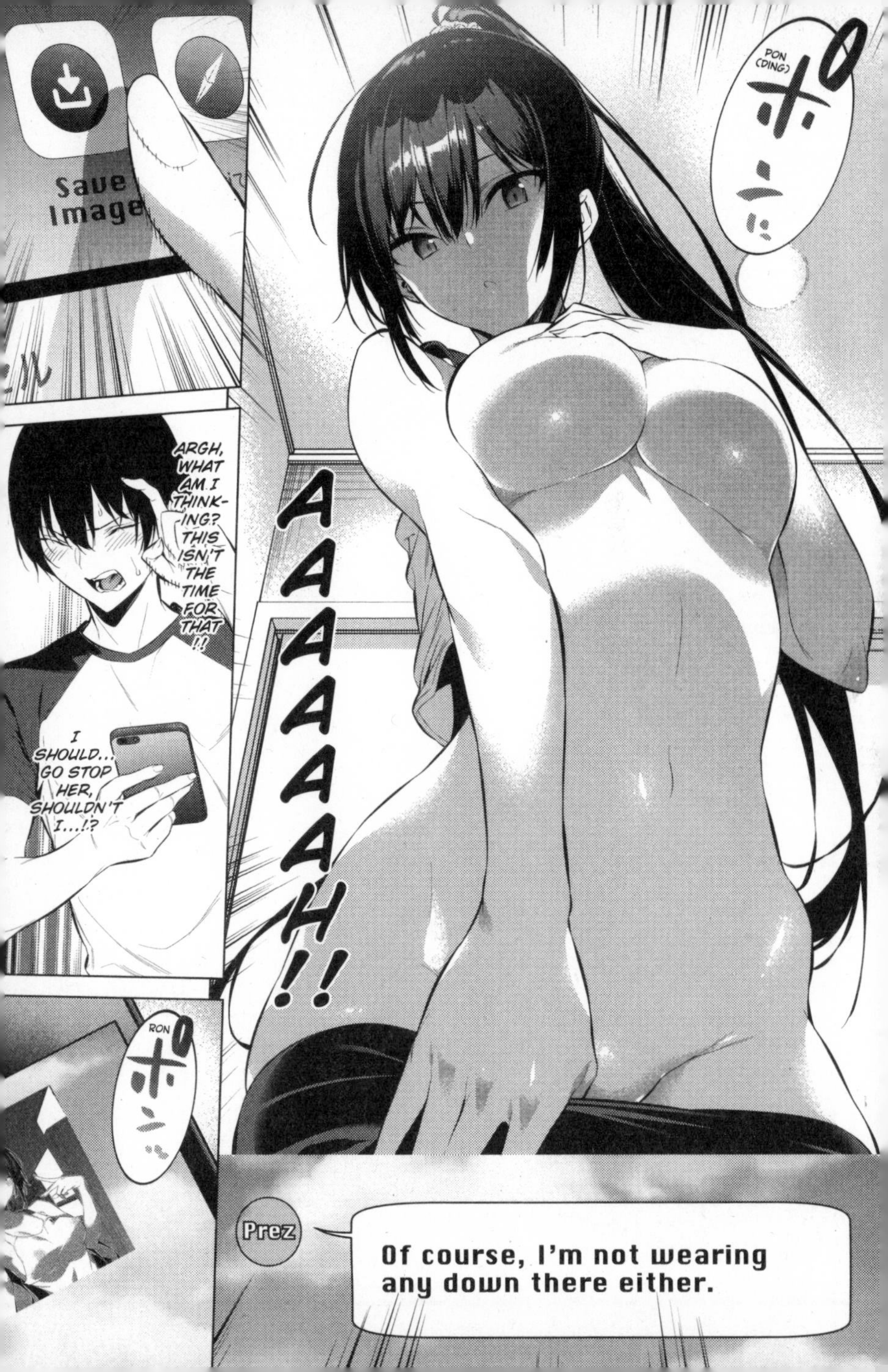
PON (DING)
AAAAAAAH!!
Prez
Of course, I'm not wearing any down there either.
Save Image
ARGH, WHAT AM I THINKING? THIS ISN'T THE TIME FOR THAT!!
I SHOULD... GO STOP HER, SHOULDN'T I...!?
RON

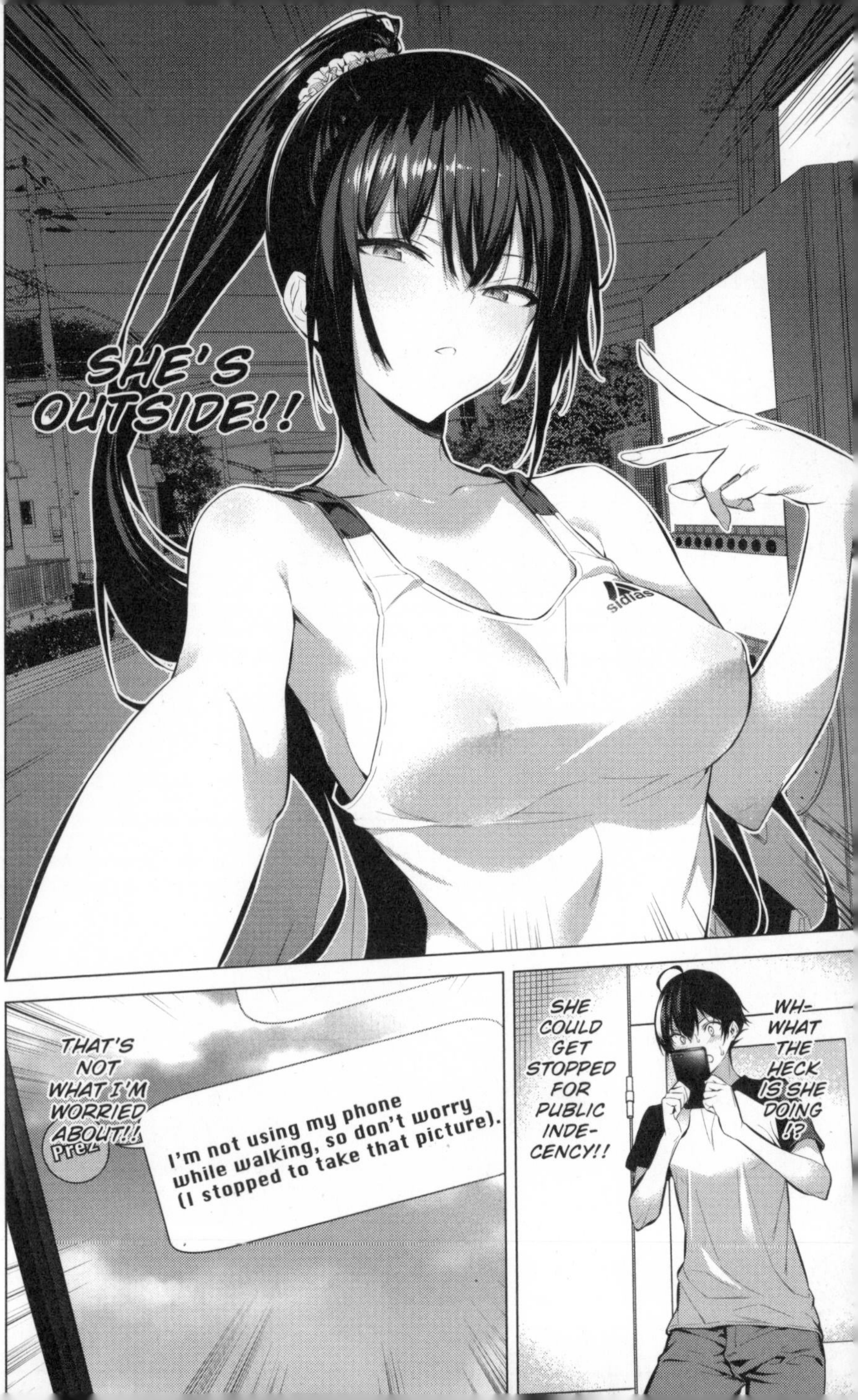
SHE'S OUTSIDE!!
sidias
WH- WHAT THE HECK IS SHE DOING!?
SHE COULD GET STOPPED FOR PUBLIC INDE-CENCY!!
Prez
I'm not using my phone while walking, so don't worry (I stopped to take that picture).
THAT'S NOT WHAT I'M WORRIED ABOUT!!

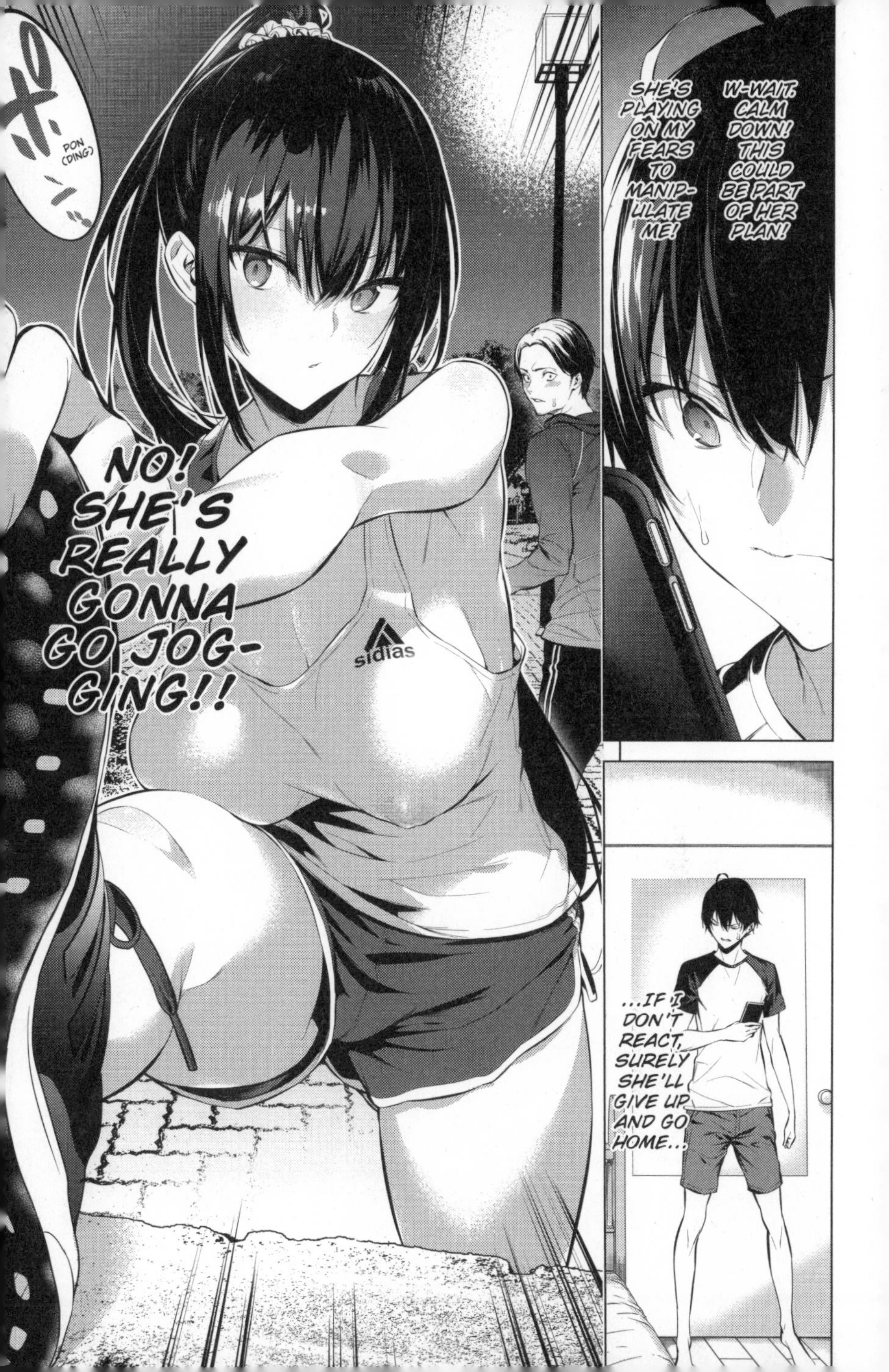
W-WAIT. CALM DOWN! THIS COULD BE PART OF HER PLAN!
SHE'S PLAYING ON MY FEARS TO MANIP-ULATE ME!
...IF I DON'T REACT, SURELY SHE'LL GIVE UP AND GO HOME...
PON (DING)
NO! SHE'S REALLY GONNA GO JOG-GING!!
sidias

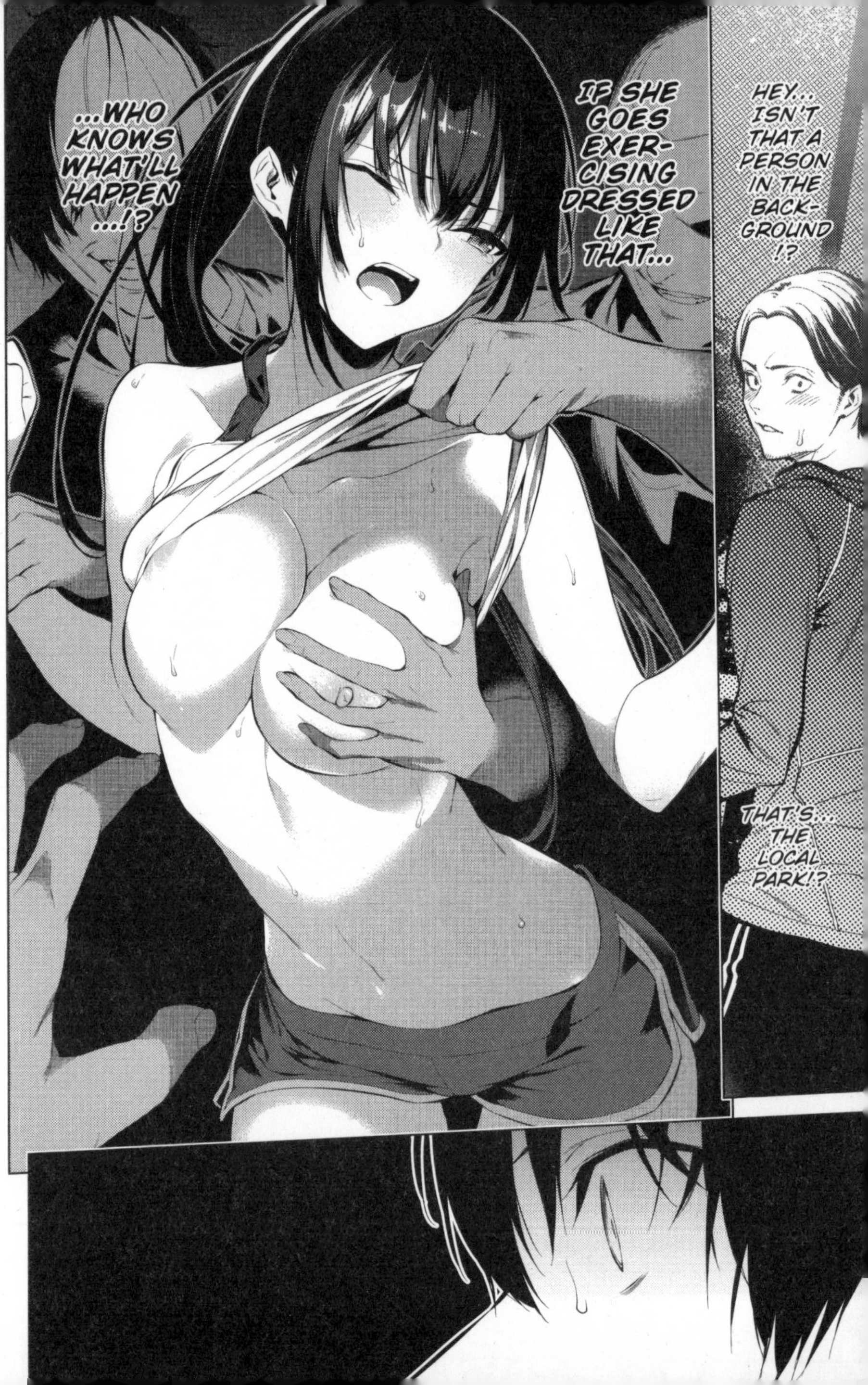
HEY... ISN'T THAT A PERSON IN THE BACK-GROUND!?
THAT'S... THE LOCAL PARK!?
IF SHE GOES EXER-CISING DRESSED LIKE THAT...
...WHO KNOWS WHAT'LL HAPPEN ...!?

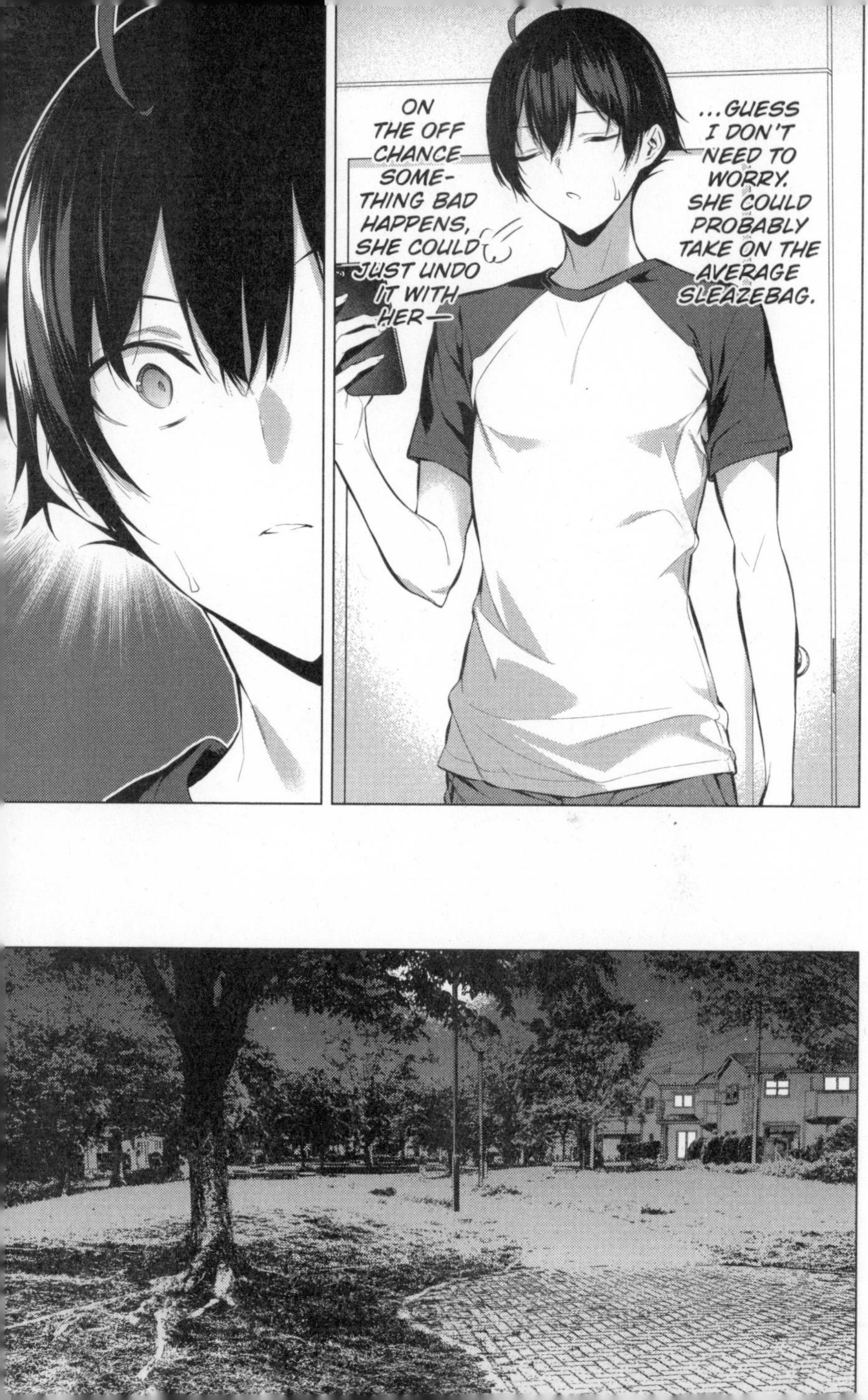
...GUESS I DON'T NEED TO WORRY. SHE COULD PROBABLY TAKE ON THE AVERAGE SLEAZEBAG.
ON THE OFF CHANCE SOME-THING BAD HAPPENS, SHE COULD JUST UNDO IT WITH HER—

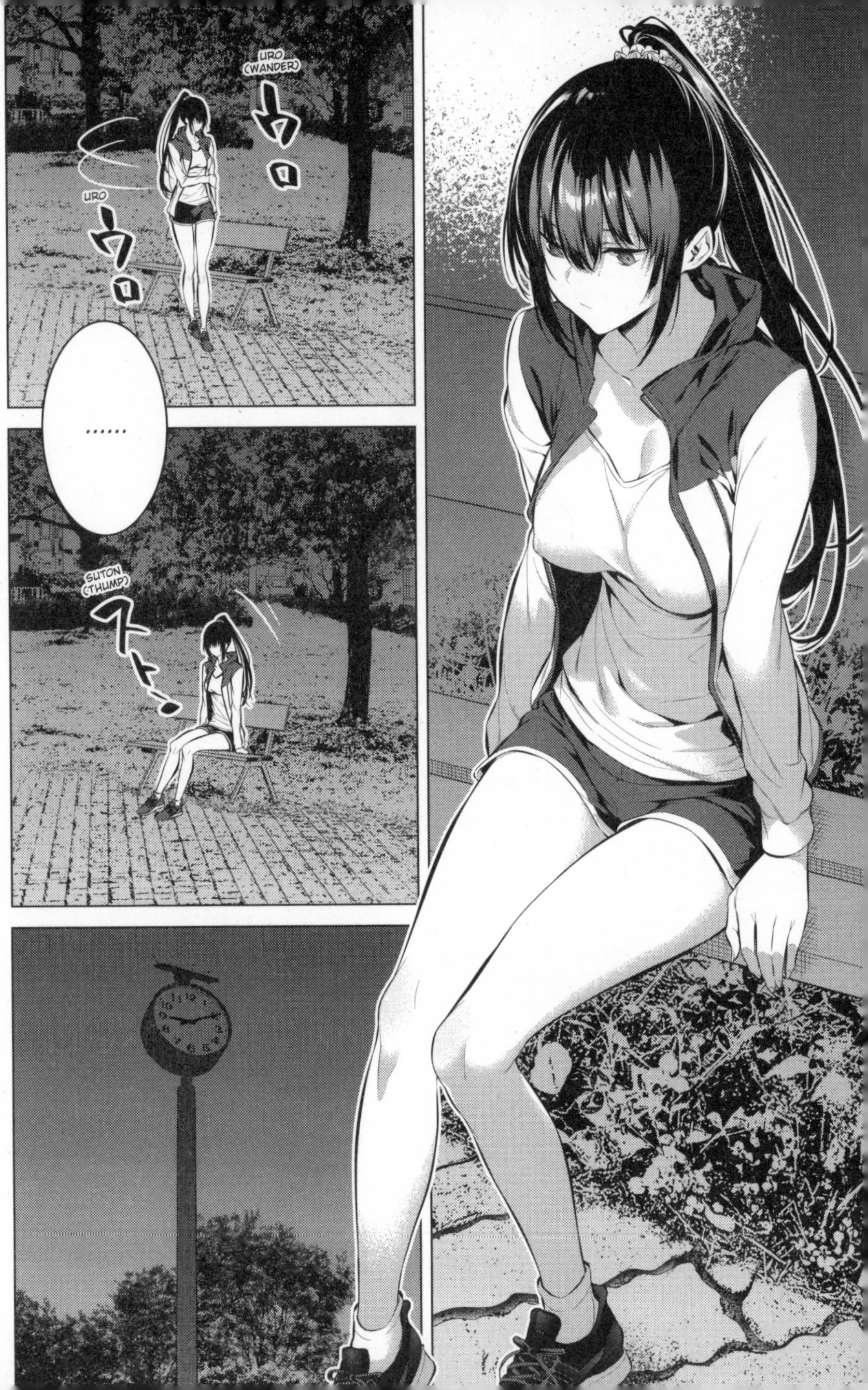
URO (WANDER)
ウロ
URO
ウロ
......
SUTON (THUMP)
ストン

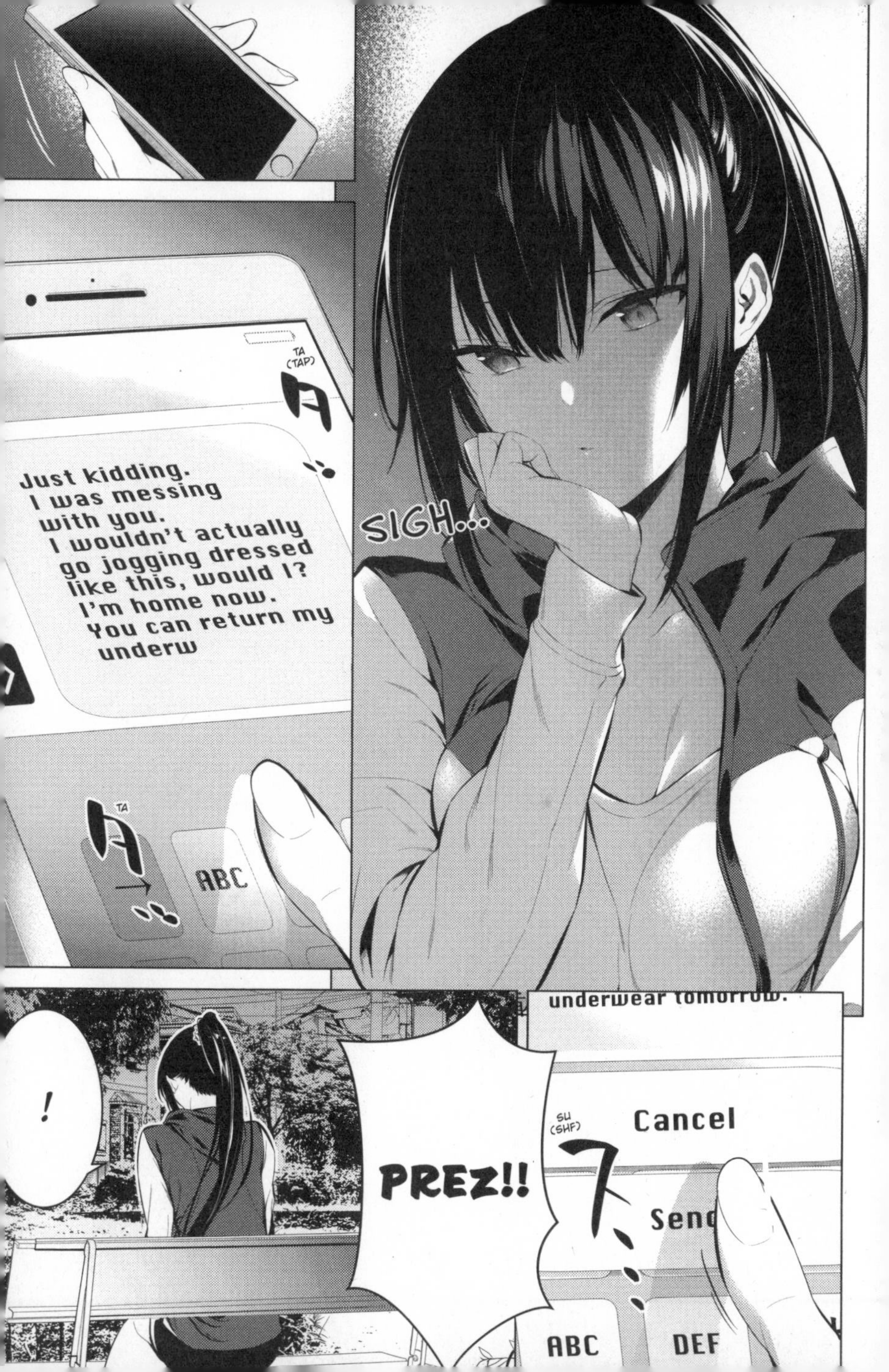
SIGH...
TA (TAP)
Just kidding. I was messing with you. I wouldn't actually go jogging dressed like this, would I? I'm home now. You can return my underw
TA
ABC
underwear tomorrow.
SU (SHF)
Cancel
Sen
ABC
DEF
PREZ!!
!

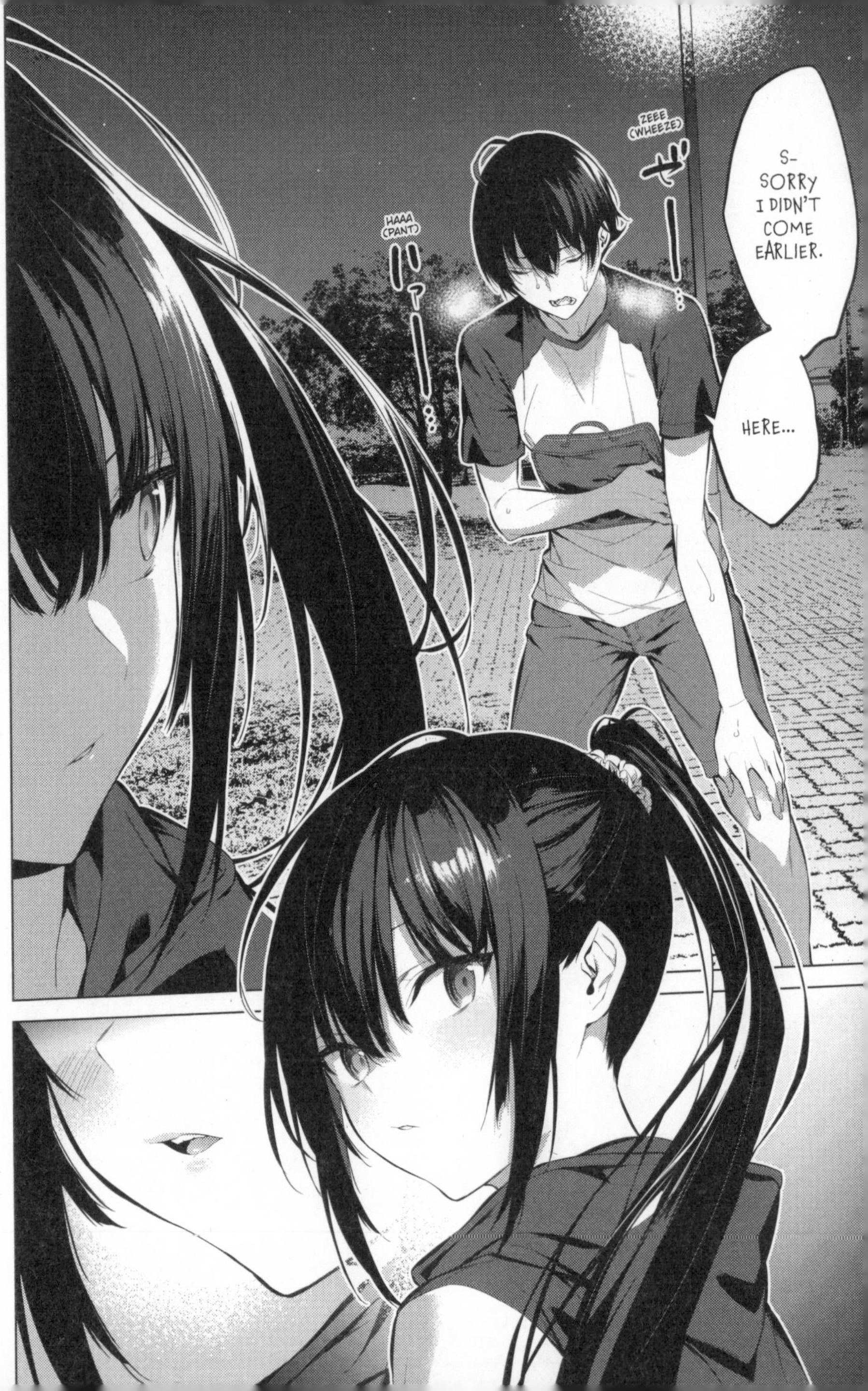
S-
SORRY
I DIDN'T
COME
EARLIER.
HERE...
ZEEE
(WHEEZE)
HAAA
(PANT)

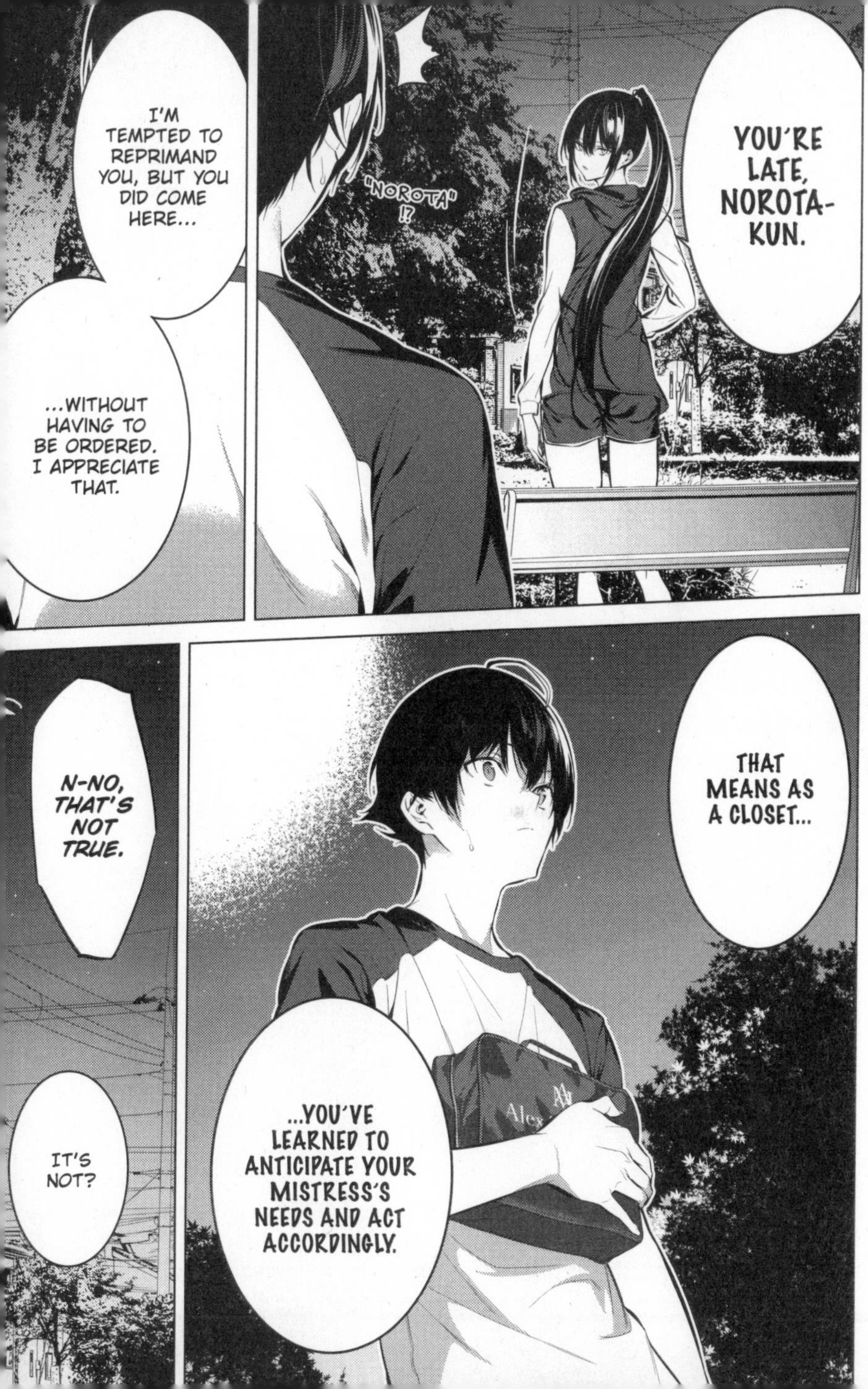
YOU'RE LATE, NOROTA-KUN.
"NOROTA" !?
I'M TEMPTED TO REPRIMAND YOU, BUT YOU DID COME HERE...
...WITHOUT HAVING TO BE ORDERED. I APPRECIATE THAT.
THAT MEANS AS A CLOSET...
...YOU'VE LEARNED TO ANTICIPATE YOUR MISTRESS'S NEEDS AND ACT ACCORDINGLY.
N-NO, THAT'S NOT TRUE.
IT'S NOT?

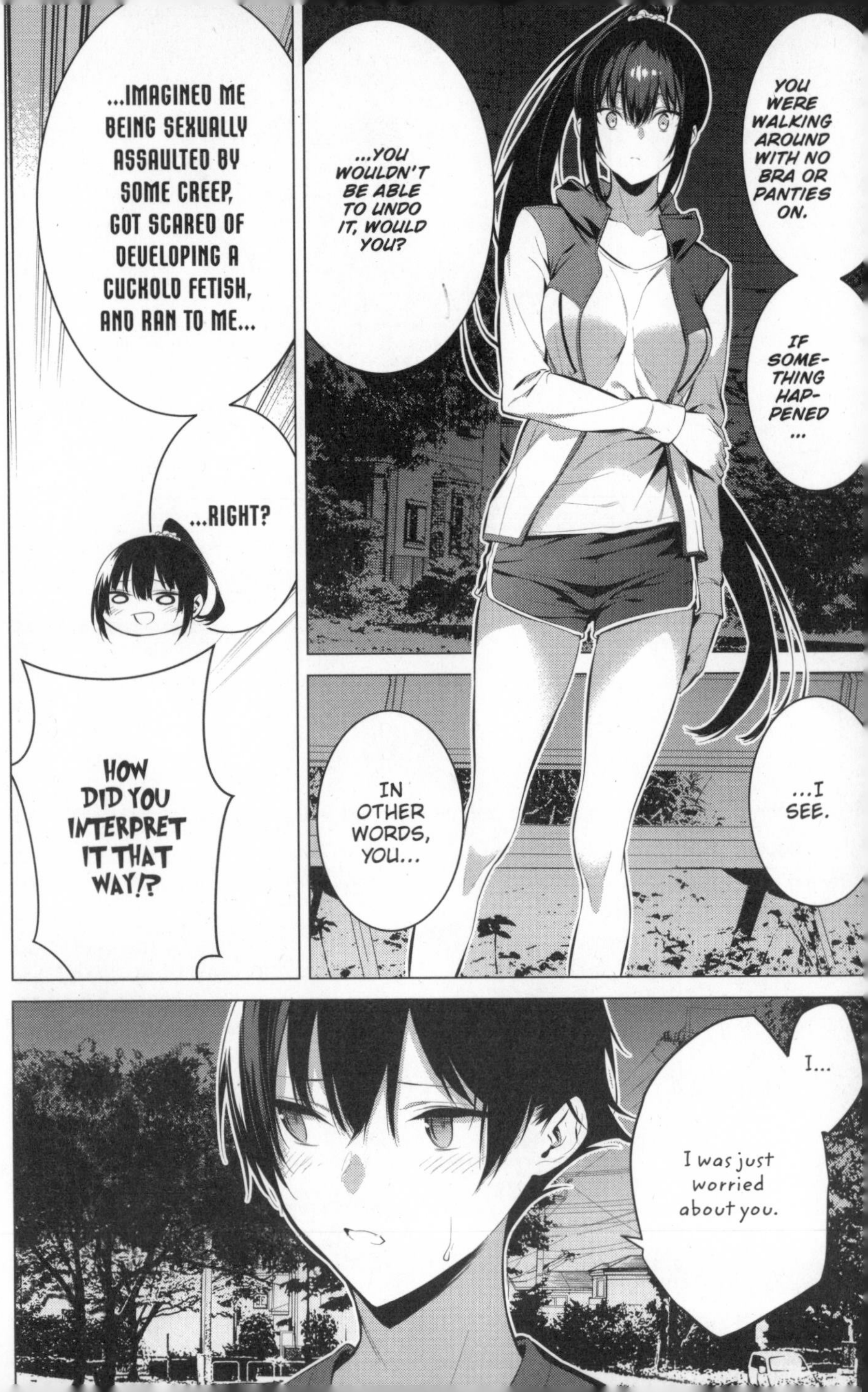
YOU WERE WALKING AROUND WITH NO BRA OR PANTIES ON.
IF SOMETHING HAPPENED...
...YOU WOULDN'T BE ABLE TO UNDO IT, WOULD YOU?
...I SEE.
IN OTHER WORDS, YOU...
...IMAGINED ME BEING SEXUALLY ASSAULTED BY SOME CREEP, GOT SCARED OF DEVELOPING A CUCKOLD FETISH, AND RAN TO ME...
...RIGHT?
HOW DID YOU INTERPRET IT THAT WAY!?
I...
I was just worried about you.

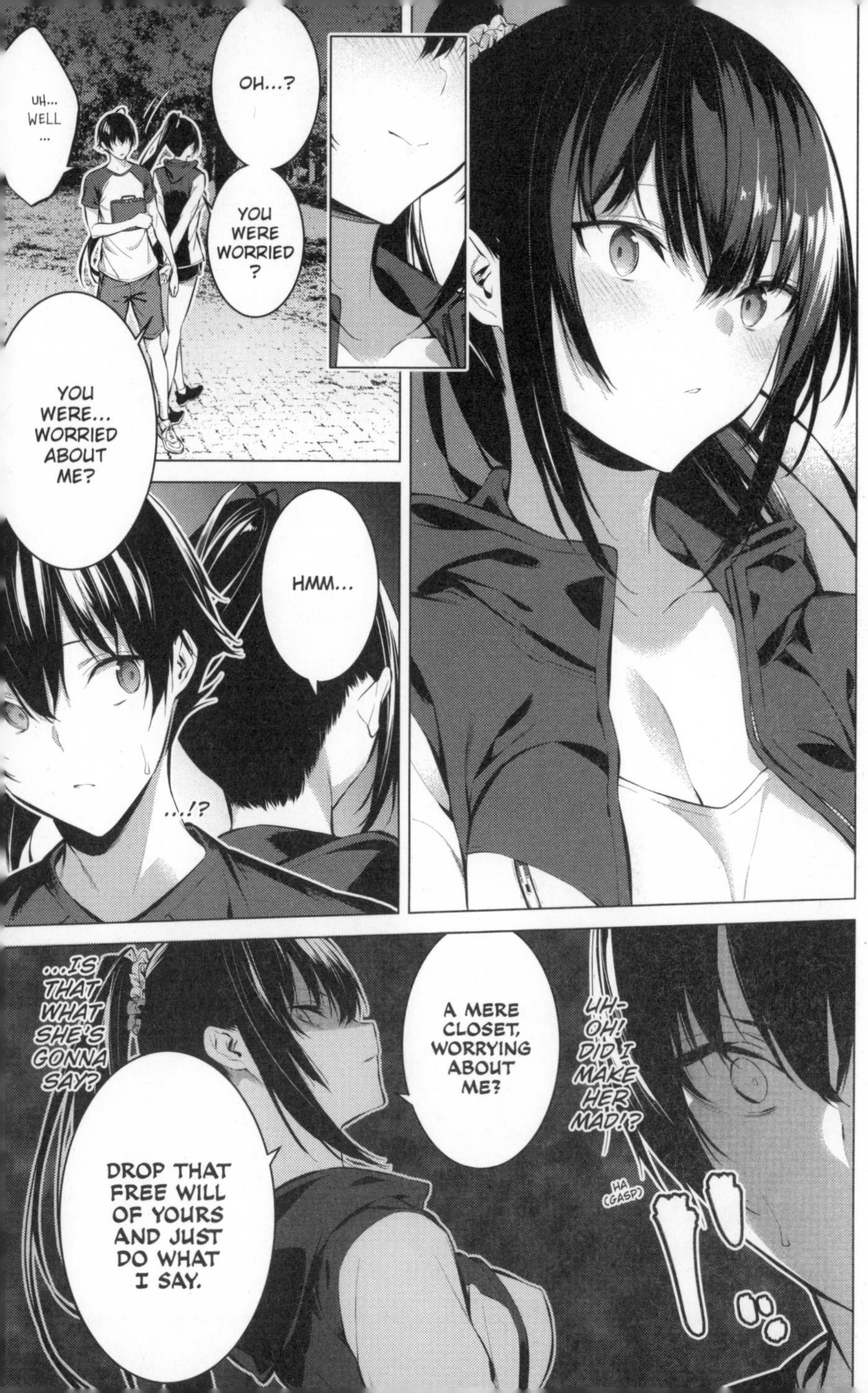
OH...?
YOU WERE WORRIED ?
UH... WELL ...
YOU WERE... WORRIED ABOUT ME?
HMM...
...!?
UH-OH! DID I MAKE HER MAD!?
HA (GASP)
A MERE CLOSET, WORRYING ABOUT ME?
...IS THAT WHAT SHE'S GONNA SAY?
DROP THAT FREE WILL OF YOURS AND JUST DO WHAT I SAY.

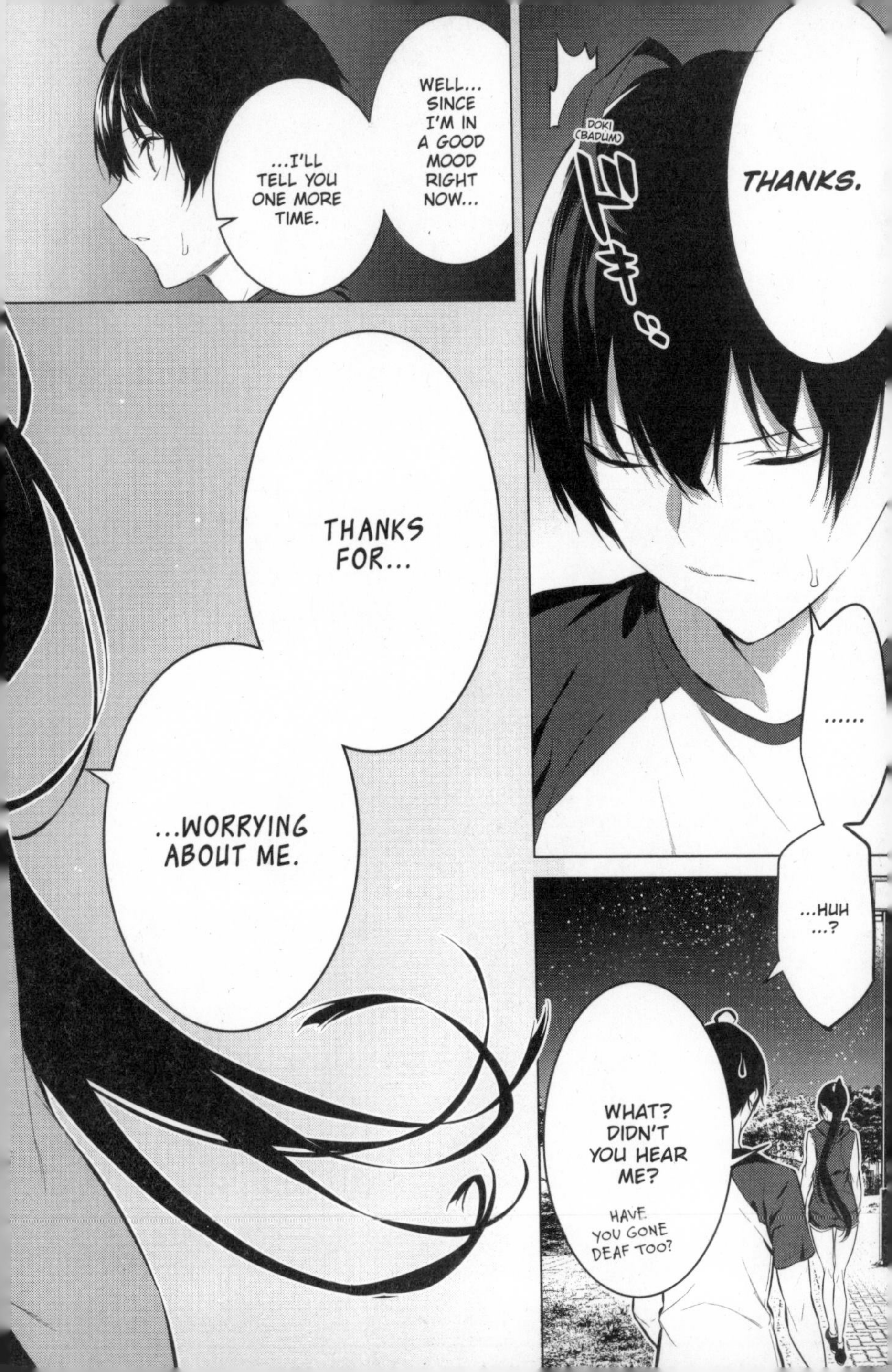
THANKS.
DOKI (BADUM)
......
...HUH ...?
WHAT? DIDN'T YOU HEAR ME?
HAVE YOU GONE DEAF TOO?
WELL... SINCE I'M IN A GOOD MOOD RIGHT NOW...
...I'LL TELL YOU ONE MORE TIME.
THANKS FOR...
...WORRYING ABOUT ME.

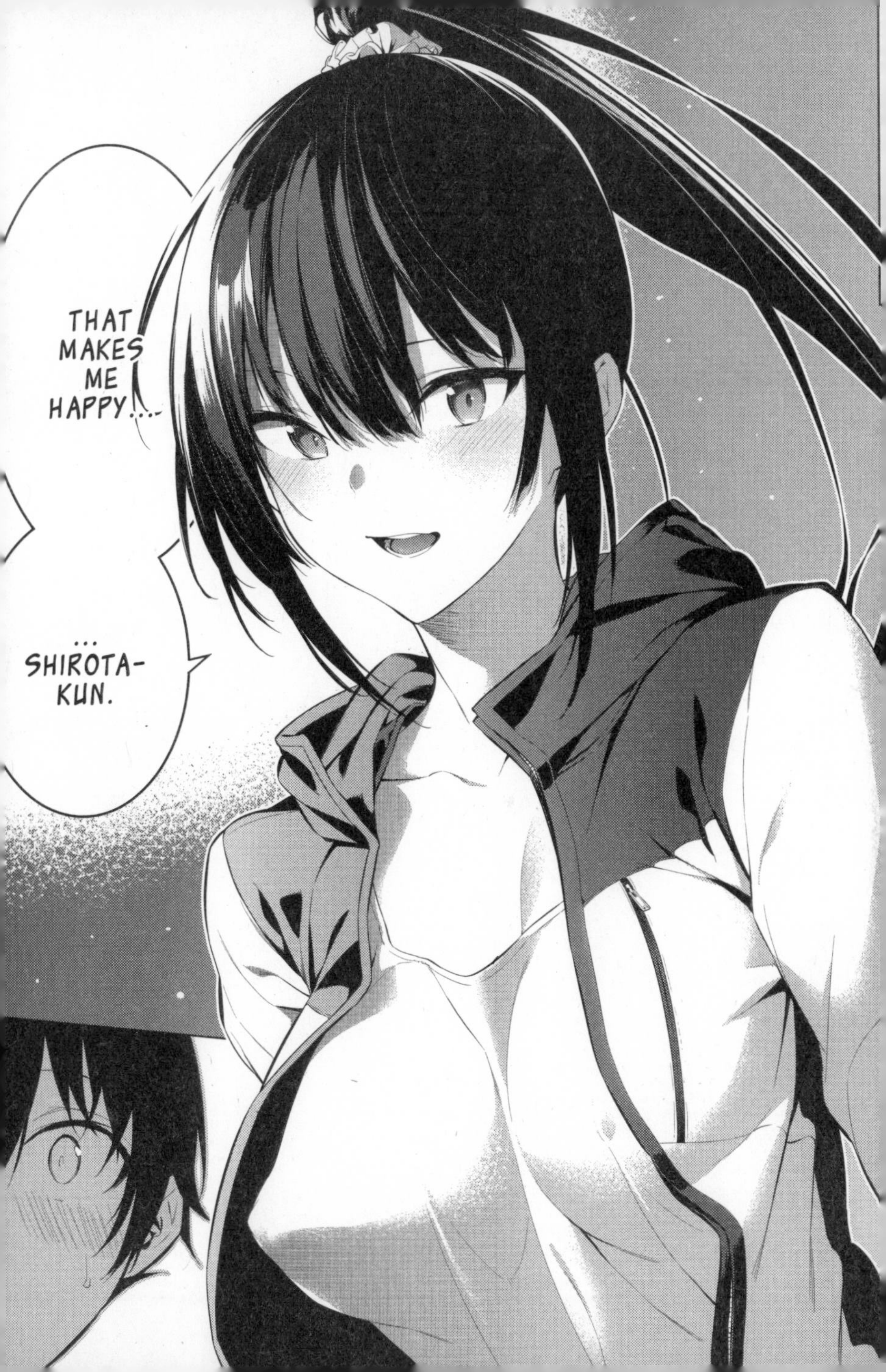
THAT MAKES ME HAPPY....
...SHIROTA-KUN.

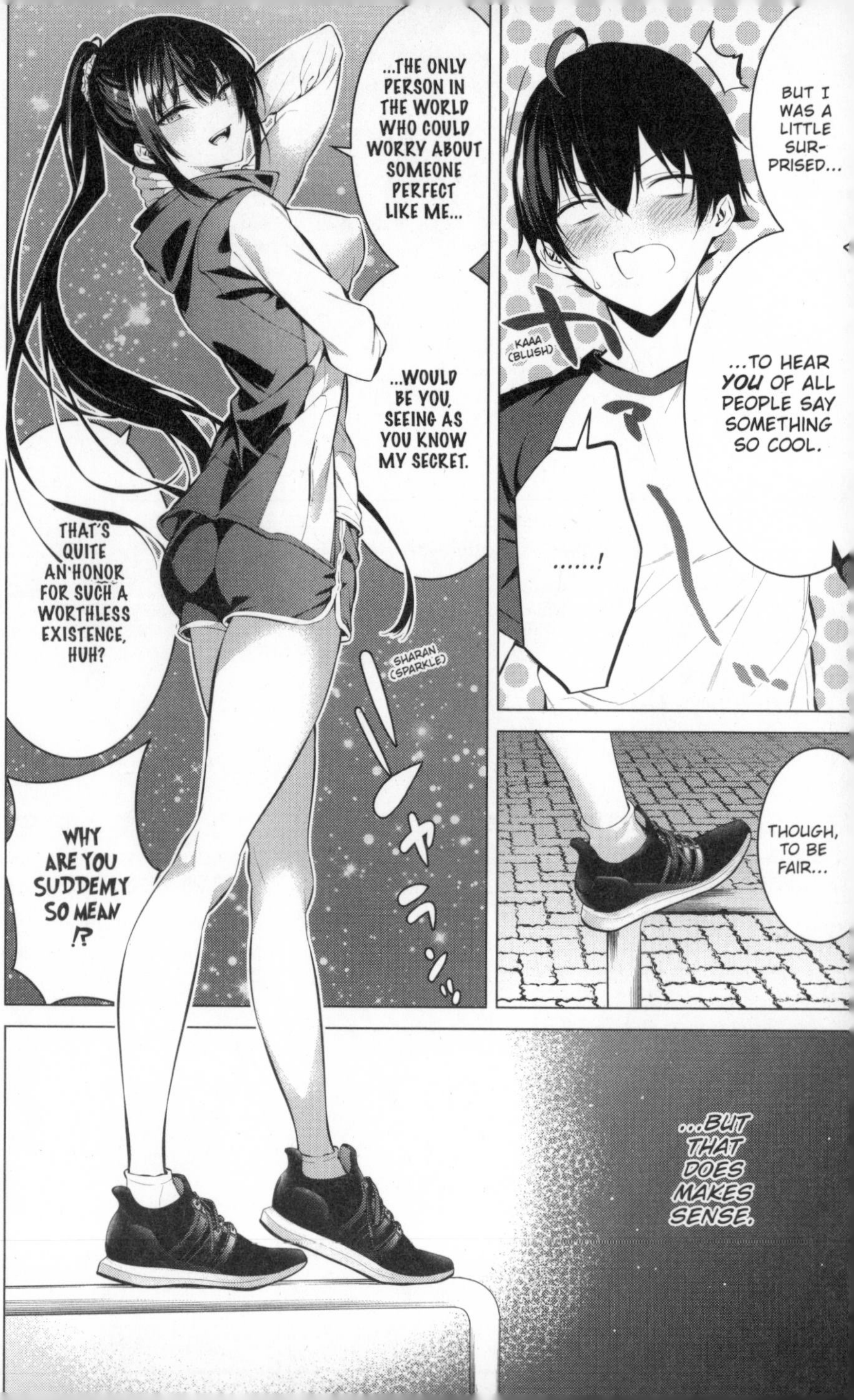
BUT I WAS A LITTLE SUR-PRISED...
KAAA (BLUSH)
...TO HEAR *YOU* OF ALL PEOPLE SAY SOMETHING SO COOL.
......!
THOUGH, TO BE FAIR...
...THE ONLY PERSON IN THE WORLD WHO COULD WORRY ABOUT SOMEONE PERFECT LIKE ME...
...WOULD BE YOU, SEEING AS YOU KNOW MY SECRET.
THAT'S QUITE AN HONOR FOR SUCH A WORTHLESS EXISTENCE, HUH?
WHY ARE YOU SUDDENLY SO MEAN!?
SHARAN (SPARKLE)
...BUT THAT DOES MAKES SENSE.

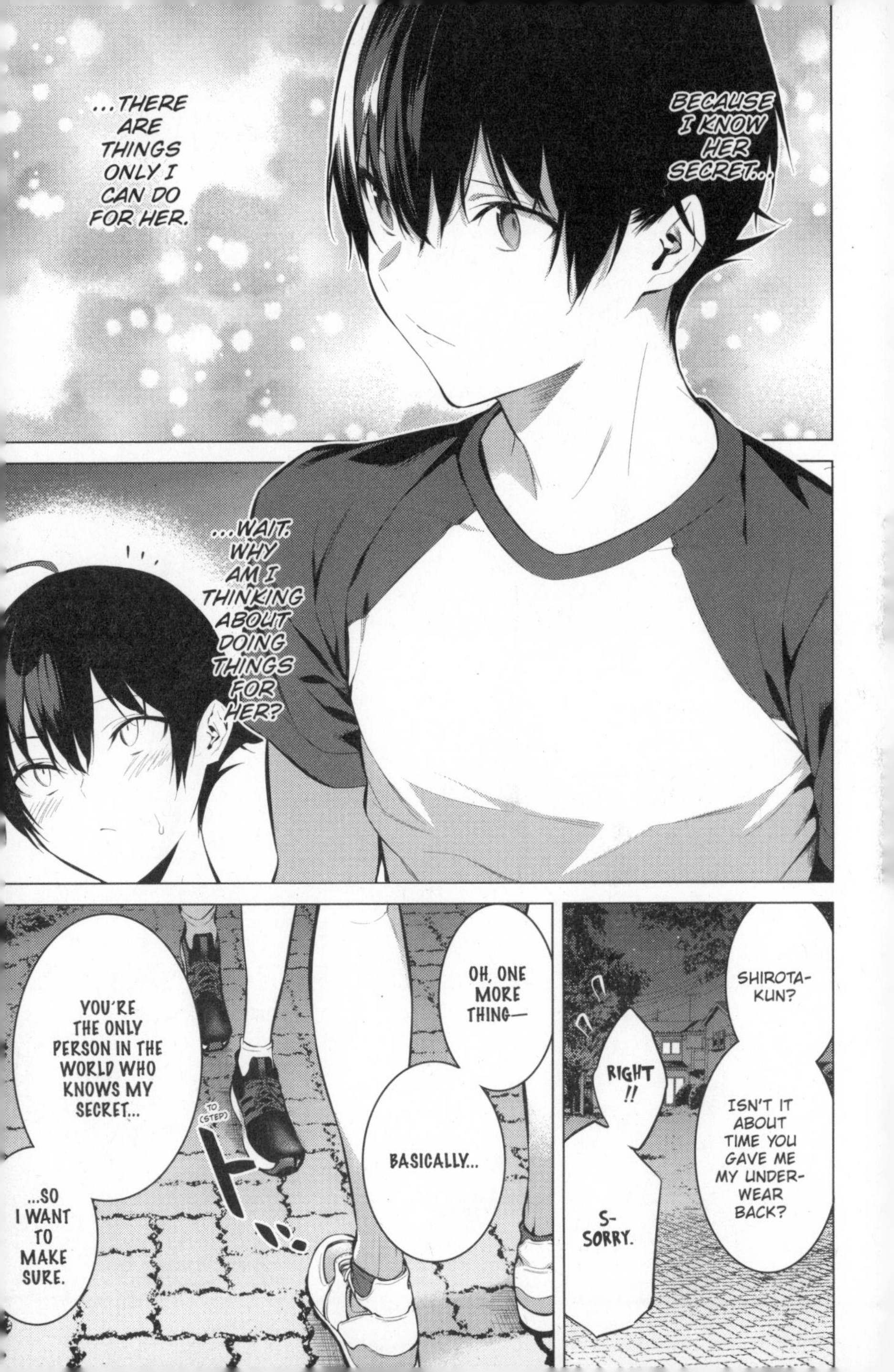
BECAUSE I KNOW HER SECRET...
...THERE ARE THINGS ONLY I CAN DO FOR HER.
...WAIT. WHY AM I THINKING ABOUT DOING THINGS FOR HER?
SHIROTA-KUN?
ISN'T IT ABOUT TIME YOU GAVE ME MY UNDER-WEAR BACK?
RIGHT!!
S-SORRY.
OH, ONE MORE THING—
BASICALLY...
YOU'RE THE ONLY PERSON IN THE WORLD WHO KNOWS MY SECRET...
TO (STEP)
...SO I WANT TO MAKE SURE.

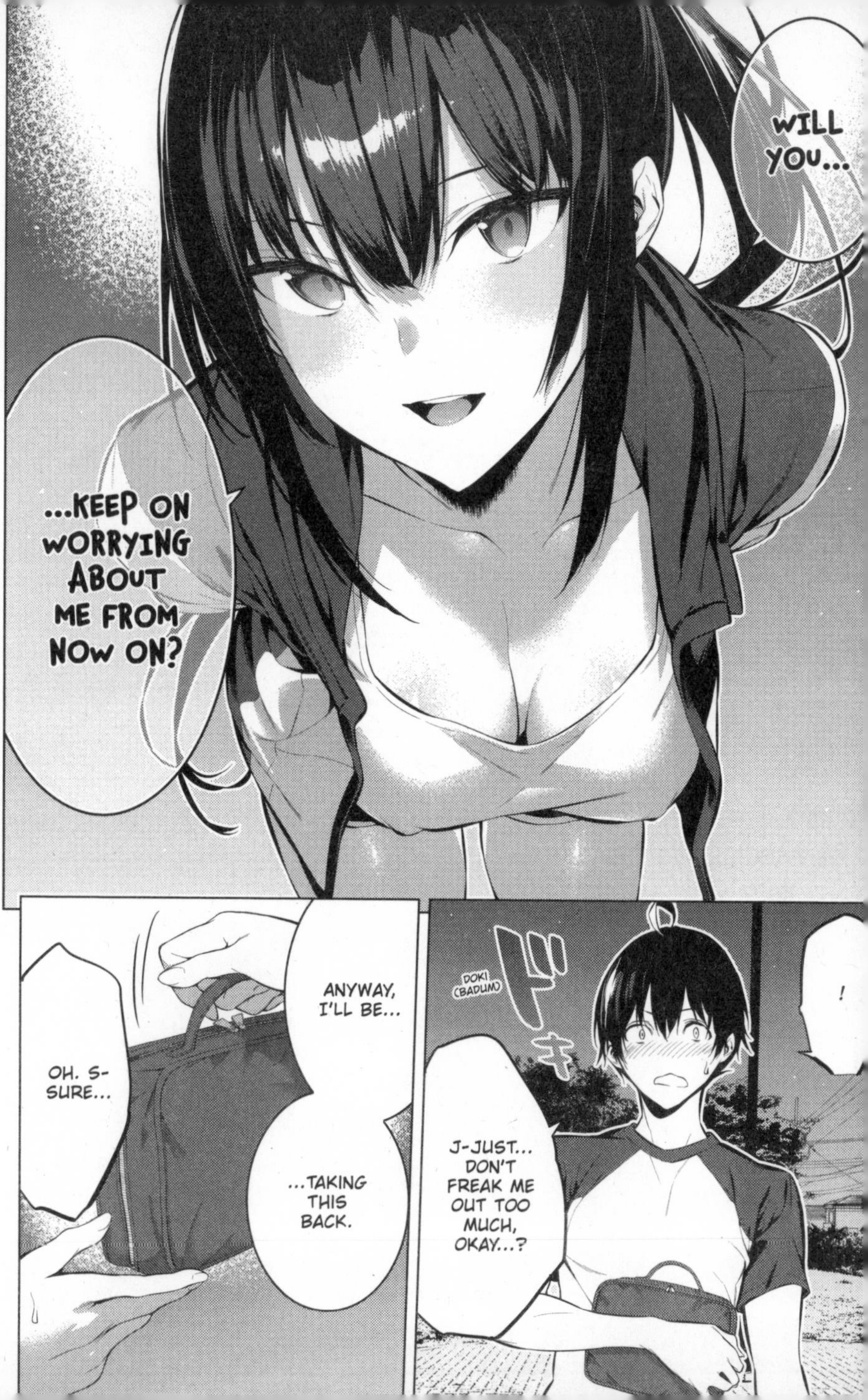
WILL YOU...
...KEEP ON WORRYING ABOUT ME FROM NOW ON?
!
DOKI (BADUM)
ドキ
J-JUST... DON'T FREAK ME OUT TOO MUCH, OKAY...?
ANYWAY, I'LL BE...
...TAKING THIS BACK.
OH. S-SURE...

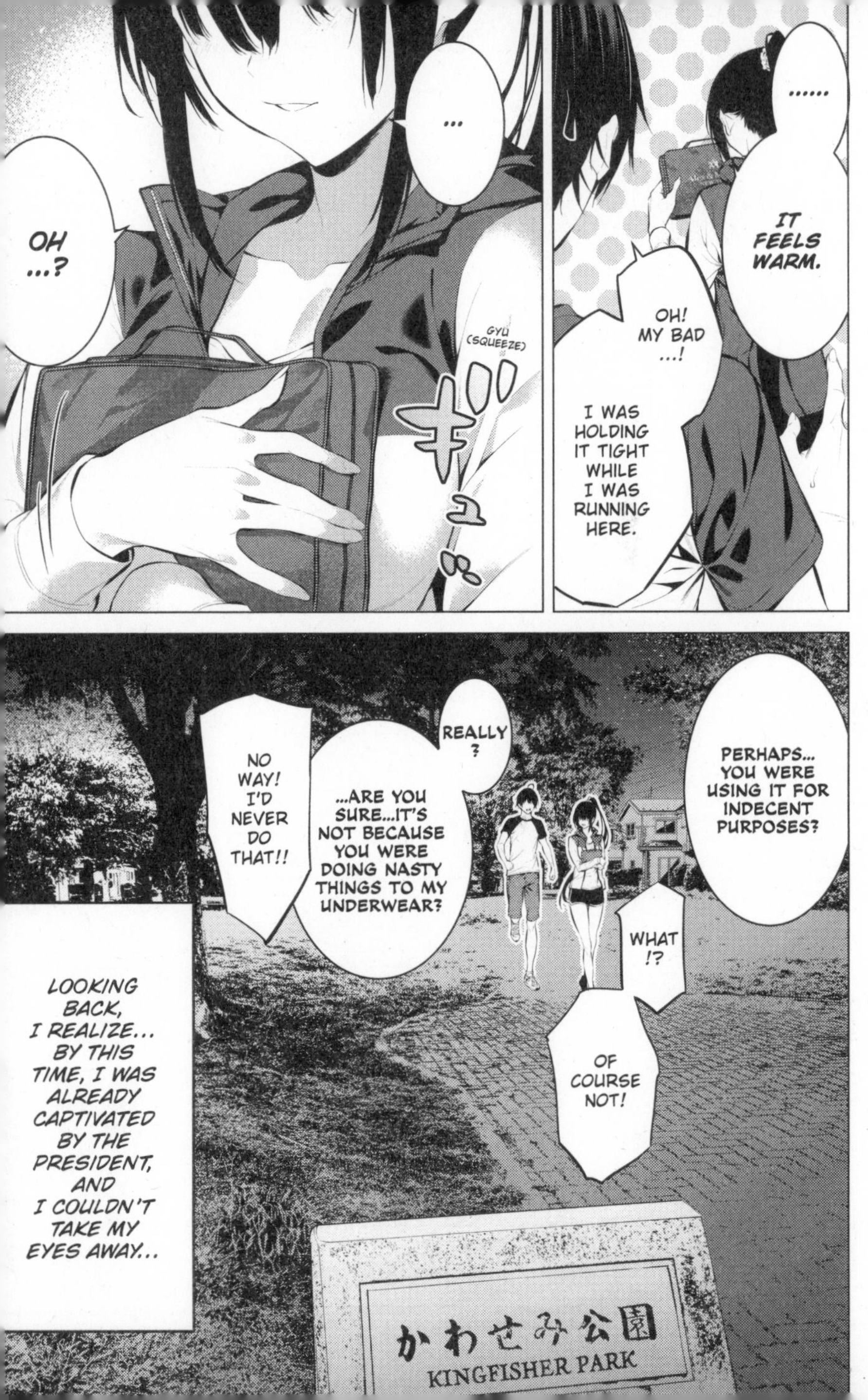
......
IT FEELS WARM.
OH! MY BAD ...!
I WAS HOLDING IT TIGHT WHILE I WAS RUNNING HERE.
...
OH ...?
GYU (SQUEEZE)
PERHAPS... YOU WERE USING IT FOR INDECENT PURPOSES?
WHAT !?
OF COURSE NOT!
REALLY ?
...ARE YOU SURE...IT'S NOT BECAUSE YOU WERE DOING NASTY THINGS TO MY UNDERWEAR?
NO WAY! I'D NEVER DO THAT!!
LOOKING BACK, I REALIZE... BY THIS TIME, I WAS ALREADY CAPTIVATED BY THE PRESIDENT, AND I COULDN'T TAKE MY EYES AWAY...
かわせみ公園
KINGFISHER PARK

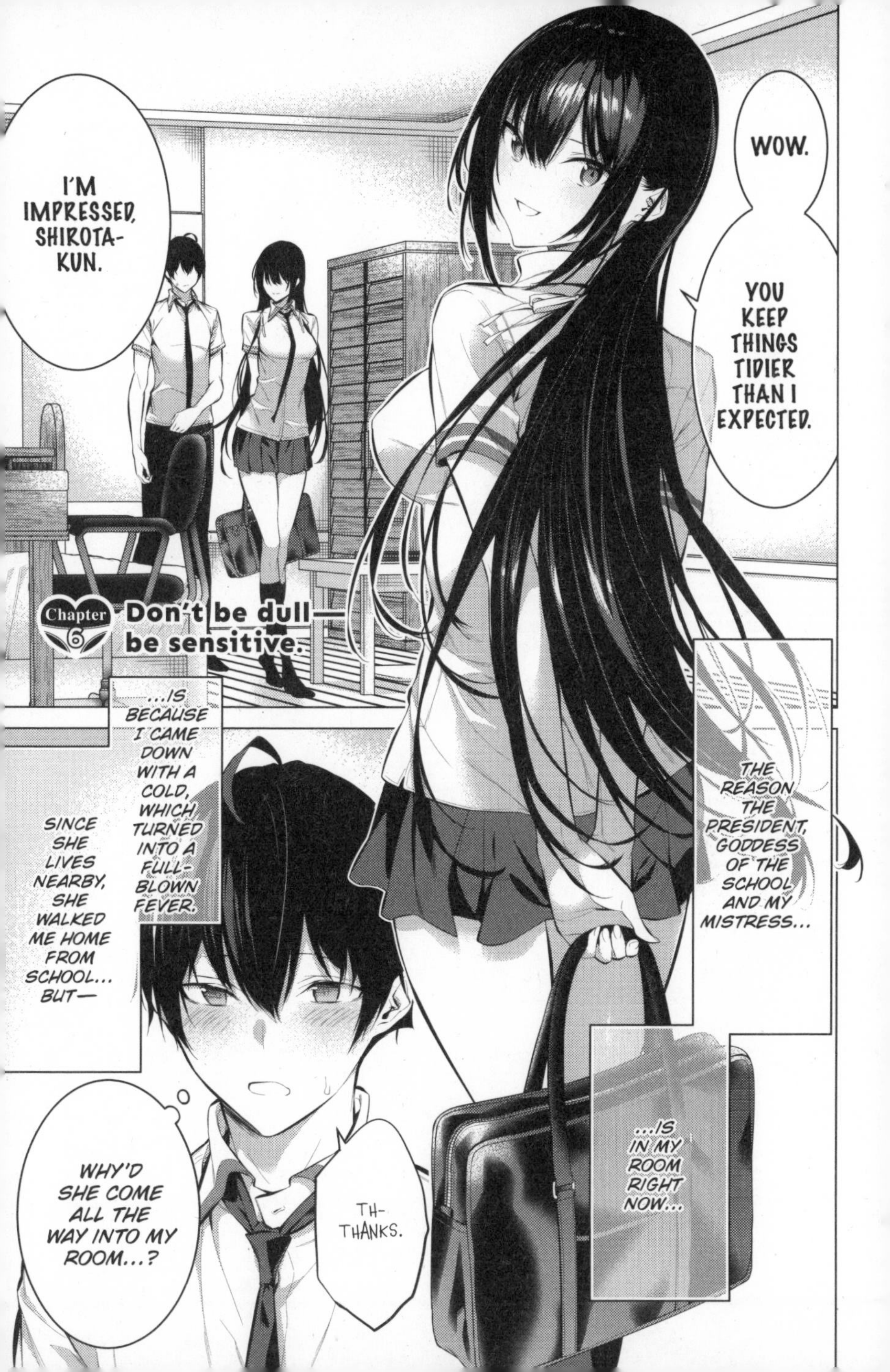
WOW.
YOU KEEP THINGS TIDIER THAN I EXPECTED.
I'M IMPRESSED, SHIROTA-KUN.
Chapter 6
Don't be dull—be sensitive.
THE REASON THE PRESIDENT, GODDESS OF THE SCHOOL AND MY MISTRESS...
...IS BECAUSE I CAME DOWN WITH A COLD, WHICH TURNED INTO A FULL-BLOWN FEVER.
SINCE SHE LIVES NEARBY, SHE WALKED ME HOME FROM SCHOOL... BUT—
...IS IN MY ROOM RIGHT NOW...
TH-THANKS.
WHY'D SHE COME ALL THE WAY INTO MY ROOM...?

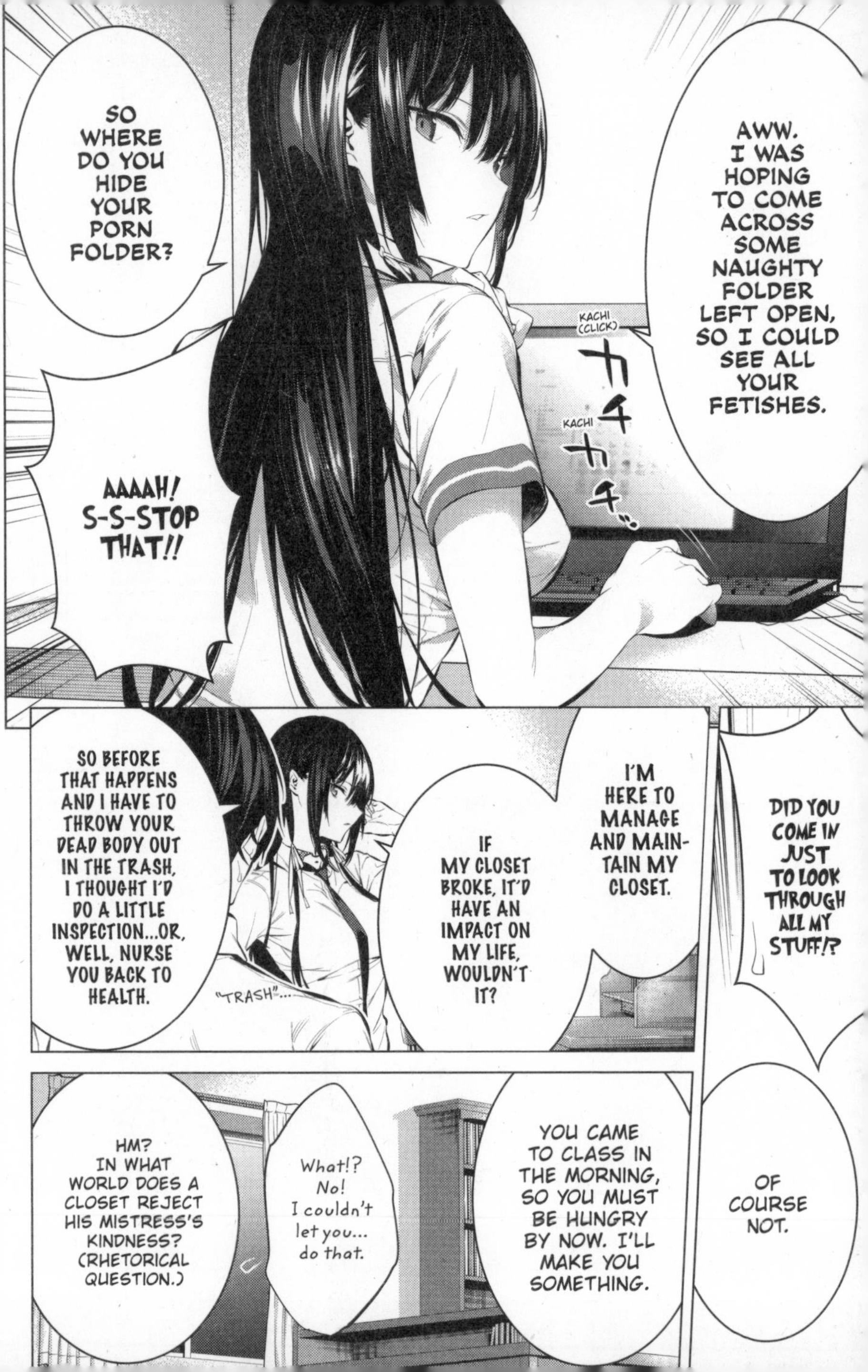
AWW. I WAS HOPING TO COME ACROSS SOME NAUGHTY FOLDER LEFT OPEN, SO I COULD SEE ALL YOUR FETISHES.
SO WHERE DO YOU HIDE YOUR PORN FOLDER?
KACHI (CLICK)
KACHI
AAAAH! S-S-STOP THAT!!
DID YOU COME IN JUST TO LOOK THROUGH ALL MY STUFF!?
OF COURSE NOT.
I'M HERE TO MANAGE AND MAIN-TAIN MY CLOSET.
IF MY CLOSET BROKE, IT'D HAVE AN IMPACT ON MY LIFE, WOULDN'T IT?
SO BEFORE THAT HAPPENS AND I HAVE TO THROW YOUR DEAD BODY OUT IN THE TRASH, I THOUGHT I'D DO A LITTLE INSPECTION...OR, WELL, NURSE YOU BACK TO HEALTH.
"TRASH"...
YOU CAME TO CLASS IN THE MORNING, SO YOU MUST BE HUNGRY BY NOW. I'LL MAKE YOU SOMETHING.
What!? No! I couldn't let you... do that.
HM? IN WHAT WORLD DOES A CLOSET REJECT HIS MISTRESS'S KINDNESS? (RHETORICAL QUESTION.)

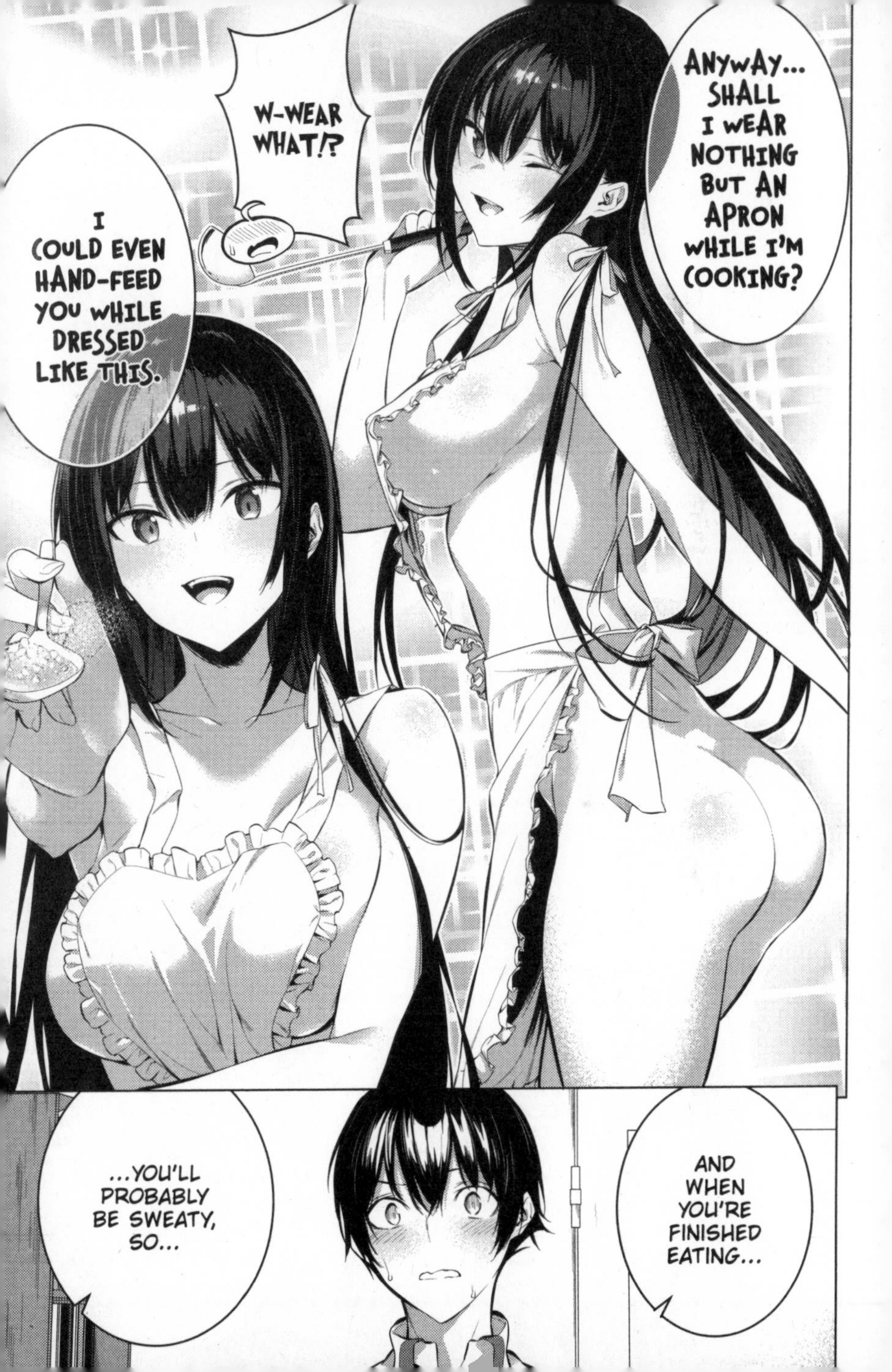
ANYWAY... SHALL I WEAR NOTHING BUT AN APRON WHILE I'M COOKING?
W-WEAR WHAT!?
I COULD EVEN HAND-FEED YOU WHILE DRESSED LIKE THIS.
AND WHEN YOU'RE FINISHED EATING...
...YOU'LL PROBABLY BE SWEATY, SO...

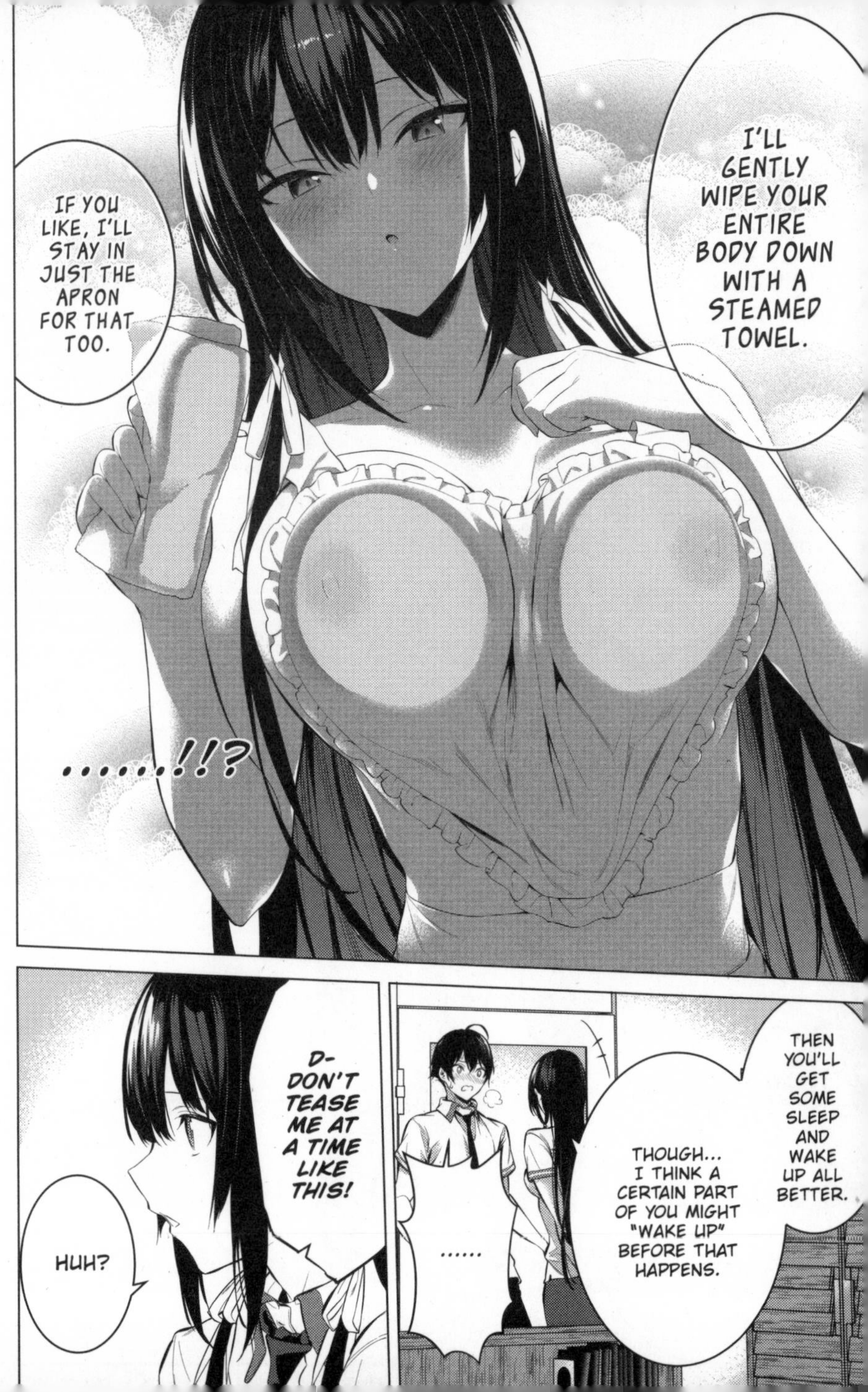
I'LL GENTLY WIPE YOUR ENTIRE BODY DOWN WITH A STEAMED TOWEL.
IF YOU LIKE, I'LL STAY IN JUST THE APRON FOR THAT TOO.
......!!?
THEN YOU'LL GET SOME SLEEP AND WAKE UP ALL BETTER.
THOUGH... I THINK A CERTAIN PART OF YOU MIGHT "WAKE UP" BEFORE THAT HAPPENS.
......
D-DON'T TEASE ME AT A TIME LIKE THIS!
HUH?

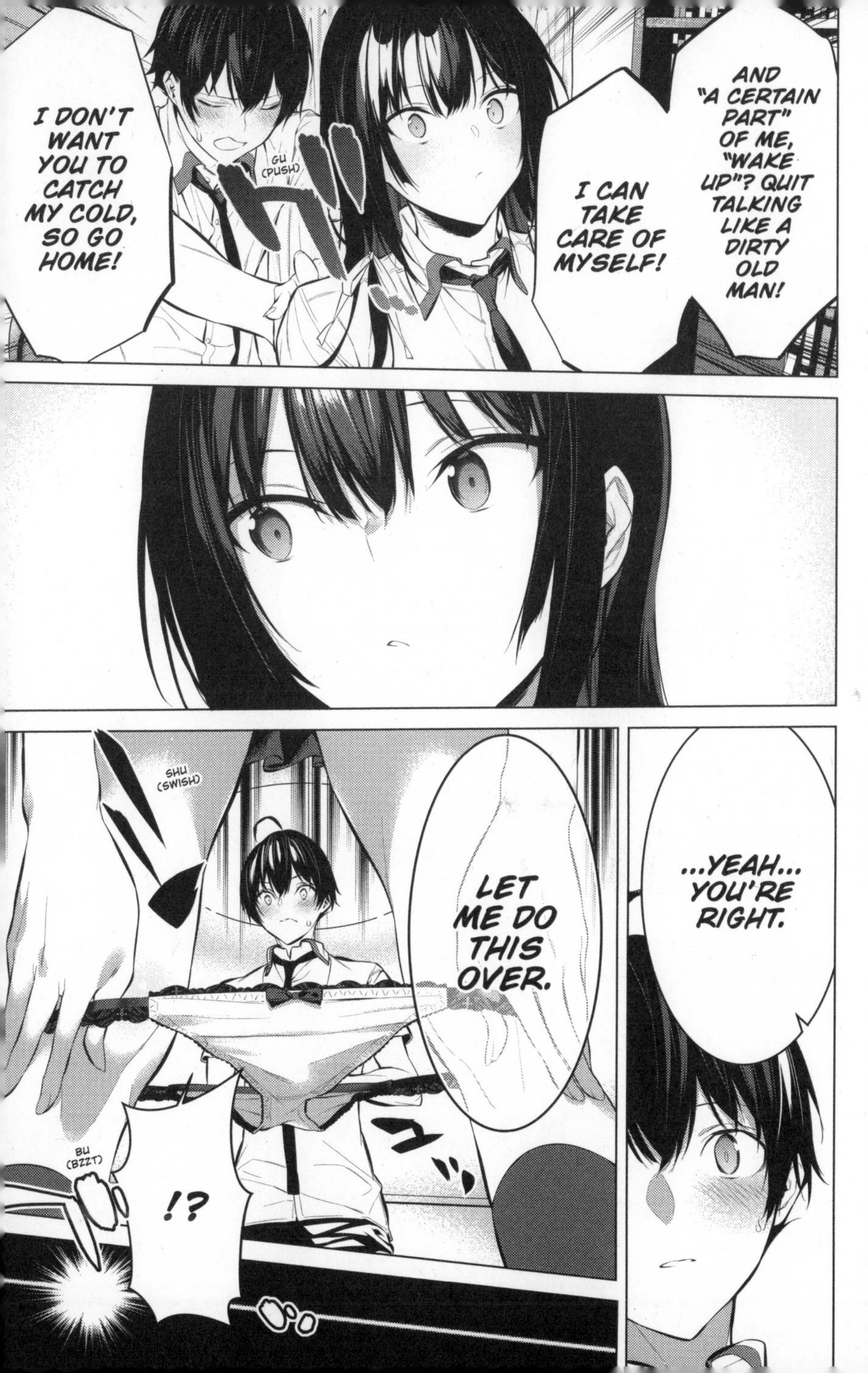
AND "A CERTAIN PART" OF ME, "WAKE UP"? QUIT TALKING LIKE A DIRTY OLD MAN!
I CAN TAKE CARE OF MYSELF!
GU (PUSH)
I DON'T WANT YOU TO CATCH MY COLD, SO GO HOME!
...YEAH... YOU'RE RIGHT.
LET ME DO THIS OVER.
SHU (SWISH)
!?
BU (BZZT)

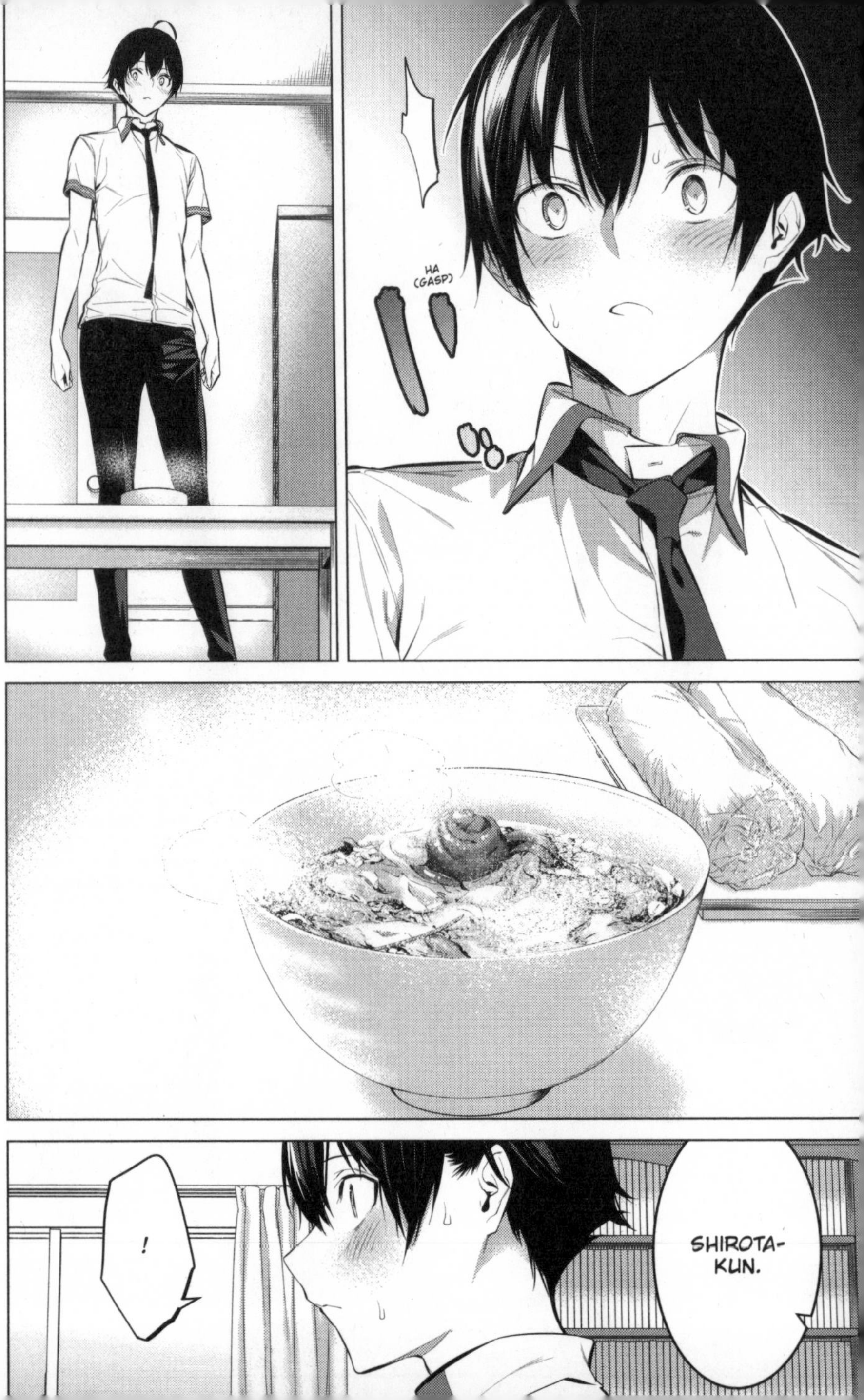
HA (GASP)
SHIROTA-KUN.
!

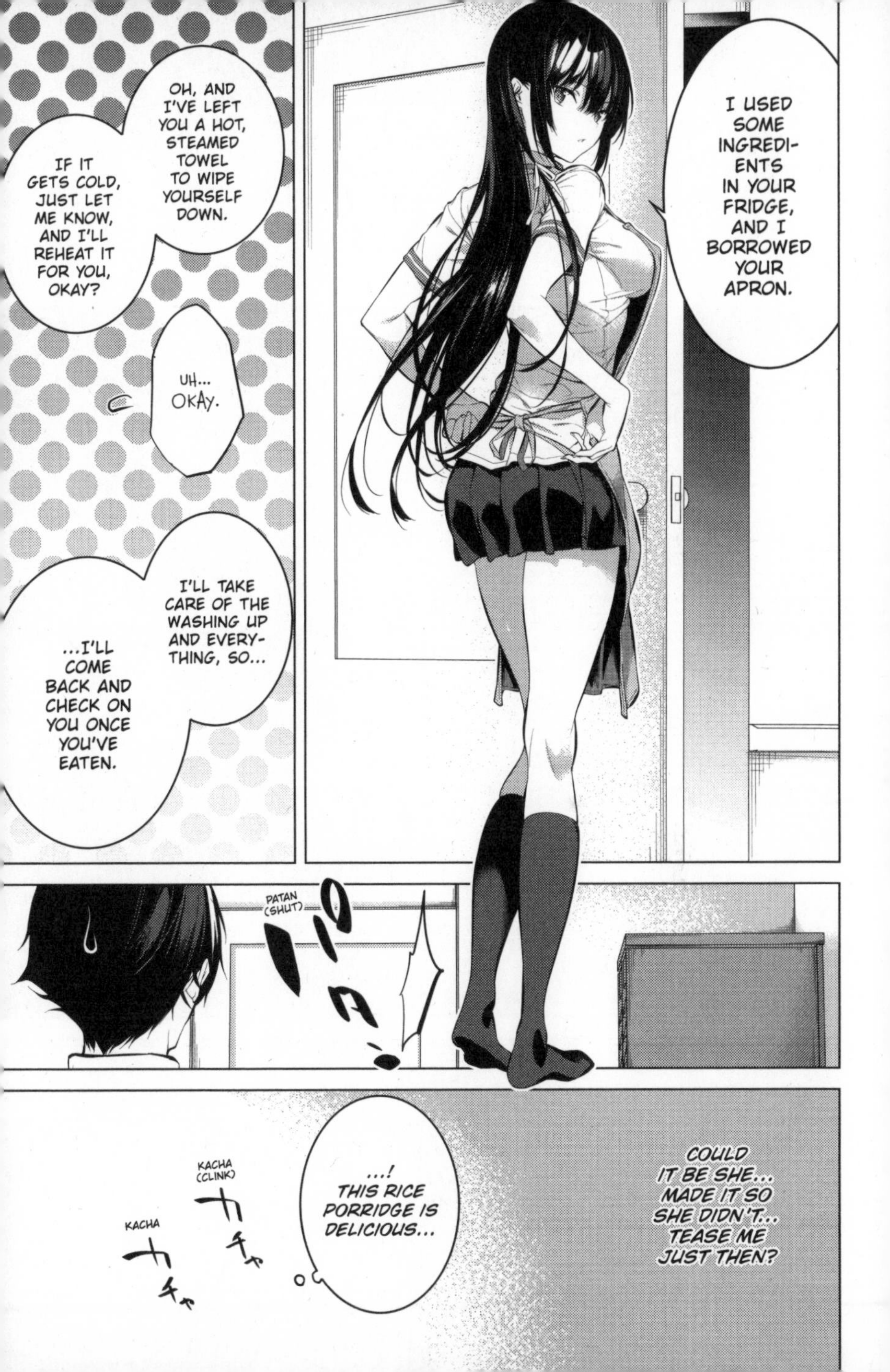
I USED SOME INGREDI-ENTS IN YOUR FRIDGE, AND I BORROWED YOUR APRON.
OH, AND I'VE LEFT YOU A HOT, STEAMED TOWEL TO WIPE YOURSELF DOWN.
IF IT GETS COLD, JUST LET ME KNOW, AND I'LL REHEAT IT FOR YOU, OKAY?
UH... OKAY.
I'LL TAKE CARE OF THE WASHING UP AND EVERY-THING, SO...
...I'LL COME BACK AND CHECK ON YOU ONCE YOU'VE EATEN.
PATAN (SHUT)
COULD IT BE SHE... MADE IT SO SHE DIDN'T... TEASE ME JUST THEN?
...! THIS RICE PORRIDGE IS DELICIOUS...
KACHA (CLINK)
KACHA

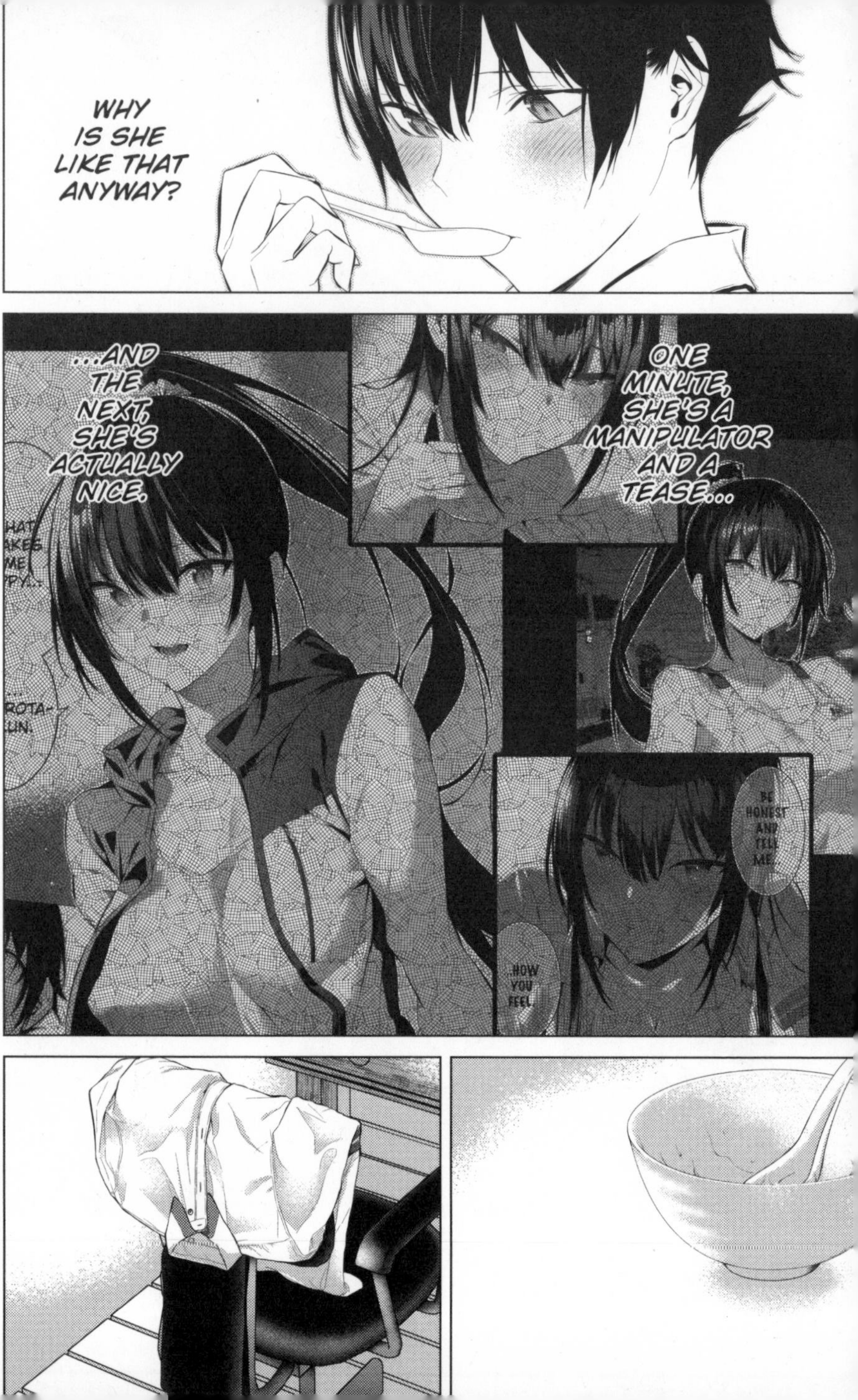
WHY IS SHE LIKE THAT ANYWAY?
ONE MINUTE, SHE'S A MANIPULATOR AND A TEASE...
BE HONEST AND TELL ME...
...HOW YOU FEEL.
...AND THE NEXT, SHE'S ACTUALLY NICE.

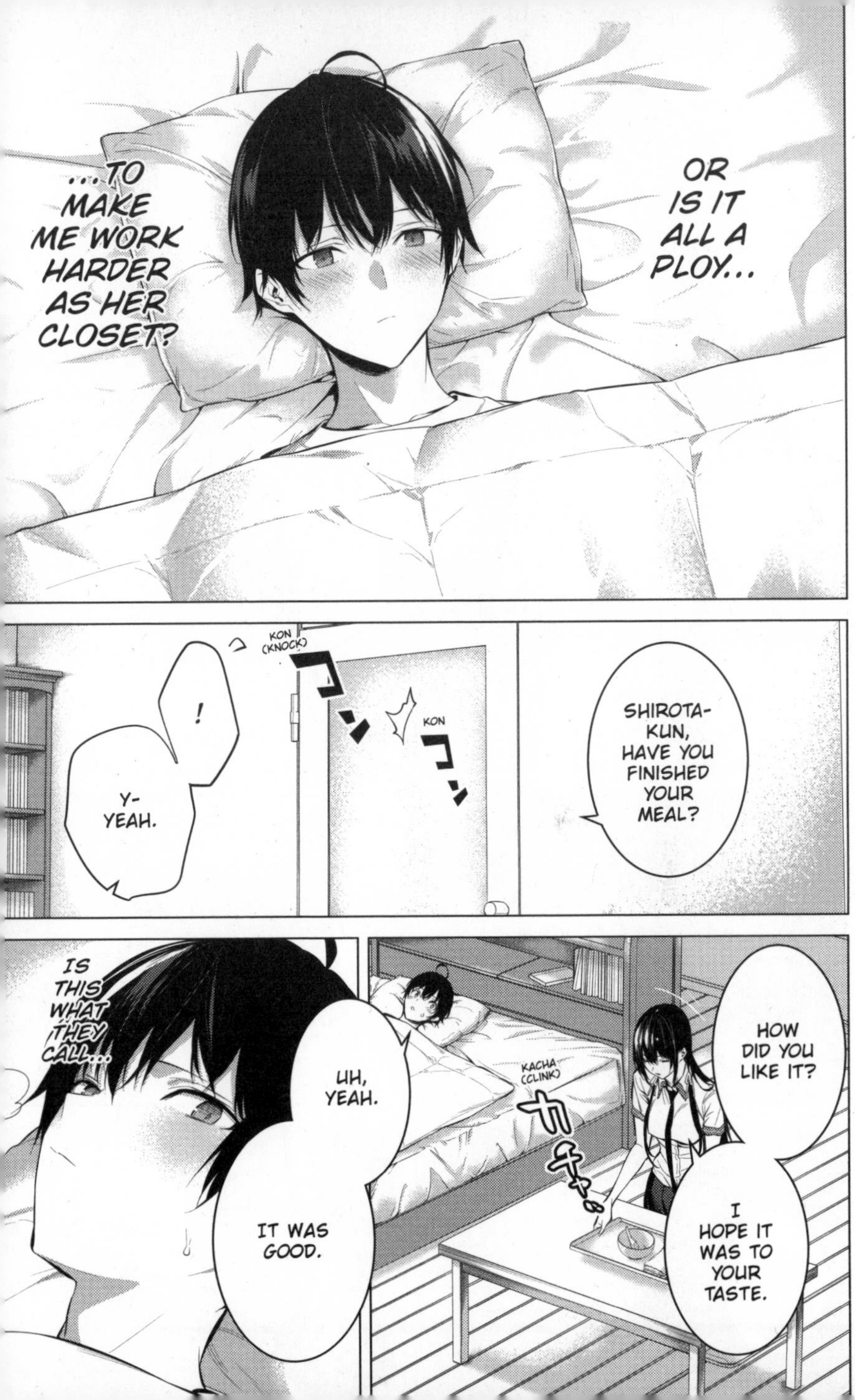
OR IS IT ALL A PLOY...
...TO MAKE ME WORK HARDER AS HER CLOSET?
SHIROTA-KUN, HAVE YOU FINISHED YOUR MEAL?
KON (KNOCK)
KON
!
Y-YEAH.
HOW DID YOU LIKE IT?
KACHA (CLINK)
I HOPE IT WAS TO YOUR TASTE.
UH, YEAH.
IT WAS GOOD.
IS THIS WHAT THEY CALL...

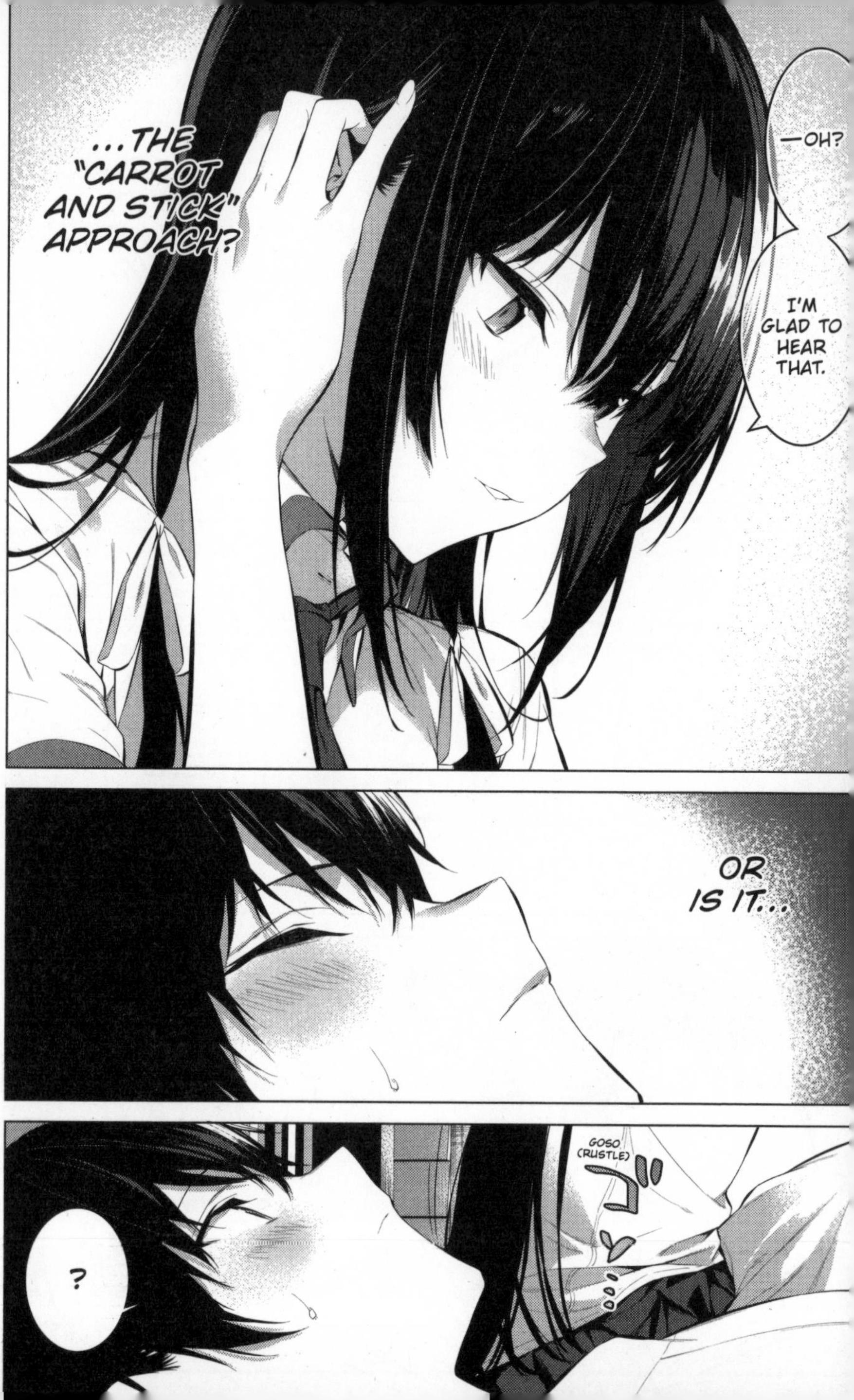
—OH?
I'M GLAD TO HEAR THAT.
...THE "CARROT AND STICK" APPROACH?
OR IS IT...
GOSO (RUSTLE)
?

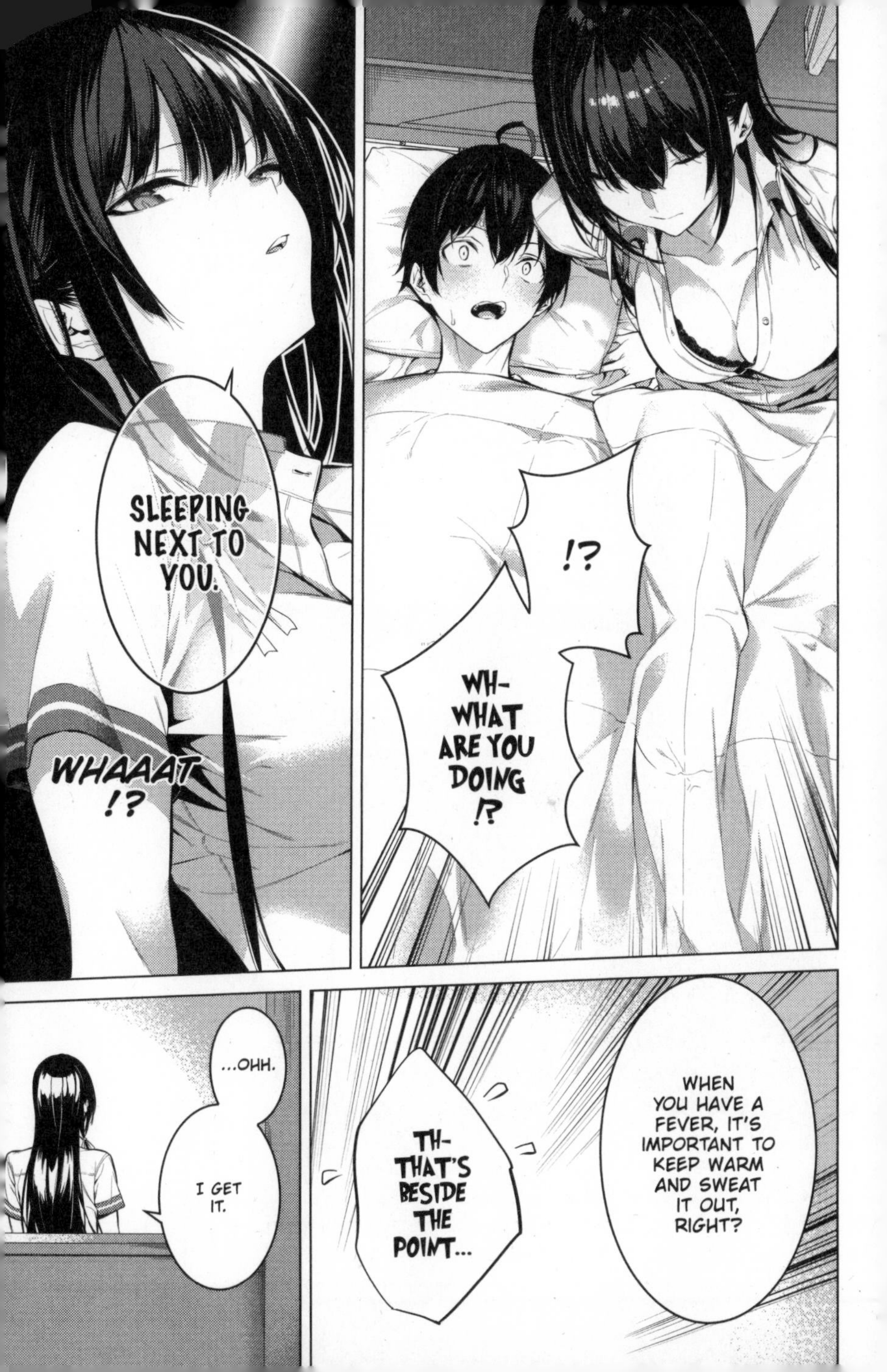
!?
WH- WHAT ARE YOU DOING !?
SLEEPING NEXT TO YOU.
WHAAAT !?
WHEN YOU HAVE A FEVER, IT'S IMPORTANT TO KEEP WARM AND SWEAT IT OUT, RIGHT?
TH- THAT'S BESIDE THE POINT...
...OHH.
I GET IT.

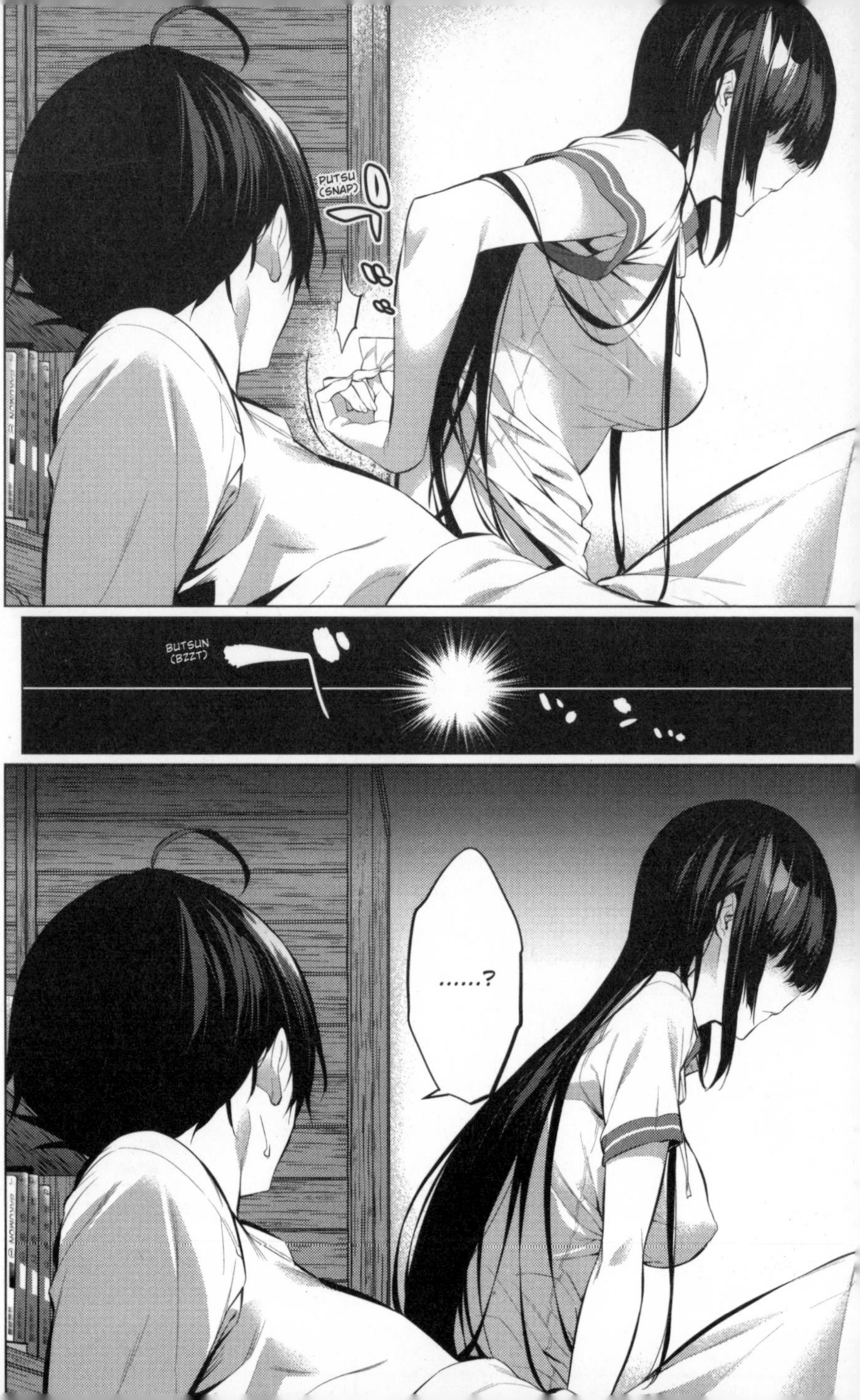
PUTSU (SNAP)
BUTSUN (BZZT)
......?

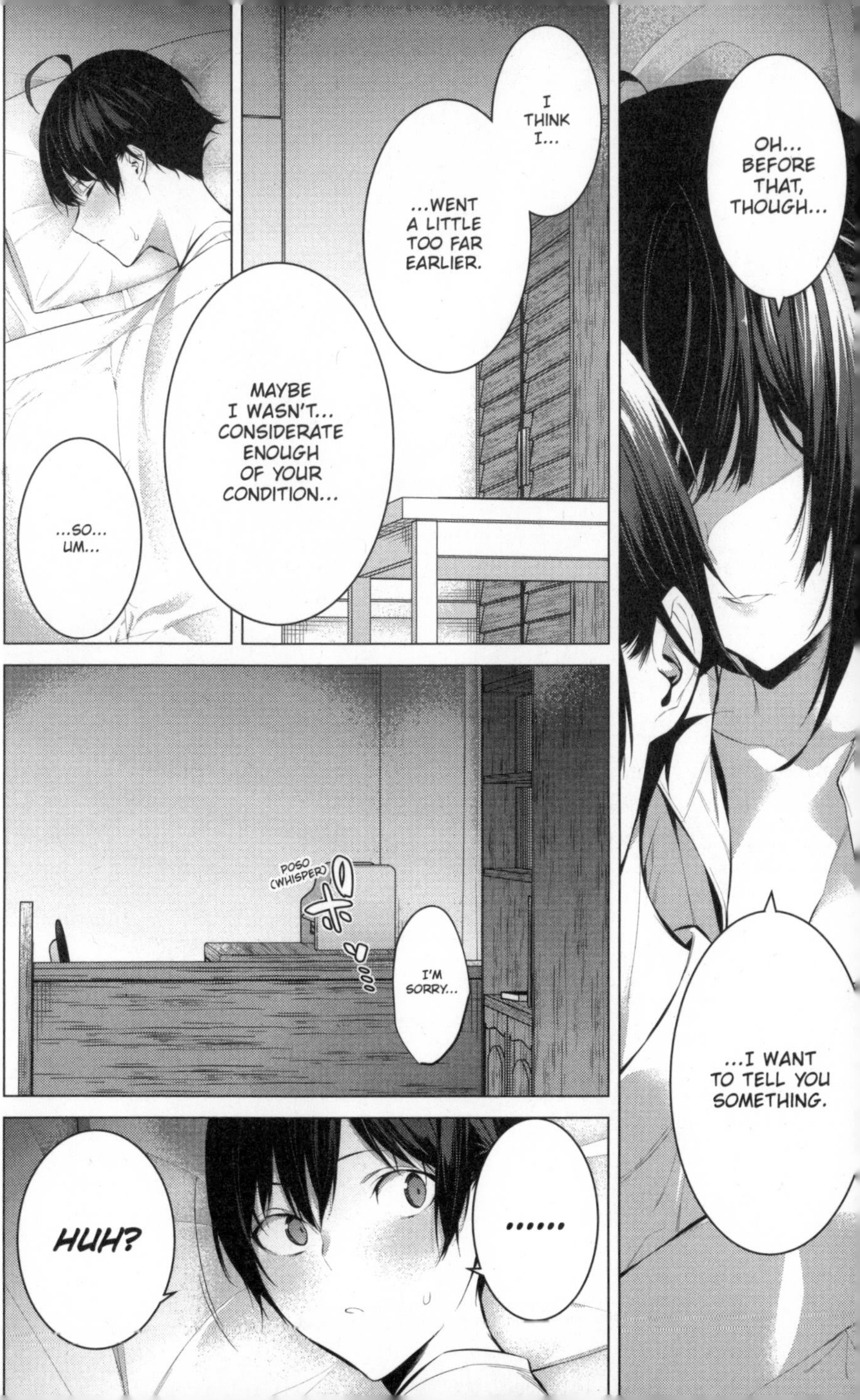
OH... BEFORE THAT, THOUGH...
...I WANT TO TELL YOU SOMETHING.
I THINK I...
...WENT A LITTLE TOO FAR EARLIER.
MAYBE I WASN'T... CONSIDERATE ENOUGH OF YOUR CONDITION...
...SO... UM...
POSO (WHISPER)
I'M SORRY...
......
HUH?

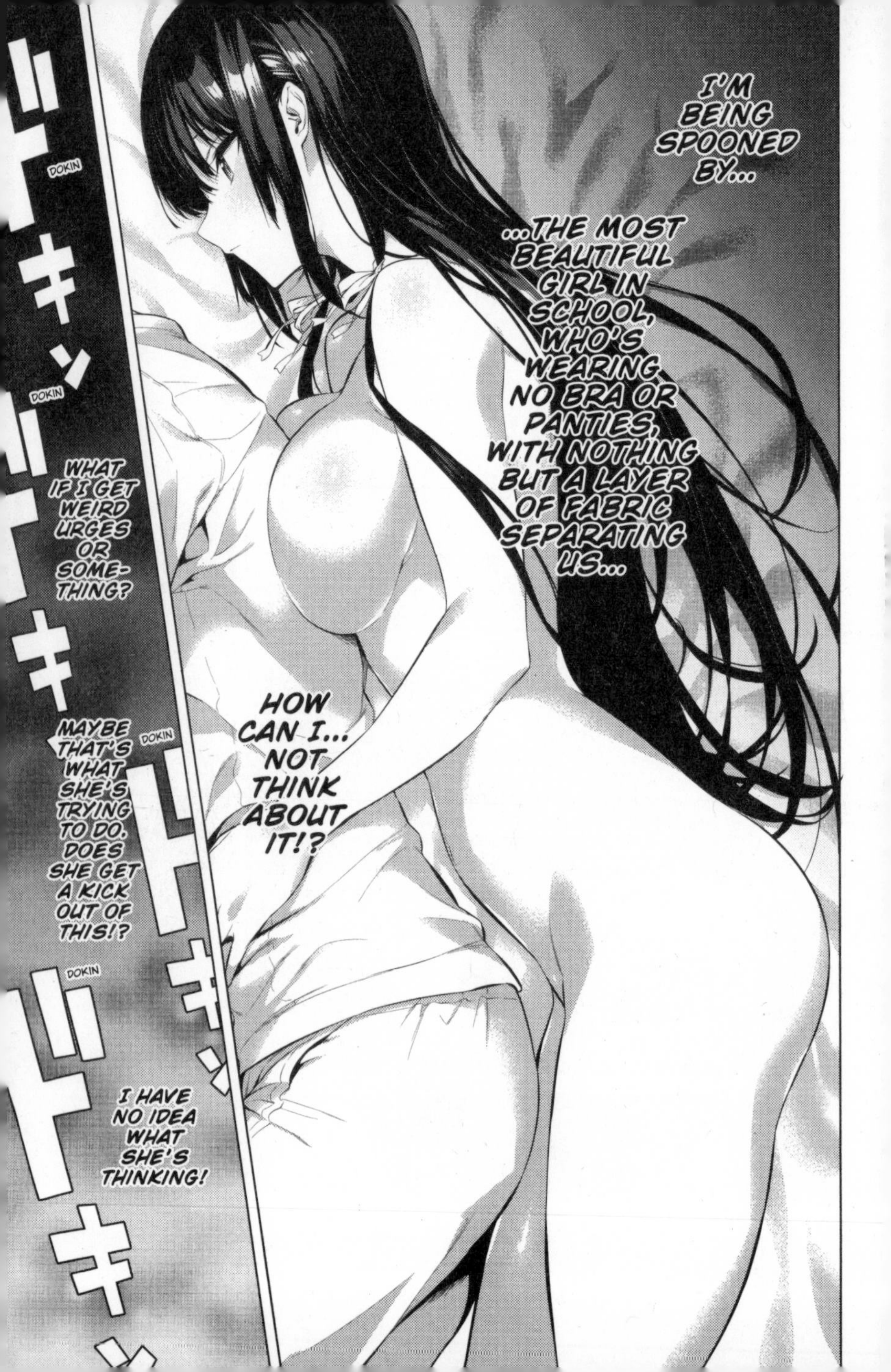

I'M BEING SPOONED BY...
...THE MOST BEAUTIFUL GIRL IN SCHOOL, WHO'S WEARING NO BRA OR PANTIES, WITH NOTHING BUT A LAYER OF FABRIC SEPARATING US...
HOW CAN I... NOT THINK ABOUT IT!?
DOKIN
DOKIN
WHAT IF I GET WEIRD URGES OR SOME-THING?
DOKIN
MAYBE THAT'S WHAT SHE'S TRYING TO DO. DOES SHE GET A KICK OUT OF THIS!?
DOKIN
I HAVE NO IDEA WHAT SHE'S THINKING!

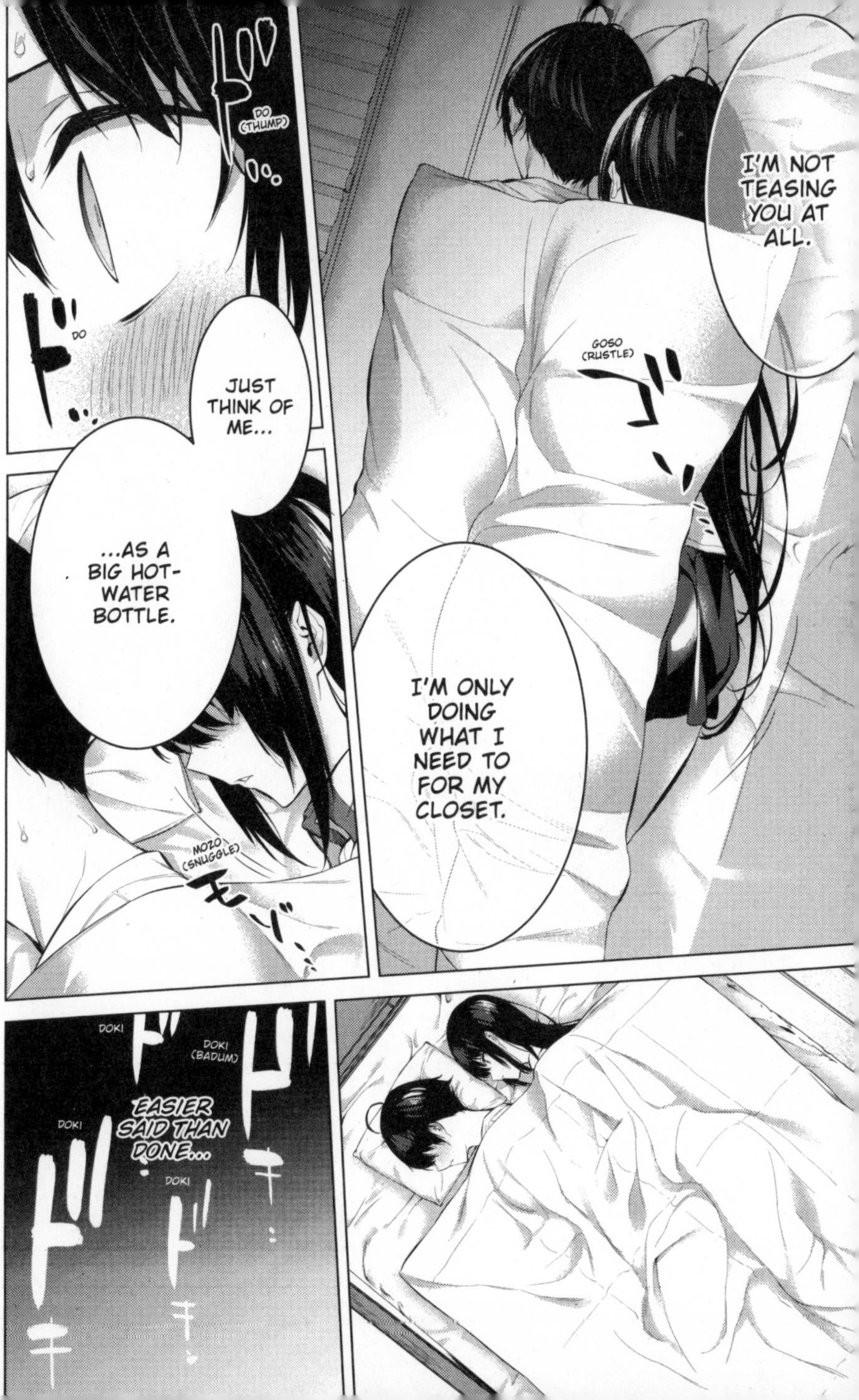
I'M NOT TEASING YOU AT ALL.
GOSO (RUSTLE)
I'M ONLY DOING WHAT I NEED TO FOR MY CLOSET.
DO (THUMP)
DO
JUST THINK OF ME...
...AS A BIG HOT-WATER BOTTLE.
MOZO (SNUGGLE)
DOKI
DOKI (BADUM)
EASIER SAID THAN DONE...
DOKI
DOKI

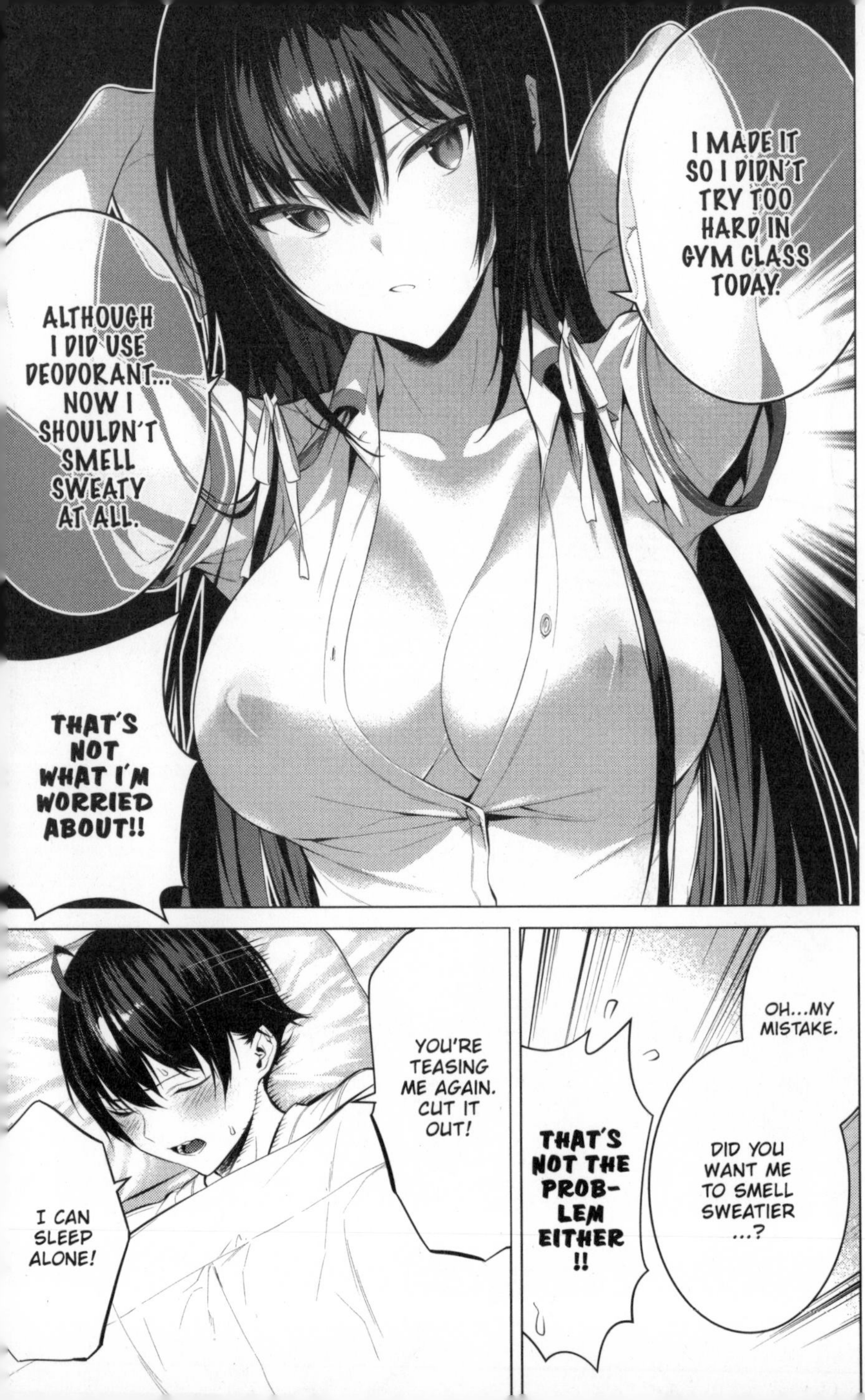
I MADE IT SO I DIDN'T TRY TOO HARD IN GYM CLASS TODAY.
ALTHOUGH I DID USE DEODORANT... NOW I SHOULDN'T SMELL SWEATY AT ALL.
THAT'S NOT WHAT I'M WORRIED ABOUT!!
OH...MY MISTAKE.
DID YOU WANT ME TO SMELL SWEATIER ...?
THAT'S NOT THE PROB-LEM EITHER !!
YOU'RE TEASING ME AGAIN. CUT IT OUT!
I CAN SLEEP ALONE!

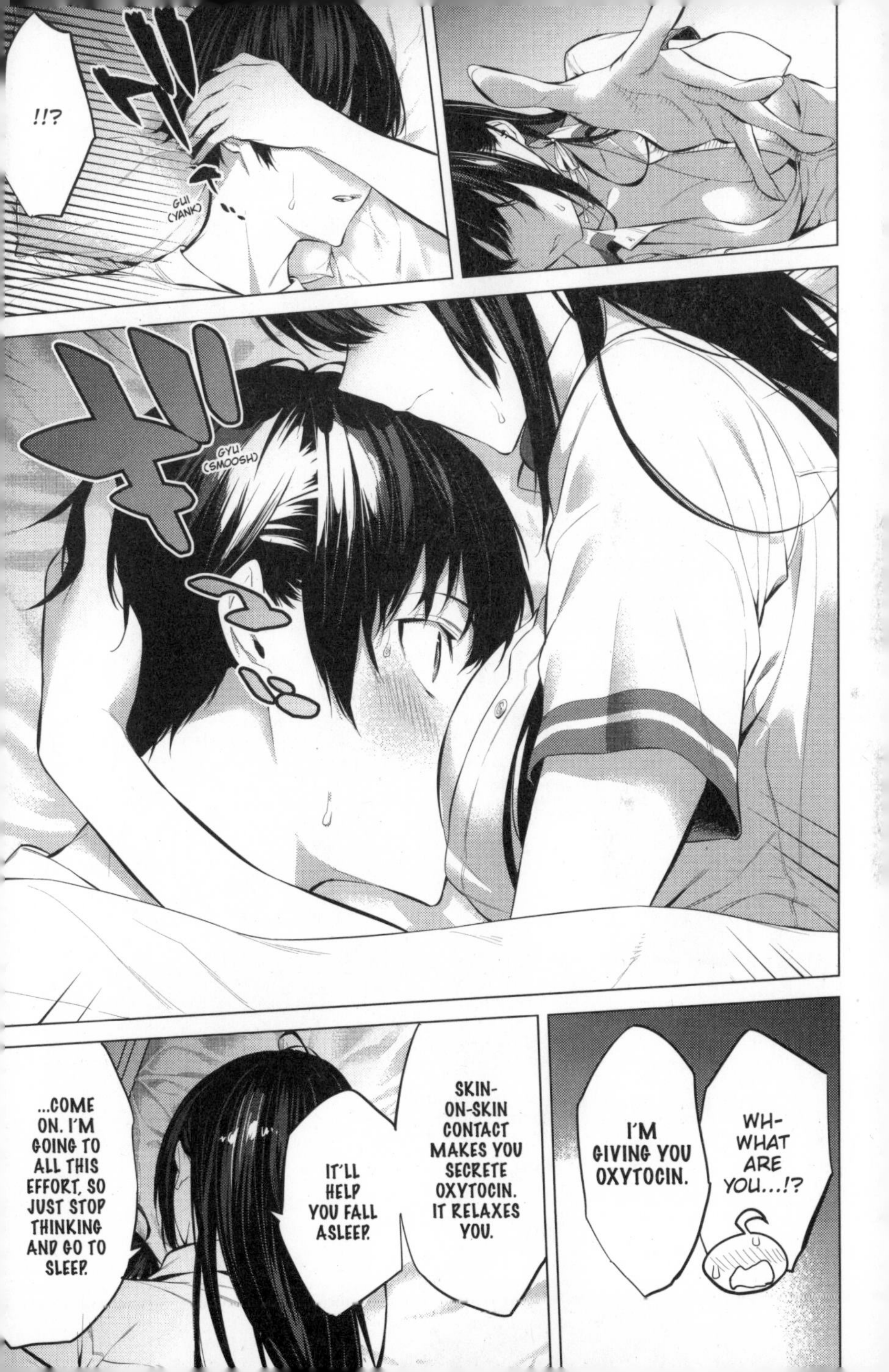
!!?
GUI (YANK)
GYU (SMOOSH)
WH-WHAT ARE YOU...!?
I'M GIVING YOU OXYTOCIN.
SKIN-ON-SKIN CONTACT MAKES YOU SECRETE OXYTOCIN. IT RELAXES YOU.
IT'LL HELP YOU FALL ASLEEP.
...COME ON. I'M GOING TO ALL THIS EFFORT, SO JUST STOP THINKING AND GO TO SLEEP.

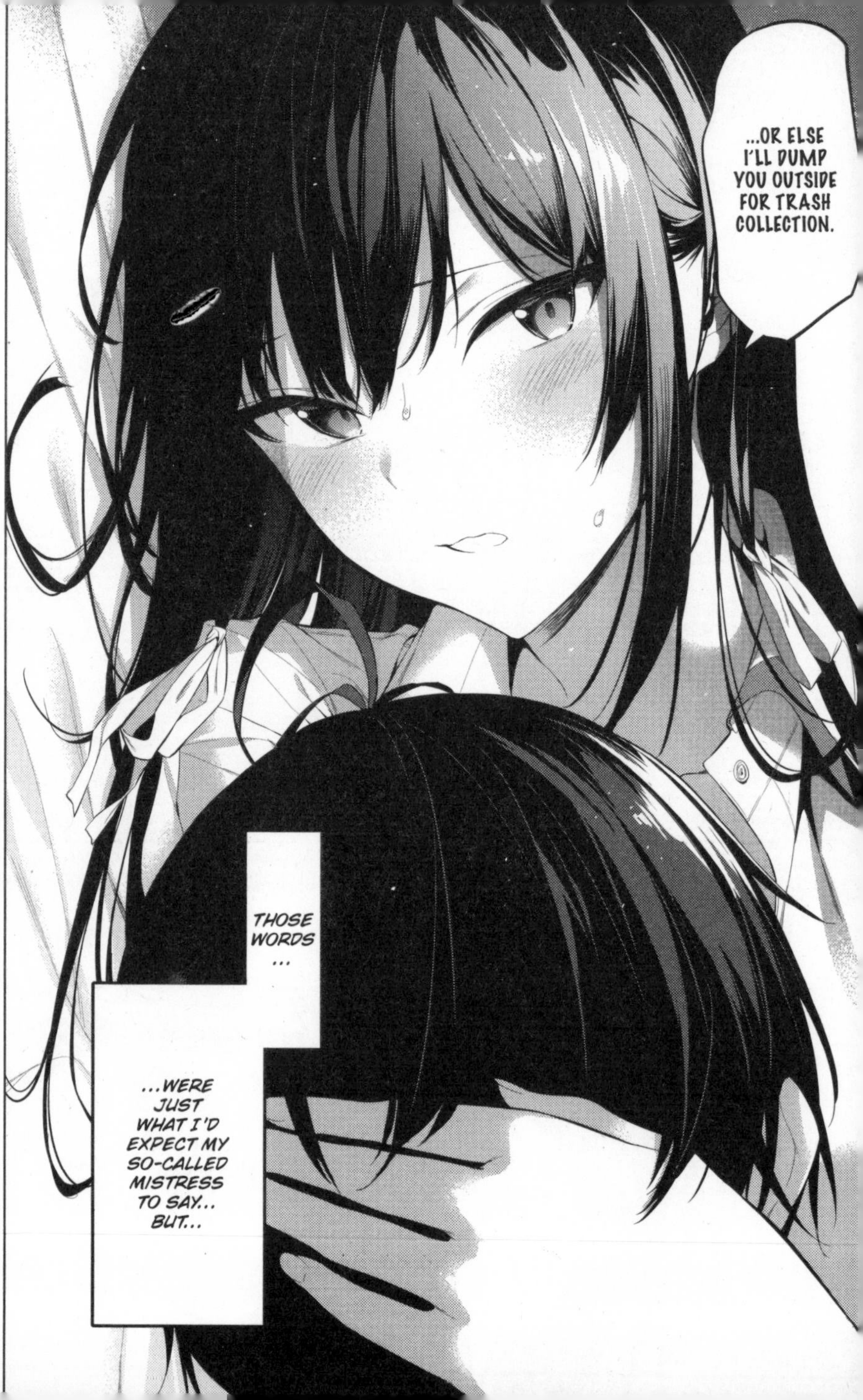
...OR ELSE I'LL DUMP YOU OUTSIDE FOR TRASH COLLECTION.
THOSE WORDS ...
...WERE JUST WHAT I'D EXPECT MY SO-CALLED MISTRESS TO SAY... BUT...

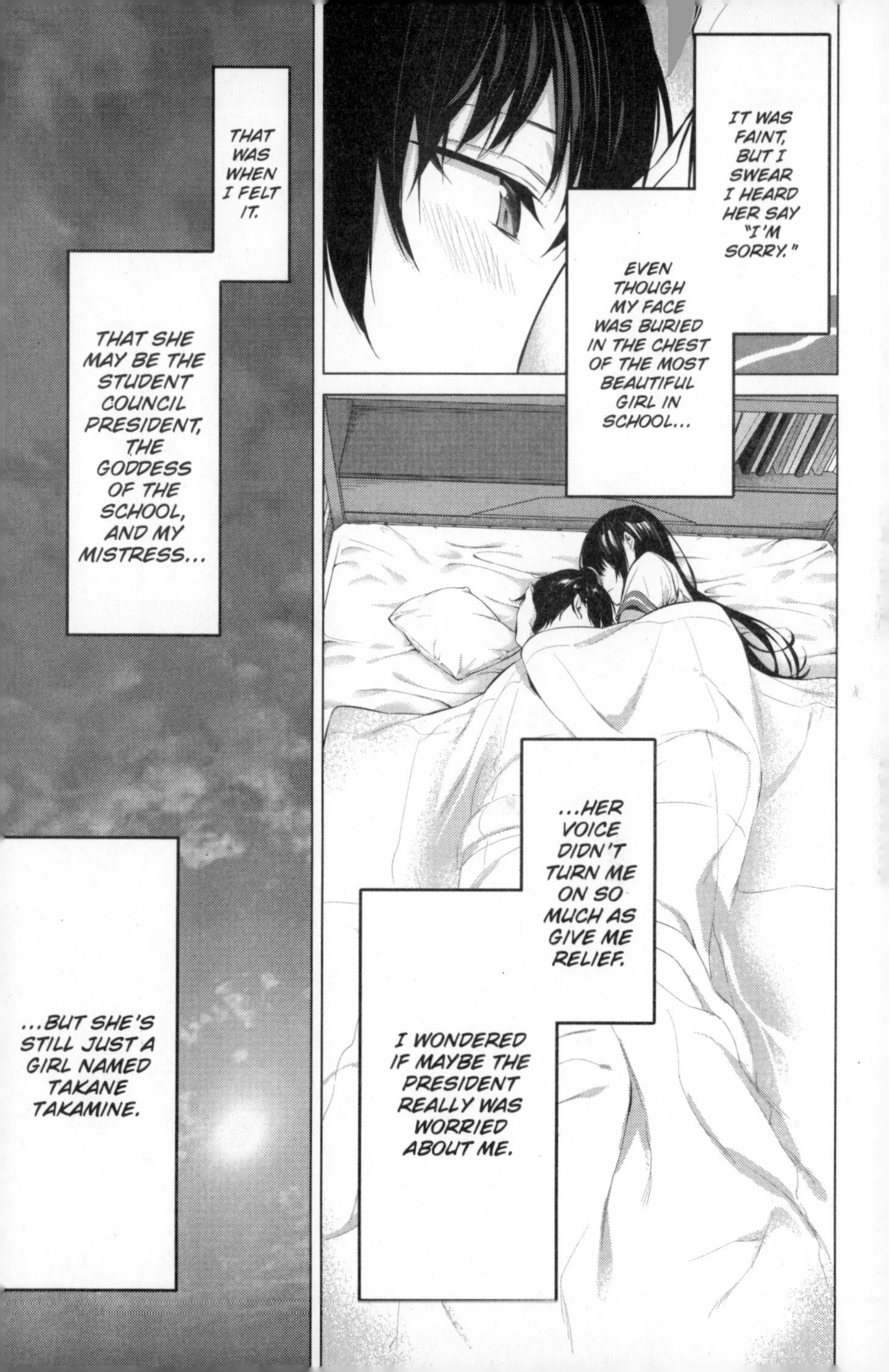
IT WAS FAINT, BUT I SWEAR I HEARD HER SAY "I'M SORRY."
EVEN THOUGH MY FACE WAS BURIED IN THE CHEST OF THE MOST BEAUTIFUL GIRL IN SCHOOL...
...HER VOICE DIDN'T TURN ME ON SO MUCH AS GIVE ME RELIEF.
I WONDERED IF MAYBE THE PRESIDENT REALLY WAS WORRIED ABOUT ME.
THAT WAS WHEN I FELT IT.
THAT SHE MAY BE THE STUDENT COUNCIL PRESIDENT, THE GODDESS OF THE SCHOOL, AND MY MISTRESS...
...BUT SHE'S STILL JUST A GIRL NAMED TAKANE TAKAMINE.

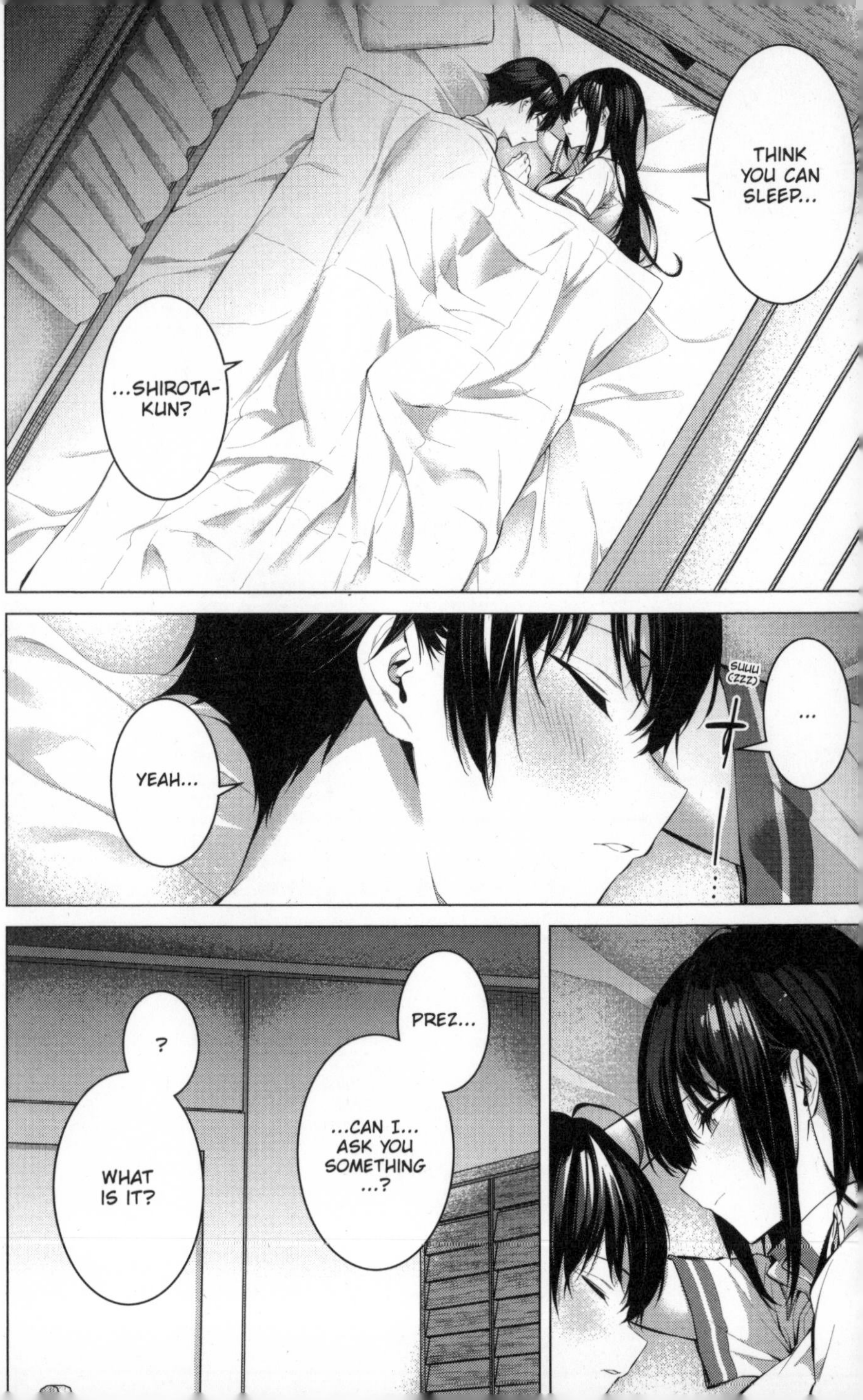
THINK YOU CAN SLEEP...
...SHIROTA-KUN?
SUUU (ZZZ)
...
YEAH...
PREZ...
...CAN I... ASK YOU SOMETHING ...?
?
WHAT IS IT?

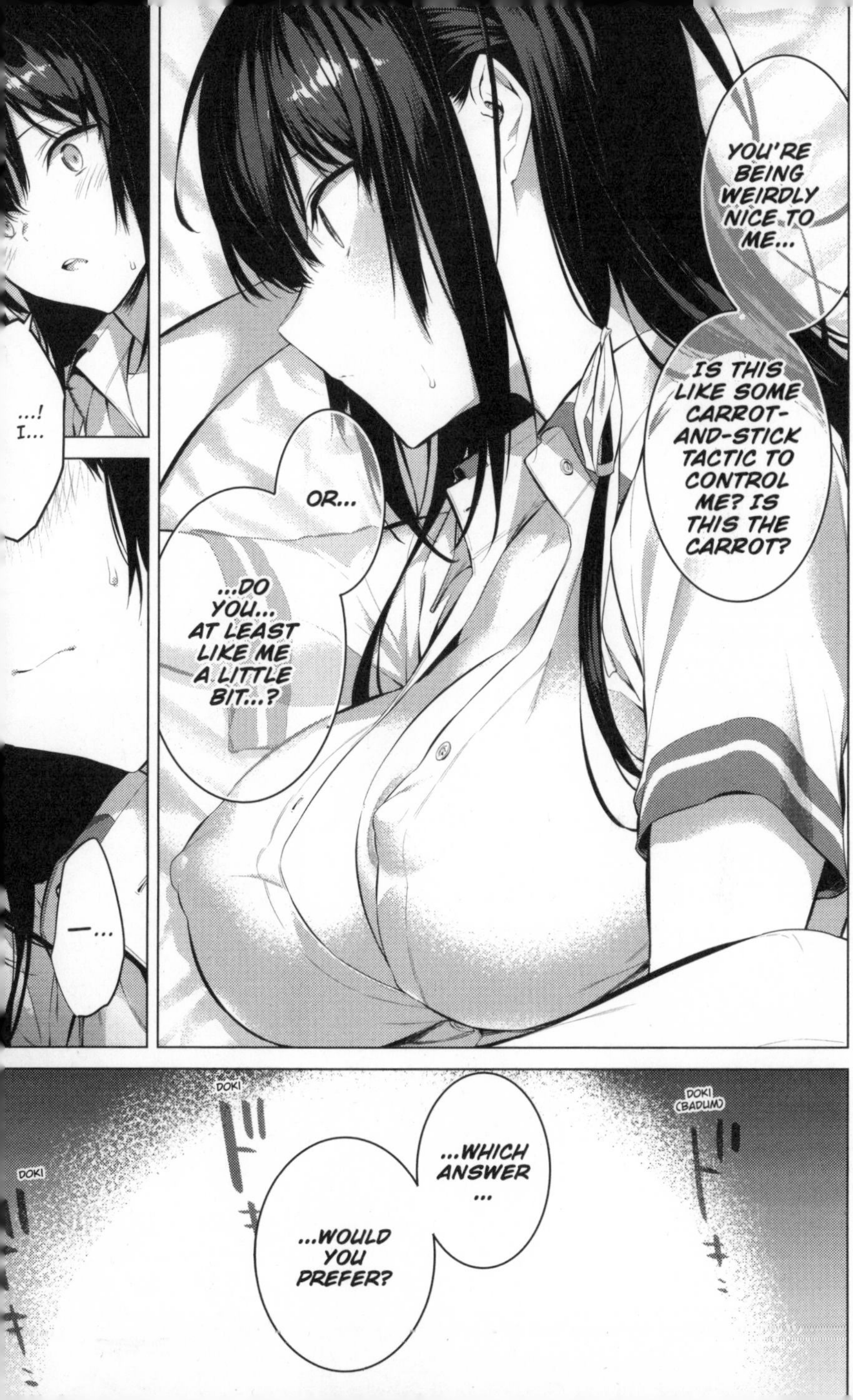

YOU'RE BEING WEIRDLY NICE TO ME...
IS THIS LIKE SOME CARROT-AND-STICK TACTIC TO CONTROL ME? IS THIS THE CARROT?
OR...
...DO YOU... AT LEAST LIKE ME A LITTLE BIT...?
...! I...
—...
DOKI (BADUM)
...WHICH ANSWER ...
...WOULD YOU PREFER?
DOKI
DOKI

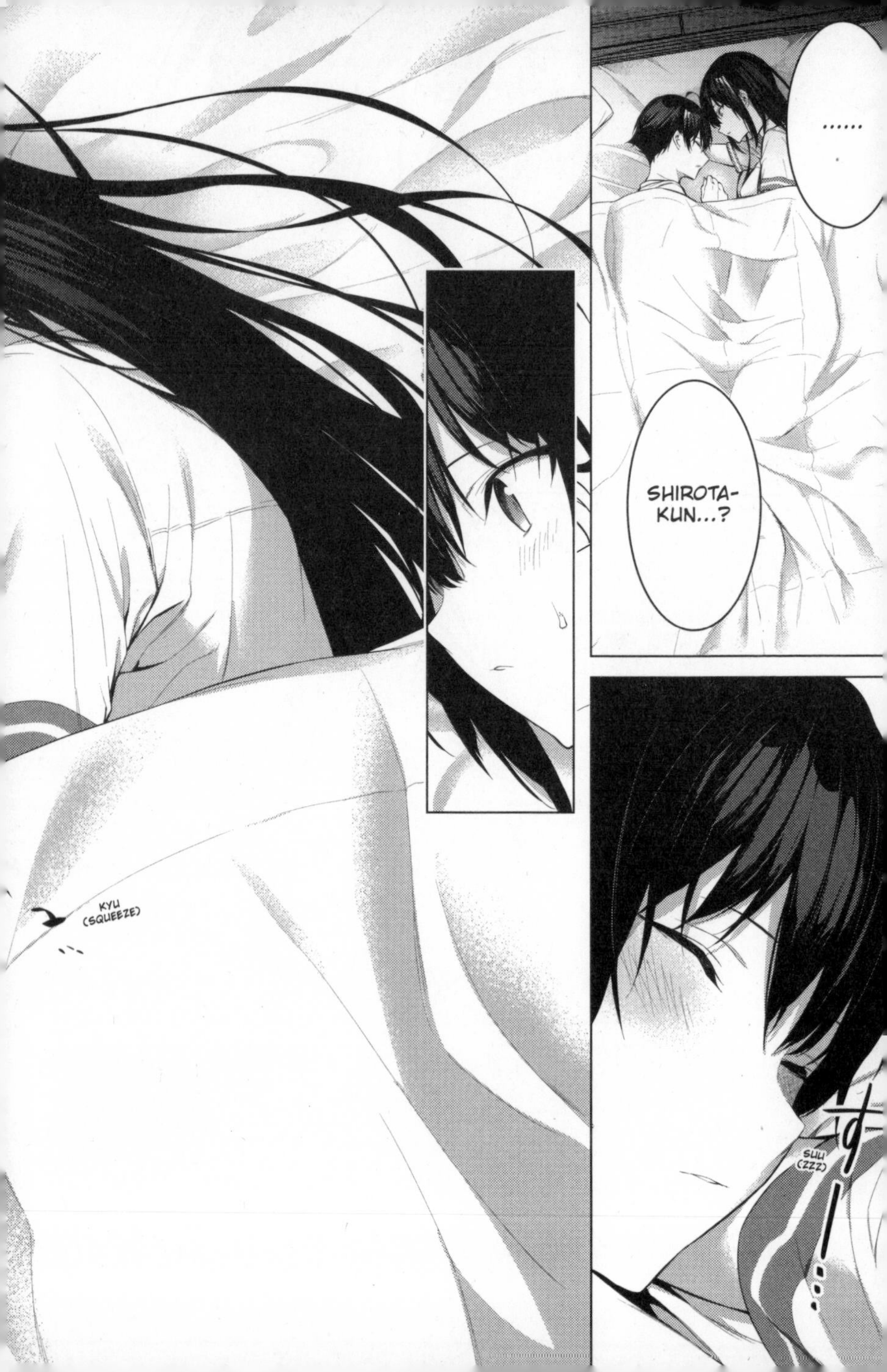
......
SHIROTA-KUN...?
SUU (ZZZ)
KYU (SQUEEZE)

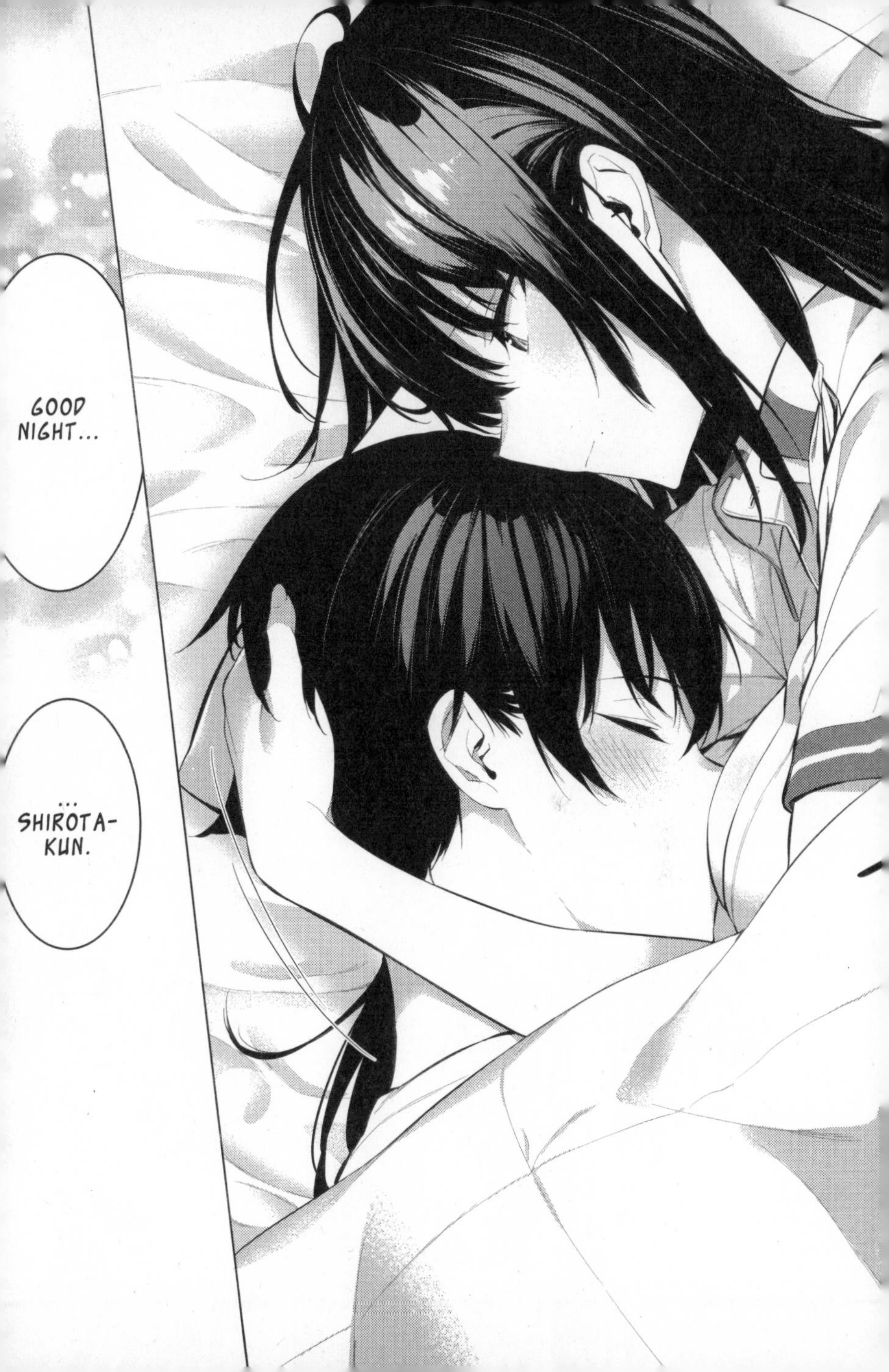
GOOD NIGHT...
...SHIROTA-KUN.

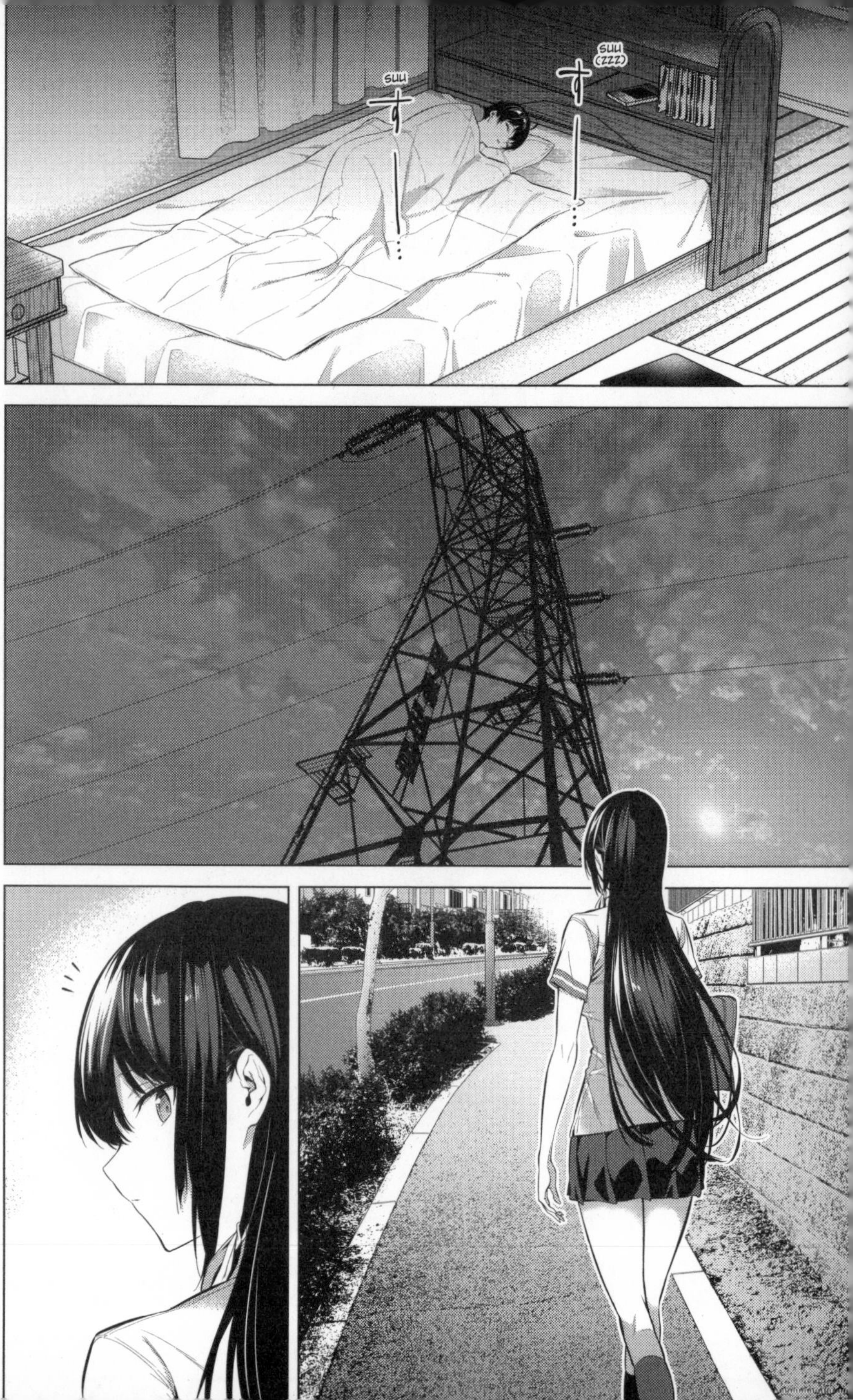
SUU (ZZZ)
すー…
SUU
すー…

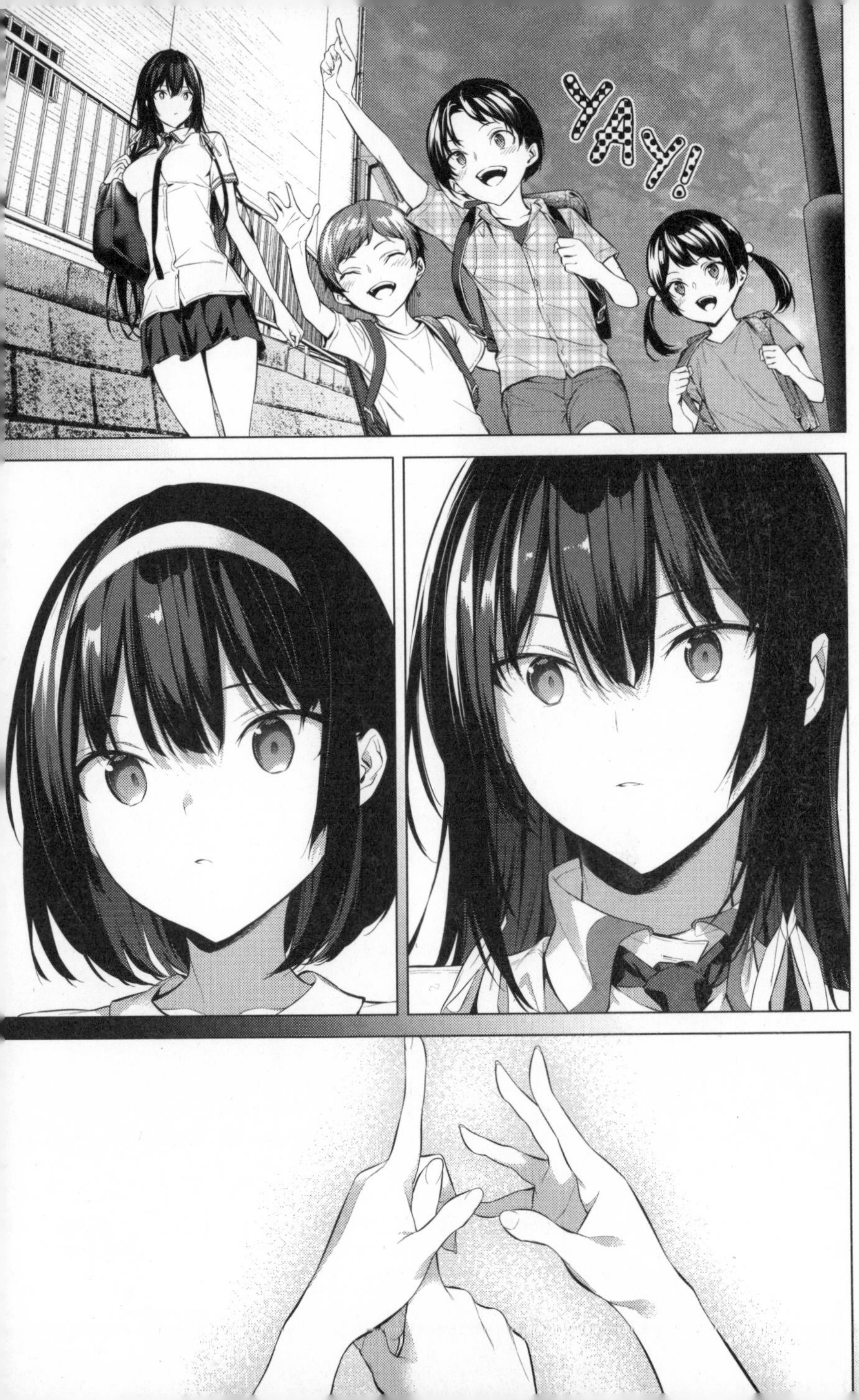
YAY!

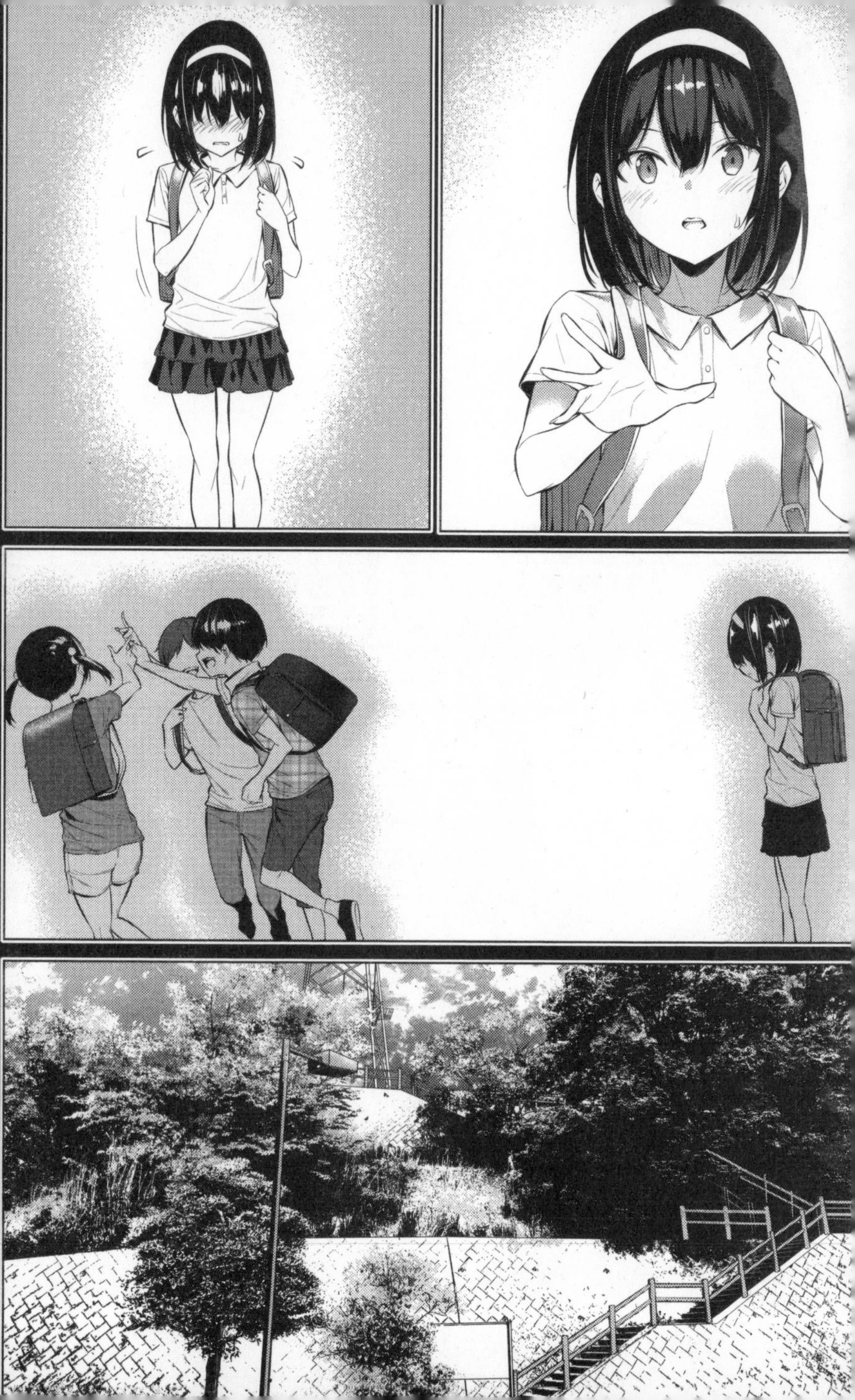

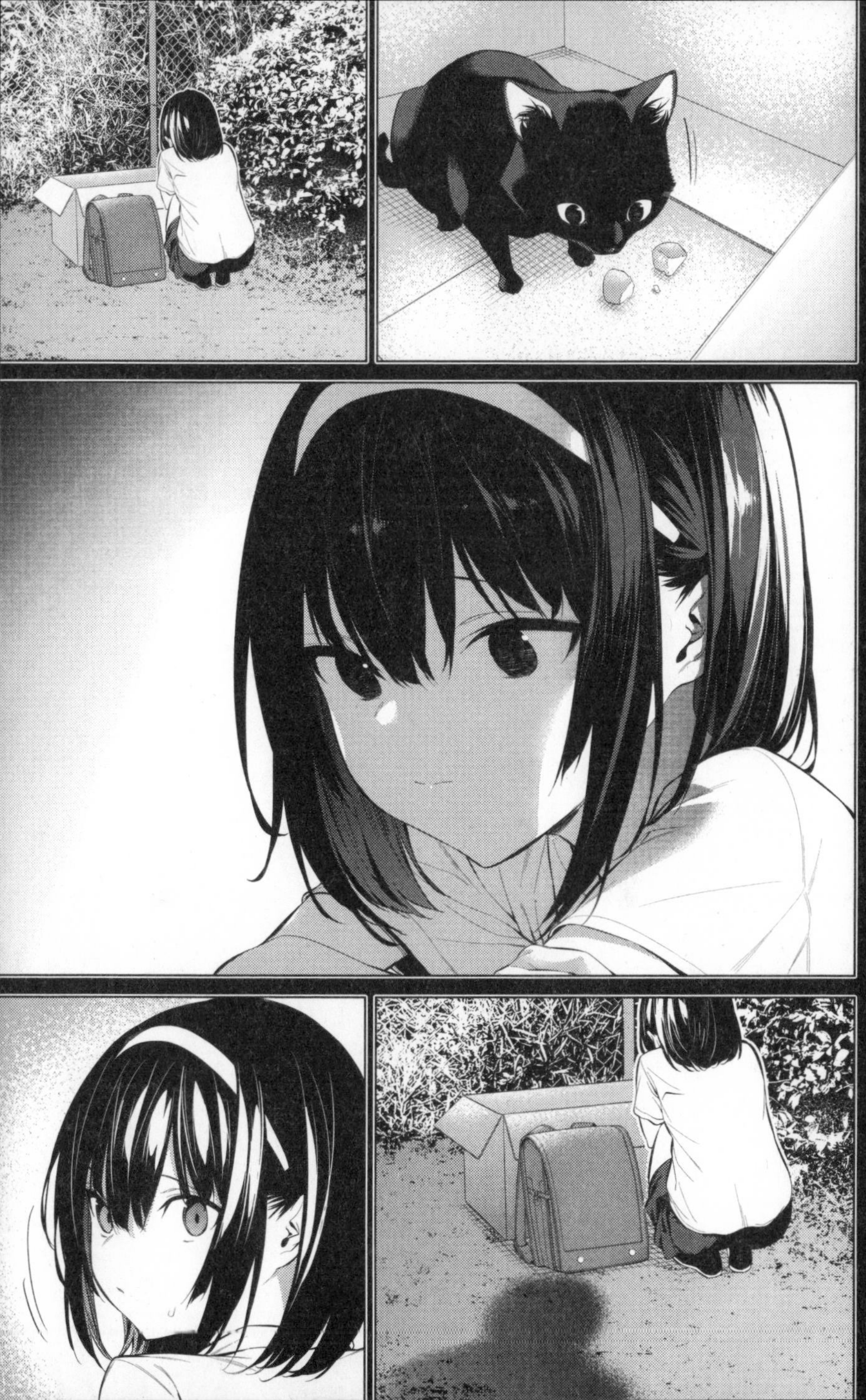

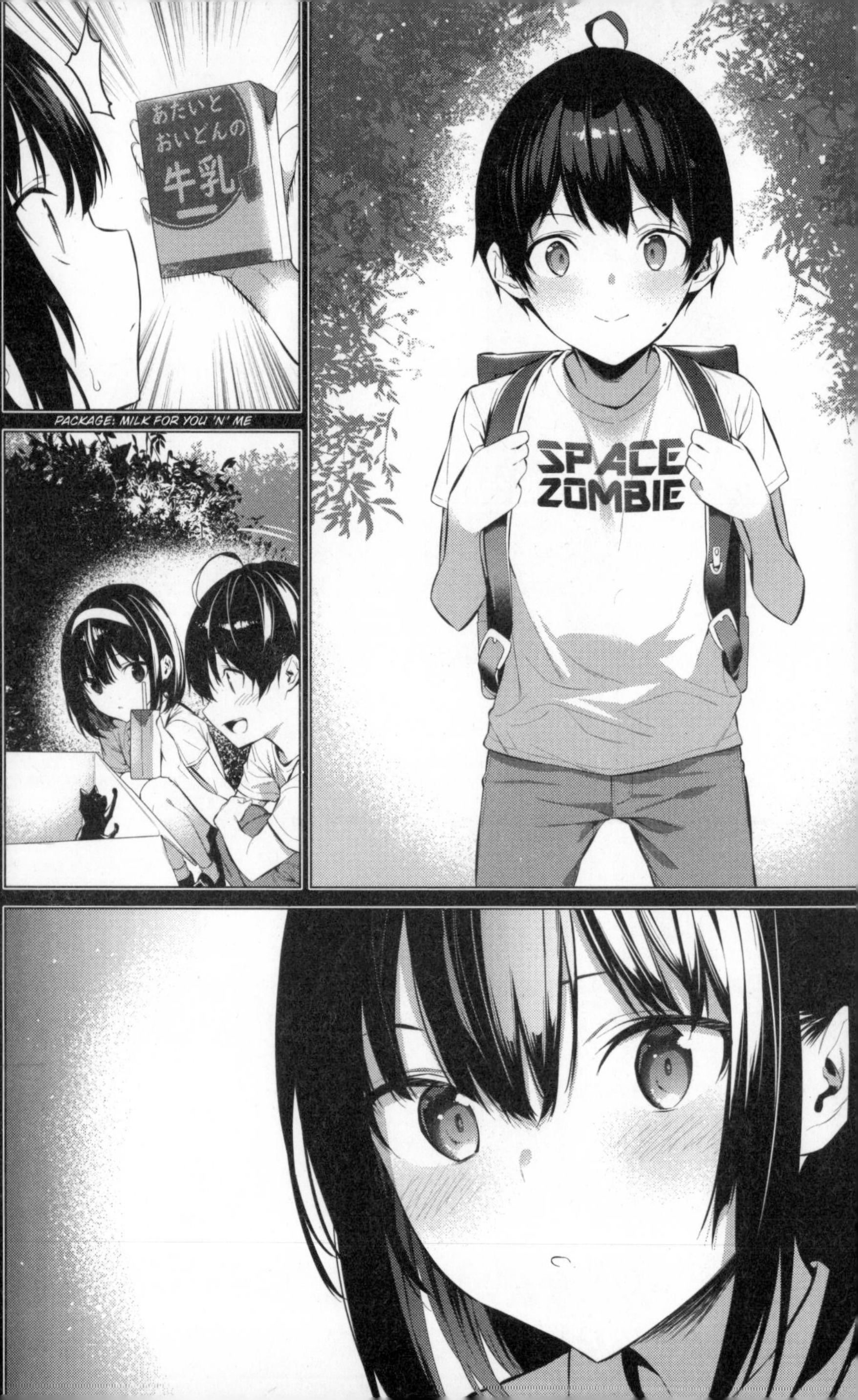
SPACE ZOMBIE
あたいとおいどんの牛乳
PACKAGE: MILK FOR YOU 'N' ME

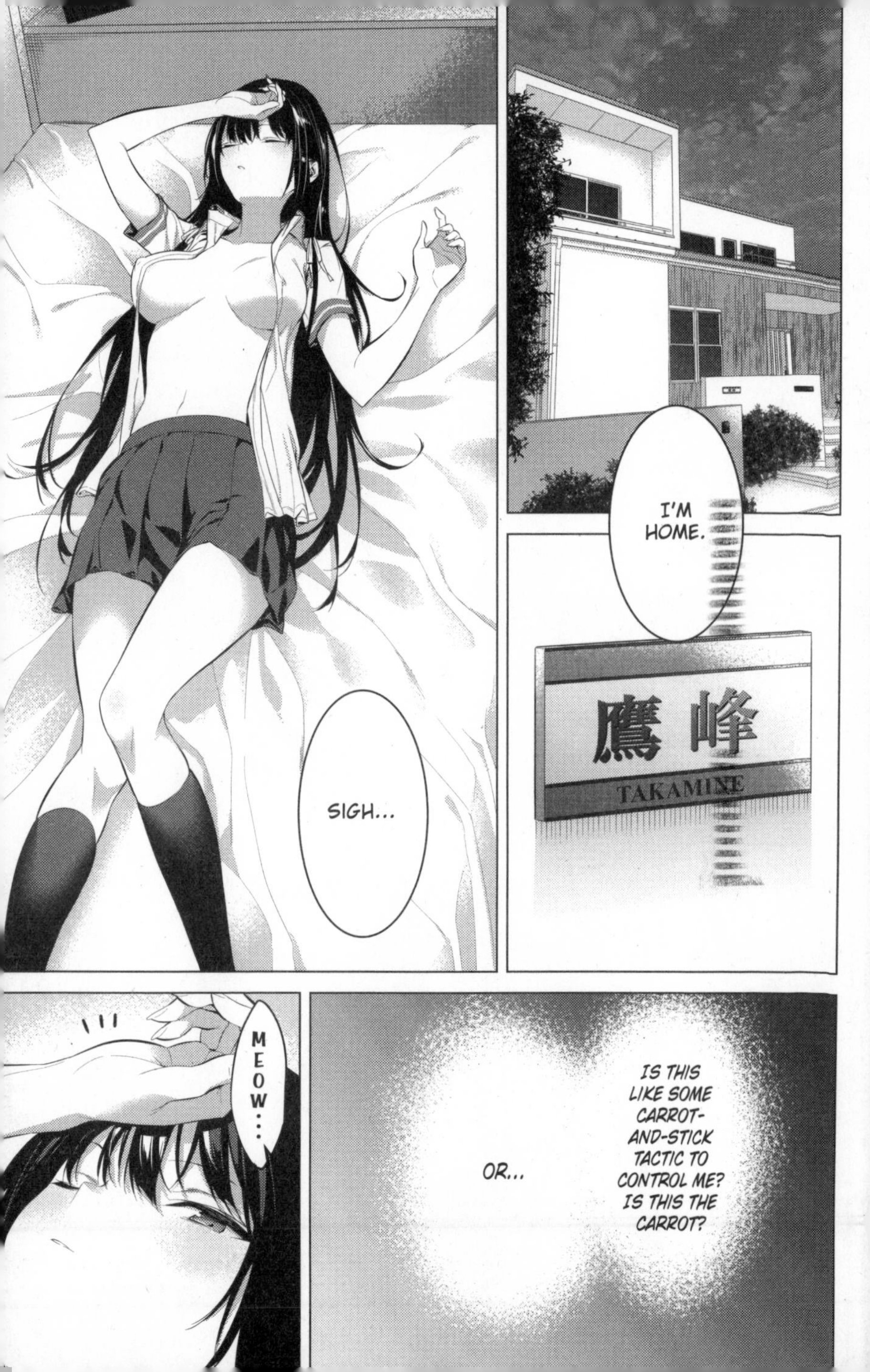
I'M HOME.
鷹峰
TAKAMINE
SIGH...
IS THIS LIKE SOME CARROT-AND-STICK TACTIC TO CONTROL ME? IS THIS THE CARROT?
OR...
MEOW...

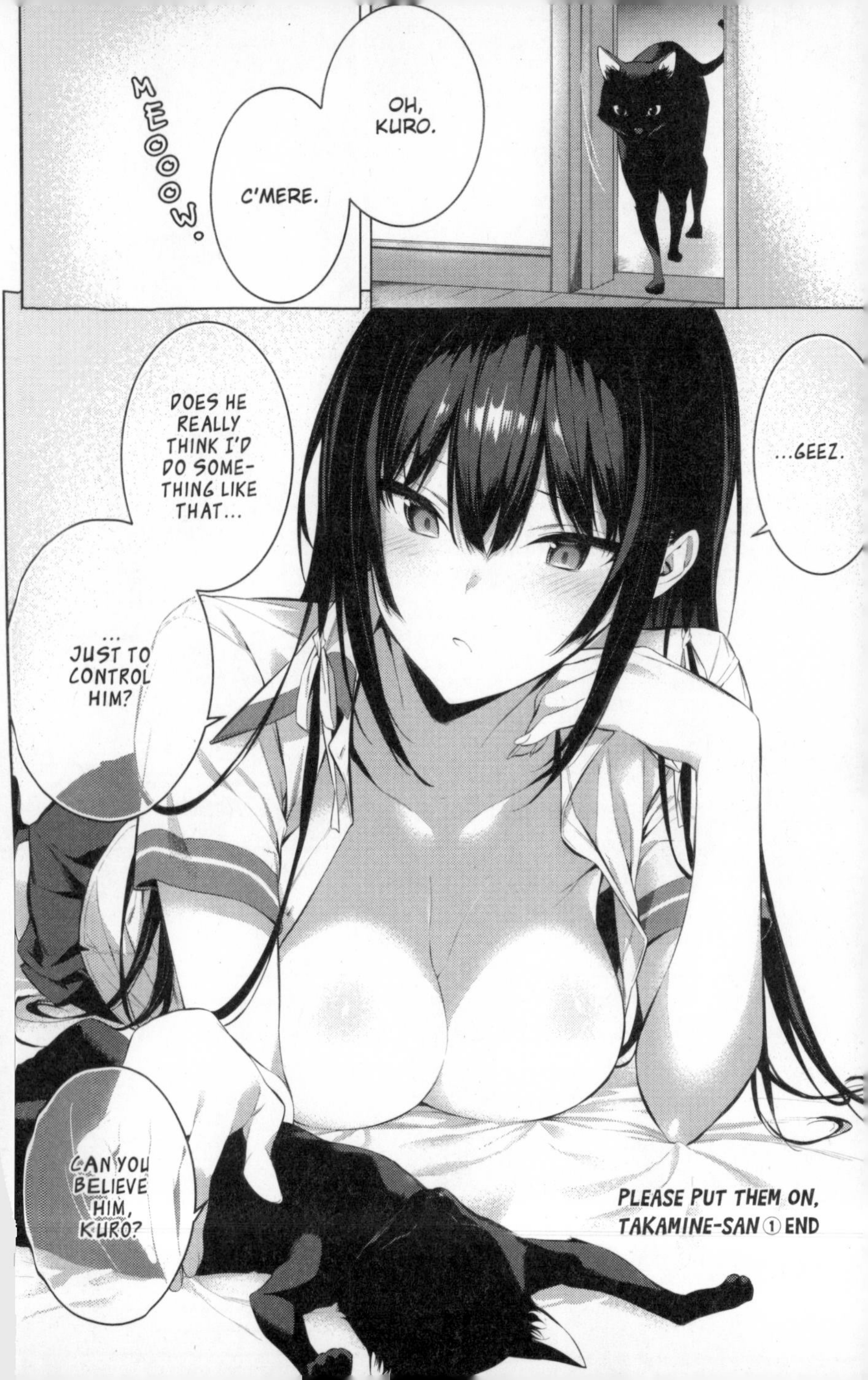
OH, KURO.
C'MERE.
MEOOOW.
...GEEZ.
DOES HE REALLY THINK I'D DO SOME-THING LIKE THAT...
... JUST TO CONTROL HIM?
CAN YOU BELIEVE HIM, KURO?
PLEASE PUT THEM ON, TAKAMINE-SAN ① END

AFTERWORD

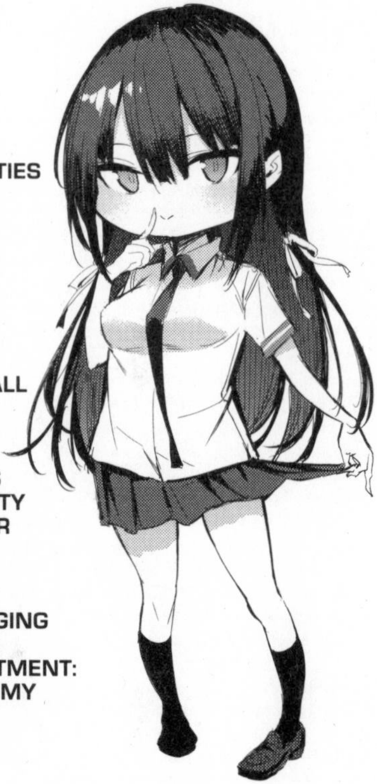

THANK YOU FOR BUYING VOLUME 1 OF *PLEASE PUT THEM ON, TAKAMINE-SAN*!

THIS BOOK WAS THE RESULT OF MANY PEOPLE'S EFFORTS. WHILE I'M DEEPLY GRATEFUL FOR THEIR WORK, I'M ALSO A LITTLE WORRIED I TOOK TOO MANY LIBERTIES JUST TO SATISFY MY OWN TASTES...

IN THE SIX MONTHS SINCE THIS SERIES BEGAN, THERE HAVE BEEN SOME HAPPY DEVELOPMENTS IN MY PERSONAL LIFE, AND IT'S BEEN PRETTY HECTIC ADAPTING TO THE CHANGES IN ENVIRONMENT THAT CAME ALONG WITH THAT. SOMEHOW, THOUGH, I MADE IT THROUGH, IN NO SMALL PART THANKS TO MY ASSISTANTS AND EDITORS.

THANK YOU SO MUCH TO MY ASSISTANTS FOR ALWAYS DRAWING SUCH HIGH-QUALITY BACKGROUNDS, AND TO MY READERS FOR READING THIS MANGA! THE FEEDBACK I OCCASIONALLY RECEIVE FROM YOU GUYS GIVES ME SO MUCH ENCOURAGEMENT. ALSO, TO MY EDITOR Y-MOTO-SAN, MANAGING EDITOR K-UCHI-SAN, AND EVERYONE ELSE IN THE *GANGAN JOKER* EDITORIAL DEPARTMENT: I'M REALLY SORRY FOR ALWAYS MISSING MY DEADLINES!!

ANYWAY,
SEE YOU AGAIN IN VOLUME 2!

YUICHI HIIRAGI

SPECIAL THANKS

TO: HASHII-SAMA,
KATAGIRI-SAMA,
SUDOU-SAMA,
MORIMOTO-SAMA,
MY EDITOR-IN-CHARGE
YUMOTO-SAMA,
EVERYONE IN THE
EDITORIAL DEPARTMENT

& YOU!!

TRANSLATION NOTES

COMMON HONORIFICS

no honorific: Indicates familiarity or closeness; if used without permission or reason, addressing someone in this manner would constitute an insult.

-san: The Japanese equivalent of Mr./Mrs./Miss. If a situation calls for politeness, this is the fail-safe honorific.

-sama: Conveys great respect; may also indicate that the social status of the speaker is lower than that of the addressee.

-shi: An impersonal honorific used in formal speech or writing (e.g., legal documents).

-dono: Roughly equivalent to "master" or "milord."

-kun: Used most often when referring to boys, this indicates affection or familiarity. Occasionally used by older men among their peers, but it may also be used by anyone referring to a person of lower standing.

-chan: An affectionate honorific indicating familiarity used mostly in reference to girls; also used in reference to cute persons or animals of either gender.

-tan: A cutesy version of -chan.

-(o)nii/(o)nee: Meaning "big brother"/"big sister," it can also refer to those older but relatively close in age to the speaker. It is typically followed by -san, -chan, or -sama.

-senpai: An honorific for one's senior classmate, colleague, etc., although not as senior or respected as a sensei ("teacher").

GENERAL

One hundred yen is roughly equal to one U.S. dollar.

Otaku is a Japanese word referring to obsessive fans. Although it often refers to fans of anime, manga, and video games, the term can apply to any sort of fandom. For example, hard-core baseball fans are called baseball *otaku*.

PAGE 6

Here, "**night and day**" is actually "the moon and a softshell turtle" in Japanese. The connection is that while both share something in common—such as being round or students—they couldn't be more different.

Likewise, "**apples and oranges**" is actually "paper lanterns and temple bells" in Japanese. They may look similar, but one is a lot stronger than the other.

PAGE 17

"**Even a master makes mistakes**" is actually "Even Kobo Daishi's handwriting contains mistakes" in Japanese. Kobo Daishi is a monk from the Heian period who was famous for founding the Shingon School of Japanese Buddhism.

PAGE 23

"**The goddess I shouldn't approach**" refers to a Japanese proverb that literally means "The spirit (god) you do not approach will not curse you." It's similar to the phrase "Let sleeping dogs lie." In this case, however, the "god" meaning is important because Koushi is referencing Takamine's status as the school's goddess.

PAGE 34

The characters used to write "**Eternal Virgin Road**" can also be read as "maiden who does not yet know indecency."

PAGE 55

Kurota-kun is actually a play on words. The "*kuro*" comes from "closet," which is written as *kuroozetto* in Japanese, and Kurota is also a surname similar to Shirota. *Shiro* means "white" and *kuro* means "black," so it's like going from Mr. White to Mr. Black.

PAGE 79

Kokinshu is short for *Kokin Wakashu*, a famous collection of Japanese poems from ancient to modern times.

Ariwara no Narihira was a poetic genius of the Heian period.

PAGE 104

The "**student council slave**" label in the original reads *seidokaichou* instead of *seitokaichou*. The difference here is that *seito* means "student," whereas *seido* means "sex slave."

In Japanese, Koushi uses the proverb "**Have a walking stick ready before stumbling,**" or more generally, "better safe than sorry."

PAGE 122

Koushi is referencing *The Girl Who Leapt Through Time*, an animated film inspired by Yasutaka Tsutsui's 1967 novel of the same name. It follows a girl who relives the same day over and over again in a time loop, not unlike the 1993 film *Groundhog Day*.

PAGE 129
Kendo is a Japanese martial art in which participants don light armor, wield bamboo swords, and square off against each other. It's similar to fencing and is widely practiced in Japan to this day.

PAGE 130
Torita is a play on Shirota's name using the word *tori*, which means "bird."

PAGE 131
Takamine is saying she would be a ***tantai*** porn actress. *Tantai* actresses are the most prestigious, starring in porn as the main attraction rather than simply appearing in a work for the purposes of the story.

PAGE 159
These **chirps** are not from birds but cicadas——a sure sign that summer has started in Japan.

PAGE 170
LIME is a play on LINE, the premier messaging app used in Japan.

PAGE 183
Takamine's penchant for giving poor Shirota derisive nicknames continues here. **Norota** is a play on his name using the word *noroi*, which means "slow."

PAGE 202
The Japanese phrase used here is actually "candy and whip" instead of **"carrot and stick."**

PAGE 209
Oxytocin, also referred to as the love hormone, plays an essential role in childbirth and is strongly associated with feelings of empathy.

Please Put Them On, Takamine-san ①

Yuichi Hiiragi

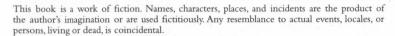

Translation: Lisa Coffman

Lettering: Chiho Christie

This book is a work of fiction. Names, characters, places, and incidents are the product of the author's imagination or are used fictitiously. Any resemblance to actual events, locales, or persons, living or dead, is coincidental.

HAITE KUDASAI, TAKAMINE-SAN Volume 1 ©2019 Yuichi Hiiragi / SQUARE ENIX CO., LTD. First published in Japan in 2019 by SQUARE ENIX CO., LTD. English translation rights arranged with SQUARE ENIX CO., LTD. and Yen Press, LLC through Tuttle-Mori Agency, Inc., Tokyo.

English translation ©2021 by SQUARE ENIX CO., LTD.

Yen Press, LLC supports the right to free expression and the value of copyright. The purpose of copyright is to encourage writers and artists to produce the creative works that enrich our culture.

The scanning, uploading, and distribution of this book without permission is a theft of the author's intellectual property. If you would like permission to use material from the book (other than for review purposes), please contact the publisher. Thank you for your support of the author's rights.

Yen Press
150 West 30th Street, 19th Floor
New York, NY 10001

Visit us at yenpress.com ♥ facebook.com/yenpress ♥ twitter.com/yenpress
yenpress.tumblr.com ♥ instagram.com/yenpress

First Yen Press Edition: April 2021

Yen Press is an imprint of Yen Press, LLC.
The Yen Press name and logo are trademarks of Yen Press, LLC.

The publisher is not responsible for websites (or their content) that are not owned by the publisher.

Library of Congress Control Number: 2020951854

ISBNs: 978-1-9753-2163-5 (paperback)
978-1-9753-2164-2 (ebook)

10 9 8 7 6 5 4 3

TPA

Printed in South Korea

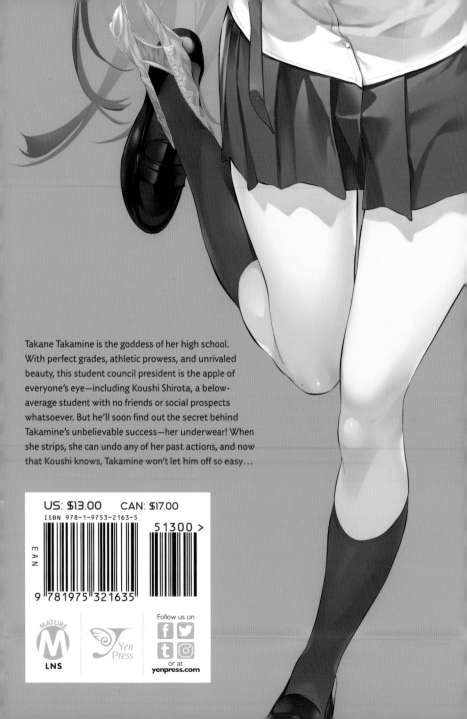

Takane Takamine is the goddess of her high school.
With perfect grades, athletic prowess, and unrivaled
beauty, this student council president is the apple of
everyone's eye—including Koushi Shirota, a below-
average student with no friends or social prospects
whatsoever. But he'll soon find out the secret behind
Takamine's unbelievable success—her underwear! When
she strips, she can undo any of her past actions, and now
that Koushi knows, Takamine won't let him off so easy…

US: $13.00   CAN: $17.00

ISBN 978-1-9753-2163-5

51300 >

E A N

9 781975 321635

MATURE
M
LNS

Yen Press

Follow us on

f 🐦
t 📷

or at
yenpress.com